D0601817

The North American Third Edition

Cambridge Latin Course
Unit 3

Revision Editor
Ed Phinney
Chair, Department of Classics, & Director, University Foreign Language Resource Center
University of Massachusetts at Amherst, U.S.A.

Consulting Editor
Patricia E. Bell
Teacher of Latin & Assistant Head of Languages
Centennial Collegiate and Vocational Institute, Guelph, Ontario, Canada

Editorial Assistant
Barbara Romaine
Amherst, Massachusetts, U.S.A.

CAMBRIDGE
UNIVERSITY PRESS

Published by the Press Syndicate of the University of Cambridge
40 West 20th Street, New York, NY 10011-4211, USA

The Cambridge Latin Course was funded and developed by the
University of Cambridge School Classics Project and SCDC Publications,
London, and is published with the sponsorship of the School Curriculum
Development Committee in London and the North American Cambridge
Classics Project. The work of the School Curriculum Development Committee
has now been taken over by the National Curriculum Council.

© SCDC Publications 1971, 1972, 1983, 1984, 1989

This edition first published 1989
Reprinted 1992, 1993, 1994, 1995, 1996, 1997, 1998 (twice), 2000, 2002, 2003

Printed in the United States of America

Library of Congress cataloging-in-publication data
Cambridge Latin course. Unit 3. - North American 3rd ed./revision
editors, Ed Phinney.
Includes indexes.
1. Latin language – Grammar – 1976-   I. Phinney, Ed.   II. Title:
Cambridge Latin course. Unit three.
PA2087.5.C335   1989
478.2'421 – dc19
88-36424 CIP

ISBN 0-521-34382-8 hardback

Stories from Unit 3 which have been recorded on the cassette tapes accompanying
the course are so indicated by the cassette symbol [⚏]

DS

Drawings by Peter Kesteven, Joy Mellor, and Leslie Jones
Maps and diagrams by Reg Piggott and David Bryant

Acknowledgments

Thanks are due to the following for permission to reproduce photographs: pp. iv, 40 Fotek, Bath;
pp. 5, 17, 21, 52 Unichrome (Bath) Ltd; pp. 9, 161, 200, 209, Cambridge School Classics Project;
pp. 13, 149, 192, 232, 240 Roger Dalladay; p. 20 Bob Wilkins (c) Bath Archaeological Trust; p. 29
SKIRA (c) Naples Museum; p. 32 Bath City Council; p. 48 Museo Civico, Piacenza; p. 49 Ecole
des Beaux Arts, Paris; pp. 60, 133, 137, 153, 173, 177, 196, 213 Societa Scala, Firenze; pp. 65, 101,
156, 181, 184, 241 Ronald Sheridan's Photo-Library; p. 66 Rheinisches Landes Museum, Trier;
p. 68 The Ermine Street Guard; pp. 73, 84, 237 The Trustees of the British Museum; p. 74
Rijksmuseum, G.M. Kam; pp. 83, 183, 240 Mansell Collection; pp. 88, 92, 100, 112, 120
Grosvenor Museum; p. 100 courtesy of the Verulamium Museum, St Albans; p. 104 Airviews;
p. 105 D. Swarbrick c/o Grosvenor Museum; p. 108 Coventry Museums; p. 140 Institute of
Archaeology, Oxford; p. 156 Peter Connolly; p. 167 Alinari; p. 169 Alberto Carpececi *Rome 200
Years Ago* pub. Bonechi; p. 221 Museum of London; p. 224 negativo Musei Capitolini – Archivio
Fotografico; p. 256 Musée Royal de Mariemont.

**Cover picture: An onyx cameo of the Roman imperial eagle, engraved around AD 40,
from Kunsthistorisches Museum, Vienna.**

Contents

Aerial view of the city of Bath (Aquae Sulis) in southwestern England. The Roman Baths can be seen just below the Abbey Church in the center of the picture.

Stage 21

Aquae Sūlis

in oppidō Aquīs Sūlis labōrābant multī fabrī, quī thermās maximās exstruēbant. architectus Rōmānus fabrōs īnspiciēbat.

Aquīs Sūlis: Aquae Sūlis *Roman name of Bath, a town in southwestern England*

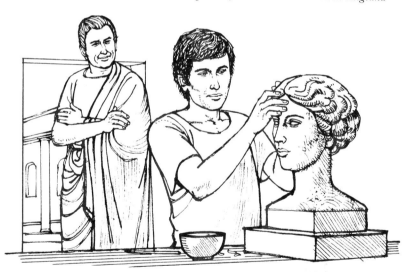

faber prīmus statuam deae Sūlis sculpēbat.
architectus fabrum laudāvit, quod perītus erat et dīligenter labōrābat.
faber, ab architectō laudātus, laetissimus erat.

deae Sūlis: dea Sūlis *the goddess Sūlis, a Celtic deity associated with healing*

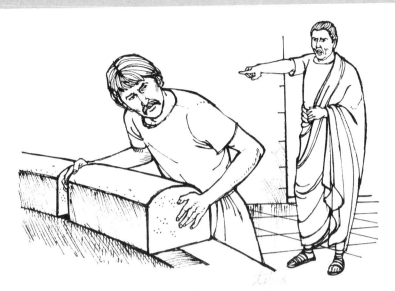

faber secundus mūrum circum fontem pōnēbat.
architectus fabrum incitāvit, quod fessus erat et lentē labōrābat.
faber, ab architectō incitātus, rem graviter ferēbat. nihil tamen
dīxit, quod architectum timēbat.

faber tertius aquam ad balneum ē fonte sacrō portābat.
architectus fabrum vituperāvit, quod ignāvus erat et minimē
labōrābat.
faber, ab architectō vituperātus, īnsolenter respondit.

architectus, ubi verba īnsolentia fabrī audīvit, servōs suōs arcessīvit.

servī, ab architectō arcessītī, fabrum comprehendērunt et in balneum dēiēcērunt.

"linguam sordidam habēs," inquit architectus cachinnāns. "melius est tibi aquam sacram bibere."

fōns sacer

Quīntus apud Salvium manēbat per tōtam hiemem. saepe ad aulam Cogidubnī ībat, ā rēge invītātus. Quīntus eī multa dē vītā suā nārrābat, quod rēx aliquid novī audīre semper volēbat.

ubi vēr appropinquābat, Cogidubnus in morbum gravem incidit. multī medicī, ad aulam arcessītī, remedium morbī quaesīvērunt. 5
ingravēscēbat tamen morbus. rēx Quīntum et Salvium dē remediō anxius cōnsuluit.

"mī Quīnte," inquit, "tū es vir magnae prūdentiae. volō tē mihi

fōns	*fountain, spring*
aliquid novī	*something new*
morbum: morbus	*illness*
gravem: gravis	*serious*
cōnsuluit: cōnsulere	*consult*
vir magnae prūdentiae	*a man of great prudence, a man of good sense*

Spring water overflowing from the hot spring at Bath.

cōnsilium dare. ad fontem sacrum īre dēbeō?"

"ubi est iste fōns?" rogāvit Quīntus. 10

"est in oppidō Aquīs Sūlis," respondit Cogidubnus. "multī aegrōtī, quī ex hōc fonte aquam bibērunt, posteā convaluērunt. architectum Rōmānum illūc mīsī, quī thermās maximās exstrūxit. prope thermās stat templum deae Sūlis, ā meīs fabrīs aedificātum. ego deam saepe honōrāvī; nunc fortasse dea mē sānāre potest. Salvī, 15 tū es vir magnae calliditātis; volō tē mihi cōnsilium dare. quid facere dēbeō?"

"tū es vir sapiēns," respondit ille. "melius est tibi testāmentum facere."

cōnsilium	advice	convaluērunt: convalēscere	get better, recover
oppidō: oppidum	town	exstrūxit: exstruere	build
aegrōtī: aegrōtus	invalid	calliditātis: calliditās	cleverness, shrewdness

When you have read section I of this story, answer the questions at the end of the section.

Lūcius Marcius Memor

I

oppidum Aquae Sūlis parvum erat, thermae maximae. prōcūrātor thermārum erat Lūcius Marcius Memor, nōtissimus haruspex, homō obēsus et ignāvus. quamquam iam tertia hōra erat, Memor in cubiculō ēbrius dormiēbat. Cephalus, haruspicis lībertus, Memorem excitāre temptābat. 5

"domine! domine!" clāmābat.

haruspex, graviter dormiēns, nihil respondit.

"dominus nimium vīnī rūrsus bibit." sibi dīxit lībertus. "domine! surge! hōra tertia est."

Memor, ā lībertō tandem excitātus, ūnum oculum aperuit. 10

"fer mihi plūs vīnī!" inquit. "tum abī!"

"domine! domine! necesse est tibi surgere," inquit Cephalus.

"cūr mē vexās, Cephale?" respondit Memor. "cūr tū rem administrāre ipse nōn potes?"

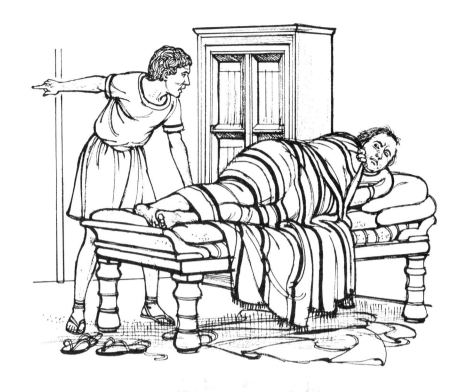

"rem huius modī administrāre nōn possum," respondit lībertus. 15
"sunt multī servī, multī fabrī, quī mandāta prōcūrātōris exspectant.
tē exspectat architectus ipse, vir magnae dignitātis. tē exspectant
aegrōtī. adstant sacerdōtēs parātī. adsunt mercātōrēs, quōs
arcessīvistī. tū rem ipse administrāre dēbēs."

"numquam dēsinit labor," clāmāvit Memor. "quam fessus sum! 20
cūr ad hunc populum barbarum umquam vēnī?"

Cephalus, quī rīsum cēlāre temptābat, Memorī respondit,
"haruspex callidissimus es. nōnne aegrōtīs remedia praebēre vīs?"

prōcūrātor	manager	huius modī	of this kind
haruspex	diviner (who reads the future by inspecting the livers and other organs of animals), soothsayer	mandāta	instructions, orders
		dignitātis: dignitās	importance, prestige
		adstant: adstāre	stand by
		dēsinit: dēsinere	end, cease
obēsus	fat	labor	work
graviter	heavily, soundly	populum: populus	people
nimium vīnī	too much wine	umquam	ever
rūrsus	again	rīsum: rīsus	smile
fer!	bring!	praebēre	provide
plūs vīnī	more wine		

nōnne Britannīs mōrēs Rōmānōs impōnere vīs?"

"es homō magnae stultitiae," respondit Memor. "aegrōtōs floccī   25
nōn faciō. Britannōs etiam minōris pretiī habeō. sed nunc mihi
commodum est hoc tam molestum officium agere. sīc enim ad
maiōrēs honōrēs ascendere possum. ego virōs potentēs colere velim.
ēheu! in hāc īnsulā sunt paucī virī potentēs, paucī clārī."

"quid vīs mē facere, Memor?" rogāvit lībertus.   30

"iubeō tē omnēs dīmittere," clāmāvit Memor. "nōlī mē iterum
vexāre!"

Memor, postquam haec verba dīxit, statim obdormīvit.
Cephalus, ā dominō īrātō territus, invītus exiit. extrā cubiculum
multitūdinem aegrōtōrum invēnit, Memorem exspectantium et   35
vehementer clāmantium. inter aegrōtōs erant nōnnūllī mīlitēs, ab
hostibus nūper vulnerātī et paene interfectī. adstābant quoque
multī fabrī, Memorem absentem vituperantēs. eōs omnēs Cephalus
dīmīsit.

mōrēs: mōs	custom
impōnere	impose
stultitiae: stultitia	stupidity
etiam minōris pretiī habeō	I care even less about
officium	duty
sīc	in this way
honōrēs: honor	honor
potentēs: potēns	powerful
colere	seek favor of, make friends with
velim	I would like
clārī: clārus	famous, distinguished
haec verba	these words
territus: terrēre	frighten
hostibus: hostis	enemy
absentem: absēns	absent

1 What is the time of day at the start of this story? What is Memor's
   freedman trying to do?
2 What does the word "rūrsus" (line 8) suggest about Memor's habits?
3 How many different groups and individuals are waiting to see Memor,
   according to Cephalus (lines 16–18)?
4 Why does Cephalus say "mandāta prōcūrātōris" (line 16) rather than
   "mandāta tua"?
5 What do you think makes Cephalus smile (line 22)? Why does he try to
   hide the smile?

6 According to Cephalus (lines 23–4), what were Memor's reasons for coming to work at Bath? Does Cephalus mean this seriously?
7 According to Memor himself (lines 27–8), what was his real reason for coming to Bath? Why has he found it hard to achieve what he wanted?
8 In line 31, Memor says "iubeō tē omnēs dīmittere." Which words in the last paragraph tell you that this order was obeyed?

Base of a statue dedicated to the goddess Sulis by Lucius Marcius Memor.

II

mox tamen, Cephalus cubiculum rūrsus intrāvit Memoremque dormientem excitāvit. Memor, simulac Cephalum vīdit, īrātus clāmāvit,

"cūr prohibēs mē dormīre? cūr mihi nōn pārēs? stultior es quam asinus."   5

"sed domine," respondit Cephalus, "aliquid novī nūntiāre volō. postquam hinc discessī, mandāta, quae mihi dedistī, effēcī. ubi tamen aegrōtōs fabrōsque dīmittēbam, senātōrem thermīs appropinquantem cōnspexī."

prohibēs: prohibēre   *prevent*
hinc   *from here*
effēcī: efficere   *carry out, accomplish*

"quis est ille senātor?" rogāvit Memor, valdē vexātus. "unde   10
vēnit? senātōrem vidēre nōlō."

"melius est tibi hunc senātōrem vidēre," respondit Cephalus.
"nam Gāius Salvius est."

"num Gāius Salvius Līberālis?" exclāmāvit Memor. "nōn crēdō
tibi."   15

Cephalus tamen facile eī persuāsit, quod Salvius iam in āream
thermārum equitābat.

Memor perterritus statim clāmāvit,

"fer mihi togam! fer calceōs! ōrnāmenta mea ubi sunt? vocā
servōs! quam īnfēlīx sum! Salvius hūc venit, vir summae   20
auctōritātis, quem colere maximē volō."

Memor celerrimē togam calceōsque induit. Cephalus eī
ōrnāmenta trādidit, ex armāriō raptim extracta. haruspex lībertum
innocentem vituperābat, lībertus Salvium.

calceōs: calceus	*shoe*
ōrnāmenta	*badges of office*
auctōritātis: auctōritās	*authority*
raptim	*hastily, quickly*

About the Language

1 In Stage 20, you met sentences like these, containing *present* participles:

servī per vīllam contendērunt, arāneās **quaerentēs**.
The slaves hurried through the house, looking for spiders' webs.

astrologus, amulētum **tenēns**, ad nōs accurrit.
The astrologer, holding an amulet, ran up to us.

2 In Stage 21, you have met sentences like these:

Memor, ā lībertō **excitātus**, īrātissimus erat.
*Memor, **having been awakened** by the freedman, was very angry.*

templum, ā fabrīs perītīs **ōrnātum**, splendidissimum erat.
*The temple, **having been decorated** by skillful craftsmen, was very impressive.*

The words in boldface are *perfect* participles.

3 A perfect participle is used to describe a noun. For instance, in the first example in paragraph 2, **excitātus** describes Memor.

4 Translate the following examples:

1 servus, ā dominō verberātus, ē vīllā fūgit.
2 saltātrīx, ā spectātōribus laudāta, rīsit.
3 nūntius, ad rēgem arcessītus, rem terribilem nārrāvit.

Pick out the perfect participle in each sentence and find the noun which it describes.

5 A perfect participle changes its ending to agree with the noun it describes. For example:

SINGULAR: fūr, ā centuriōne superātus, veniam petīvit.
PLURAL: fūrēs, ā centuriōne superātī, veniam petīvērunt.

6 Translate the following examples and pick out the perfect participle in each sentence:

1 senex, ab astrologō monitus, nāvigāre nōluit.
2 prīncipēs, ā rēge vocātī, celeriter ad aulam vēnērunt.
3 cēna, ā coquō Graecō parāta, omnēs hospitēs dēlectāvit.

Find the noun which each perfect participle is describing and say whether each noun-and-participle pair is singular or plural.

7 There are two kinds of perfect participle in Latin. The one described in this Stage is known as the *perfect passive* participle. You will meet the other kind in Stage 22.

8 Notice two different ways of translating perfect passive participles:

architectus, ā Cogidubnō ipsō missus, thermās maximās exstrūxit.
The architect, having been sent by Cogidubnus himself, built some very large baths.
   or, in more natural English,
The architect, sent by Cogidubnus himself, built some very large baths.

mercātōrēs, ā latrōnibus graviter vulnerātī, in fossā iacēbant.
The merchants, having been seriously wounded by robbers, were lying in the ditch.
The merchants, seriously wounded by robbers, were lying in the ditch.

Memor rem suscipit

Salvius et Memor, in hortō sōlī ambulantēs, sermōnem gravem habent.

Salvius: Lūcī Marcī Memor, vir summae prūdentiae es. volō tē
                rem magnam suscipere.

Memor: tālem rem suscipere velim, sed occupātissimus sum.
                exspectant mē aegrōtī et sacerdōtēs. vexant mē   5
                architectus et fabrī. sed quid vīs mē facere?

Salvius: Tiberius Claudius Cogidubnus, rēx Rēgnēnsium, hūc
                nūper advēnit. Cogidubnus, quī in morbum gravem
                incidit, aquam ē fonte sacrō bibere vult.

Memor: difficile est mihi tē adiuvāre, mī senātor. Cogidubnus est   10
                vir octōgintā annōrum. difficile est deae Sūlī Cogi-
                dubnum sānāre.

Salvius: nōlō tē reddere Cogidubnum sānum. volō tē rem
                contrāriam efficere.

Memor: quid dīcis? num mortem Cogidubnī cupis?   15

Salvius: ita vērō! porrō, quamquam tam occupātus es, volō tē
                ipsum hanc rem efficere.

Memor: vīsne mē mortem eī parāre? rem huius modī facere nōn
                ausim. Cogidubnus enim est vir clārissimus, ā populō
                Rōmānō honōrātus.   20

Salvius: es vir summae calliditātis. hanc rem efficere potes. nōn
                sōlum ego, sed etiam Imperātor, hoc cupit. Cogidubnus
                enim Rōmānōs saepe vexāvit. Imperātor mihi, nōn
                Cogidubnō, cōnfīdit. Imperātor tibi praemium dignum
                prōmittit. num praemium recūsāre vīs, tibi ab   25
                Imperātōre prōmissum?

Memor: quō modō id facere possum?

Salvius: nescio. hoc tantum tibi dīcō: Imperātor mortem
                Cogidubnī exspectat.

Memor: ō mē miserum! rem difficiliōrem numquam fēcī.   30

Salvius: vīta, mī Memor, est plēna rērum difficilium.
                (exit Salvius.)

Memor: Cephale! Cephale! *(lībertus, ā Memore vocātus, celeriter*
                intrat. pōculum vīnī fert.) cūr mihi vīnum offers? nōn
                vīnum, sed cōnsilium quaerō. iubeō tē mihi cōnsilium   35
                quam celerrimē dare. rēx Cogidubnus hūc vēnit,

remedium morbī petēns. Imperātor, ā Cogidubnō saepe vexātus, iam mortem eius cupit. Imperātor ipse iubet mē hoc efficere. quam difficile est!

Cephalus: minimē, facile est! pōculum venēnātum habeō, mihi ā   40
            latrōne Aegyptiō ōlim datum. venēnum, in pōculō
            cēlātum, vītam celerrimē exstinguere potest.

Memor: cōnsilium, quod mihi prōpōnis, perīculōsum est.
            Cogidubnō venēnum dare timeō.

Cephalus: nihil perīculī est. rēx, quotiēns ē balneō exiit, ad fontem   45
            deae īre solet. tum necesse est servō prope fontem deae
            stāre et pōculum rēgī offerre.

Memor: (dēlectātus) cōnsilium optimum est. nūllīs tamen servīs
            cōnfīdere ausim. sed tibi cōnfīdō, Cephale. iubeō tē
            ipsum Cogidubnō pōculum offerre.   50

Cephalus: ēheu! vīta lībertī dūra est. mihi rem difficillimam
            impōnis.

Memor: vīta, mī Cephale, est plēna rērum difficilium.

tālem: tālis	such		nescio: nescīre	not know
octōgintā	eighty		venēnātum: venēnātus	poisoned
reddere	make		datum: dare	give
sānum: sānus	well, healthy		venēnum	poison
rem contrāriam:			exstinguere	extinguish, destroy
rēs contrāria	the opposite		prōpōnis: prōpōnere	propose, put forward
porrō	what's more,		nihil perīculī	no danger
	furthermore		quotiēns	whenever
nōn ausim	I wouldn't dare		balneō: balneum	bath
nōn sōlum . . .			difficillimam:	
sed etiam	not only . . . but also		difficillimus	very difficult
dignum: dignus	worthy, appropriate			

About the Language

1 Study the following examples:

plūs cibī   *more food*
nimium vīnī   *too much wine*

Each example is made up of two words:

Ⱶ a word like **plūs** or **nimium** which indicates an *amount* or *quantity*,
2 a noun in the *genitive* case.

2 Further examples:

satis pecūniae   nimium perīculī
nimium cibī   plūs sanguinis
plūs labōris   satis aquae

Practicing the Language

1 Study the forms and meanings of the following words, and give the meanings of the untranslated ones:

laetus	*happy*	laetē	*happily*
perītus	*skillful*	perītē	*skillfully*
stultissimus	*very foolish*	stultissimē	*very foolishly*
tacitus	*silent*	tacitē	
cautus	*cautious*	cautē	
probus		probē	*honestly*
callidus		callidē	*cleverly*
superbus	*proud*	superbē	
crūdēlissimus	*very cruel*	crūdēlissimē	
sevērissimus	*very severe*	sevērissimē	
līberālissimus		līberālissimē	*very generously*

The words in the left-hand pair of columns are *adjectives*. Adjectives were described in Stage 14 and the Language Information Section of Unit 2.

The words in the right-hand pair of columns are known as *adverbs*.

Give the meaning of each of the following adverbs:

intentē, firmē, stultē, saevē, dīligentissimē

2 Complete each sentence with the right word and then translate.

1 omnēs aegrōtī . . . . . vīsitāre volēbant. (fōns, fontem, fontis)
2 plūrimī servī in fundō . . . . . labōrābant. (dominus, dominum, dominī)
3 "fortasse . . . . . morbum meum sānāre potest," inquit rēx. (dea, deam, deae)
4 . . . . . Cogidubnum laudāvērunt, quod līberālis et sapiēns erat. (prīncipēs, prīncipum)
5 mercātor, postquam . . . . . in saccō posuit, ē forō discessit. (dēnāriī, dēnāriōs, dēnāriōrum)
6 senex, quī in Arabiā diū habitāverat, magnum numerum . . . . . collēgerat. (gemmae, gemmās, gemmārum)

3 Complete each sentence with the right word from the list below and then translate.

parāvī, rapuērunt, amīcōrum, hastam, nūntius, hospitibus

1 puer, in cubiculō dormiēns, vōcēs . . . . . nōn audīvit.
2 "optimam cēnam tibi . . . . ., domine," inquit coquus.
3 senex, quī avārus erat, ... vīnum offerre nōlēbat.
4 in rīpā flūminis stābat servus, quī . . . . . in manibus tenēbat.
5 subitō latrōnēs irrūpērunt et pecūniam . . . . . .
6 . . . . ., quem rēx mīserat, epistulam in itinere āmīsit.

4 Translate each English sentence into Latin by selecting correctly from the pairs of Latin words.

For example: *The messenger heard the voice of the old man.*

         nūntius   vōcem   senem   audīvī
         nūntium vōcī   senis   audīvit

Answer: nūntius vōcem senis audīvit.

1 *The priests showed the statue to the architect.*
    sacerdōtēs   statuam architectum   ostendit
    sacerdōtibus statuās   architectō   ostendērunt

2 *The king praised the skillful doctor.*
    rēx   medicus   perītum   laudāvit
    rēgēs   medicum   perītī   laudāvērunt

3 *A friend of the soldiers was visiting the temple.*
    amīcus   mīlitis   templum   vīsitābat
    amīcō   mīlitum templī   vīsitāvit

4 *The shouts of the invalids had annoyed the soothsayer.*
     clāmōrem   aegrōtī   haruspicem vexāverant
     clāmōrēs   aegrōtōrum haruspicēs vexāvērunt

5 *We handed over the master's money to the farmers.*
     pecūnia   dominum   agricolās trādidimus
     pecūniam dominī   agricolīs trādidērunt

5 Complete each sentence with the right word and then translate.

1 tū ipse hanc rem administrāre . . . . . .(dēbeō, dēbēs, dēbet)
2 "domine! surge!" clāmāvit Cephalus. "nam Gāius Salvius thermīs
   . . . . . ." (appropinquō, appropinquās, appropinquat)
3 cūr mē vituperās? heri per tōtum diem . . . . . . (labōrāvī, labōrāvistī, labōrāvit)
4 ego, quod fontem sacrum vidēre . . . . ., iter ad oppidum Aquās Sūlis fēcī. (cupiēbam, cupiēbās, cupiēbat)
5 lībertus, quī senātōrem . . . . ., in cubiculum haruspicis ruit. (cōnspexeram, cōnspexerās, cōnspexerat)
6 ubi poēta versum scurrīlem recitāvit, amīcus meus īrātus erat; ego tamen . . . . . . (rīsī, rīsistī, rīsit)
7 ē lectō surrēxī, quod dormīre nōn . . . . . . (poteram, poterās, poterat)
8 in hāc vīllā . . . . . Memor, haruspex nōtissimus. (habitō, habitās, habitat)

Aquae Sulis and its Baths

The modern city of Bath lies in the valley of the river Avon, just to the east of Bristol in the southwest of England. In a small area of low-lying ground, enclosed by a bend in the river, mineral springs of hot water emerge from underground at the rate of a quarter of a million gallons (over one million liters) a day. The water has a temperature of between 104 and 121 degrees Fahrenheit (40 and 49 degrees centigrade). It has a low mineral content (calcium, magnesium, and sodium are the main minerals) and microscopic traces of radium. It was here that the Celts who lived in the surrounding hills came to worship the goddess of the spring, Sulis, long before the Romans arrived in Britain. The Celts clearly recognized the power of the goddess to produce hot water from the ground, but they also saw the power of the goddess in the healing properties of the spring water.

As Roman settlers moved gradually westwards after the invasion of A.D. 43, they soon brought changes to the region. Much of the rich farmland owned by Celtic farmers was taken over and turned into villa estates in the Roman style. The Romans recognized that the springs of Sulis were an important religious center and they erected huge public baths and other buildings so that visitors might enjoy the healing properties of the hot mineral waters in comfort. No doubt the heat helped relieve conditions such as rheumatism and arthritis, but many people must have visited the baths in the hope of miraculous cures for all kinds of diseases. During the latter part of the first century A.D., the new Romano-British town of Aquae Sulis began to grow up. The Roman writer, Pliny the Elder, said in his *Natural History* that healing springs help to encourage the growth of towns. Aquae Sulis was no exception. The healing springs, a mild climate, and a sheltered position were all reasons why the town developed as an important spa.

The steaming waters of the Great Bath. The existing surroundings date from the 19th century AD.

The Roman masons had good supplies of limestone quarried locally, and the nearby Mendip Hills provided the lead needed for lining the baths. The main building was a long, rectangular structure, larger and more magnificent than any other set of baths west of Rome at this date. It contained three main plunge baths filled with a constant supply of water at a pleasant temperature. The water was brought from the hot spring through lead pipes. The pool nearest the spring naturally contained the hottest water, whereas the furthest pool was the coolest, since the water lost much of its heat on the way to it. To provide a focal point for visitors to the baths, the Romans surrounded the spring with a lead-lined reservoir some 40–50 feet (12–15 meters) across. At a later date, they built a viewing platform and roofed the entire structure.

Aquae Sulis lay within tribal territory over which Cogidubnus may have had control. It is just possible that he himself was responsible for or at least had a hand in the development of the town. This building project certainly matched the splendor of the palace at Fishbourne which was erected at about the same time.

At the time of our story (A.D. 83), Aquae Sulis was a small but growing community. The bath buildings were still being erected but were already the most impressive feature of the town. There were probably a few other public buildings, such as a **basilica** (*court building*)

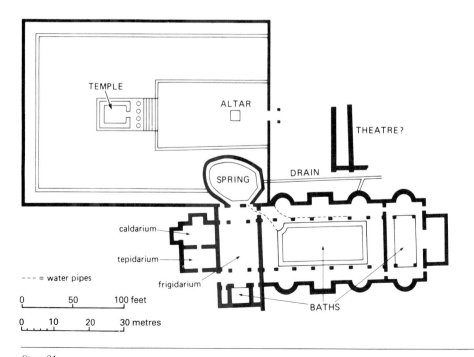

for the administration of law and local government, and possibly a theater, but most of the other buildings would have been houses for those who had already made their home in the town, and inns for the town's many visitors.

Some people traveled long distances to Aquae Sulis, attracted by the fame of its spring and hoping that the healing power of the waters would cure their illnesses. One elderly woman, Rusonia Aventina, came from Metz in eastern Gaul. Her tombstone shows that she died at Aquae Sulis at the age of fifty-eight, perhaps from the illness which she had hoped the spring would cure. Julius Vitalis was a soldier serving as armorer to the Twentieth Legion, based at Chester in northwestern England, 130 miles (200 kilometers) north-northwest of Bath. His tombstone shows that he had served for just nine years when he died at the age of twenty-nine; possibly his commanding officer had sent him to Aquae Sulis on sick leave. But many visitors came and departed in good health.

The Roman authorities were quick to realize that Aquae Sulis was becoming a popular place of pilgrimage. Visitors entering the new bath buildings and seeing the mysterious hot waters bubbling in the newly built reservoir would feel that they were entering a holy place. They thought that a cure for their ailments depended as much on divine favor as on the medicinal powers of the water. A temple was therefore constructed next to the bath buildings and dedicated to the goddess Sulis Minerva. By linking the two names in this way, the Romans encouraged the British people to worship Minerva, goddess of healing and the arts, together with their own goddess, Sulis. The temple stood in a specially enclosed area, with a magnificent altar in front and a bronze statue of the goddess inside.

The appointment of a Roman official, Lucius Marcius Memor, to take charge of the religious activities at Aquae Sulis is another example of the Romans' efforts to spread Roman ways and customs among the Britons. In the story on page 8 he complains of having to live and work in Britain, but he reluctantly accepts that this is necessary if he is to further his career back in Rome. Clearly, Memor has been posted to the province of Britain to help promote the Roman way of life. Many such officials must have contributed to the policy of "Romanization" in this way.

Aquae Sulis was, of course, something of a tourist center as well as a place of religious pilgrimage, and one can imagine the entrance to the baths crowded with souvenir stalls and sellers of lucky charms. Visitors would often buy such offerings to throw into the sacred spring with a prayer for future good health. These offerings were sometimes expensive:

they included, for example, beautifully carved gemstones and other items of jewelry.

The full extent of the bath and temple buildings is only gradually becoming known to us from the work of archaeologists. The most recent excavations have revealed the details of construction of the Roman reservoir surrounding the hot spring itself, and important work was carried out in 1982 on the temple precinct. The results of these excavations are on display in the museum. Many thousands of Roman coins have been recovered from the spring, together with silver and pewter vessels used for pouring offerings to the goddess. Many small sheets of lead or pewter were also found with Latin inscriptions on them. Their translations show that some people were anxious to use the powers of Sulis Minerva for more sinister purposes than good health, as we shall see in Stage 22.

Inscribed pewter and silver bowls thrown as offerings into the sacred spring.

Tin mask discovered in the sacred spring.

Words and Phrases Checklist

From now on, most verbs in the checklists are listed as in the Language Information Section of this Unit (i.e. perfect passive participles are usually included).

ā, ab	*by*
adiuvō, adiuvāre, adiūvī	*help*
annus, annī	*year*
ascendō, ascendere, ascendī	*climb, rise*
barbarus, barbarī	*barbarian*
cēlō, cēlāre, cēlāvī, cēlātus	*hide*
circum	*around*
cōnfīdō, cōnfīdere	*trust*
dēiciō, dēicere, dēiēcī, dēiectus	*throw down*
dūrus, dūra, dūrum	*harsh, hard*
efficiō, efficere, effēcī, effectus	*carry out, accomplish*
extrahō, extrahere, extrāxī, extractus	*drag out, pull out*
fōns, fontis	*fountain, spring*
gravis, grave	*heavy, serious*
haruspex, haruspicis	*diviner, soothsayer*
hōra, hōrae	*hour*
īnfēlīx, *gen.* īnfēlīcis	*unlucky*
iubeō, iubēre, iussī, iussus	*order*
morbus, morbī	*illness*
nōnnūllī, nōnnūllae	*some, several*
nūper	*recently*
occupātus, occupāta, occupātum	*busy*
oppidum, oppidī	*town*
perītus, perīta, perītum	*skillful*
plēnus, plēna, plēnum	*full*
plūs, *gen.* plūris	*more*
pretium, pretiī	*price*
sapiēns, *gen.* sapientis	*wise*
suscipiō, suscipere, suscēpī, susceptus	*undertake, take on*
unde	*from where*

Word Search

Match each definition with one of the words given below.

annually, barbaric, confidence, effect, endure, morbid, sapient

1 . . . . .: crude or savage
2 . . . . .: a result (as a noun); to bring about or cause (as a verb)
3 . . . . .: psychologically unhealthy
4 . . . . .: on a yearly basis
5 . . . . .: to persevere despite hardship
6 . . . . .: trust; certainty
7 . . . . .: possessing wisdom or knowledge

dēfīxiō

fūr thermīs cautē
appropinquāvit.
fūr, thermās ingressus, ad
fontem sacrum festīnāvit. .

fūr, prope fontem stāns,
circumspectāvit.
fūr, senem cōnspicātus, post
columnam sē cēlāvit.

senex, amulētum aureum tenēns,
ad fontem prōcessit.
senex oculōs ad caelum sustulit
et deae Sūlī precēs adhibuit.

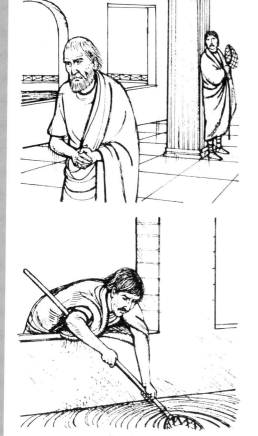

senex, deam precātus, amulētum
in fontem iniēcit et exiit.

fūr, quī amulētum aureum
vīderat, ad fontem iterum
festīnāvit.
fūr, ad fontem regressus,
amulētum in aquā quaesīvit.

fūr, amulētum adeptus, attonitus lēgit:

fūr amulētum dēiēcit et ē thermīs perterritus fūgit.

Vilbia

Vilbia et Rubria, pōcula sordida lavantēs, in culīnā tabernae garriēbant. hae puellae erant fīliae Latrōnis. Latrō, quī tabernam tenēbat, erat vir magnae dīligentiae sed minimae prūdentiae. Latrō, culīnam ingressus, puellās castīgābat.

"multa sunt pōcula sordida. iubeō vōs pōcula quam celerrimē 5
lavāre. labōrāte! nōlīte garrīre! loquāciōrēs estis quam psittacī."

Latrō, haec verba locūtus, exiit.

Vilbia, tamen, quae pulchra et obstināta erat, patrem floccī nōn faciēbat. pōcula nōn lāvit, sed Rubriae fībulam ostendit. Rubria fībulam, quam soror tenēbat, avidē spectāvit. 10

Rubria: quam pulchra, quam pretiōsa est haec fībula, mea Vilbia! eam īnspicere velim. quis tibi dedit? num argentea est?

Vilbia: sānē argentea est. Modestus, mīles Rōmānus, eam mihi dedit.

Rubria: quālis est hic mīles? estne homō mendāx, sīcut cēterī 15
mīlitēs Rōmānī? multī mīlitēs vulnera fingunt, quod perīcula bellī vītāre volunt. Modestus quoque ignāvus est?

Vilbia: minimē! est vir maximae virtūtis. ōlim tria mīlia hostium occīdit. nunc lēgātum ipsum custōdit.

Rubria: Herculēs alter est! ego autem tālēs fābulās saepe ex aliīs 20
mīlitibus audīvī.

Vilbia: cēterī mīlitēs mendācēs sunt, Modestus probus. Modestus hūc vēnit aeger. Modestus, in thermās ingressus, aquam sacram bibit. Modestus, deam Sūlem precātus, statim convaluit. 25

Rubria: dissentīre nōn ausim. quō modō huic tam mīrābilī mīlitī occurristī?

Vilbia: simulac tabernam nostram intrāvit Modestus, eum statim amāvī. quantī erant lacertī eius! quanta bracchia!

Rubria: tibi favet fortūna, mea Vilbia. quid autem dē Bulbō dīcis, 30
quem ōlim amābās? tibi perīculōsum est Bulbum contemnere, quod rēs magicās intellegit.

Vilbia: nōlī illam pestem commemorāre! Bulbus, saepe dē mātrimōniō locūtus, nihil umquam effēcit. sed Modestus,

qui fortissimus et audācissimus est, mē cūrāre potest.
Modestus nunc est suspīrium meum.

dīligentiae: dīligentia	*industry, hard work*	lēgātum: lēgātus	*commander*
minimae: minimus	*very little*	alter	*another, a second*
ingressus	*having entered*	autem	*but*
locūtus	*having spoken*	precātus	*having prayed to*
fībulam: fībula	*brooch*	huic	*this (dative of* hic)
avidē	*eagerly*	occurristī: occurrere	*meet*
quālis?	*what sort of man?*	quantī: quantus	*how big*
vulnera fingunt	*pretend to be wounded,*	lacertī: lacertus	*muscle*
	invent wounds	bracchia	*arms*
bellī: bellum	*war*	contemnere	*reject, despise*
virtūtis: virtūs	*courage*	mātrimōniō:	
tria mīlia	*three thousand*	mātrimōnium	*marriage*
occīdit: occīdere	*kill*	suspīrium	*heart-throb*

Latrōnis: Latrō	*father of Vilbia and Rubria, and innkeeper (What does his name mean?)*
Bulbō: Bulbus	*Vilbia's boyfriend (His name means "onion.")*
Modestus	*a soldier in the Roman Second Legion (What does his name mean?)*

Modestus

Modestus et Strȳthiō ad tabernam Latrōnis ambulant. Strȳthiō, quamquam amīcus Modestī est, eum dērīdet.

Modestus: ubi es, Strȳthiō? iubeō tē prope mē stāre.

Strȳthiō: adsum. hercle! quam fortūnātus sum! prope virum summae virtūtis sum. tū enim fortior es quam Mārs   5
ipse.

Modestus: vērum dīcis. ōlim tria mīlia hostium occīdī.

Strȳthiō: tē omnēs puellae amant, quod tam fortis et pulcher es. illa Vilbia, heri tē cōnspicāta, statim amāvit. multa dē tē rogāvit.   10

Modestus: quid dīxit?

Strȳthiō: mē avidē rogāvit, "estne Herculēs?" "minimē! est frāter eius," respondī. tum fībulam, quam puella alia tibi dederat, Vilbiae trādidī. "Modestus, vir benignus et

vērum	*the truth*	cōnspicāta: cōnspicātus	*having caught sight of*
Strȳthiō	*a soldier in the Roman Second Legion (His name means "ostrich.")*		
Mārs	*Mars (Roman god of war)*		

---

nōbilis," inquam, "tibi hanc fībulam grātīs dat." Vilbia,   15
fībulam adepta, mihi respondit, "quam pulcher
Modestus est! quam līberālis! velim cum eō colloquium
habēre."

Modestus: ēheu! nōnne molestae sunt puellae? mihi difficile est
puellās vītāre. nimis pulcher sum.   20

Strȳthiō: ecce! ad tabernam Latrōnis advēnimus. fortasse inest
Vilbia, quae tē tamquam deum adōrat.
(tabernam intrant.)

inquam	*I said*	colloquium	*talk, chat*
grātīs	*free*	nimis	*too*
adepta: adeptus	*having received,*	inest: inesse	*be inside*
	having obtained	tamquam	*as, like*

About the Language

1 In Stage 21 you met sentences containing *perfect passive* participles:

rēx, ā Rōmānīs **honōrātus**, semper fidēlis manēbat.
*The king, **having been honored** by the Romans, always remained loyal.*

puerī, ā custōde **monitī**, ad vīllam rediērunt.
*The boys, **having been warned** by the guard, returned to the house.*

2 In Stage 22, you have met another kind of perfect participle. Study the
way it is translated in the following examples:

Vilbia, culīnam **ingressa**, sorōrī fībulam ostendit.
*Vilbia, **having entered** the kitchen, showed the brooch to her sister.*

senex, haec verba **locūtus**, abiit.
*The old man, **having said** these words, went away.*

This kind of participle is a *perfect active* participle.

3 Translate the following examples and pick out the perfect active
participle in each sentence:

1 iuvenis, ad thermās regressus, amīcum quaesīvit.
2 puellae, leōnem cōnspicātae, ad vīllam statim ruērunt.
3 mercātōrēs, pecūniam adeptī, ad nāvēs contendērunt.
4 ancilla, deam precāta, ā templō discessit.

Find the noun which each participle is describing.

amor omnia vincit

scaena prīma

Bulbus et amīcus in tabernā Latrōnis sunt. vīnum bibunt āleamque lūdunt.
Bulbus amīcō multam pecūniam dēbet.

Gutta (*amīcus Bulbī*): quam īnfēlīx es! nōn sōlum puellam, sed etiam
        pecūniam āmīsistī.

Bulbus: pecūniam floccī nōn faciō, sed puellam, quam maximē   5
        amō, āmittere nōlō.

amor	*love*	scaena	*scene*
omnia	*all, everything*	āleam . . . lūdunt	*are playing dice*

Wall-painting of a dice game from Pompeii.

Gutta: quō modō eam retinēre potes? mīles Rōmānus, vir summae
virtūtis, eam petit. heus! Venerem iactāvī! caupō! iubeō tē
plūs vīnī ferre.

Bulbus: mīles, quī eam dēcēpit, homō mendāx, prāvus, ignāvus est. 10
Vilbia, ab eō dēcepta, nunc mē contemnit. eam saepe
monuī, nōlī mīlitibus crēdere, praesertim Rōmānīs. Vilbia
tamen, hunc Modestum cōnspicāta, statim eum amāvit.

Gutta: puellīs nōn tūtum est per viās huius oppidī īre. tanta est
arrogantia hōrum mīlitum. hercle! tū etiam īnfēlīcior es. 15
canem iterum iactāvistī. alium dēnārium mihi dēbēs.

Bulbus: dēnārium libenter trādō, nōn puellam. ōdī istum mīlitem.
Modestus tamen puellam retinēre nōn potest, quod
auxilium ā deā petīvī. thermās ingressus, tabulam in
fontem sacrum iniēcī. dīra imprecātiō, in tabulā scrīpta, 20
iam in fonte deae iacet. (*intrant Modestus et Strȳthiō*.) exitium
Modestī laetus exspectō. nihil mihi obstāre potest.

Gutta: hercle! īnfēlīcissimus es. ecce! nōbīs appropinquat ipse
Modestus. necesse est mihi quam celerrimē exīre.
(*exit currēns*.) 25

iactāvī: iactāre	*throw*
praesertim	*especially*
arrogantia	*arrogance, excessive pride*
canem: canis	*dog (lowest throw at dice)*
ōdī	*I hate*
tabulam: tabula	*tablet, writing-tablet*
imprecātiō	*curse*
scrīpta: scrībere	*write*
exitium	*ruin, destruction*
Gutta	*friend of Bulbus (The name means "drop" or "droplet")*
Venerem: Venus	*Venus (highest throw at dice)*

scaena secunda

Modestus īrātus Bulbum vituperat, quod verba eius audīvit.

Modestus: quid dīcēbās, homuncule? exitium meum exspectās?
asine! tū, quod mīlitem Rōmānum vituperāvistī, in
magnō perīculō es. mihi facile est tē, tamquam hostem,
dīlaniāre. Strȳthiō! tē iubeō hanc pestem verberāre. 5
postquam eum verberāvistī, ē tabernā ēice!

Strȳthiō invītus Bulbum verberāre incipit. Bulbus, fortiter sē dēfendēns, vīnum in caput Strȳthiōnis fundit. Modestus Bulbum, simulac tergum vertit, ferōciter pulsat. Bulbus exanimātus prōcumbit. Vilbia, quae clāmōrēs audīvit, intrat. ingressa, Bulbum humī iacentem videt et Modestum mollīre incipit. 10

Vilbia: dēsine, mī Modeste. iste Bulbus, ā tē verberātus, iterum mē vexāre nōn potest. tū es leō, iste rīdiculus mūs. volō tē clēmentem esse et Bulbō parcere. placetne tibi?

Modestus: mihi placet. victōribus decōrum est victīs parcere. tē, nōn istum, quaerō. 15

Vilbia: ō Modeste, quam laeta sum! cūr mē ex omnibus puellīs ēlēgistī?

Modestus: necesse est nōbīs in locō sēcrētō noctū convenīre.

Vilbia: id facere nōn ausim. pater mē sōlam exīre nōn vult. ubi est hic locus? 20

Modestus: prope fontem deae Sūlis. nōnne tibi persuādēre possum?

Vilbia: mihi difficile est iussa patris neglegere, sed tibi resistere nōn possum.

Modestus: dā mihi ōsculum. 25

Vilbia: ēheu! ō suspīrium meum! mihi necesse est ad culīnam redīre, tibi noctem exspectāre.

exeunt. Bulbus, quī magnam partem huius colloquiī audīvit, surgit. quam celerrimē ēgressus, Guttam petit, cui cōnsilium callidum prōpōnit.

dīlaniāre	*tear to pieces*
ēice: ēicere	*throw out*
humī	*on the ground*
mollīre	*soothe*
clēmentem: clēmēns	*merciful*
parcere	*spare*
victīs: victī	*the conquered*
sēcrētō: sēcrētus	*secret*
noctū	*by night*
iussa	*orders, instructions*
neglegere	*neglect*
ēgressus	*having gone out*
cui	*to whom (dative of* quī*)*

The sacred spring in Bath as it is today. Visitors still come to "take the waters".

scaena tertia

per silentium noctis thermās intrant Bulbus et Gutta. prope fontem sacrum sē cēlant. Bulbus Guttae stolam et pallium, quod sēcum tulit, ostendit.

Bulbus: Gutta, volō tē haec vestīmenta induere. volō tē persōnam Vilbiae agere. nōbīs necesse est dēcipere Modestum, quem brevī exspectō.   5

Gutta: vah! virō nōn decōrum est stolam gerere. praetereā barbam habeō.

Bulbus: id minimī mōmentī est, quod in tenebrīs sumus. nōnne tibi persuādēre possum? ecce! decem dēnāriōs tibi dō. nunc tacē! indue stolam palliumque! stā prope fontem   10 deae! ubi Modestus fontī appropinquat, dīc eī verba suāvissima!

Gutta, postquam stolam invītus induit, prope fontem stat. Modestus, sōlus thermās ingressus, fontī appropinquat.

Modestus: Vilbia, mea Vilbia! Modestus, fortissimus mīlitum,   15 adest.

Gutta: ō dēliciae meae! venī ad mē.

Modestus:	quam rauca est vōx tua! num lacrimās, quod tardus adveniō?
Gutta:	ita vērō! tam sollicita eram. 20
Modestus:	lacrimās tuās siccāre possum. (*Modestus ad Guttam advenit.*) dī immortālēs! Vilbia! barbam habēs? quid tibi accidit? ō!

tum Bulbus Modestum in fontem dēicit. Vilbia, thermās ingressa, ubi clāmōrēs
audīvit, prope iānuam perterrita manet. 25

Modestus:	pereō! pereō! parce! parce!
Bulbus:	furcifer! Vilbiam meam, quam valdē amō, auferre audēs? nunc mihi facile est tē interficere.
Modestus:	reddō tibi Vilbiam. nōn amō Vilbiam. eam ā tē auferre nōn ausim. nōlī mē innocentem interficere. Vilbiam 30 floccī nōn faciō.

Vilbia, simulatque haec audīvit, īrāta fontī appropinquat. Modestum
vituperāre incipit.

Vilbia:	mē floccī nōn facis? ō hominem ignāvum! ego ipsa tē dīlaniāre velim. 35
Bulbus:	mea Vilbia, victōribus decōrum est victīs parcere.
Vilbia:	mī Bulbe, dēliciae meae, miserrima sum! longē errāvī.
Bulbus:	nōlī lacrimāre! ego tē cūrāre possum.
Vilbia:	ō Bulbe! ō suspīrium meum!

Bulbus et Vilbia domum redeunt. Gutta stolam palliumque exuit. dēnāriōs laetē 40
numerat. Modestus ē fonte sē extrahit et madidus abit.

pallium	*cloak*
vestīmenta	*clothes*
persōnam Vilbiae agere	*play the part of Vilbia*
brevī	*in a short time*
vah!	*ugh!*
praetereā	*besides*
mōmentī: mōmentum	*importance*
tenebrīs: tenebrae	*darkness*
siccāre	*dry*
auferre	*take away, steal*
longē errāvī: longē errāre	*make a big mistake*
exuit: exuere	*take off*

About the Language

1 Study the following examples:

homō ingeniī prāvī   *a man of evil character*
fēmina magnae dignitātis   *a woman of great prestige*

In each example, a word like **homō** or **fēmina** is described by a noun and adjective in the *genitive* case.

2 Notice the different ways of translating such phrases:

puella magnae prūdentiae
a girl of great sense; or, in more natural English: *a very sensible girl*

vir summae virtūtis
a man of the utmost courage; or, in more natural English: *a very courageous man,* or *a very brave man*

3 Further examples:

vir magnae auctōritātis   fābula huius modī
homō minimae prūdentiae   iuvenis ingeniī optimī
vir octōgintā annōrum   puella maximae calliditātis

Practicing the Language

1 Study the forms and meanings of the following adjectives and adverbs, and give the meanings of the untranslated words:

brevis	*short, brief*	breviter	*shortly, briefly*
ferōx	*fierce*	ferōciter	*fiercely*
cōmis	*polite*	cōmiter	
levis		leviter	*lightly, slightly*
suāvis	*sweet*	suāviter	
celer		celeriter	*quickly*
crūdēlis	*cruel*	crūdēliter	
mollis	*soft, gentle*	molliter	
pār		pariter	*equally*
dīligēns	*careful*	dīligenter	
neglegēns		neglegenter	*carelessly*
prūdēns	*shrewd, sensible*	prūdenter	
audāx	*bold*	audācter	

Give the meaning of each of the following adverbs:

fidēliter, fortiter, līberāliter, sapienter, īnsolenter

2 Complete each sentence with the right word and then translate.

1 Modestus per viās . . . . . ambulābat, puellās quaerēns. (oppidī, oppidō)
2 Gutta, vir benignus, auxilium . . . . . saepe dabat. (amīcī, amīcō)
3 Rubria, quae in tabernā labōrābat, ... vīnum obtulit. (iuvenis, iuvenī)
4 in vīllā . . . . ., turba ingēns conveniēbat. (haruspicis, haruspicī)
5 tabernārius . . . . . multās rēs pretiōsās ostendit. (ancillārum, ancillīs)
6 dea Sūlis precēs . . . . . audīre solēbat. (aegrōtōrum, aegrōtīs)
7 centuriō gladiōs hastāsque . . . . . īnspicere coepit. (mīlitum, mīlitibus)
8 caupō pessimum vīnum . . . . . praebēbat. (hospitum, hospitibus)

3 Make up six Latin sentences using some of the words in the lists below. Some of your sentences should contain four words, but others may contain only three, or two. Write out each sentence and then translate it.

For example:
    puer senī pōculum trādidit.   *The boy handed the cup to the old man.*

    cīvēs agricolam salūtāvērunt.   *The citizens greeted the farmer.*

    nautās vīdit.   *He saw the sailors.*

NOMINATIVES	ACCUSATIVES	DATIVES	VERBS
servus	pecūniam	ancillīs	vīdit
servī	equōs	fabrō	vīdērunt
gladiātor	dominum	iuvenibus	trādidit
gladiātōrēs	nautās	centuriōnī	trādidērunt
cīvis	leōnem	hominibus	interfēcit
cīvēs	gemmās	senī	interfēcērunt
fēmina	agricolam	spectātōribus	obtulit
fēminae	librōs	medicō	obtulērunt
puer	mīlitem	amīcīs	salūtāvit
puerī	pōculum	rēgī	salūtāvērunt

Magic and Curses

When Roman religious sites are excavated, archaeologists sometimes find lead or pewter tablets inscribed with curses. These are known as **dēfīxiōnēs**. Many Romans believed it was possible to put a curse on a personal enemy by dedicating him or her to the gods in this way.

Many defixiones have been found in Britain. They include, for example, a defixio placed by a man on a gang that had beaten him up. In another one, a woman curses someone who has falsely accused her of poisoning her husband. Many are directed at thieves.

The method of putting a defixio on somebody was as follows. The name of the offender was written on a small tablet together with details of the crime and the hoped-for punishment. The tablet was then fastened to a tomb with a long nail, or thrown into a well or a spring. To increase the mystery, the name was often written backwards and apparently meaningless magical words, such as BESCU, BEREBESCU, BAZAGRA, were also added for effect. Sometimes we find a figure roughly drawn on the tablet, as in the illustration opposite. It depicts a bearded demon, carrying an urn and a torch, which were symbols of death. The boat in which he stands may represent the boat of Charon, the ferryman of the Underworld, who took the souls of the dead across the river Styx.

The wording of the curse can be very simple, just "I dedicate," followed by the intended victim's name. But sometimes it can be ferociously eloquent, as in the following example: "May burning fever seize all her limbs, kill her soul and her heart. O Gods of the Underworld, break and smash her bones, choke her, let her body be twisted and shattered—phrix, phrox."

It may seem strange that religion should be used to bring harm to people in this very direct and spiteful way, but the Romans tended to see their gods as possible allies in the struggles of life. When they wished to injure an enemy, they thought it natural and proper to seek the gods' powerful help.

CVCSEV
CENSEV
CINBEV
PERFZEV
DIARVNCO
YASTA
BESCV
BEREBESCL
ARVRARA
BASASRA

ΓΑRITMO
ΑRAIT
TO

NOCTIVASVS
TIBERIS OCEANVS

Words and Phrases Checklist

adeptus, adepta, adeptum	*having received, having obtained*
amor, amōris	*love*
aureus, aurea, aureum	*golden, made of gold*
avidē	*eagerly*
caelum, caelī	*sky*
dēcipiō, dēcipere, dēcēpī, dēceptus	*deceive, trick*
dīrus, dīra, dīrum	*dreadful, awful*
dissentiō, dissentīre, dissēnsī	*disagree*
ēligō, ēligere, ēlēgī, ēlēctus	*choose*
exitium, exitiī	*ruin, destruction*
fundō, fundere, fūdī, fūsus	*pour*
hostis, hostis	*enemy*
iactō, iactāre, iactāvī, iactātus	*throw*
incipiō, incipere, incēpī, inceptus	*begin*
ingressus, ingressa, ingressum	*having entered*
iniciō, inicere, iniēcī, iniectus	*throw in*
lacrima, lacrimae	*tear*
minimus, minima, minimum	*very little, least*
molestus, molesta, molestum	*troublesome*
moneō, monēre, monuī, monitus	*warn, advise*
parcō, parcere, pepercī	*spare*
precātus, precāta, precātum	*having prayed (to)*
prūdentia, prūdentiae	*prudence, good sense*
quantus, quanta, quantum	*how big*
quō modō?	*how?*
tardus, tarda, tardum	*late*
tūtus, tūta, tūtum	*safe*
verbum, verbī	*word*
virtūs, virtūtis	*courage*
vītō, vītāre, vītāvī, vītātus	*avoid*

Word Search

dire, hostile, inception, molest, monitor, retard, suffuse

1 . . . . .: a beginning, origin
2 . . . . .: to spread through or over
3 . . . . .: to keep track of by electronic device
4 . . . . .: terrible, disastrous
5 . . . . .: to assault or harass
6 . . . . .: unfriendly, antagonistic
7 . . . . .: to delay

haruspex

in thermīs

I

prope thermās erat templum, ā fabrīs Cogidubnī aedificātum. in hōc templō aegrōtī deam Sūlem adōrāre solēbant. rēx Cogidubnus cum multīs prīncipibus servīsque prō templō sedēbat. Quīntus prope sellam rēgis stābat. rēgem prīncipēsque manus mīlitum custōdiēbat. prō templō erat āra ingēns, quam omnēs aspiciēbant.   5
Memor, togam praetextam gerēns, prope āram stābat.

duo sacerdōtēs, agnam nigram dūcentēs, ad āram prōcessērunt. postquam rēx signum dedit, ūnus sacerdōs agnam sacrificāvit. deinde Memor, quī iam tremēbat sūdābatque, alterī sacerdōtī dīxit,

"iubeō tē ōmina īnspicere. dīc mihi: quid vidēs?"   10

sacerdōs, postquam iecur agnae īnspexit, anxius,

"iecur est līvidum," inquit. "nōnne hoc mortem significat? nōnne mortem virī clārī significat?"

Memor, quī perterritus pallēscēbat, sacerdōtī respondit,

"minimē. dea Sūlis, quae precēs aegrōtōrum audīre solet, nōbīs   15
ōmina optima mīsit."

haec verba locūtus, ad Cogidubnum sē vertit et clāmāvit,

"ōmina sunt optima! ōmina tibi remedium mīrābile significant, quod dea Sūlis Minerva tibi favet."

tum rēgem ac prīncipēs Memor in apodytērium dūxit.   20

manus mīlitum	*a band of soldiers*
aspiciēbant: aspicere	*look towards*
praetextam: praetextus	*with a purple border*
agnam: agna	*lamb*
ōmina	*omens (signs from the gods)*
iecur	*liver*
līvidum: līvidus	*lead-colored*
significat: significāre	*mean, indicate*
pallēscēbat: pallēscere	*grow pale*
ac	*and*

Gorgon's head from the pediment of the temple at Bath.

II

deinde omnēs in eam partem thermārum intrāvērunt, ubi balneum
maximum erat. Quīntus, prīncipēs secūtus, circumspectāvit et
attonitus dīxit,

    "hae thermae maiōrēs sunt quam thermae Pompēiānae!"

  servī cum magnā difficultāte Cogidubnum in balneum dēmittere   5
coepērunt. maximus clāmor erat. rēx prīncipibus mandāta dabat.
prīncipēs lībertōs suōs vituperābant, lībertī servōs.

  tandem rēx, ē balneō ēgressus, vestīmenta, quae servī tulerant,
induit. tum omnēs fontī sacrō appropinquāvērunt.

  "ubi est pōculum?" rogāvit Cogidubnus. "nōbīs decōrum est   10
aquam sacram bibere. aqua est amāra, sed remedium potentis-
simum."

  haec verba locūtus, rēx ad fontem sacrum prōcessit. Cephalus,
quī anxius tremēbat, prope fontem stābat, pōculum ōrnātissimum
tenēns. rēgī pōculum obtulit. rēx pōculum ad labra sustulit. subitō   15

secūtus	*having followed*
difficultāte: difficultās	*difficulty*
dēmittere	*let down, lower*
amāra: amārus	*bitter*
labra	*lips*

Quīntus, pōculum cōnspicātus, manum rēgis prēnsāvit et clāmāvit,

"nōlī bibere! hoc est pōculum venēnātum. pōculum huius modī in urbe Alexandrīā vīdī."

"longē errās," respondit rēx. "nēmō mihi nocēre vult. nēmō umquam mortem mihi parāre temptāvit."   20

"rēx summae virtūtis es," respondit Quīntus. "sed, quamquam nūllum perīculum timēs, tūtius est tibi vērum scīre. pōculum īnspicere velim. dā mihi!"

tum pōculum Quīntus īnspicere coepit. Cephalus tamen pōculum ē manibus Quīntī rapere temptābat. maxima pars   25 spectātōrum stābat immōta. sed Dumnorix, prīnceps Rēgnēnsium, saeviēbat tamquam leō furēns. pōculum rapuit et Cephalō obtulit.

"facile est nōbīs vērum cognōscere," clāmāvit. "iubeō tē pōculum haurīre. num aquam bibere timēs?"

Cephalus pōculum haurīre nōluit, et ad genua rēgis prōcubuit.   30
rēx immōtus stābat. cēterī prīncipēs lībertum frūstrā resistentem prēnsāvērunt. Cephalus, ā prīncipibus coāctus, venēnum hausit. deinde, vehementer tremēns, gemitum ingentem dedit et mortuus prōcubuit.

prēnsāvit: prēnsāre   *take hold of, clutch*
genua   *knees*
coāctus: cōgere   *force, compel*

epistula Cephalī

postquam Cephalus periit, servus eius rēgī epistulam trādidit, ā Cephalō ipsō scrīptam:

"rēx Cogidubne, in maximō perīculō es. Memor īnsānit. mortem tuam cupit. iussit mē rem efficere. invītus Memorī pāruī. fortasse mihi nōn crēdis. sed tōtam rem tibi nārrāre velim.   5

ubi tū ad hās thermās advēnistī, remedium quaerēns, Memor mē ad vīllam suam arcessīvit. vīllam ingressus, Memorem perterritum invēnī. attonitus eram. numquam Memorem adeō perterritum vīderam. Memor mihi,

'Imperātor mortem Cogidubnī cupit,' inquit. 'iubeō tē hanc rem   10
administrāre. iubeō tē venēnum parāre. tibi necesse est eum

interficere. Cogidubnus enim est homō ingeniī prāvī.'

Memorī respondī,

'longē errās. Cogidubnus est vir ingeniī optimī. tālem rem facere nōlō.'

15

Memor īrātus mihi respondit,

'sceleste! lībertus meus es, et servus meus erās. tē līberāvī et tibi multam pecūniam dedī. mandāta mea facere dēbēs. cūr mihi obstās?'

rēx Cogidubne, diū recūsāvī obstinātus. diū beneficia tua commemorāvī. tandem Memor custōdem arcessīvit, quī mē verberāvit. ā custōde paene interfectus, Memorī tandem cessī.

20

ad casam meam regressus, venēnum invītus parāvī. scrīpsī tamen hanc epistulam et servō fidēlī trādidī. iussī servum tibi epistulam trādere. veniam petō, quamquam facinus scelestum parāvī. Memor nocēns est. Memor coēgit mē hanc rem efficere. Memorem, nōn mē, pūnīre dēbēs."

25

| īnsānit: īnsānīre | *be crazy, be insane* | facinus | *crime* |
| beneficia | *acts of kindness, favors* | coēgit: cōgere | *force, compel* |

About the Language

1 You have now met the plural of neuter nouns like **templum** and **nōmen**:

sunt multa **templa** in hāc urbe.
*There are many **temples** in this city.*

lībertus **nōmina** prīncipum recitāvit.
*The freedman read out the **names** of the chieftains.*

2 Study the nominative and accusative forms of the following neuter nouns:

| | SINGULAR | | PLURAL | |
	NOMINATIVE	ACCUSATIVE	NOMINATIVE	ACCUSATIVE
2ND DECLENSION	templum	templum	templa	templa
	aedificium	aedificium	aedificia	aedificia
3RD DECLENSION	nōmen	nōmen	nōmina	nōmina
	caput	caput	capita	capita
	mare	mare	maria	maria

3 Further examples:
  1 aedificium erat splendidissimum.
  2 ubi haec verba audīvit, Memor tacēbat.
  3 fēlēs caput hominis rāsit.
  4 Cephalus cōnsilium subitō cēpit.
  5 haec cubicula sunt sordidissima.
  6 servī pōcula ad prīncipēs tulērunt.

When you have read this, answer the questions at the end.

Britannia perdomita

Salvius cum Memore anxius colloquium habet. servus ingressus ad Memorem currit.

servus: domine, rēx Cogidubnus hūc venit. rēx togam
            praetextam ōrnāmentaque gerit. magnum numerum
            mīlitum sēcum dūcit.   5
Memor: rēx mīlitēs hūc dūcit? togam praetextam gerit?
Salvius: Cogidubnus, nōs suspicātus, ultiōnem petit. Memor,
            tibi necesse est mē adiuvāre. nōs enim Rōmānī
            sumus, Cogidubnus barbarus.
            (*intrat Cogidubnus. in manibus epistulam tenet, ā Cephalō*   10
            scrīptam.)
Cogidubnus: Memor, tū illās īnsidiās parāvistī. tū iussistī
            Cephalum venēnum comparāre et mē necāre. sed
            Cephalus, lībertus tuus, mihi omnia patefēcit.
Memor: Cogidubne, id quod dīcis, absurdum est. mortuus est   15
            Cephalus.
Cogidubnus: Cephalus homō magnae prūdentiae erat. tibi nōn
            crēdidit. invītus tibi pāruit. simulac mandāta ista
            dedistī, scrīpsit Cephalus epistulam in quā omnia
            patefēcit. servus, ā Cephalō missus, epistulam mihi   20
            tulit.
Memor: epistula falsa est, servus mendācissimus.
Cogidubnus: tū, nōn servus, es mendāx. servus enim, multa
            tormenta passus, in eādem sententiā mānsit.
Salvius: Cogidubne, cūr mīlitēs hūc dūxistī?   25
Cogidubnus: Memorem ē cūrā thermārum iam dēmōvī.

Memor:	quid dīcis? tū mē dēmōvistī? innocēns sum. Salv- . . .
Salvius:	rēx Cogidubne, quid fēcistī? tū, quī barbarus es,

Memor: quid dīcis? tū mē dēmōvistī? innocēns sum. Salv- . . .
Salvius: rēx Cogidubne, quid fēcistī? tū, quī barbarus es,
           haruspicem Rōmānum dēmovēre audēs? nimium
           audēs! tū, summōs honōrēs ā nōbīs adeptus,   30
           numquam contentus fuistī. nōs diū vexāvistī. nunc
           dēnique, cum mīlitibus hūc ingressus, perfidiam
           apertē ostendis. Imperātor Domitiānus, arrogantiam
           tuam diū passus, ad mē epistulam nūper mīsit. in hāc
           epistulā iussit mē rēgnum tuum occupāre. iubeō tē   35
           igitur ad aulam statim redīre.
Cogidubnus: ēn iūstitia Rōmāna! ēn fidēs! nūllī perfidiōrēs sunt
           quam Rōmānī. stultissimus fuī, quod Rōmānīs adhūc
           crēdidī. amīcōs meōs prōdidī; rēgnum meum āmīsī.
           ōlim, ā Rōmānīs dēceptus, ōrnāmenta honōrēsque   40
           Rōmānōs accēpī. hodiē ista ōrnāmenta, mihi ā
           Rōmānīs data, humī iaciō. Salvī, mitte nūntium ad
           istum Imperātōrem, "nōs Cogidubnum tandem
           vīcimus. Britannia perdomita est."
           (senex, haec locūtus, lentē per iānuam exit.)   45

perdomita: perdomitus	*conquered*	perfidiam: perfidia	*treachery*
suspicātus	*having suspected*	apertē	*openly*
ultiōnem: ultiō	*revenge*	rēgnum	*kingdom*
patefēcit: patefacere	*reveal*	occupāre	*seize, take over*
absurdum: absurdus	*absurd*	ēn iūstitia!	*so this is justice!*
falsa: falsus	*false, untrue*	fidēs	*loyalty, trustworthiness*
tormenta	*torture*	perfidiōrēs: perfidus	*treacherous, untrustworthy*
passus	*having suffered*	adhūc	*until now*
eādem	*the same*	prōdidī: prōdere	*betray*
dēmōvī: dēmovēre	*dismiss*	vīcimus: vincere	*conquer*

DE BRITANNIS

1 When Memor and Salvius hear of Cogidubnus' arrival, do they think this is an ordinary visit, or a special one? What makes them think so?
2 What reason does Salvius give for saying that Memor ought to support him against Cogidubnus?
3 How has Cogidubnus found out about the poison plot?
4 What action has Cogidubnus taken against Memor? Was this action wise or foolish?
5 Which word in line 29 is used by Salvius to contrast with "barbarus" in line 28?
6 What orders does Salvius say he has recently received? From whom?
7 Why does Cogidubnus fling his "ōrnāmenta" to the ground?

Practicing the Language

1 Study the forms and meanings of the following verbs and nouns, and give the meanings of the untranslated words. The verb is given in its infinitive form; sometimes the perfect passive participle has been added in parentheses.

arāre	*to plow*	arātor	*plowman*
pingere (pictus)	*to paint*	pictor	*painter*
vincere (victus)	*to win*	victor	
emere (ēmptus)		ēmptor	*buyer, purchaser*
praecurrere	*to run ahead*	praecursor	
dūcere (ductus)	*to lead*	ductor	
legere (lēctus)		lēctor	*reader*
gubernāre	*to steer*	gubernātor	
amāre	*to love*	amātor	
spectāre		spectātor	
favēre		fautor	
		(*written in early Latin as* "favitor")	

Give the meaning of each of the following nouns:

dēfēnsor, oppugnātor, vēnditor, saltātor, prōditor

2 Complete each sentence with the right word and then translate.

1 nōs ancillae fessae sumus; semper in vīllā . . . . . . (labōrāmus, labōrātis, labōrant)
2 "quid faciunt illī servī?" "saxa ad plaustrum . . . . . ." (ferimus, fertis, ferunt)

3 fīlius meus vōbīs grātiās agere vult, quod mē . . . . . . (servāvimus, servāvistis, servāvērunt)

4 quamquam prope āram . . . . ., sacrificium vidēre nōn poterāmus. (stābāmus, stābātis, stābant)

5 ubi prīncipēs fontī . . . . ., Cephalus prōcessit, pōculum tenēns. (appropinquābāmus, appropinquābātis, appropinquābant)

6 in maximō perīculō estis, quod fīlium rēgis . . . . . . (interfēcimus, interfēcistis, interfēcērunt)

7 nōs, quī fontem sacrum numquam . . . . ., ad thermās cum rēge īre cupiēbāmus. (vīderāmus, vīderātis, vīderant)

8 dominī nostrī sunt benignī; nōbīs semper satis cibī . . . . . . (praebēmus, praebētis, praebent)

3 Translate the verbs in the left-hand column. Then, keeping the person and number unchanged, use the verb in parentheses to form a phrase with the infinitive and translate again. For example:

respondēmus.   (volō)   This becomes: respondēre volumus.
We reply.   *We want to reply.*
festīnat.   (dēbeō)   This becomes: festīnāre dēbet.
He hurries.   *He ought to hurry.*

The present tense of **volō** and **possum** is set out on page 282 of the Review Grammar; **dēbeō** is a second conjugation verb like **doceō** (see Review Grammar, p.275).

1 dormītis.   (dēbeō)
2 sedēmus.   (volō)
3 pugnat.   (possum)
4 labōrant.   (dēbeō)
5 revenīmus.   (possum)
6 num nāvigās? (volō)

4 Complete each sentence with the most suitable participle from the list below and then translate.

locūtus, ingressus, missus, excitātus, superātus

1 Cogidubnus, haec verba . . . . ., ab aulā discessit.
2 nūntius, ab amīcīs meīs . . . . ., epistulam mihi trādidit.
3 fūr, vīllam . . . . ., cautē circumspectāvit.
4 Bulbus, ā Modestō . . . . ., sub mēnsā iacēbat.
5 haruspex, ā Cephalō . . . . ., invītus ē lectō surrēxit.

Roman Religion

The stories in Stages 22 and 23 have mentioned two ways in which religion played a part in Roman life. In Stage 22, Bulbus sought the help of the gods against his enemy Modestus by means of a defixio; in Stage 23, Memor has been carrying out his duties as a **haruspex** or *soothsayer*, by supervising a sacrifice and ordering the examination of the victim's internal organs (entrails). This was one of the ways in which the Romans tried to foretell the future and discover what the gods had in store for them. An invalid hoping for a cure, a general about to fight a battle, and a merchant just before a long business journey, might all consult a haruspex to try to discover their chances of success.

An animal would be sacrificed to the appropriate god or goddess; it was hoped that this would please the deity and encourage him or her to look favorably on the sacrificer. The haruspex and his assistants would make careful observations. They would watch the way in which the victim fell; they would observe the smoke and flames when parts of the victim were placed on the altar fire; and, above all, they would cut the victim open and examine its entrails, especially the liver. They would look for anything unusual about the liver's size or shape, observe its color and texture, and note whether it had spots on its surface. They would then interpret what they saw and announce to the sacrificer whether the signs from the gods were favorable or not.

Such attempts to discover the future were known as divination. Another type of divination was performed by priests known as **augurēs** (augurs) who based their predictions on observations of the flight of birds. Augurs would note the direction of flight, and observe whether the

Bronze liver marked with the different areas to be observed by the haruspex.

birds flew together or separately, what kind of birds they were, and what noises they made.

Roman religion involved many other beliefs, habits, and ceremonies, and it developed over many centuries. The early Romans, in common with many primitive peoples, believed that all things were controlled by spirits which they called **nūmina**. They had looked at fire and been terrified by its power to burn and destroy, yet excited by its power to cook, warm, and provide light. They had seen the regular sequence of day and night and of the seasons of the year but were unable to explain their causes scientifically. Not surprisingly, therefore, they believed that the power of numina was at work, and they soon realized it was important to ensure that the numina used their power for good rather than harm. For this reason, the early Romans presented them with offerings of food and wine. At special times of the year, such as seed-time or harvest, an animal would be slaughtered and offered as a sacrifice to the numina. In this way ceremonies and rituals developed at fixed points in the year and gradually communities began to construct calendars to record them.

"The Rape of Proserpina," painted in the 18th century AD by Charles de Lafosse. It depicts Proserpina's abduction by Pluto.

When the Romans came into contact with the peoples of the Greek world, they began to realize that their own vague and shapeless spirits were imagined by the Greeks as all-powerful gods and goddesses who had not only names and physical shapes but also human characteristics. The Roman goddess of grain, Ceres, became identified with the Greek goddess, Demeter, mother of all life-giving nourishment. The Greeks told stories (myths) about their gods and goddesses which helped to explain more vividly the workings of the world. For example, they said that Demeter's daughter, Persephone (in Roman myth, Proserpina), had been carried off by her wicked uncle, Hades (also called Pluto), ruler of the Underworld, and was only allowed to return to the earth for six months of the year. In this way a myth was used to explain the rebirth of nature each spring: as Persephone returned each year, Demeter stopped grieving and allowed life back to the countryside.

The Romans were also in contact with the Etruscans, a powerful race who lived in central Italy to the north of Rome. From them they borrowed the practice of divination, described above.

The worship of the gods and goddesses and the practice of divination became central features of the Roman state religion. The rituals and ceremonies were organized by supervisory committees of priests and other religious officials, and the festivals and sacrifices were carried out by them on behalf of the state. The emperor always held the position of **Pontifex Maximus**, or Chief Priest. Great attention was paid to the details of worship. Every word had to be pronounced correctly, otherwise the whole ceremony had to be restarted; a pipe-player was employed to drown noises and cries which were thought to be unlucky for the ritual. Everyone who watched the ceremonies had to stand quite still and silent, like Plancus in the Stage 17 story.

In addition to these public ceremonies, many citizens kept up the practice of private family worship. This included offerings to Vesta, the spirit of the hearth, and to the **lārēs** and **penātēs**, the spirits of the household and storage-cupboard. Such practices were probably more common in the country districts than they were in Rome itself. The head of the household (**paterfamiliās**) was responsible for performing the rituals and chanting the prayers. Even here everything had to be done correctly and many Roman prayers are worded to make sure that no god or goddess was forgotten or left out by mistake. It was important to address the god or goddess by the right name, as in this example from a poem by Catullus:

You are called Juno Lucina
by women in childbirth,
you are called nightly Trivia, and Luna
whose light is not your own.
. . . may you be hallowed
by whatever name pleases you . . .

Catullus was, in fact, addressing the goddess Diana, but he used some of her other names to make sure she would attend to his prayer.

The Romans tended to regard prayer as a means of asking for favors from the gods and accompanied their prayers with promises of offerings if the favors were granted. These promises were known as **vōta**. It would not be an exaggeration to say that many Romans saw religion as a kind of "business deal" with the gods. A common phrase in prayers was: "dō ut dēs"—"I give so that you may give."

When the Romans arrived in Britain, they found that the Celtic religion was very similar to their own earlier belief in numina. Under Roman influence, the Celts began to identify their spirits with the Roman gods and goddesses, just as the Romans had adopted the Greek gods and goddesses several centuries earlier. The following inscription is a good example of this: "Peregrinus, son of Secundus, a Treveran, to Mars Loucetius and Nemetona willingly and with good cause fulfilled his vow." The Roman god Mars and the Celtic god Loucetius are presented here as one god with one name, just as Sulis and Minerva had merged into one goddess at Aquae Sulis. The Romans made no attempt to convert the Celts to a belief in Roman religion. However, they knew that by identifying Roman gods with Celtic ones, they would encourage the British to accept Roman rule more readily.

Another feature of Roman religion which was intended to encourage acceptance of Roman rule was the worship of the emperor. In Rome itself, emperor worship was officially discouraged. However, the peoples of the eastern provinces of the Roman empire had always regarded their kings and rulers as divine and were equally ready to pay divine honors to the Roman emperors. Gradually the Romans introduced this idea in the west as well. The Britons and other western peoples were encouraged to worship the **genius** (*protecting spirit*) of the emperor, linked with the goddess Roma. Altars were erected in honor of "Rome and the emperor." When an emperor died it was usual to deify him (make him a god), and temples were often built to honor the deified emperor in the provinces.

One such temple, that of Claudius in Colchester, was destroyed by the British before it was even finished, during the revolt led by Queen Boudica in A.D. 60. The historian Tacitus tells us why:

> The temple dedicated to the deified Emperor Claudius seemed to the British a symbol of everlasting oppression, and the chosen priests used religion as an excuse for wasting British money.

Clearly the British found it hard to accept the idea of emperor worship at first.

Bronze head of the goddess Minerva, found at Bath in 1727.

Words and Phrases Checklist

administrō, administrāre, administrāvī	*manage*
cēdō, cēdere, cessī	*give in, give way*
clārus, clāra, clārum	*famous*
commemorō, commemorāre, commemorāvī, commemorātus	*mention, recall*
cōnspicātus, cōnspicāta, cōnspicātum	*having caught sight of*
cūra, cūrae	*care*
enim	*for*
errō, errāre, errāvī	*make a mistake*
gerō, gerere, gessī, gestus	*wear*
honor, honōris	*honor*
iaciō, iacere, iēcī, iactus	*throw*
immōtus, immōta, immōtum	*still, motionless*
induō, induere, induī, indūtus	*put on*
ingenium, ingeniī	*character*
locūtus, locūta, locūtum	*having spoken*
mandātum, mandātī	*instruction, order*
modus, modī	*manner, way, kind*
rēs huius modī	*a thing of this kind*
nimium	*too much*
numerus, numerī	*number*
ōrnō, ōrnāre, ōrnāvī, ōrnātus	*decorate*
pāreō, pārēre, pāruī	*obey*
potēns, *gen.* potentis	*powerful*
prāvus, prāva, prāvum	*evil*
regressus, regressa, regressum	*having returned*
sciō, scīre, scīvī	*know*
tālis, tāle	*such*
tamquam	*as, like*
umquam	*ever*
venēnum, venēnī	*poison*
venia, veniae	*mercy*

Word Search

aberrant, concede, depravity, elocution, potentate, regress, venial

1 . . . . .: pardonable
2 . . . . .: to yield or grant
3 . . . . .: moral corruption
4 . . . . .: the art of public speaking
5 . . . . .: deviating from the norm
6 . . . . .: a monarch or ruler
7 . . . . .: to go back; to revert to a previous condition or state

---

fuga

in itinere

Modestus et Strȳthiō, ex oppidō Aquīs Sūlis ēgressī, Dēvam equitābant. in itinere ad flūmen altum vēnērunt, ubi erat pōns sēmirutus. cum ad pontem vēnissent, equus trānsīre nōluit.

"equus trānsīre timet," inquit Modestus. "Strȳthiō, tū prīmus trānsī!"   5

cum Strȳthiō trānsiisset, equus trānsīre etiam tum nōlēbat. Modestus igitur ex equō dēscendit. cum dēscendisset, equus statim trānsiit.

"eque! redī!" inquit Modestus. "mē dēseruistī."

equus tamen in alterā rīpā immōtus stetit. Modestus cautissimē   10
trānsīre coepit. cum ad medium pontem vēnisset, dēcidit pōns, dēcidit Modestus. mediīs ex undīs clāmāvit,

"caudicēs, vōs pontem labefēcistis."

altum: altus	*deep*
sēmirutus	*rickety*
labefēcistis: labefacere	*weaken*

Dēvam *to Chester (town in northwestern England)*

When you have read this story, answer the questions at the end.

Quīntus cōnsilium capit

cum Cogidubnus trīstis īrātusque ē vīllā Memoris exiisset, Salvius
mīlitēs quīnquāgintā arcessīvit. eōs iussit rēgem prīncipēsque
Rēgnēnsium comprehendere et in carcere retinēre. hī mīlitēs, tōtum
per oppidum missī, mox rēgem cum prīncipibus invēnērunt. eōs
statim comprehendērunt. Dumnorix tamen, ē manibus mīlitum   5
ēlāpsus, per viās oppidī noctū prōcessit et Quīntum quaesīvit.
Quīntō enim crēdēbat.

cubiculum Quīntī ingressus, haec dīxit:

"amīce, tibi crēdere possum. adiuvā mē, adiuvā Cogidubnum.
paucīs Rōmānīs crēdō; plūrimī sunt perfidī. nēmō quidem perfidior   10
est quam iste Salvius quī Cogidubnum interficere nūper temptāvit.
nunc Cogidubnus, ā mīlitibus Salviī comprehēnsus, in carcere iacet.
Salvius crīmen maiestātis in eum īnferre cupit. rēx, in carcere
inclūsus, omnīnō dē vītā suā dēspērat.

"tū tamen es vir summae virtūtis magnaeque prūdentiae.   15
quamquam Salvius potentissimus et īnfestissimus est, nōlī rēgem
dēserere. nōlī eum, ab homine scelestō oppugnātum, relinquere. tū
anteā eum servāvistī. nōnne iterum servāre potes?"

cum Dumnorix haec dīxisset, Quīntus rem sēcum anxius
cōgitābat. auxilium Cogidubnō ferre volēbat, quod eum valdē   20
dīligēbat; sed rēs difficillima erat. subitō cōnsilium cēpit.

"nōlī dēspērāre!" exclāmāvit. "rēgī auxilium ferre possumus.
hanc rem ad lēgātum Gnaeum Iūlium Agricolam clam referre
dēbēmus. itaque nōbīs festīnandum est ad ultimās partēs
Britanniae ubi Agricola bellum gerit. eī vēra patefacere possumus. 25
Agricola sōlus Salviō obstāre potest, quod summam potestātem in
Britanniā habet. nunc nōbīs hinc effugiendum est."

Dumnorix, cum haec audīvisset, cōnsilium audāx magnopere
laudāvit. tum Quīntus servum fidissimum arcessīvit, cui mandāta
dedit. servus exiit. mox regressus, cibum sex diērum Quīntō et   30
Dumnorigī trādidit. illī, ē vīllā ēlāpsī, per viās dēsertās cautē
prōcessērunt.

vīllam Memoris praetereuntēs, Quīntus et Dumnorix duōs equōs

cōnspexērunt, ad pālum dēligātōs. Quīntus, quī fūrtum committere
nōlēbat, haesitāvit.   35

    Dumnorix rīdēns "nōlī haesitāre," inquit. "hī sunt equī Salviī."

    Quīntus et Dumnorix equōs cōnscendērunt et ad ultimās partēs
īnsulae abiērunt.

carcere: carcer	*prison*	potestātem: potestās	*power*
ēlāpsus	*having escaped*	magnopere	*greatly*
quidem	*indeed*	fīdissimum: fīdus	*trustworthy*
crīmen maiestātis	*charge of treason*	diērum: diēs	*day*
īnferre	*bring against*	praetereuntēs:	
inclūsus	*shut up, imprisoned*	praeterīre	*pass by, go past*
omnīnō	*completely*	pālum: pālus	*stake, post*
sēcum . . . cōgitābat	*considered . . . to himself*	fūrtum	*theft, robbery*
dīligēbat: dīligere	*be fond of*	committere	*commit*
nōbīs festīnandum est	*we must hurry*	haesitāvit: haesitāre	*hesitate*
ultimās: ultimus	*furthest*	cōnscendērunt:	
bellum gerit: bellum		cōnscendere	*mount, climb on*
gerere	*wage war, campaign*		

1 How many soldiers does Salvius send for? What does he tell them to
   do?

2 Which British chieftain escapes? Whose help does he seek, and why?

3 What further action does Salvius intend to take against Cogidubnus?

4 What events is Dumnorix referring to when he says "tū anteā eum
   servāvistī" (lines 17–18)?

5 What does Quintus suggest? Why does he think Agricola can stop
   Salvius?

6 How many days' food do Quintus and Dumnorix take with them?
   How do they obtain horses?

7 Why does Quintus support a British king and a British chieftain,
   instead of supporting his fellow-Roman Salvius?

About the Language

1 Study the following sentences:

    cum Modestus ad pontem **advēnisset**, equus cōnstitit.
    *When Modestus **had arrived** at the bridge, the horse stopped.*

    cum coquus omnia **parāvisset**, mercātor amīcōs in triclīnium dūxit.
    *When the cook **had gotten** everything **ready**, the merchant led his friends into
    the dining-room.*

    The form of the verb in boldface is known as the *subjunctive*.

2 The subjunctive is often used with the word **cum** meaning *when*, as in the examples above.

3 Further examples:

1 cum rēx exiisset, Salvius mīlitēs ad sē vocāvit.
2 cum gladiātōrēs leōnem interfēcissent, spectātōrēs plausērunt.
3 cum dominus haec mandāta dedisset, fabrī ad aulam rediērunt.
4 fūrēs, cum cubiculum intrāvissent, tacitī circumspectāvērunt.

4 The examples of the subjunctive in paragraphs 1 and 3 are all in the same tense: the *pluperfect subjunctive*. Compare the pluperfect subjunctive with the ordinary form of the pluperfect:

PLUPERFECT	PLUPERFECT SUBJUNCTIVE	
3RD PERSON SINGULAR	3RD PERSON SINGULAR	3RD PERSON PLURAL
trāxerat	trāxisset	trāxissent
ambulāverat	ambulāvisset	ambulāvissent
dormīverat	dormīvisset	dormīvissent
voluerat	voluisset	voluissent
fuerat	fuisset	fuissent

Salvius cōnsilium cognōscit

postrīdiē mīlitēs Dumnorigem per oppidum quaerēbant. cum eum nusquam invenīre potuissent, rem dēnique Salviō nūntiāvērunt. ille, cum dē fugā Dumnorigis cognōvisset, vehementer saeviēbat; omnēs mīlitēs, quī Dumnorigem custōdīverant, poenās dare iussit. Quīntum quoque quaesīvit; invenīre tamen nōn poterat. tum   5
Belimicum, prīncipem Cantiacōrum, arcessīvit.

"Belimice," inquit, "iste Dumnorix ē manibus meīs effūgit; abest quoque Quīntus Caecilius. neque Dumnorigī neque Quīntō crēdō. Quīntus enim saepe Dumnorigī favēbat, saepe cum eō colloquium habēbat. ī nunc; dūc mīlitēs tēcum; illōs quaere in omnibus partibus   10
oppidī. quaere servōs quoque eōrum. facile est nōbīs servōs torquēre et vērum ita cognōscere."

Belimicus, multīs cum mīlitibus ēgressus, per oppidum dīligenter

quaerēbat. intereā Salvius anxius reditum eius exspectābat. cum
Salvius rem sēcum cōgitāret, Belimicus subitō rediit exsultāns.   15
servum Quīntī in medium ātrium trāxit.

"fūgērunt illī scelestī," clāmāvit, "sed hic servus, captus et
interrogātus, vērum patefēcit."

Salvius ad servum trementem conversus,

"ubi est Quīntus Caecilius?" inquit. "quō fūgit Dumnorix?"   20

"nescio," inquit servus quī, multa tormenta passus, iam vix
quicquam dīcere poterat. "nihil scio," iterum inquit.

Belimicus, cum haec audīvisset, gladium dēstrictum ad iugulum
servī tenuit.

"melius est tibi," inquit, "vērum Salviō dīcere."   25

servus quī iam dē vītā suā dēspērābat,

"cibum sex diērum tantum parāvī," inquit susurrāns. "nihil aliud
fēcī. dominus meus cum Dumnorige in ultimās partēs Britanniae
discessit."

nusquam	*nowhere*	exsultāns: exsultāre	*exult, be triumphant*
fugā: fuga	*escape*	conversus	*having turned*
ī: īre	*go*	quicquam	*anything*
torquēre	*torture*	dēstrictum: dēstringere	*draw*
reditum: reditus	*return*	iugulum	*throat*

Salvius "hercle!" inquit. "ad Agricolam iērunt. Quīntus, ā 30
Dumnorige incitātus, mihi obstāre temptat; homō tamen magnae
stultitiae est; mihi resistere nōn potest, quod ego maiōrem
auctōritātem habeō quam ille."

Salvius, cum haec dīxisset, Belimicō mandāta dedit. eum iussit
cum ducentīs equitibus exīre et fugitīvōs comprehendere. servum 35
carnificibus trādidit. deinde scrībam arcessīvit cui epistulam
dictāvit. ūnum ē servīs suīs iussit hanc epistulam quam celerrimē ad
Agricolam ferre.

intereā Belimicus, Quīntum et Dumnorigem per trēs diēs
secūtus, eōs tandem invēnit. equitēs statim impetum in eōs fēcērunt. 40
amīcī, ab equitibus circumventī, fortiter resistēbant. dēnique
Dumnorix humī cecidit mortuus; Quīntus vulnerātus magnā cum
difficultāte effūgit.

fugitīvōs: fugitīvus   *fugitive*   scrībam: scrība   *secretary*

Agricolam: Agricola   *Roman governor of Britain, A.D. 78–84*

About the Language

1 At the beginning of this Stage, you met sentences with **cum** and the *pluperfect subjunctive*:

senex, cum pecūniam **invēnisset**, ad vīllam laetus rediit.
When the old man had found the money, he returned happily to the villa.

cum rem **cōnfēcissent**, abiērunt.
When they had finished the job, they went away.

2 Now study the following examples:

cum custōdēs **dormīrent**, captīvī ē carcere effūgērunt.
*When the guards **were sleeping**, the prisoners escaped from the prison.*

Modestus, cum in Britanniā **mīlitāret**, multās puellās amābat.
*When Modestus **was serving in the army** in Britain, he loved many girls.*

In these sentences, **cum** is being used with a different tense of the subjunctive: the *imperfect subjunctive*.

3 Further examples:

1 cum hospitēs cēnam cōnsūmerent, fūr cubiculum intrāvit.
2 cum prīnceps rem cōgitāret, nūntiī subitō revēnērunt.
3 iuvenēs, cum bēstiās agitārent, mīlitem vulnerātum cōnspexērunt.
4 puella, cum epistulam scrīberet, sonitum mīrābilem audīvit.

4 Compare the imperfect subjunctive with the infinitive:

INFINITIVE	IMPERFECT SUBJUNCTIVE	
	3RD PERSON SINGULAR	3RD PERSON PLURAL
trahere	traheret	traherent
ambulāre	ambulāret	ambulārent
dormīre	dormīret	dormīrent
velle	vellet	vellent
esse	esset	essent

Practicing the Language

1 Study the forms and meanings of the following, and give the meanings of the untranslated words:

volō	*I want*	nōlō	*I do not want*
scīre	*to know*	nescīre	*not to know*
umquam	*ever*	numquam	
usquam	*anywhere*	nusquam	
fās	*right, lawful*	nefās	
patiēns		impatiēns	*impatient*
mortālis		immortālis	
sānus	*of sound mind*	īnsānus	
memor	*remembering*	immemor	
fēlīx		īnfēlīx	*unlucky*
amīcus	*friend*	inimīcus	
ūtilis		inūtilis	*useless*
pavidus		impavidus	*fearless*
nōtus	*known, well-known*	ignōtus	
aequus	*fair, equal*	inīquus	
cōnsentīre	*to agree*	dissentīre	
facilis		difficilis	*difficult*
similis		dissimilis	*unlike*

Notice again the meanings of three pairs of words which you have already met:

ōtium	*leisure*	neg-ōtium	*non-leisure*, i.e. *business*
legere	*to read, to attend to*	neg-legere	*not to attend to,* i.e. *to neglect*
homō	*man*	nēmō	*no man*, i.e. *nobody*

Give the meaning of each of the following words:

immōtus, incertus, incrēdibilis, indignus, ingrātus, innocēns

2 With the help of paragraph 6 on page 271 of the Review Grammar, replace the words in boldface with the correct form of the pronoun **is** and then translate. For example:

Rūfilla in hortō ambulābat. Quīntus **Rūfillam** salūtāvit.
This becomes:
Rūfilla in hortō ambulābat. Quīntus eam salūtāvit.
Rūfilla was walking in the garden. Quintus greeted her.

In sentences 7 and 8, you may need to look up the gender of a noun in the Complete Vocabulary part of the Language Information Section.

1 Quīntus mox ad aulam advēnit. ancilla **Quīntum** in ātrium dūxit.
2 Salvius in lectō recumbēbat. puer **Salviō** plūs cibī obtulit.
3 Rūfilla laetissima erat; marītus **Rūfillae** tamen nōn erat contentus.
4 Britannī ferōciter pugnāvērunt, sed legiōnēs nostrae tandem **Britannōs** vīcērunt.
5 barbarī impetum in nōs fēcērunt. **barbarīs** autem restitimus.
6 multae fēminae prō templō conveniēbant. līberī **fēminārum** quoque aderant.
7 in illō oppidō est fōns sacer; **fontem** saepe vīsitāvī.
8 in Britanniā sunt trēs legiōnēs; imperātor **legiōnēs** iussit barbarōs vincere.

3 Complete each sentence with the right word and then translate.

1 subitō ancilla . . . . . in ātrium irrūpit. (perterrita, perterritae)
2 rēx, postquam hoc audīvit, fabrōs . . . . . dīmīsit. (fessum, fessōs)
3 centuriō quī adstābat custōdēs . . . . . laudāvit. (callidum, callidōs)
4 omnēs cīvēs nāvem . . . . . spectābant. (sacram, sacrās)
5 ubi in magnō perīculō eram, amīcus . . . . . mē servāvit. (fidēlis, fidēlēs)
6 "in illā īnsulā," inquit senex, "habitant multī virī . . . . . ." (ferōx, ferōcēs)

4 Make up six Latin sentences using some of the words listed below. Write out each sentence and then translate it. Include *two* sentences which do not contain nominatives.

NOMINATIVES	DATIVES	ACCUSATIVES	VERBS
senātor	fīliae	flōrēs	emō
centuriōnēs	uxōrī	dōna	emit
prīnceps	mīlitibus	gladiōs	emunt
nūntius	agricolae	fēlem	ostendō
amīcī	dominō	plaustra	ostendit
marītus	hospitibus	vīnum	ostendunt
puella	fēminīs	cibum	dat
iuvenēs	imperātōrī	epistulās	damus
virī	carnificibus	fūrem	dant
ancillae	servīs	cēram	trādit
			trāditis
			trādunt

Travel and Communication

Judged by modern Western standards, traveling in the Roman world was neither easy nor comfortable; nevertheless, people traveled extensively and there was much movement of goods throughout the provinces of the empire. This was made possible by a remarkable network of straight, well-surfaced roads which connected all major towns by the shortest possible routes. Travelers went on horseback, or

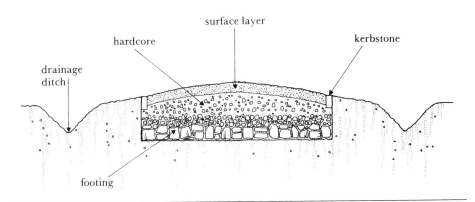

surface layer

hardcore

kerbstone

drainage
ditch

footing

Via Appia, near Rome, showing Roman paving.

used carts or other wheeled vehicles, or they walked. Such journeys were limited by the freshness of horse or traveler. They could cover 40–50 miles (60–70 km) in a day by carriage, perhaps 25 miles (35 km) on foot.

The line of a Roman road was first laid out by surveyors. By taking sightings from high points using smoke from fires, it was possible to ensure that each section of road took the shortest practicable distance between the points. River valleys and impassable mountains forced the roads to make diversions, but once past the obstructions, the roads usually continued along their original line. After the line had been chosen, an embankment of earth, called an **agger** was raised to act as a firm foundation. An agger could be as high as 4–5 feet (1.2–1.5 meters). In this was embedded a footing of large stones. This was covered with a layer of smaller stones, rubble, and packed stone, and the surface was faced with local materials: large flat stones, small flints, or slag from iron mines. This final surface is known as metaling and was curved or "cambered" to provide effective drainage. On either side of the agger, ditches were dug for the same purpose. Roman road-building was generally carried out with great skill and thoroughness, and the remains of a number of roads still exist today. Many modern roads still follow the Roman alignments and these can be seen very clearly on British Ordnance Survey maps.

The roads' original purpose was to allow rapid movement of Roman troops and so ensure military control of the provinces. Other travelers included Roman government officials, who made use of a system known as the Imperial Post (**cursus pūblicus**). A traveler with a government warrant (**diplōma**) who was making a journey on official business was supplied with fresh horses at posting stations which were sited at frequent intervals along all main roads; every effort was made to speed such a traveler on his way. In particular, the cursus publicus was used for carrying government correspondence. It has been estimated that by means of the cursus publicus an official message could travel from Britain to Rome (a distance of some 1100 miles, 1800 kilometers) in about seven days. Private letters carried by a person's own slave took much longer.

Relief showing a Roman lightweight carriage approaching a milestone.

Travelers would break long journeys with overnight stays at roadside inns. These were, for the most part, small, dirty, and uncomfortable, and were frequented by thieves, prostitutes, and drunks. The innkeepers, too, were often dishonest. The poet Horace, describing his stay at one inn, comments tersely: "perfidus hīc caupō." Wealthy travelers would try to avoid using these inns by arranging to stay with friends or acquaintances, where possible.

Traveling by sea was generally more popular, although it was restricted to the sailing season (March to November) and was fraught with danger from pirates, storms, and shipwrecks. Most sea journeys were undertaken on merchant ships; passenger shipping as we know it did not exist, except for the occasional ferry. A traveler could either charter a boat or wait until a merchant ship was about to put to sea and bargain with the captain for an acceptable fare.

Words and Phrases Checklist

adstō, adstāre, adstitī	*stand by*
auctōritās, auctōritātis	*authority*
audāx, *gen.* audācis	*bold, daring*
carcer, carceris	*prison*
colloquium, colloquiī	*talk, chat*
comprehendō, comprehendere, comprehendī, comprehēnsus	*arrest*
cōnscendō, cōnscendere, cōnscendī	*climb on, mount*
cum	*when*
dēscendō, dēscendere, dēscendī	*go down, come down*
dēserō, dēserere, dēseruī, dēsertus	*desert*
ēgressus, ēgressa, ēgressum	*having gone out*
eques, equitis	*horseman*
flūmen, flūminis	*river*
humī	*on the ground*
īnfestus, īnfesta, īnfestum	*hostile*
intereā	*meanwhile*
magnopere	*greatly*
maximē	*very greatly, most of all*
neque . . . neque	*neither . . . nor*
nusquam	*nowhere*
oppugnō, oppugnāre, oppugnāvī, oppugnātus	*attack*
passus, passa, passum	*having suffered*
patefaciō, patefacere, patefēcī, patefactus	*reveal*
perfidus, perfida, perfidum	*treacherous, untrustworthy*
pōns, pontis	*bridge*
rīpa, rīpae	*river bank*
tantum	*only*
trānseō, trānsīre, trānsiī	*cross*
trīstis, trīste	*sad*
vērum, vērī	*the truth*

Word Search

colloquy, flume, impassive, incarcerate, perfidy, transition, veritable

1 . . . . .: formal conversation
2 . . . . .: a narrow gorge, usually with a stream running through it
3 . . . . .: to imprison
4 . . . . .: a process of change
5 . . . . .: treachery, betrayal
6 . . . . .: unquestionable, actual
7 . . . . .: devoid of or not subject to emotion

Legionary soldiers from the Ermine Street Guard (modern amateur enthusiasts), here on parade at Lunt Roman Fort in the Midlands of England.

mīlitēs

explōrātor Britannicus

mīles legiōnis secundae per castra ambulābat. subitō iuvenem
ignōtum prope horreum latentem cōnspexit.
"heus tū," clāmāvit mīles, "quis es?" iuvenis nihil respondit.
mīles iuvenem iterum rogāvit quis esset. iuvenis fūgit.

ignōtum: ignōtus *unknown*   castra   *military camp*

mīles iuvenem petīvit et facile superāvit. "furcifer!" exclāmāvit.
"quid prope horreum facis?"
iuvenis dīcere nōlēbat quid prope horreum faceret. mīles eum ad
centuriōnem dūxit.

centurió, iuvenem cónspicátus, "hunc agnóscó!" inquit. "explórátor Britannicus est, quem saepe prope castra cónspexī. quó modó eum cēpistī?"

tum mīles explicāvit quó modó iuvenem cēpisset.

centurió, ad iuvenem conversus, "cūr in castra vēnistī?" rogāvit. iuvenis tamen tacēbat.

centurió, ubi cognóscere nón poterat cūr iuvenis in castra vēnisset, mīlitem iussit eum ad carcerem dūcere.

iuvenis, postquam verba centuriónis audīvit, "ego sum Vercobrix," inquit, "fīlius prīncipis Deceanglórum. vóbīs nón decórum est mē in carcere tenēre." "fīlius prīncipis Deceanglórum?" exclāmāvit centurió. "libentissimē tē videó. nós tē diū quaerimus, cellamque optimam tibi in carcere parāvimus."

Deceanglórum: Deceanglī *name of a tribe who inhabited an area of Britain that is now part of northern Wales*

Strȳthiō

optiō per castra ambulat. Strȳthiōnem, iam ad castra regressum, cōnspicit.

optiō: heus Strȳthiō! hūc venī! tibi aliquid dīcere volō.

Strȳthiō: nōlī mē vexāre! occupātus sum. Modestum quaerō, quod
           puella eum exspectat. hercle! puellam pulchriōrem
           numquam vīdī. vōx eius est suāvissima; oculī eius . . .   5

optiō: mī Strȳthiō, quamquam occupātissimus es, dēbēs
           maximā cum dīligentiā mē audīre. ā centuriōne nostrō
           missus sum. centuriō tē iubet ad carcerem statim
           festīnāre.

Strȳthiō: īnsānit centuriō! innocēns sum.   10

optiō: tacē! centuriō Modestum quoque iussit ad carcerem
           festīnāre.

Strȳthiō: deōs testēs faciō. innocentēs sumus. nūllum facinus
           commīsimus.

optiō: caudex! tacē! difficile est rem tibi explicāre! Valerius,   15
           centuriō noster, vōs ambōs carcerem custōdīre iussit.

Strȳthiō: nōlī mē vituperāre! rem nunc intellegō! Valerius nōs vult
           custōdēs carceris esse. decōrum est Valeriō nōs ēligere,
           quod fortissimī sumus. ego et Modestus, cum in Āfricā
           mīlitārēmus, sōlī tōtam prōvinciam custōdiēbāmus.   20

optiō: quamquam fortissimī estis, dīligentiam quoque
           maximam praestāre dēbētis. nam inter captīvōs est
           Vercobrix, iuvenis magnae dignitātis, cuius pater est
           prīnceps Deceanglōrum. necesse est vōbīs Vercobrigem
           dīligentissimē custōdīre.   25

Strȳthiō: nōlī anxius esse, mī optiō. nōbīs nihil difficile est, quod
           fortissimī sumus, ut anteā dīxī. tū redī ad Valerium. dīc
           Valeriō haec omnia verba. nōlī quicquam omittere!
           "Strȳthiō, mīles legiōnis secundae, Valeriō, centuriōnī
           legiōnis secundae, salūtem plūrimam dīcit. optiō, ā tē   30
           missus, mandāta tua nōbīs tulit. nōs mandātīs tuīs
           pārentēs, ad statiōnem prōcēdimus."

exeunt. optiō centuriōnem quaerit, Strȳthiō amīcum.

optiō	optio (military officer,	prōvinciam: prōvincia	*province*
	ranking below centurion)	praestāre	*show, display*
ambōs: ambō *both*		captīvōs: captīvus	*prisoner, captive*

cuius	*whose (genitive of* quī)	pārentēs: pārēre	*obey*
omittere	*leave out, omit*	statiōnem: statiō	*post*
salūtem plūrimam dīcit	*sends his best wishes*		

Valerius   *a centurion in the Roman Second Legion*

Legionary helmet from the River Thames, with a shield boss from the VIIIth legion, found in the River Tyne.

Modestus custōs

Modestus et Strȳthiō, carcerem ingressī, cellās in quibus captīvī erant īnspiciēbant. habēbat Strȳthiō libellum in quō nōmina captīvōrum scrīpta erant. Modestus eum rogāvit in quā cellā Vercobrix inclūsus esset. Strȳthiō, libellum īnspiciēns, cognōvit ubi Vercobrix iacēret, et Modestum ad cellam dūxit. Modestus, cum ad   5 portam cellae advēnisset, haesitāns cōnstitit.

Strȳthiō "num cellam intrāre timēs?" inquit. "vīnctus est fīlius prīncipis Deceanglōrum. tē laedere nōn potest."

cum Strȳthiō haec dīxisset, Modestus īrātus exclāmāvit,

"caudex, prīncipis fīlium nōn timeō! cōnstitī quod tē   10 exspectābam. volō tē mihi portam aperīre!"

cum portam Strȳthiō aperuisset, Modestus rūrsus haesitāvit.

"obscūra est cella," inquit Modestus anxius. "fer mihi lucernam."

Strȳthiō, vir summae patientiae, lucernam tulit amīcōque   15 trādidit. ille, cellam ingressus, ē cōnspectū discessit.

cōnstitit: cōnsistere	*halt, stop*	patientiae: patientia	*patience*
vīnctus: vincīre	*bind, tie up*	cōnspectū: cōnspectus	*sight*
lucernam: lucerna	*lamp*		

in angulō cellae iacēbat Vercobrix. Modestus, cum eum vīdisset, gladium dēstrīnxit. tum, ad mediam cellam prōgressus, Vercobrigem vituperāre coepit. Vercobrix tamen contumēliās Modestī audīre nōn poterat, quod graviter dormiēbat. Modestus   20
Vercobrigī dormientī exsultāns appropinquāvit, et gladium ante ōs eius vibrābat. iterum magnā cum vōce eum vituperābat. Strȳthiō, quī extrā cellam stābat, attonitus erat. nesciēbat enim cūr Modestus clāmāret. dormiēbat tamen Vercobrix, ignārus clāmōrum Modestī.

subitō arānea, ē tēctō cellae lāpsa, in nāsum Modestī incidit et   25
trāns ōs cucurrit. Modestus, ab arāneā territus, ē cellā fūgit.

"Strȳthiō! Strȳthiō!" clāmāvit. "claude portam cellae. nōbīs necesse est summā cum dīligentiā Vercobrigem custōdīre. etiam arāneae eum adiuvant!"

Strȳthiō cum portam clausisset, Modestum territum rogāvit quid   30
accidisset.

"Modeste," inquit, "quam pallidus es! num captīvum timēs?"
"minimē! pallidus sum, quod nōn cēnāvī," respondit.
"vīsne mē ad culīnam īre et tibi cēnam ferre?" rogāvit Strȳthiō.
"optimum cōnsilium est!" inquit alter. "tū tamen hīc manē.   35
melius est mihi ipsī ad culīnam īre, quod coquus decem dēnāriōs mihi dēbet."

haec locūtus, ad culīnam statim cucurrit.

angulō: angulus	*corner*	tēctō: tēctum	*ceiling, roof*
prōgressus	*having advanced*	lāpsa: lāpsus	*having fallen*
contumēliās: contumēlia	*insult, abuse*	trāns	*across*
ante ōs eius	*in front of his face*	pallidus	*pale*
ignārus	*not knowing, unaware*	hīc	*here*
arānea	*spider*		

About the Language

1 In Unit 1, you met sentences like this:

"quis clāmōrem audīvit?"   "ubi est captīvus?"
"Who heard the shout?"   *"Where is the prisoner?"*

In each example, a question is being *asked*. These examples are known as *direct* questions.

2 In Stage 25, you have met sentences like this:

centuriō nesciēbat quis clāmōrem audīvisset.
The centurion did not know who had heard the shout.

equitēs cognōvērunt ubi captīvus esset.
The horsemen found out where the prisoner was.

In each of these examples, the question is not being asked, but is being *reported* or *mentioned*. These examples are known as *indirect* questions. The verb in an indirect question in Latin is normally subjunctive.

3 Compare the following examples:

DIRECT QUESTIONS	INDIRECT QUESTIONS
"quid Vercobrix fēcit?"	mīlitēs intellēxērunt quid Vercobrix fēcisset.
"What has Vercobrix done?"	*The soldiers understood what Vercobrix had done.*
"cūr Britannī fūgērunt?"	optiō rogāvit cūr Britannī fūgissent.
"Why did the Britons run away?"	*The optio asked why the Britons had run away.*
"quis appropinquat?"	custōs nesciēbat quis appropinquāret.
"Who is approaching?"	*The guard did not know who was approaching.*

4 Further examples of direct and indirect questions:

1 "quis puerum interfēcit?"
2 nēmō sciēbat quis puerum interfēcisset.
3 Salvius tandem intellēxit quō Quīntus et Dumnorix fūgissent.
4 nūntius scīre voluit ubi rēx habitāret.
5 "quō modō pecūniam invēnistī?"
6 iūdex mē rogāvit quō modō pecūniam invēnissem.
7 Salvius nesciēbat cūr Quīntus rēgem adiūvisset.
8 Salvius nesciēbat cūr Quīntus rēgem adiuvāret.

Modestus perfuga

I

Modestus, ēgressus ē culīnā ubi cēnam optimam cōnsūmpserat, ad
carcerem redībat. cum ambulāret, sīc cōgitābat,

"numquam cēnam meliōrem gustāvī; numquam vīnum suāvius
bibī. sollicitus tamen sum. nam coquus illam cēnam et mihi et
Strȳthiōnī parāvit, sed ego sōlus cōnsūmpsī. nunc mihi necesse est   5
hanc rem Strȳthiōnī explicāre. fortūna tamen mihi favet, quod
Strȳthiō est vir magnae patientiae, minimīque cibī."

ubi carcerī appropinquāvit, portam apertam vīdit.

"dī immortālēs!" clāmāvit permōtus. "Strȳthiō, num portam
carceris apertam relīquistī? nēminem neglegentiōrem quam tē   10
nōvī."

carcerem ingressus, portās omnium cellārum apertās invēnit.
cum hoc vīdisset, exclāmāvit,

"ēheu! omnēs portae apertae sunt! captīvī, ē cellīs ēlāpsī, omnēs
fūgērunt!"   15

Modestus rem anxius cōgitāvit. nesciēbat enim quō captīvī
fūgissent; intellegere nōn poterat cūr Strȳthiō abesset.

"quid facere dēbeō? perīculōsum est hīc manēre ubi mē centuriō invenīre potest. ūna est spēs salūtis. mihi fugiendum est. ō Strȳthiō, Strȳthiō! coēgistī mē statiōnem dēserere. mē perfugam fēcistī. sed   20
deōs testēs faciō. invītus statiōnem dēserō, invītus centuriōnis īram fugiō."

perfuga	*deserter*	permōtus	*alarmed, disturbed*	īram: īra *anger*
et . . . et	*both . . . and*	spēs	*hope*	

II

Modestus, haec locūtus, subitō sonitum audīvit. aliquis portam cellae Vercobrigis aperīre et exīre temptābat!

"mihi ē carcere fugiendum est," aliquis ē cellā clāmāvit.

Modestus, cum haec audīvisset, ad portam cellae cucurrit et clausit.   5

"Vercobrix, tibi in cellā manendum est!" clāmāvit Modestus. "euge! nōn effūgit Vercobrix! eum captīvum habeō! euge! nunc mihi centuriō nocēre nōn potest, quod captīvum summae dignitātis in carcere retinuī."

Modestus autem anxius manēbat; nesciēbat enim quid Strȳthiōnī   10 accidisset. subitō pugiōnem humī relictum cōnspexit.

"heus, quid est? hunc pugiōnem agnōscō! est pugiō Strȳthiōnis! Strȳthiōnī dedī, ubi diem nātālem celebrābat. ēheu! cruentus est pugiō. ō mī Strȳthiō! nunc rem intellegō. mortuus es! captīvī, ē cellīs ēlāpsī, tē necāvērunt. ēheu! cum ego tuam cēnam in culīnā   15 cōnsūmerem, illī tē oppugnābant! ō Strȳthiō! nēmō īnfēlīcior est quam ego. nam tē amābam sīcut pater fīlium. tū tamen nōn inultus periistī. Vercobrix, quī in hāc cellā etiam nunc manet, poenās dare dēbet. heus! Vercobrix, mē audī! tibi moriendum est, quod Strȳthiō meus mortuus est."   20

haec locūtus, in cellam furēns irrūpit. captīvum, quī intus latēbat, verberāre coepit.

captīvus: Modeste! mī Modeste! dēsine mē verberāre! nōnne mē agnōscis? Strȳthiō sum, quem tū amās sīcut pater fīlium.   25

Modestus: Strȳthiō? Strȳthiō! num vīvus es? cūr vīvus es? sceleste! furcifer! ubi sunt captīvī quōs custōdiēbās?

aliquis	*someone*	inultus	*unavenged*
relictum: relinquere	*leave*	tibi moriendum est	*you must die*
cruentus	*bloody, covered with blood*	vīvus	*alive, living*

Strȳthiō:	fūgērunt, Modeste. mē dēcēpērunt. coēgērunt mē portās omnium cellārum aperīre.	
Modestus:	ēheu! quid facere dēbēmus?	30
Strȳthiō:	nōbīs statim ē carcere fugiendum est: centuriōnem appropinquantem audiō.	
Modestus:	ō Strȳthiō! ō, quam īnfēlīx sum!	
Strȳthiō:	nōlī dēspērāre. cōnsilium habeō. tibi necesse est mihi cōnfīdere.	35

amīcī ē carcere quam celerrimē fūgērunt.

About the Language

1 The examples of the imperfect and pluperfect subjunctive that you have met so far have nearly all ended in **-t** or **-nt**, meaning **he** . . . or **they** . . .:

nēmō sciēbat ubi Britannī **latērent**.
Nobody knew where the Britons were lying hidden.

centuriō, cum hoc **audīvisset**, saeviēbat.
When the centurion had heard this, he was furious.

2 The imperfect and pluperfect subjunctive can also end in **-m**, **-mus**, **-s** or **-tis**, meaning **I** . . ., **we** . . . or **you** . . .:

custōdēs nōs rogāvērunt cūr **clāmārēmus**.
*The guards asked us why **we were shouting.***

cum patrem **excitāvissem**, ad cubiculum rediī.
*When **I had awakened** my father, I returned to my bedroom.*

3 Further examples:

1 nesciēbam quō fūgissēs.
2 cum in Britanniā mīlitārem, oppidum Aquās Sūlis saepe vīsitāvī.
3 cum cēnam tuam cōnsūmerēs, centuriō tē quaerēbat.
4 cum nōmina recitāvissem, hospitēs ad rēgem dūxī.
5 amīcus meus cognōscere voluit ubi habitārētis.
6 puella nōs rogāvit cūr rem tam difficilem suscēpissēmus.

4 The imperfect and pluperfect tenses of the subjunctive are set out in full on page 279 of the Review Grammar.

Practicing the Language

1 Study the forms and meanings of the following nouns and give the meanings of the untranslated ones:

deus	*god*	dea	*goddess*
fīlius	*son*	fīlia	
ursus		ursa	*she-bear*
lupus		lupa	
leō		leaena	
captīvus	*prisoner (male)*	captīva	
avus	*grandfather*	avia	
saltātor	*dancer*	saltātrīx	*dancing-girl*
vēnātor	*hunter*	vēnātrīx	
victor		victrīx	*winner (female)*

Give the meaning of each of the following nouns:

rēgīna, domina, equa, nūntia

2 Complete the sentences of this story with the most suitable word from the list below, and then translate.

clāmāvit, cucurrit, invēnit, coxit, bibit, cōnsūmpsit, exiit

Modestus ad culīnam īrātus . . . . . . culīnam ingressus, coquum occupātum . . . . . . coquus cibum parābat.

"ubi sunt dēnāriī quōs mihi dēbēs?" . . . . . Modestus.

coquus, ubi Modestum īrātum vīdit, eī pōculum vīnī obtulit. Modestus libenter vīnum . . . . . deinde coquus cēnam . . . . . et Modestō obtulit. Modestus, simulac cēnam gustāvit, avidus . . . . . .

postrēmō Modestus, optimē cēnātus, ē culīnā ēbrius . . . . ., immemor pecūniae. coquus in culīnā stābat cachinnāns.

3 Translate the following sentences and then, with the help of the tables on pages 262–63 of the Review Grammar, change their meaning by turning each nominative into a dative and each dative into a nominative, then translate again.

For example: imperātor rēgibus dōna dedit.
The emperor gave gifts to the kings.
This becomes: rēgēs imperātōrī dōna dedērunt.
The kings gave gifts to the emperor.

Notice that in some sentences, as in the example above, you will have to change the verb from singular to plural, or plural to singular.

1 puella puerō gemmam ostendit.
2 mercātor amīcō dōnum ēmit.
3 servus puellīs respondit.
4 rēx cīvibus haec verba dīxit.
5 puerī cīvī nōn crēdidērunt.
6 mīlitēs fēminīs auxilium dedērunt.
7 custōdēs centuriōnī pecūniam trādidērunt.
8 ego tibi nōn fāvī.

4 This exercise is based on the story "Modestus custōs" on page 73. Read the story again. Complete each of the sentences below with one of the following groups of words and then translate. Use each group of words once only.

cum Modestus ad culīnam abiisset
cum carcerem intrāvissent
cum arānea dē tēctō dēcidisset
cum lucernam tulisset
cum Modestus gladium vibrāret

1 Modestus et Strȳthiō, ..., cellās captīvōrum īnspiciēbant.
2 Strȳthiō, ..., Modestō trādidit.
3 . . . . ., Vercobrix graviter dormiēbat.
4 . . . . ., Modestus fūgit perterritus.
5 . . . . ., Strȳthiō in carcere mānsit.

5 Complete each sentence with the right word and then translate.

1 medicus puellae . . . . . pōculum dedit. (aegram, aegrae)
2 hospitēs coquum . . . . . laudāvērunt. (callidum, callidō)
3 faber mercātōrī . . . . . dēnāriōs reddidit. (īrātum, īrātō)
4 ancillae dominō . . . . . pārēre nōlēbant. (crūdēlem, crūdēlī)
5 centuriō mīlitēs . . . . . castīgābat. (ignāvōs, ignāvīs)
6 puer stultus nautīs . . . . . crēdidit. (mendācēs, mendācibus)
7 stolās . . . . . emēbat fēmina. (novās, novīs)
8 . . . . . amīcīs pecūniam obtulī. (omnēs, omnibus)

The Legionary Soldier

The crack troops of the Roman army were the soldiers who served in the legions. They were all Roman citizens and full-time professionals who had signed on for twenty-five years. They were highly trained in the skills of infantry warfare and were often specialists in other things as well. In fact a Roman legion, consisting normally of about 5,000 foot soldiers, was a miniature army in itself, capable of constructing forts and camps, manufacturing its weapons and equipment and building roads. On its staff were engineers, architects, carpenters, smiths, doctors, medical orderlies, clerks, and accountants.

A legion

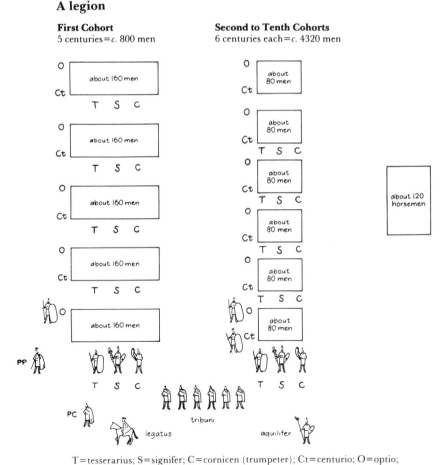

First Cohort
5 centuries=c. 800 men

Second to Tenth Cohorts
6 centuries each=c. 4320 men

T=tesserarius; S=signifer; C=cornicen (trumpeter); Ct=centurio; O=optio;
PP=primus pilus; PC=praefectus castrorum

Recruitment

When he joined the army a new recruit would first be interviewed to ensure that he had the proper legal status, i.e. that he was a Roman citizen; he was also given a medical examination. The army was inclined to favor recruits who came from certain trades, preferring "blacksmiths, wagon-makers, butchers, and huntsmen," and disapproving of "confectioners, weavers, and those who have been employed in occupations appropriate to the women's quarters."

Training

After being accepted and sworn in, the new recruit was sent to his unit to begin training. This was thorough, systematic, and physically hard. First the young soldier had to learn to march at the regulation pace for distances of up to 24 Roman miles (about 22 statute miles or 35 kilometers). Physical fitness was further developed by running, jumping, swimming, and carrying heavy packs. Next came weapon training, starting with a wooden practice-sword and wicker shield. The soldier learned to handle the shield correctly and to attack a dummy target with the point of his sword. When he had mastered the basic skills with dummy weapons, he went on to the real thing and finally practiced individual combat in pairs, probably with a leather button on the point of his sword.

The second phase of weapon training was to learn to throw the javelin (**pīlum**). This had a wooden shaft 5 feet (1.5 meters) long and a pointed iron head of 2 feet (0.6 meters). This head was cleverly constructed. The first 10 inches (25 centimeters) were finely tempered to give it penetrating power, but the rest was left untempered so that it was fairly soft and liable to bend. Thus, when the javelin was hurled at an enemy, from a distance of 25–30 yards (23–28 meters), its point penetrated and stuck into his shield, while the neck of the metal head bent and the shaft hung down. This not only made the javelin unusable, so that it could not be thrown back, but also made the encumbered shield so difficult to manage that the enemy might have to abandon it altogether.

When he had reached proficiency in handling his weapons and was physically fit, the soldier was ready to leave the barracks for training in the open countryside. This began with route marches on which he carried not only his body armor and weapons but also several days'

Relief from Trajan's column showing soldiers building a fort.

ration of food, together with equipment for making an overnight camp, such as a saw, an axe, and also a basket for moving earth, as shown in the picture above. Much importance was attached to the proper construction of the camp at the end of the day's march, and the young soldier was given careful instruction and practice. Several practice camps and forts have been found in Britain. For example, at Cawthorn in Yorkshire (in the north of England) the soldiers under training did rather more than just dig ditches and ramparts; they also constructed platforms for catapults (**ballistae**) and even built camp ovens.

Work

The fully trained legionary did not spend all or even much of his time on active service. Most of it was spent on peacetime duties, such as building or roadmaking, and, during the first century A.D. at least, he had good prospects of surviving till his discharge. He was generally stationed in a large legionary fortress somewhere near the frontiers of the empire in places such as Deva (Chester), Bonna (Bonn), and Vindobona (Vienna) which were key points in the Roman defenses against the barbarians.

Many of the daily duties were the same wherever he was stationed. A duty roster, written on papyrus, has come down to us and lists the names of thirty-six soldiers, all members of the same century in one of the legions stationed in Egypt. It covers the first ten days in October possibly in the year A.D. 87. A selection of the entries is given on page 86 below. For example, C. Julius Valens was to spend October 2nd on guard duty in the tower of the fortress, October 4th repairing boots, and October 8th acting as orderly (servant) to one of the officers.

Pay

In both war and peacetime the soldier received the same rate of pay. In the first century A.D., up to the time of the Emperor Domitian (A.D. 81–96), this amounted to 225 denarii per annum; Domitian improved the

rate to 300 denarii. These amounts were gross pay, and before any money was handed to the soldier certain deductions were made. Surprising though it may seem, he was obliged to pay for his food, clothing, and equipment. He would also leave some money in the military savings bank. What he actually received in cash may have been only a quarter or a fifth of his gross pay. Whether he felt badly treated is difficult to say. Certainly we know of cases of discontent, but pay and conditions of service were apparently not bad enough to discourage recruits. The soldier could look forward to some promotion and eventually an honorable discharge with a gratuity of 3,000 denarii or an allocation of land.

Promotion

If a soldier was promoted his life began to change in several ways. He was paid more and he was exempted from many of the fatigues performed by the ordinary soldier. Each century was commanded by a centurion and he was assisted by an optio who was waiting for a vacancy in the ranks of the centurions. There was also in each century a *standard-bearer* (**signifer**), a **tesserārius** who commanded the guard-pickets, and one or two clerks. The centurions, who were roughly equivalent to non-commissioned warrant officers in a modern army, were the backbone of the legion. There were sixty of them, each responsible for the training and discipline of a century, and their importance was reflected in their pay, which was probably about 1,500 denarii per annum. Most of them had risen from the ranks by virtue of courage and ability. The senior centurion of the legion (**prīmus pīlus**) was a highly respected figure; he was at least fifty years old and had worked his way up through the various grades of centurion. He held office for one year, then received a large gratuity and was allowed to retire; or he might go on still further to become **praefectus castrōrum** (*commander of the camp*).

Senior Officers

The men mentioned so far would expect to spend the whole of their working lives serving as professional soldiers. The senior officers, on the other hand, spent a much shorter period of time in the legion, possibly three or four years, without any previous service as centurion or ordinary legionary.

The officer commanding the legion was called a **lēgātus**. He was a member of the Senate in Rome and usually fairly young, in his middle thirties. He was assisted by six military tribunes. Of these, one was usually a young man of noble birth, serving his military apprenticeship before starting a political career. The other five were members of a slightly lower social class (**equitēs**) and they too would be in their thirties. They were generally able, wealthy, and educated men, often aiming at important posts in the imperial civil service.

	1 Oct.	2 Oct.	3 Oct.	4 Oct.	5 Oct.	6 Oct.	7 Oct.	8 Oct.	9 Oct.	10 Oct.
C. Julius Valens	training arena	tower	drainage	boots	armory	armory	baths	orderly	in century	baths
L. Sextilius Germanus	gate guard	standards	baths	tower	duty in D. Decrius' century	→	→	→	→	→
M. Antonius Crispus	baths	stretchers	in century	plain clothes	in century	—	tribune's escort	→	→	→
T. Flavius	baths	—	—	baths	baths	baths	gate guard	—	—	
M. Domitius	—	—	detachment to the granaries at Neapolis	→	→	→	→	→	→	→

Words and Phrases Checklist

accidō, accidere, accidī	*happen*
aliquis	*someone*
aperiō, aperīre, aperuī, apertus	*open*
autem	*but*
captīvus, captīvī	*prisoner, captive*
castra, castrōrum	*military camp*
cōgō, cōgere, coēgī, coāctus	*force, compel*
dēpōnō, dēpōnere, dēposuī, dēpositus	*put down, take off*
dēsinō, dēsinere	*end, cease*
dignitās, dignitātis	*importance, prestige*
dīligentia, dīligentiae	*industry, hard work*
explicō, explicāre, explicāvī, explicātus	*explain*
extrā	*outside*
furēns, *gen.* furentis	*furious, in a rage*
haesitō, haesitāre, haesitāvī	*hesitate*
immemor, *gen.* immemoris	*forgetful*
immortālis, immortāle	*immortal*
dī immortālēs!	*heavens above!*
laedō, laedere, laesī, laesus	*harm*
lateō, latēre, latuī	*lie hidden*
legiō, legiōnis	*legion*
nescio, nescīre, nescīvī	*not know*
nōmen, nōminis	*name*
ōs, ōris	*face*
poena, poenae	*punishment*
poenās dare	*pay the penalty, be punished*
rūrsus	*again*
scelestus, scelesta, scelestum	*wicked*
statiō, statiōnis	*post*
suāvis, suāve	*sweet*
testis, testis	*witness*

Word Search

aperture, captivate, depose, indignity, latent, suave, testify

1 . . . . .: to give evidence
2 . . . . .: an opening
3 . . . . .: humiliation, degradation
4 . . . . .: having a smooth or charming manner
5 . . . . .. underlying
6 . . . . .: to remove from office; to dethrone
7 . . . . .: to fascinate or mesmerize

Artist's impression of Deva (modern Chester) and its surroundings.

Agricola

adventus Agricolae

mīlitēs legiōnis secundae, quī Dēvae in castrīs erant, diū et strēnuē labōrābant. nam Gāius Iūlius Sīlānus, lēgātus legiōnis, adventum Agricolae exspectābat. mīlitēs, ā centuriōnibus iussī, multa et varia faciēbant. aliī arma poliēbant; aliī aedificia pūrgābant; aliī plaustra reficiēbant. Sīlānus neque quiētem neque commeātum mīlitibus   5
dedit.

mīlitēs, ignārī adventūs Agricolae, rem graviter ferēbant. trēs continuōs diēs labōrāvērunt; quārtō diē Sīlānus adventum Agricolae nūntiāvit. mīlitēs, cum hoc audīvissent, maximē gaudēbant quod Agricolam dīligēbant.   10

tertiā hōrā Sīlānus mīlitēs in ōrdinēs longōs īnstrūxit, ut Agricolam salūtārent. mīlitēs, cum Agricolam castra intrantem vīdissent, magnum clāmōrem sustulērunt.

"iō, Agricola! iō, iō, Agricola!"

Agricola ad tribūnal prōcessit ut pauca dīceret. omnēs statim   15
tacuērunt ut contiōnem Agricolae audīrent.

"gaudeō," inquit, "quod hodiē vōs rūrsus videō. nūllam legiōnem fidēliōrem habeō, nūllam fortiōrem. disciplīnam studiumque vestrum valdē laudō."

mīlitēs ita hortātus, per ōrdinēs prōcessit ut eōs īnspiceret. deinde   20
prīncipia intrāvit ut colloquium cum Sīlānō habēret.

adventus	*arrival*	gaudēbant: gaudēre	*be pleased, rejoice*
strēnuē	*hard, energetically*	tertiā hōrā	*at the third hour*
aliī . . . aliī . . . aliī	*some . . . others*	iō!	*hurrah!*
	. . . others	tribūnal	*platform*
arma	*arms, weapons*	contiōnem: contiō	*speech*
poliēbant: polīre	*polish*	disciplīnam: disciplīna	*discipline,*
pūrgābant: pūrgāre	*clean*		*orderliness*
quiētem: quiēs	*rest*	studium	*enthusiasm, zeal*
commeātum: commeātus	*leave*	vestrum: vester	*your*
trēs . . . diēs	*for three days*	hortātus	*having encouraged*
continuōs: continuus	*continuous, on end*	prīncipia	*headquarters*
quārtō diē	*on the fourth day*		
Dēvae	*at Chester*		

When you have read this story, answer the questions at the end.

in prīncipiīs

Salvius ipse paulō prius ad castra advēnerat. iam in legiōnis secundae prīncipiīs sedēbat, Agricolam anxius exspectāns. sollicitus erat quod in epistulā, quam ad Agricolam mīserat, multa falsa scrīpserat. in prīmīs Cogidubnum sēditiōnis accūsāverat. in animō volvēbat num Agricola sibi crēditūrus esset. Belimicum   5
sēcum dūxerat ut testis esset.

subitō Salvius, Agricolam intrantem cōnspicātus, ad eum festīnāvit ut salūtāret. deinde renovāvit ea quae in epistulā scrīpserat. Agricola, cum haec audīvisset, diū tacuit. dēnique maximē commōtus,   10

"quanta perfidia!" inquit. "quanta īnsānia! id quod mihi patefēcistī, vix intellegere possum. īnsānīvit Cogidubnus. īnsānīvērunt prīncipēs Rēgnēnsium. numquam nōs oportet barbarīs crēdere; tūtius est eōs omnēs prō hostibus habēre. nunc mihi necesse est rēgem opprimere quem quīnque annōs prō amīcō   15
habeō."

haec locūtus, ad Sīlānum, lēgātum legiōnis, sē vertit.

"Sīlāne," inquit, "nōs oportet rēgem prīncipēsque Rēgnēnsium quam celerrimē opprimere. tibi statim cum duābus cohortibus proficīscendum est."   20

Sīlānus, ē prīncipiīs ēgressus, centuriōnibus mandāta dedit. eōs iussit cohortēs parāre. intereā Agricola plūra dē rēgis perfidiā rogāre coepit. Salvius eī respondit,

"ecce Belimicus, vir ingeniī optimī summaeque fideī, quem iste Cogidubnus corrumpere temptābat. Belimicus autem, quī   25
blanditiās rēgis spernēbat, omnia mihi patefēcit."

paulō prius	*a little earlier*	īnsānia	*insanity, madness*
in prīmīs	*in particular*	nōs oportet	*we must*
sēditiōnis: sēditiō	*rebellion*	prō hostibus habēre	*consider as enemies*
in animō volvēbat:		opprimere	*crush*
in animō volvere	*wonder, turn over*	tibi . . . proficīscendum est	*you must set out*
	in the mind	cohortibus: cohors	*cohort*
num	*whether*	corrumpere	*corrupt*
crēditūrus	*going to believe*	blanditiās: blanditiae	*flatteries*
renovāvit: renovāre	*repeat, renew*	spernēbat: spernere	*despise, reject*

"id quod Salvius dīxit vērum est," inquit Belimicus. "rēx Rōmānōs ōdit. Rōmānōs ē Britanniā expellere tōtamque īnsulam occupāre cupit. nāvēs igitur comparat. mīlitēs exercet. etiam bēstiās saevās colligit. nūper bēstiam in mē impulit ut mē interficeret." 30

Agricola tamen hīs verbīs diffīsus, Salvium dīligentius rogāvit quae indicia sēditiōnis vīdisset. cognōscere voluit quot essent armātī, num Britannī cīvēs Rōmānōs interfēcissent, quās urbēs dēlēvissent.

subitō magnum clāmōrem omnēs audīvērunt. per iānuam 35 prīncipiōrum perrūpit homō squālidus. ad Agricolam praeceps cucurrit genibusque eius haesit.

"cīvis Rōmānus sum," inquit. "Quīntum Caecilium Iūcundum mē vocant. ego multās iniūriās passus hūc tandem advēnī. hoc ūnum dīcere volō. Cogidubnus est innocēns." 40

haec locūtus humī prōcubuit exanimātus.

diffīsus	*having distrusted*	perrūpit: perrumpere	*burst through, burst in*
indicia: indicium	*sign, evidence*	squālidus	*covered with dirt, filthy*
armātī: armātus	*armed*		

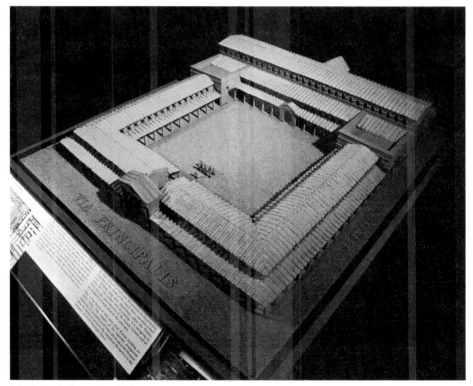

Model of the principia at Chester.

1 Why has Salvius come to Chester?
2 Why has he brought Belimicus with him?
3 Why do you think Agricola stays silent for a long time (line 9)?
4 What orders does he give to Silanus?
5 Why does Agricola feel doubtful about Belimicus' statement?
6 What questions does Agricola put to Salvius? Would Salvius find Agricola's questions easy to answer? Do you think Agricola ought to have asked these questions *before* sending out the cohorts?
7 What happens before Salvius can answer Agricola?
8 What is the first thing Quintus says? Why does he say this first?

About the Language

1 Study the following examples:

mīlitēs ad prīncipia convēnērunt **ut Agricolam audīrent**.
*The soldiers gathered at the headquarters **in order that they might hear Agricola**.*

per tōtam noctem labōrābat medicus **ut vulnera mīlitum sānāret**.
*The doctor worked all night **in order that he might treat the soldiers' wounds**.*

The groups of words in boldface are known as *purpose clauses*, because they indicate the *purpose* for which an action was done. For instance, in the second example above, the group of words **ut vulnera mīlitum sānāret** indicates the purpose of the doctor's work. The verb in a purpose clause in Latin is always subjunctive.

2 Further examples:

1 dominus stilum et cērās poposcit ut epistulam scrīberet.
2 omnēs cīvēs ad silvam contendērunt ut leōnem mortuum spectārent.
3 dēnique ego ad patrem rediī ut rem explicārem.
4 pugiōnem rapuī ut captīvum interficerem.

3 Instead of translating **ut** and the subjunctive as *in order that s/he (they) might . . .*, it is often possible to use a simpler form of words:

mīlitēs ad prīncipia convēnērunt ut Agricolam audīrent.
The soldiers gathered at the headquarters in order to hear Agricola.
    or, simpler still:
The soldiers gathered at the headquarters to hear Agricola.

tribūnus

Agricola, ubi hoc vīdit, custōdēs iussit Quīntum auferre medicumque arcessere. tum ad tribūnum mīlitum, quī adstābat, sē vertit.

"mī Rūfe," inquit, "prūdentissimus es omnium tribūnōrum quōs habeō. tē iubeō hunc hominem summā cum cūrā interrogāre."   5

Salvius, cum Rūfus exiisset, valdē commōtus,

"cūr tempus terimus?" inquit. "omnia explicāre possum. nōtus est mihi hic homō. nūper in vīllā mē vīsitāvit, quamquam nōn invītāveram. trēs mēnsēs apud mē mānsit, opēs meās dēvorāns. duōs tripodas argenteōs habēbam, quōs abstulit ut Cogidubnō   10
daret. sed eum nōn accūsāvī, quod hospes erat. ubi tamen Aquās Sūlis mēcum advēnit, facinus scelestum committere temptāvit. venēnum parāvit ut Memorem, haruspicem Rōmānum, necāret. postquam rem nōn effēcit, mē ipsum accūsāvit. nōlī eī crēdere. multō perfidior est quam Britannī."   15

haec cum audīvisset, Agricola respondit,

"sī tālia fēcit, eī moriendum est."

mox revēnit Rūfus valdē attonitus.

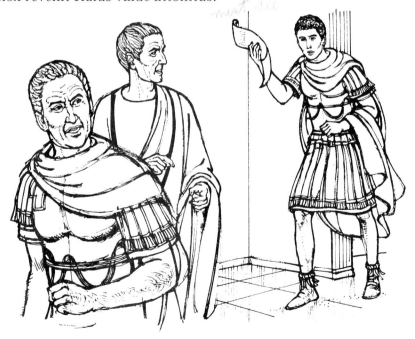

"Quīntus Caecilius," inquit, "est iuvenis summae fideī. patrem meum, quem Alexandrīae relīquī, bene nōverat. hoc prō certō habeō quod Quīntus hanc epistulam mihi ostendit, ā patre ipsō scrīptam."

Agricola statim Quīntum ad sē vocāvit, cēterōsque dīmīsit. Salvius, Quīntum dētestātus, anxius exiit. Agricola cum Quīntō colloquium trēs hōrās habēbat.

20

25

tribūnus	*tribune (high-ranking officer)*
prūdentissimus: prūdēns	*shrewd, intelligent*
tempus terimus: tempus terere	*waste time*
opēs	*money, wealth*
dēvorāns: dēvorāre	*devour, eat up*
multō perfidior	*much more treacherous*
tālia	*such things*
prō certō habeō: prō certō habēre	*know for certain*
dētestātus	*having cursed*

Rūfe: Rūfus *son of Barbillus and Plotina (see Unit 2, Stage 20)*

About the Language

1 From Stage 14 onwards you have met sentences of this kind:

necesse est mihi cēnam parāre.   *I must prepare the dinner.*
necesse est vōbīs labōrāre.   *You must work.*

2 You have now met another way of expressing the same idea:

necesse est nōbīs currere. ⎫
nōbīs **currendum** est.   ⎬   *We must run.*
                           ⎭

necesse est eī revenīre. ⎫
eī **reveniendum** est.   ⎬   *He must come back.*
                           ⎭

The word in boldface is known as the *gerundive*.

3 Further examples:

1 mihi fugiendum est.
2 nōbīs ambulandum est.
3 tibi hīc manendum est.
4 omnibus servīs labōrandum est.

contentiō

Agricola, cum Quīntum audīvisset, vehementer saeviēbat. Salvium furēns arcessīvit. quī, simulatque intrāvit, aliquid dīcere coepit. Agricola tamen, cum silentium iussisset, Salvium vehementer accūsāvit.

"dī immortālēs! Cogidubnus est innocēns, tū perfidus. cūr tam   5
īnsānus eram ut tibi crēderem? quīnque annōs hanc prōvinciam iam administrō. rēgem Cogidubnum bene cognōvī. saepe rēx mihi auxiliō fuit. neque perfidum neque mendācem umquam sē praestitit. cūr tū crīmen falsum in eum intulistī? accūsāvistīne eum ut potentiam tuam augērēs? simulatque ad hanc prōvinciam   10
vēnistī, amīcī mē dē calliditāte tuā monuērunt. nunc rēs ipsa mē docuit. num Imperātor Domitiānus hanc tantam perfidiam ferre potest? ego sānē nōn possum. in hāc prōvinciā summam potestātem habeō. iubeō tē hās inimīcitiās dēpōnere. iubeō tē ad Cogidubnī aulam īre, veniamque ab eō petere. praetereā tē oportet Imperātōrī   15
ipsī rem explicāre."

haec ubi dīxit Agricola, Salvius respondit īrātus,

"quam caecus es! quam longē errās! tē ipsum oportet Imperātōrī id quod in Britanniā fēcistī explicāre. quīnque annōs hanc prōvinciam pessimē administrās. tū enim in ultimīs Britanniae 20 partibus bellum geris et victōriās inānēs ē Calēdoniā refers; sed Imperātor pecūniās opēsque accipere cupit. itaque rēgnum Cogidubnī occupāre cōnstituit; Calēdoniam floccī nōn facit. tū sānē hoc nescīs. in magnō perīculō es, quod cōnsilium meum spernis. nōn sōlum mihi sed Imperātōrī ipsī obstās." 25

cum hanc contentiōnem inter sē habērent, subitō nūntius prīncipia ingressus exclāmāvit,

"mortuus est Cogidubnus!"

auxiliō fuit	*was a help, was helpful*
potentiam: potentia	*power*
augērēs: augēre	*increase*
inimīcitiās: inimīcitia	*feud, dispute*
tē oportet	*you must*
caecus	*blind*
pessimē	*very badly*
victōriās: victōria	*victory*
inānēs: inānis	*empty, meaningless*
cōnstituit: cōnstituere	*decide*

Imperātor Domitiānus	*the Emperor Domitian (reigned A.D. 81–96)*
Calēdoniā: Calēdonia	*Scotland*

Practicing the Language

1 Study the forms and meanings of the following verbs and nouns, and give the meanings of the untranslated words:

amāre	*to love*	amor	*love*
timēre	*to be afraid*	timor	*fear*
honōrāre	*to honor*	honor	
clāmāre		clāmor	
labōrāre		labor	
fulgēre		fulgor	*brightness*
pavēre	*to be alarmed*	pavor	
furere		furor	*madness, fury*
tremere		tremor	*a shaking, a tremor*
dolēre (1)	*to hurt, to be painful*	dolor (1)	
dolēre (2)	*to be sad*	dolor (2)	

Give the meaning of each of the following nouns:

favor, pallor, sūdor

2 Complete each sentence with the right word and then translate.

1 Agricola, ubi verba . . . . . audīvit, Salvium arcessīvit. (Quīntum, Quīntī, Quīntō)
2 omnēs hospitēs . . . . . saltātrīcis laudāvērunt. (artem, artis, artī)
3 iter nostrum difficile erat, quod tot cīvēs . . . . . complēbant. (viās, viārum, viīs)
4 prō prīncipiīs stābat magna turba . . . . . . (mīlitēs, mīlitum, mīlitibus)
5 lēgātus, postquam mandāta . . . . . dedit, legiōnem ad montem proximum dūxit. (centuriōnēs, centuriōnum, centuriōnibus)
6 iūdex, quī . . . . . nōn crēdēbat, īrātissimus fīēbat. (puerōs, puerōrum, puerīs)

3 Translate each English sentence into Latin by selecting correctly from the list of Latin words.

1 *The kind citizens had provided help.*
    cīvis   benignī   auxilium   praebuērunt
    cīvēs   benignōs   auxiliī   praebuerant

2 *They arrested the soldier in the kitchen of an inn.*
    mīlitem   per culīnam   tabernae   comprehendunt
    mīlitis   in culīnā   tabernārum   comprehendērunt

3 *Master! Read this letter!*
    domine   haec   epistula   lege
    dominus   hanc   epistulam   legis

4 *The old men departed, praising the brave messenger.*
    senēs   discēdunt   fortem   nūntium   laudāns
    senum   discessērunt   fortī   nūntiōs   laudantēs

5 *How can we avoid the punishments of the gods?*
    quō modō   poenae   deōrum   vītantēs   possumus
    quis   poenās   deīs   vītāre   poterāmus

6 *The words of the soothsayer frightened him.*
    verbum   haruspicis   eam   eum   terruit
    verba   haruspicī   eōs   terruērunt

4 Complete each sentence with the most suitable word from the list below, and then translate.

epistulam, audīvisset, ēgressus, invēnērunt, equīs, captī

1 Salvius, ē prīncipiīs . . . . ., Belimicum quaesīvit.
2 Agricola, cum haec verba . . . . ., ad Rūfum sē vertit.
3 dominus . . . . . ē manibus servī impatiēns rapuit.
4 custōdēs nūntium humī iacentem . . . . . .
5 quattuor Britannī, in pugnā . . . . ., vītam miserrimam in carcere agēbant.
6 aliī mīlitēs . . . . . aquam dabant, aliī frūmentum in horrea īnferēbant.

Agricola, Governor of Britain

With the abbreviated words written out, this reads:
imperatore Vespasiano VIIII Tito imperatore VII consule Cnaeo Iulio Agricola legato Augusti propraetore.

The two inscriptions above both contain the name of Gnaeus Julius Agricola. The first comes from a lead water-pipe found at Chester, the second from the forum of Verulamium (St. Albans). These inscriptions might have been virtually all that we knew about the man if his life-story had not been written by his son-in-law, the historian Tacitus. Because of Tacitus' biography we possess a very detailed picture of Agricola.

He was born on June 13, A.D. 40 in the Roman colony of Forum Iulii in southeast Gaul. The town had been founded by Julius Caesar for his veteran soldiers, and most of its inhabitants were Italian-born citizens rather than native Gauls. (It is today the French town of Fréjus.) He came from a distinguished family. His grandfathers had both held important government posts and his father had been made a senator by the Emperor Tiberius, but later fell foul of the Emperor Gaius Caligula and was executed in A.D. 40, shortly after Agricola was born.

Agricola went to school at Massilia (Marseilles), which was the cultural and educational center of southern Gaul. He followed the normal curriculum for the young sons of upper-class Roman families: public speaking (taught by a **rhētor**) and philosophy. He enjoyed the latter, but Tacitus records his mother's reaction:

"I remember that Agricola often told us that in his youth he was more enthusiastic about philosophy than a Roman and a senator was expected to be, and his mother thought it wise to put a damper on such a passionate interest."

At the age of eighteen, Agricola served in the Roman army in Britain with the rank of **tribūnus**, like Barbillus Rufus in the story on p.94. He used this opportunity to become familiar with the province. The soldiers under his command had a similar opportunity to get to know him. Two years later, during the revolt of Boudica in A.D. 60, he witnessed the grim realities of warfare. Agricola was by now very knowledgeable about the province of Britain and this knowledge was to stand him in good stead during his governorship some eighteen years later.

Back in Rome, he continued his political career. In A.D. 70, he returned to Britain to take command of the Twentieth Legion which was stationed at Viroconium (Wroxeter, in the west of England, about 40 miles (64 kilometers) south of Chester) and had become undisciplined and troublesome. His success in handling this difficult task was rewarded by promotion to the governorship of Aquitania (the central region of modern France) in Gaul. In A.D. 77 he became consul and the following year returned to Britain for a third time, as governor of the province. The political experience and military skill which he had acquired by then equipped him to face an exciting, if demanding, situation.

Agricola rose to the challenge in many different ways. He actively promoted a policy of Romanization; he extended a network of roads and forts across northern Britain, including the legionary fortress at Chester; and during his governorship he virtually doubled the area of Roman-held territory in Britain.

Career of Agricola

A.D. 58	Tribunus Militum in Britain
64	Quaestor in Asia
66	Tribunus Plebis in Rome
68	Praetor in Rome
70	Commander of Twentieth Legion in Britain
74	Governor of Aquitania
77	Consul
78	Governor of Britain

Words and Phrases Checklist

accūsō, accūsāre, accūsāvī, accūsātus — *accuse*
auferō, auferre, abstulī, ablātus — *take away, steal*
bellum, bellī — *war*
  bellum gerere — *wage war, campaign*
cohors, cohortis — *cohort*
colligō, colligere, collēgī, collēctus — *gather, collect*
commōtus, commōta, commōtum — *moved, excited, upset*
doceō, docēre, docuī, doctus — *teach*
facinus, facinoris — *crime*
falsus, falsa, falsum — *false, dishonest*
fidēs, fideī — *loyalty, trustworthiness*
īnsānus, īnsāna, īnsānum — *crazy, insane*
īnstruō, īnstruere, īnstrūxī, īnstrūctus — *draw up*
lēgātus, lēgātī — *commander*
num — *whether*
occupō, occupāre, occupāvī, occupātus — *seize, take over*
oportet — *it is right*
  mē oportet — *I must*
perfidia, perfidiae — *treachery*
praebeō, praebēre, praebuī, praebitus — *provide*
prīncipia, prīncipiōrum — *headquarters*
prōvincia, prōvinciae — *province*
quot? — *how many?*
referō, referre, rettulī, relātus — *bring back, deliver*
rēgnum, rēgnī — *kingdom*
saevus, saeva, saevum — *savage, cruel*
sānē — *obviously*
sī — *if*
tribūnus, tribūnī — *tribune (high-ranking officer)*
ultimus, ultima, ultimum — *furthest*
ut — *that, in order that*

Word Search

belligerent, commotion, delegate, doctor, infidel, provincial, ultimate

1 . . . . .: to entrust (e.g. authority or responsibility) to an agent
2 . . . . .: an unbeliever
3 . . . . .: aggressive
4 . . . . .: a person who has obtained the highest academic degree in a particular field
5 . . . . .: limited in perspective; narrowminded
6 . . . . .: final
7 . . . . .: disturbance, uproar

Aerial view of Chester, showing clearly how the river has altered its course. The main bridge, however, crosses the river at the same point as the Roman one did.

Stage 27

in castrīs

"fuge mēcum ad horreum!"

extrā carcerem, Modestus et
Strȳthiō sermōnem anxiī
habēbant.
Modestus Strȳthiōnem monēbat
ut ad horreum sēcum fugeret.

"invenīte Modestum Strȳthiōnemque!"

prō prīncipiīs, centuriō Valerius
mīlitibus mandāta dabat.
centuriō mīlitibus imperābat ut
Modestum Strȳthiōnemque
invenīrent.

"castra Rōmāna oppugnāte!
horrea incendite!"

in silvā proximā, Vercobrix
contiōnem apud Britannōs
habēbat.
Vercobrix Britannōs incitābat ut
castra Rōmāna oppugnārent et
horrea incenderent.

When you have read this story, answer the questions at the end.

sub horreō

Modestus et Strȳthiō, ē carcere ēgressī, ad horreum fūgērunt. per
aditum angustum rēpsērunt et sub horreō cēlātī manēbant. centuriō
Valerius, cum portās cellārum apertās carceremque dēsertum
vīdisset, īrātissimus erat. mīlitibus imperāvit ut Modestum et
Strȳthiōnem caperent. mīlitēs tamen, quamquam per tōta castra   5
quaerēbant, eōs invenīre nōn poterant. illī quīnque diēs mānsērunt
cēlātī. sextō diē Modestus tam miser erat ut rem diūtius ferre nōn
posset.

Modestus: quam īnfēlīx sum! mālim in illō carcere esse potius
           quam sub hōc horreō latēre. quālis est haec vīta?   10
           necesse est mihi grāna quae mūrēs relīquērunt
           cōnsūmere. adest Strȳthiō, comes exiliī, sed mē nōn
           adiuvat. nam Strȳthiō est vir maximī silentiī,
           minimīque iocī. ēheu! mē taedet huius vītae.
Strȳthiō: mī Modeste, difficile est nōbīs sub horreō diūtius   15
           manēre. nunc tamen advesperāscit. vīsne mē, ex horreō
           ēgressum, cibum quaerere? hominibus miserrimīs cibus
           sōlācium semper affert.
Modestus: id est cōnsilium optimum. nōbīs cēnandum est.
           Strȳthiō, tē huic reī praeficiō. ī prīmum ad coquum.   20
           eum iubē cēnam splendidam coquere et hūc portāre.
           deinde quaere Aulum et Pūblicum, amīcōs nostrōs!
           invītā eōs ad cēnam! iubē Aulum amphoram vīnī ferre,
           Pūblicum lucernam āleāsque. tum curre ad vīcum;

aditum: aditus	*entrance*	mē taedet	*I am tired, I am bored*
angustum: angustus	*narrow*	advesperāscit:	
rēpsērunt: rēpere	*crawl*	advesperāscere	*get dark, become dark*
imperāvit: imperāre	*order, command*	sōlācium	*comfort*
sextō: sextus	*sixth*	affert: afferre	*bring*
mālim	*I would prefer*	praeficiō: praeficere	*put in charge*
potius	*rather*	prīmum	*first*
grāna: grānum	*grain*	vīcum: vīcus	*town, village*
exiliī: exilium	*exile*		

Aulum: Aulus	*soldier in the Roman Second Legion*
Pūblicum: Pūblicus	*soldier in the Roman Second Legion*

Nigrīnam quaere! optima est saltātrīcum; mihi 25
saltātrīcēs quoque sōlācium afferunt.
Strȳthiō: quid dīcis? vīsne mē saltātrīcem in castra dūcere?
Modestus: abī caudex!

Strȳthiō, ut mandāta Modestī efficeret, invītus discessit. coquō
persuāsit ut cēnam splendidam parāret; Aulō et Pūblicō persuāsit 30
ut vīnum et lucernam āleāsque ferrent; Nigrīnam ōrāvit ut ad
horreum venīret, sed eī persuādēre nōn poterat.

ōrāvit: ōrāre *beg*

Nigrīnam: Nigrīna *a dancer from the village* (vīcus) *near the fortress at Deva*

Reconstructed Roman granary from the fort at Lunt in central England.

1 What was the purpose of a "horreum"? Why was its floor raised above
  ground level? What does this enable Modestus and Strythio to do?
2 After five days, what has Modestus been forced to do?
3 What makes Strythio think he can go outside without getting caught?
4 Who is to bring the dinner to the granary? What are Aulus and
  Publicus to bring? Who else is to come to the dinner? Where is she to be
  found?
5 Why is Strythio "invītus" (line 29)? How successful is he in carrying
  out Modestus' instructions?
6 Which would you expect to be built first, the "castra" or the "vīcus"?

About the Language

1 In Unit 1, you met sentences like this:

"redīte!"   "pecūniam trāde!"
"Go back!"   *"Hand over the money!"*

In each example, an order or command is being *given*. These examples are known as *direct* commands.

2 In Stage 27, you have met sentences like this:

lēgātus mīlitibus imperāvit **ut redīrent**.
*The commander ordered his soldiers **that they should go back**.*
   or, in more natural English:
*The commander ordered his soldiers **to go back**.*

latrōnēs mercātōrī imperāvērunt **ut pecūniam trāderet**.
*The robbers ordered the merchant **that he should hand over the money**.*
   or, in more natural English:
*The robbers ordered the merchant **to hand over the money**.*

In each of these examples, the command is not being given, but is being *reported* or *mentioned*. These examples are known as *indirect* commands. The verb in an indirect command in Latin is usually subjunctive.

3 Compare the following examples:

DIRECT COMMANDS	INDIRECT COMMANDS
"contendite!"	iuvenis amīcīs persuāsit ut contenderent.
"Hurry!"	*The young man persuaded his friends to hurry.*
"dā mihi aquam!"	captīvus custōdem ōrāvit ut aquam sibi daret.
"Give me water!"	*The prisoner begged the guard to give him water.*
"fuge!"	mē monuit ut fugerem.
"Run away!"	*He warned me to run away.*

---

4 Further examples of direct and indirect commands:

1 nēmō ancillae persuādēre poterat ut saltāret.
2 "tacē!"
3 centuriō mihi imperāvit ut tacērem.
4 vōs saepe monēbam ut dīligenter labōrārētis.
5 "parcite mihi!"
6 senex nōs ōrābat ut sibi parcerēmus.
7 coquus servīs imperāvit ut vīnum in mēnsam pōnerent.
8 comitēs mercātōrem monuērunt ut ab oppidō clam discēderet.

Modestus prōmōtus

cum Strȳthiō cēnam et amīcōs quaereret, decem Britannī ā
Vercobrige ductī, castrīs cautē appropinquābant. Vercobrix enim
eīs persuāserat ut castra oppugnārent. Britannī, postquam custōdēs
vītāvērunt, vallum tacitē trānscendērunt et castra intrāvērunt. in
manibus facēs tenēbant ut horrea incenderent. celeriter ad horrea   5
advēnērunt quod prius cognōverant ubi sita essent.

Modestus, ignārus adventūs Britannōrum, sub horreō sedēbat.
adeō ēsuriēbat ut dē vītā paene dēspērāret. per rīmam prōspiciēbat,
reditum Strȳthiōnis exspectāns.

"trēs hōrās Strȳthiōnem iam exspectō. quid eī accidit?"   10
subitō manum hominum per tenebrās cōnspexit.

"euge! tandem vēnērunt amīcī! heus, amīcī, hūc venīte!"

Britannī, cum Modestī vōcem audīvissent, erant tam attonitī, ut
immōtī stārent. respondēre nōn audēbant. Vercobrix tamen, quī
raucam Modestī vōcem agnōverat, ad comitēs versus,   15

"nōlīte timēre," inquit susurrāns. "nōtus est mihi hic mīles.
stultior est quam asinus. nōbīs nocēre nōn potest."

tum Britannī per aditum tacitī rēpsērunt. simulatque intrāvērunt, Modestus eīs obviam iit, ut salūtāret.

"salvēte, amīcī! nunc nōbīs cēnandum ac bibendum est."   20
tum Britannus quīdam, vir ingēns, in Modestum incurrit.

"ō Nigrīna, dēliciae meae!" clāmāvit Modestus. "tē nōn agnōvī!
quam longī sunt capillī tuī! age! cōnsīde prope mē! dā mihi ōsculum!
quis lucernam habet?"

Vercobrix, cum Modestum lucernam rogantem audīvisset, 25
Britannīs imperāvit ut facēs incenderent. Modestus, Vercobrigem
Britannōsque cōnspicātus, palluit.

"dī immortālēs!" inquit. "abiit Nigrīna, appāruērunt Britannī!
mihi statim effugiendum est."

Vercobrix tamen suīs imperāvit ut Modestum comprehenderent. 30
ūnus ē Britannīs Modestō appropinquāvit ut dēligāret. fax, tamen,
quam tenēbat, tunicam Modestī forte incendit.

"ēheu!" ululāvit ille. "ardeō! mē dēvorant flammae!"

tum ē manibus Britannōrum ēlāpsus fūgit praeceps. simulac per
aditum ērūpit, Strȳthiōnī amīcīsque occurrit. amphoram vīnī ē 35
manibus Aulī ēripuit et vīnum in tunicam fūdit.

"īnsānit Modestus!" clāmāvit Strȳthiō attonitus.

Modestus tamen, Strȳthiōnis clāmōrum neglegēns, amphoram in

prōmōtus: prōmovēre	*promote*	prōspiciēbat: prōspicere	*look out*
vallum	*rampart*	versus	*having turned*
trānscendērunt: trānscendere	*climb over*	obviam iit: obviam īre	*meet, go to meet*
facēs: fax	*torch*	incurrit: incurrere	*bump into*
ēsuriēbat: ēsurīre	*be hungry*	suīs: suī	*his men*
rīmam: rīma	*crack, chink*	ēripuit: ēripere	*snatch, tear*

aditum impulit. tum in amphoram innīxus, magnōs clāmōrēs
sustulit.   40

"subvenīte! subvenīte! Britannōs cēpī!"

statim manus mīlitum, ā Valeriō ducta, ad horrea contendit.
tantī erant clāmōrēs Modestī ut tōta castra complērent. praefectus
castrōrum ipse accurrit ut causam strepitūs cognōsceret.

Modestus exsultāns "īnsidiās Britannīs parāvī," inquit.   45
"Vercobrix ipse multīs cum Britannīs sub horreō inclūsus est."

breve erat certāmen. tantus erat numerus mīlitum Rōmānōrum
ut Britannōs facile superārent. Rōmānī Britannōs ex horreō
extractōs ad carcerem redūxērunt. tum lēgātus legiōnis ipse
Modestum arcessītum laudāvit.   50

"Modeste," inquit, "mīlitem fortiōrem quam tē numquam anteā
vīdī. sōlus decem hostibus īnsidiās parāvistī. nōs decet praemium
tibi dare."

Modestus, ā lēgātō ita laudātus, adeō gaudēbat ut vix sē
continēre posset. pecūniam laetus exspectābat.   55

"carcerī tē praeficiō," inquit lēgātus.

innīxus	*having leaned*	breve: brevis	*short, brief*
subvenīte: subvenīre	*help, come to help*	certāmen	*struggle, contest, fight*
praefectus	*commander*	redūxērunt: redūcere	*lead back*
causam: causa	*reason, cause*	nōs decet	*it is proper for us*
strepitūs: strepitus	*noise, din*	continēre	*contain*

**Antefix bearing the name and emblem
of the Twentieth Legion who were
stationed at Chester after AD 87.
(Antefixes were made of terracotta and
set along the edge of roof-tiling, as
shown on p.54, to keep the rain out.)**

About the Language

1 In Stage 11, you met the verb **placet**. Notice again how it is used:

mihi placet hoc dōnum accipere.
It pleases me to receive this present.
   or, in more natural English:
I am glad to receive this present.

nōbīs placet.
It pleases us.
   or, in more natural English:
We like it.

2 The following verbs are used in a similar way:

nōs **decet** praemium Modestō dare.
It is proper for us to give a reward to Modestus.
   or, more naturally:
We ought to give a reward to Modestus.

mē **taedet** huius vītae.
It makes me tired of this life.
   or, more naturally:
I am tired of this life.

Rōmānōs numquam **oportet** hostibus crēdere.
It is never right for Romans to trust the enemy.
   or, more naturally:
Romans must never trust the enemy.

3 These verbs are known as *impersonal* verbs.

4 Further examples:

   1 tibi placet?
   2 saltātrīcem spectāre volō! mē taedet cibī et vīnī!
   3 semper pluit!
   4 Britannōs decet extrā aulam manēre.
   5 nunc advesperāscit.
   6 nōs oportet rēgnum Cogidubnī occupāre.

Practicing the Language

1 Study the forms and meanings of the following adjectives and nouns, and give the meanings of the untranslated words:

altus	*high, deep*	altitūdō	*height, depth*
magnus	*big*	magnitūdō	*size*
pulcher	*beautiful*	pulchritūdō	
sollicitus		sollicitūdō	
lātus	*wide*	lātitūdō	
mānsuētus	*tame*	mānsuētūdō	
sōlus		sōlitūdō	

Give the meaning of each of the following nouns:

fortitūdō, longitūdō, multitūdō

Notice some slightly different examples:

cupere	*to desire*	cupīdō	*a desire*
		Cupīdō	*god of Love, god of Desire*
valēre	*to be well*	valētūdō	*health:* (1) *good health*
			(2) *bad health, illness*

The imperative of **valēre** has a special meaning which you have often met:

valē   *be well*, i.e. *farewell, good-by*

2 Complete each sentence with the right word from the list below and then translate.

missōs, līberātī, territa, regressam, tenentēs, passus

1 captīvī, ē cellīs subitō . . . . ., ad portam carceris ruērunt.
2 Britannī, hastās in manibus . . . . ., in īnsidiīs latēbant.
3 ancilla, ā dominō īrātō . . . . ., respondēre nōn audēbat.
4 Cogidubnus, tot iniūriās . . . . ., omnēs Rōmānōs ōdit.
5 māter puellam, ē tabernā tandem . . . . ., vehementer vituperāvit.
6 centuriō mīlitēs, ex Ītaliā nūper ab Imperātōre . . . . ., īnspexit.

3 Translate the following sentences, then change the words in boldface from singular to plural, and translate again. You will sometimes need to look up the gender of a noun in the Complete Vocabulary part of the Language Information Section, and you may need to refer to the table of nouns on pages 262–63 of the Review Grammar, especially to check the endings of *neuter* nouns.

1 imperātor **īnsulam** vīsitābat.
2 **nauta** pecūniam poscēbat.
3 iuvenēs **captīvum** custōdiēbant.
4 fūr **pōculum** īnspiciēbat.
5 ōmina **haruspicem** terrēbant.
6 **plaustrum** in agrō stābat.

4 With the help of the table of nouns on pages 262–63 of the Review Grammar, complete the sentences of this exercise with the right form of each unfinished word, and then translate.

1 servus prope iānuam stābat. serv. . . pecūniam dedimus.
2 puerī per viam currēbant. clāmōrēs puer. . . mē excitāvērunt.
3 puella tabernam meam intrāvit. puell. . . multās gemmās ostendī.
4 Salvius ad aulam rēg. . . quam celerrimē contendit.
5 Memor, ubi nōm. . . tuum audīvit, perterritus erat.
6 in hāc viā sunt duo templ. . . .
7 mercātor ad fundum meum herī vēnit. frūmentum meum mercātor. . . vēndidī.
8 magna multitūdō cīv. . . nōbīs obstābat.
9 barbarī prōvinciam oppugnāvērunt, multāsque urb. . . dēlēvērunt.
10 leōnēs saeviēbant; nam servus stultus nūllum cibum leō. . . dederat.
11 serv. . . dēnāriōs quōs tenēbam rapuērunt.
12 iūdex mercātor. . ., quī fēminam dēcēperat, pūnīvit.

About the Language

1 Study the following examples:

tanta erat multitūdō **ut tōtam aulam complēret**.
So great was the crowd **that it filled the whole palace**.

iuvenis gemmās adeō cupiēbat **ut pecūniam statim trāderet**.
The young man wanted the jewels so much **that he handed over the money immediately**.

The groups of words in boldface are known as *result clauses,* because they indicate a *result.* For instance, in the first example above, **ut tōtam aulam complēret** indicates the result of the crowd being large. The verb in a result clause in Latin is always subjunctive.

2 Further examples:

1 tam stultus erat puer ut omnēs eum dērīdērent.
2 tantus erat clāmor ut nēmō iussa centuriōnum audīret.
3 Agricola tot mīlitēs ēmīsit ut hostēs fugerent.
4 adeō saeviēbat Valerius ut sē continēre nōn posset.

The Legionary Fortress

If the legion itself was like an army in miniature, the fortress in which it lived when not on campaign may be compared to a fortified town. It covered about 50–60 acres (20–25 hectares), about one third of the area of Pompeii. The design of the fortress always followed a standard pattern, illustrated opposite.

The chief buildings, grouped in the center, were the headquarters (**prīncipia**), the living-quarters of the commanding officer (**praetōrium**), the hospital (**valētūdinārium**), and the granaries (**horrea**). Numerous streets and alleys criss-crossed the fortress, but there were three main streets: the **via praetōria** ran from the main gate to the front entrance of the principia; the **via prīncipālis** extended across the whole width of the fortress, making a T-junction with the via praetoria just in front of the principia; the **via quīntāna** passed behind

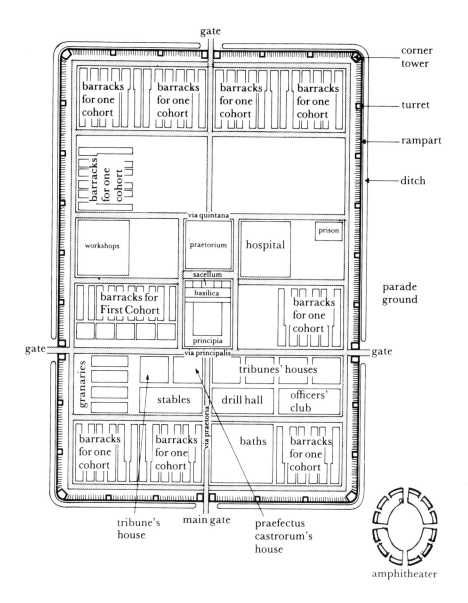

gate

corner tower

turret

rampart

ditch

barracks for one cohort

barracks for one cohort

barracks for one cohort

barracks for one cohort

barracks for one cohort

via quintana

workshops

praetorium

hospital

prison

parade ground

sacellum

basilica

barracks for First Cohort

barracks for one cohort

principia

via principalis

gate

gate

granaries

tribunes' houses

stables

drill hall

officers' club

via praetoria

barracks for one cohort

barracks for one cohort

baths

barracks for one cohort

tribune's house

main gate

praefectus castrorum's house

amphitheater

the principia and extended across the width of the fortress. The fortress was surrounded by a ditch, rampart and battlements, with towers at the corners and at intervals along the sides. Each side had a fortified gateway.

The principia was the heart of the legion and was therefore a large, complex, and impressive building. A visitor would first enter a stone-flagged courtyard surrounded on three sides by a colonnade and storerooms. On the far side of the courtyard was the great hall or basilica, where the commander worked with his officers, interviewed important local people, and administered military justice. It was a surprisingly large hall and would have looked rather like the interior of a Norman cathedral. The one at Chester, for example, was about 240 feet (73 meters) long; its central nave, bounded by tall columns supporting a vaulted roof, was 40 feet (12 meters) wide and flanked by two aisles each of 20 feet (6 meters). If each man had stood shoulder to shoulder, it would just have been possible to squeeze the entire legion into it. Whether this was ever done we do not know.

In the center of the far long wall of the basilica and directly facing the main gate was the most sacred place in the fortress, the **sacellum**, or chapel. This housed the standard of the legion, the **aquila**, an image of an eagle perched with outspread wings on the top of a pole. It was made of gold and in its talons it clutched a bundle of golden darts that represented the thunderbolts of Jupiter. The aquila represented "the spirit of the legion" and aroused feelings of intense loyalty and an almost religious respect. To lose it in battle was the worst possible disgrace and misfortune; it rarely happened. The soldier who looked after the aquila and carried it in battle (see the picture on p.69) was called the **aquilifer** (*eagle-bearer*). He was always a soldier of the first cohort.

On either side of the sacellum were the rooms where the clerks kept the payrolls and attended to all the paperwork that was needed to run a large unit. Close by and usually underground was the legion's strong-room, in which pay and savings were kept under lock and key.

The praetorium was situated by the side of or just behind the principia. It was a fine house in the style of an Italian **domus urbāna** and it provided the **lēgātus** and his family with those comforts which they would regard as necessary for a civilized life: central heating, a garden, and a private suite of baths. These luxuries were provided for the legatus, partly because he was the commander and partly because he was a member of the highest social class and would therefore expect it. But there was probably another reason, namely to demonstrate the attractions of Roman civilization to local civilian leaders, who were no doubt entertained in the praetorium from time to time. However, whether this display of wealth made them any happier about the taxes which they had to pay to the Romans is another question.

The valetudinarium contained many small wards for the sick and injured. There was also a large reception hall and a small operating theater equipped with running water.

The horrea were skillfully designed to keep grain dry and cool for long periods. In the first century A.D., like many other buildings in the fortress, they were built mainly of wood, but from the second century stone was the regular material. A granary was a long and narrow building; the roof had wide overhanging eaves to carry the rain-water away from the walls; and to prevent damp rising from the ground the floor was supported on small piers or low walls which allowed air to circulate freely underneath. There were several of these granaries in a fortress, often arranged side by side in pairs, and they could contain stocks of grain sufficient at least for one year and possibly two.

Clearly the barrack blocks, housing 5,000–6,000 men, occupied the largest area. They too were long and narrow; and they were divided into pairs of rooms, each pair providing accommodation for an eight-man section (**contubernium**). Along the front of the block ran a colonnaded verandah. Each section cooked for itself on a hearth in the front living-room, which was slightly the smaller of the two rooms, and slept in the larger room at the back. Each block housed a century (80 men). At the end of the block a larger suite of rooms was provided for the centurion, who may have shared it with his optio. The blocks themselves were arranged in pairs facing each other across an alleyway, as in the diagram below.

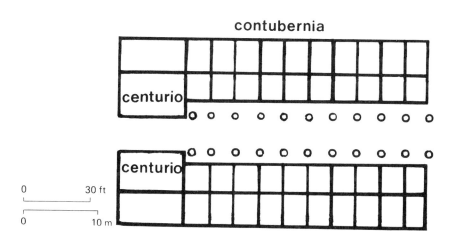

The bathhouse was regarded as an important part of military hygiene; every fortress and many smaller forts had one. Like the civilian baths, it consisted of a tepidarium, caldarium, and frigidarium and served as a social club. Sometimes the military baths were outside the fortress, by a nearby stream or river, sometimes inside.

One other building, always outside, should be mentioned: the amphitheater. It had the same shape and layout as the civilian amphitheater and could seat the whole legion. It was used for ceremonial parades, weapon training, and displays of tactics, as well as for occasional gladiatorial shows.

Not surprisingly, civilians also tended to gather around military bases. At first they were traders who set up little bars to sell appetizing food and drink to supplement the plain rations served in the barracks. Naturally, too, these bars gave soldiers opportunities to meet the local girls. Legally soldiers were not allowed to marry, but the army tolerated unofficial unions. While the father lived in barracks his family grew up just outside; and his sons when they were eighteen or nineteen often followed his profession and enlisted. Many such settlements (**vīcī**) developed

A model reconstruction of the amphitheater at Chester.

gradually into towns. A few became large, self-governing cities, such as Eboracum (York: see the map on p. 138). Thus the military fortress, which had begun as a means of holding down newly conquered territory, ended by playing an important part in the development of civilian town life.

Words and Phrases Checklist

adeō	*so much, so greatly*
aditus, aditūs	*entrance*
adventus, adventūs	*arrival*
anteā	*before*
appāreō, appārēre, appāruī	*appear*
ardeō, ardēre, arsī	*burn, be on fire*
certāmen, certāminis	*struggle, contest, fight*
comes, comitis	*comrade, companion*
decet	*it is proper*
mē decet	*I ought*
fax, facis	*torch*
gaudeō, gaudēre	*be pleased, rejoice*
ignārus, ignāra, ignārum	*not knowing, unaware*
imperō, imperāre, imperāvī	*order, command*
incendō, incendere, incendī, incēnsus	*burn, set fire to*
īnsidiae, īnsidiārum	*trap, ambush*
iocus, iocī	*joke*
iussum, iussī	*order*
manus, manūs	*band (of men)*
noceō, nocēre, nocuī	*hurt*
occurrō, occurrere, occurrī	*meet*
ōsculum, ōsculī	*kiss*
praeceps, *gen.* praecipitis	*headlong*
praemium, praemiī	*prize, reward*
proximus, proxima, proximum	*nearest*
quālis, quāle	*what sort of*
silentium, silentiī	*silence*
sub	*under, beneath*
tacitus, tacita, tacitum	*silent*
taedet	*it is tiring*
mē taedet	*I am tired, I am bored*
tantus, tanta, tantum	*so great, such a great*

Word Search

apparition, approximate, ardent, concomitant, imperious, insidious, tedious

1 . . . . .: passionate, fervent
2 . . . . .: to come close to, be nearly the same as
3 . . . . .: treacherous, underhand
4 . . . . .: a sudden or unusual sight
5 . . . . .: accompanying, attendant
6 . . . . .: tiresome, dull
7 . . . . .: domineering

imperium

post mortem Cogidubnī, Salvius rēgnum eius occupāvit. pecūniam
ā Britannīs extorquēre statim coepit. Salvium adiuvābat Belimicus,
prīnceps Cantiacōrum.

prope aulam habitābat agricola Britannicus, quī Salviō
pecūniam trādere nōluit. Salvius igitur mīlitibus imperāvit ut
casam agricolae dīriperent. centuriōnem mīlitibus praefēcit.

mīlitēs, gladiīs hastīsque
armātī, casam agricolae
oppugnāvērunt.

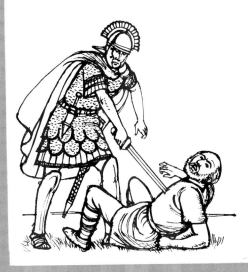

agricola, gladiō centuriōnis
vulnerātus, exanimātus
dēcidit.

servī, clāmōribus territī,
fūgērunt.

fīlius agricolae, fūste armātus,
frūstrā restitit.

Belimicus, spē praemiī
adductus, mīlitēs Rōmānōs
adiuvābat et incitābat.

mīlitēs casam intrāvērunt et
arcam, pecūniā complētam,
extulērunt.

deinde mīlitēs fēminās, catēnīs
vīnctās, abdūxērunt.

postrēmō mīlitēs casam
incendērunt. flammae, ventō
auctae, casam celeriter
cōnsūmpsērunt.

pāstōrēs, quī prope casam habitābant, immōtī stābant, spectāculō
attonitī.
casam vīdērunt, flammīs cōnsūmptam.
fīlium agricolae vīdērunt, hastā graviter vulnerātum.
agricolam ipsum vīdērunt, gladiō centuriōnis interfectum.
tandem abiērunt, timōre īrāque commōtī, Belimicum
Rōmānōsque vituperantēs.

testāmentum

ego, Tiberius Claudius Cogidubnus, rēx magnus Britannōrum, morbō gravī afflīctus, hoc testāmentum fēcī.

ego Titum Flāvium Domitiānum, optimum Imperātōrum, hērēdem meum faciō. mandō T. Flāviō Domitiānō rēgnum meum cīvēsque Rēgnēnsēs. iubeō cīvēs Rēgnēnsēs lēgibus pārēre et vītam   5
quiētam agere. nam prīncipēs Rēgnēnsium mē saepe vexāvērunt.
aliī, spē praedae adductī, inter sē pugnāvērunt; aliī, īnsāniā affectī, sēditiōnem contrā Rōmānōs facere temptāvērunt. nunc tamen eōs omnēs oportet discordiam huius modī dēpōnere.

dō lēgō Cn. Iūliō Agricolae statuam meam, ā fabrō Britannicō   10
factam. sīc Agricola mē per tōtam vītam in memoriā habēre potest.

dō lēgō C. Salviō Līberālī, fidēlissimō amīcōrum meōrum, duōs tripodas argenteōs. Salvius vir summae prūdentiae est.

dō lēgō L. Marciō Memorī vīllam meam prope Aquās Sūlis sitam.
L. Marcius Memor, ubi aeger ad thermās vēnī, ut auxilium ā deā   15
Sūle peterem, benignē mē excēpit.

dō lēgō Dumnorigī, prīncipī Rēgnēnsium, quem sīcut fīlium dīlēxī, mīlle aureōs aulamque meam. sī forte Dumnorix mortuus est, haec C. Salviō Līberālī lēgō.

dō lēgō Belimicō, prīncipī Cantiacōrum, quīngentōs aureōs et   20
nāvem celerrimam. Belimicus enim mē ab ursā ōlim servāvit, quae per aulam meam saeviēbat.

mandō C. Salviō Līberālī cūram fūneris meī. volō Salvium corpus meum sepelīre. volō eum mēcum sepelīre gemmās meās, paterās aureās, omnia arma quae ad bellum vēnātiōnemque comparāvī.   25

mandō C. Salviō Līberālī hoc testāmentum, manū meā scrīptum ānulōque meō signātum. dolus malus ab hōc testāmentō abestō!

lēgibus: lēx	*law*	mīlle	*a thousand*
praedae: praeda	*booty, plunder, loot*	celerrimam: celer	*quick, fast*
adductī: addūcere	*lead on, encourage*	corpus	*body*
affectī: afficere	*affect*	sepelīre	*bury*
discordiam: discordia	*strife*	dolus . . . abestō!	*may . . .*
in memoriā habēre	*keep in mind, remember*		*trickery keep away!*
benignē	*kindly*	malus	*evil, bad*
excēpit: excipere	*receive*		

When you have read each section, answer the questions that follow it.

in aulā Salviī

I

Salvius, cum dē morte Cogidubnī audīvisset, ē castrīs discessit. per
prōvinciam iter fēcit ad aulam quam ē testāmentō accēperat. ibi
novem diēs manēbat ut rēs Cogidubnī administrāret. decimō diē,
iterum profectus, pecūniās opēsque ā Britannīs extorquēre incēpit.
plūrimī prīncipēs, avāritiā et metū corruptī, Salvium adiuvābant.   5

Belimicus, prīnceps Cantiacōrum, spē praemiī adductus, Salviō
summum auxilium dedit. Britannōs omnia bona trādere coēgit. aliī,
quī potentiam Salviī timēbant, Belimicō statim cessērunt; aliī, quī eī
resistēbant, poenās gravēs dedērunt.

Belimicus autem, quamquam prō hōc auxiliō multa praemia   10
honōrēsque ā Salviō accēpit, haudquāquam contentus erat. rēx
enim Rēgnēnsium esse cupiēbat. hāc spē adductus, cum paucīs
prīncipibus coniūrāre coepit. quī tamen, Belimicō diffīsī, rem Salviō
rettulērunt.

Salvius, audāciā Belimicī incēnsus, eum interficere cōnstituit.   15
amīcōs igitur, quibus maximē cōnfīdēbat, ad sē vocāvit; eōs in
aulam ingressōs rogāvit utrum vim an venēnum adhibēret. amīcī, ut
favōrem Salviī conciliārent, multa et varia cōnsilia prōposuērunt.

tandem ūnus ex amīcīs, vir callidissimus,

"venēnum," inquit, "Belimicō, hostī īnfestō, aptissimum est."   20

"sed quō modō tālem rem efficere possumus?" inquit Salvius.
"nam Belimicus, vir magnae prūdentiae, nēminī cōnfīdit."

"hunc homunculum dēcipere nōbīs facile est," inquit ille.
"venēnum cibō mixtum multōs virōs callidiōrēs quam Belimicum
iam fefellit. ipse sciō venēnum perītē dare."   25

"euge!" inquit Salvius, cōnsiliō amīcī dēlectātus. "facillimum est
mihi illum ad cēnam sūmptuōsam invītāre. mē oportet epistulam
blandam eī mittere. verbīs enim mollibus ac blandīs resistere nōn
potest."

Salvius igitur Belimicum ad aulam sine morā invītāvit. quī,   30
epistulā mendācī dēceptus neque ūllam fraudem suspicātus, ad
aulam nōnā hōrā vēnit.

decimō: decimus	*tenth*	īnfestō: īnfestus	*dangerous*
profectus	*having set out*	aptissimum: aptus	*suitable*
avāritiā: avāritia	*greed*	mixtum: miscēre	*mix*
metū: metus	*fear*	fefellit: fallere	*deceive*
bona	*goods*	sūmptuōsam: sūmptuōsus	*expensive, lavish*
prō	*for, in return for*	blandam: blandus	*flattering*
haudquāquam	*not at all*	mollibus: mollis	*soft*
rettulērunt: referre	*tell, report*	morā: mora	*delay*
audāciā: audācia	*boldness, audacity*	neque	*and not*
incēnsus	*inflamed, angered*	ūllam: ūllus	*any*
utrum . . . an	*whether . . . or*	fraudem: fraus	*trick*
favōrem: favor	*favor*	nōnā: nōnus	*ninth*
conciliārent: conciliāre	*win, gain*		

1 Where does Salvius travel to when he hears of Cogidubnus' death?
2 How long does Salvius stay there? Why?
3 What does Salvius do next? How does Belimicus help him?
4 Why does Belimicus stop helping Salvius and start plotting?
5 How does Salvius find out about Belimicus' plot?
6 What decision does Salvius make when he hears of Belimicus' treachery? What question does he put to his friends?
7 Which suggestion does Salvius accept? What are the advantages of this method?
8 How does he lure Belimicus into his trap?

II

Belimicum aulam intrantem Salvius benignē excēpit et in triclīnium addūxit. ibi sōlī sūmptuōsē atque hilarē cēnābant. Belimicus, Salvium rīdentem cōnspicātus vīnōque solūtus, audācter dīcere coepit.

"mī Salvī, multa et magna beneficia ā mē accēpistī. postquam   5
effūgērunt Quīntus et Dumnorix, ego sōlus tē adiūvī; multōs continuōs diēs eōs persecūtus Dumnorigem occīdī; multa falsa Agricolae dīxī ut Cogidubnum perfidiae damnārem; post mortem eius, Britannōs pecūniam bonaque sua trādere coēgī. prō hīs tantīs beneficiīs praemium meritum rogō."   10

Salvius, ubi haec audīvit, arrogantiā Belimicī incēnsus, īram tamen cēlāvit et cōmiter respondit.

addūxit: addūcere	*lead*	vīnō . . . solūtus	*relaxed by the wine*
sūmptuōsē	*lavishly*	persecūtus	*having pursued*
atque	*and*	damnārem: damnāre	*condemn*
hilarē	*in high spirits*	meritum: meritus	*well-deserved*

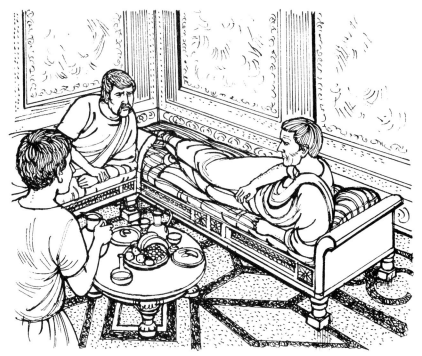

"praemium meritum iam tibi parāvī. sed cūr nihil cōnsūmis, mī amīce? volō tē garum exquīsitissimum gustāre quod ex Hispāniā importāvī. puer! fer mihi et Belimicō illud garum!" 15

cum servus garum ambōbus dedisset, Salvius ad hospitem versus,

"dīc mihi, Belimice," inquit, "quid prō hīs tantīs beneficiīs repetis?"

"iam ex testāmentō Cogidubnī," respondit ille, "quīngentōs 20 aureōs accēpī. id haudquāquam satis est. rēgnum ipsum repetō."

quod cum audīvisset, Salvius "ego," inquit, "nōn Cogidubnus, aureōs tibi dedī. cūr haud satis est?"

"quid dīcis?" exclāmāvit Belimicus. "hoc nōn intellegō."

"illud testāmentum," respondit Salvius, "est falsum. nōn 25 Cogidubnus sed ego scrīpsī."

repetis: repetere   *claim*   haud   *not*
Hispāniā: Hispānia   *Spain*

1 How is Belimicus received and treated when he comes to the palace?
2 What makes Salvius angry (line 11)? Why do you think he hides his anger?

3 What does Belimicus think Salvius means by a "praemium meritum" (line 13)? What does Salvius really mean?
4 During the meal, Belimicus changes his tactics: instead of continuing with his plot, he asks Salvius directly for the kingship. What has encouraged him to do this?
5 What has Belimicus already received? How? What does he now learn about the will?

About the Language

1 Study the following sentences:

iuvenis, **gladiō** armātus, ad castra contendit.
The young man, armed **with a sword**, *hurried to the camp.*

Britannī, **tantā iniūriā** incēnsī, sēditiōnem fēcērunt.
The Britons, angered **by such great injustice**, *revolted.*

mīles, **vulnere** impedītus, tandem cessit.
The soldier, hindered **by his wound**, *gave in at last.*

senex, **multīs cūrīs** vexātus, dormīre nōn poterat.
The old man, troubled **by many cares**, *was unable to sleep.*

cīvēs, **clāmōribus** excitātī, ē lectīs surrēxērunt.
The citizens, awakened **by the shouts**, *rose from their beds.*

The words in boldface are in the *ablative* case.

2 Compare the nominative singular with the ablative singular and ablative plural in the first, second, and third declensions:

	NOMINATIVE SINGULAR	ABLATIVE SINGULAR	ABLATIVE PLURAL
1ST DECLENSION	puella	puellā	puellīs
2ND DECLENSION	servus	servō	servīs
	puer	puerō	puerīs
	templum	templō	templīs
3RD DECLENSION	mercātor	mercātōre	mercātōribus
	leō	leōne	leōnibus
	cīvis	cīve	cīvibus
	rēx	rēge	rēgibus
	urbs	urbe	urbibus
	nōmen	nōmine	nōminibus

3 Further examples:

1 Salvius, audāciā Belimicī attonitus, nihil dīxit.
2 mercātor, fūstibus verberātus, in fossā exanimātus iacēbat.
3 mīlitēs, vallō dēfēnsī, barbarīs diū resistēbant.
4 uxor mea ānulum, gemmīs ōrnātum, ēmit.
5 hospitēs, arte ancillae dēlectātī, plausērunt.

Belimicus rēx

Belimicus, cum haec audīvisset, adeō attonitus erat ut nihil
respondēre posset. Salvius autem haec addidit rīdēns,

"mī amīce, cūr tam attonitus es? tū et Cogidubnus semper inimīcī
erātis. num quicquam ab illō spērāvistī? nōs autem in amīcitiā
sumus. tibi multum dēbeō, ut dīxistī. itaque rēgem tē creāre in   5
animō habeō. sed rēgnum quod tibi dēstinō multō maius est quam
Cogidubnī. heus! puer! plūs garī!"

servus, cui Salvius hoc imperāvit, statim exiit. brevī regressus,
garum venēnō mixtum intulit atque in Belimicī pateram effūdit.
tam laetus erat ille, ubi verba Salviī audīvit, ut garum cōnsūmeret,   10
ignārus perīculī mortis.

"quantum est hoc rēgnum quod mihi prōmīsistī? ubi gentium
est?" rogāvit Belimicus.

Salvius cachinnāns "multō maius est," inquit, "quam imperium
Rōmānum."   15

Belimicus hīs verbīs perturbātus,

"nimium bibistī, mī amīce," inquit. "nūllum rēgnum nōvī maius
quam imperium Rōmānum."

"rēgnum est, quō omnēs tandem abeunt," respondit Salvius.
"rēgnum est, unde nēmō redīre potest. Belimice, tē rēgem creō   20
mortuōrum."

Belimicus, metū mortis pallidus, surrēxit. haerēbat lingua in
gutture; tintinnābant aurēs; ventrem, quī iam graviter dolēbat,
prēnsāvit. metū īrāque commōtus exclāmāvit,

"tū mihi nocēre nōn audēs, quod omnia scelera tua Agricolae   25
dēnūntiāre possum."

"mē dēnūntiāre nōn potes, Belimice, quod nunc tibi imminet

mors. nunc tibi abeundum est in rēgnum tuum. avē atque valē, mī
Belimice."

Belimicus, venēnō excruciātus, pugiōnem tamen in Salvium   30
coniēcit, spē ultiōnis adductus. deinde magnum gemitum dedit et
humī dēcidit mortuus. Salvius, pugiōne leviter vulnerātus, servō
imperāvit ut medicum arcesseret. aliī servī corpus Belimicī ē
triclīniō extractum quam celerrimē cremāvērunt. sīc Belimicus
arrogantiae poenās dedit; sīc Salvius cēterīs prīncipibus persuāsit ut   35
in fidē manērent.

spērāvistī: spērāre	*hope, expect*	graviter dolēbat:	
creāre	*make, create*	graviter dolēre	*be extremely painful*
dēstinō: dēstināre	*intend*	scelera: scelus	*crime*
effūdit: effundere	*pour out*	dēnūntiāre	*denounce, reveal*
ubi gentium?	*where in the world?*	imminet: imminēre	*hang over*
perturbātus: perturbāre	*disturb, alarm*	tibi abeundum est	*you must go away*
lingua	*tongue*	avē atque valē	*hail and farewell*
gutture: guttur	*throat*	excruciātus: excruciāre	*torture, torment*
tintinnābant: tintinnāre	*ring*	leviter	*slightly*
ventrem: venter	*stomach*	cremāvērunt: cremāre	*cremate*

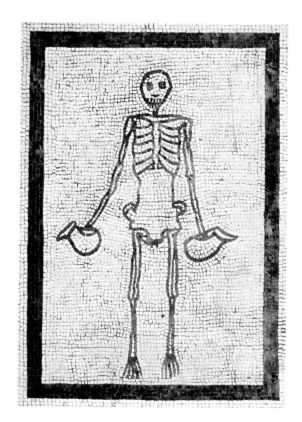

**The skeleton slave, from a
mosaic at Pompeii.**

About the Language

1 Study the following examples:

lēgātus sermōnem cum Quīntō **duās hōrās** habēbat.
*The commander talked with Quintus **for two hours***.

quattuor diēs fugitīvus in silvā latēbat.
***For four days**, the runaway lay hidden in the woods*.

In each of these sentences, the words in boldface indicate *how long* something went on; for this, Latin uses the *accusative* case.

2 Now study the following:

tertiā hōrā nūntiī advēnērunt.
***At the third hour**, the messengers arrived*.

quīntō diē Agricola pugnāre cōnstituit.
***On the fifth day**, Agricola decided to fight*.

In these sentences, the words in boldface indicate *when* something happened; for this, Latin uses the *ablative* case.

3 Further examples:

1 hospitēs trēs hōrās cēnābant.
2 quārtō diē revēnit rēx.
3 Agricola prōvinciam septem annōs administrāvit.
4 secundā hōrā lībertus Memorem excitāre temptāvit.
5 mediā nocte hostēs castra nostra oppugnāvērunt.
6 sex diēs nāvigābāmus; septimō diē ad portum advēnimus.

Practicing the Language

1 Study the forms and meanings of the following adjectives and nouns, and give the meanings of the untranslated words:

avārus	*greedy, miserly*	avāritia	*greed*
amīcus	*friendly*	amīcitia	*friendship*
superbus	*proud*	superbia	
trīstis		trīstitia	
perītus		perītia	*skill, experience*
sapiēns		sapientia	
prūdēns		prūdentia	*sense*
perfidus	*treacherous, untrustworthy*	perfidia	
ēlegāns	*elegant, tasteful*	ēlegantia	
benevolēns	*kind*	benevolentia	

Give the meaning of each of the following nouns:

laetitia, audācia, arrogantia, īnsānia, potentia

2 Complete each of the sentences below with one of the following groups of words and then translate. Use each group of words once only.

ut nēmō centuriōnem audīret
ut Belimicum interficeret
ut ad castra redīrent
quō modō Cogidubnus periisset
cum tabernam intrāvissent

1 Salvius cibum venēnō mixtum parāvit . . . . . .
2 Quīntus nesciēbat . . . . . .
3 cīvēs, ..., vīnum poposcērunt.
4 tantus erat clāmor . . . . . .
5 Agricola mīlitibus imperāvit . . . . . .

3 Complete each sentence with the most suitable word from the list below, and then translate.

audāciā, vīnō, gladiō, īrā, catēnīs

1 nūntius, ... graviter vulnerātus, effugere nōn poterat.
2 Salvius, ... eius attonitus, diū tacēbat.
3 captīvī, ... vīnctī, in longīs ōrdinibus stābant.
4 dominus, ... commōtus, omnēs servōs carnificibus trādidit.
5 hospitēs, ... solūtī, clāmāre et iocōs facere coepērunt.

About the Language

1 From Stage 1 onwards, you have met phrases of the following kind:

ad fundum   *to the farm*
ex ātriō   *out of the hall*
per viās   *through the streets*
cum amīcīs   *with friends*

The words in boldface are *prepositions*. A preposition is normally used with a noun in the accusative or ablative case.

2 The prepositions **ad**, **per**, and **prope** are used with the *accusative*:

ad **rēgem**   *to the king*
per **flammās**   *through the flames*
prope **sellam**   *near the chair*

Other prepositions used with the accusative are **ante**, **circum**, **contrā**, **extrā**, **inter**, **post**, and **trāns**.

3 The prepositions **ā**, **ab**, **cum**, **ē**, and **ex** are used with the *ablative*:

ab **amphitheātrō**   *from the amphitheater*
ex **oppidō**   *out of the town*
cum **hospitibus**   *with the guests*

Other prepositions used with the ablative are **dē**, **prō**, and **sine**.

4 Notice how the preposition **in** is used:

cīvēs **in forum** cucurrērunt.   *The citizens ran into the forum.*
mercātōrēs **in forō** negōtium agēbant.   *The merchants were doing business in the forum.*

ancilla centuriōnem **in tabernam** dūxit.   *The slave-girl led the centurion into the inn.*
canis **in tabernā** dormiēbat.   *The dog was sleeping in the inn.*

in meaning *into* is used with the accusative.
in meaning *in* is used with the ablative.

5 Further examples:

1 duo amīcī ad urbem iter faciēbant.
2 prope templum deae erat fōns sacer.
3 prīncipēs dē morte Belimicī sermōnem habēbant.
4 prō aulā stābant quattuor custōdēs.
5 mīlitēs in castrīs labōrābant.
6 Agricola in castra contendit.
7 centuriō sine mīlitibus revēnit.
8 gubernātor nāvem circum saxum dīrēxit.

Interpreting the Evidence : Our Knowledge of Roman Britain

Our knowledge of the Roman occupation of Britain is based on three types of evidence:

(1) *literary* evidence: what the Romans wrote about Britain;

(2) *archaeological* evidence: what archaeologists have discovered during excavations, including:

(3) *inscriptional* evidence: inscriptions in Latin (and sometimes Greek) from tombstones, altars, public buildings and monuments, and from private objects such as writing-tablets, defixiones, etc.

Girl with stylus and writing tablets.

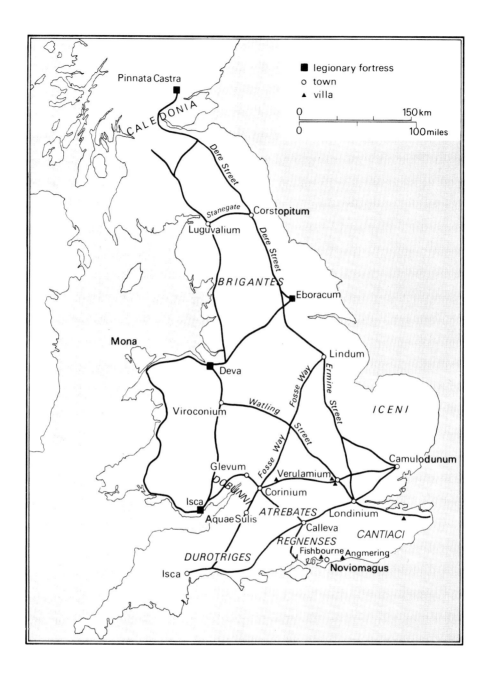

All of this material has to be interpreted before we can begin to understand it. The writings have to be translated and the exact meanings of technical terms have to be found; discoveries made on an archaeological site have to be noted down and different periods identified so that remains can be dated; inscriptions have to be deciphered, translated and, where possible, dated. It is a long and complicated process, in which one type of evidence can often help us to understand another type. To see how it works in practice, we shall examine examples from each type of evidence.

Literary Evidence

There are two well-known Latin writings about Roman Britain. One is Julius Caesar's account in which he describes his brief reconnaissance mission to the Kent coast in southeastern Britain in 55 B.C. and his return in greater force the following year when he stormed the fortress of a British king before withdrawing again. The other is Tacitus' account of the life of his father-in-law, Agricola. More than half of this is devoted to Agricola's governorship of Britain, including such exploits as the circumnavigation of Britain and the defeat of the Scots in the great battle of Mons Graupius.

Both pieces of writing are to some extent biased. Caesar wrote his account in order to justify his actions to the Senate in Rome and place himself in a favorable light; Tacitus was anxious to preserve the memory of his father-in-law and to praise his success as governor.

In chapter 21 of his biography, Tacitus tells us that under Agricola an extensive program of Romanization was carried out, including the building of **fora**, or town centers, in some of the larger and well-established settlements in the southeast of Britain. This was confirmed by the discovery, during an excavation, of fragments of an inscription which was designed to stand over the entrance to the new forum at Verulamium (St. Albans, northwest of London). It mentions the name of Agricola in connection with the building of the forum. (A reproduction of the inscription appears on p. 100.)

Tacitus also tells us of Roman plans to improve the education of the British:

"Agricola arranged for the sons of British chiefs to receive a broad education. He made it clear that he preferred the natural abilities of the British to the skill and training of the Gauls. As a result, instead of hating the language of the Romans, they became very eager to learn it."

This may sound as if Tacitus is exaggerating. However, we know from inscriptions that Salvius, who was a distinguished lawyer, was sent to

Britain at about this time, and one of his tasks may have been to help the British bring their laws into line with Roman law. If this was so, there may be a link between Salvius' presence in Britain and Tacitus' statement that the British were eager to learn Latin; they may have wished not only to have conversations with the occupying forces, but also to understand the complexities of Roman law.

Archaeological Evidence

The task of an archaeologist is to uncover and to help us understand the remains of the past. To do this he or she must first decide on a suitable site to excavate. Some sites are already well-known but have not been completely excavated; sometimes sites are found by accident. A workman digging a drain across a field in 1962 hit fragments of a mosaic

Archaeological excavation in the Sacred Spring, Bath, 1979.

floor and this chance discovery led to the excavation of the palace at Fishbourne. Building and road works can often uncover evidence of a site. In such cases archaeologists may have a very limited time in which to excavate before the bulldozers move in and destroy the evidence forever.

Once the site has been located, the archaeologist has to plan and carry out a careful excavation of the area. This means uncovering the foundations of buildings, mosaic floors, and other large structures, and carefully sifting the soil for pieces of pottery, items of jewelry, coins and other small objects. However, the purpose of an excavation is not simply to find precious objects but to discover as much as possible about the people who used the buildings, what their life was like, when they lived there, and even perhaps what happened to them. In order to do this, an archaeologist must be trained, rather like a detective, to observe every small detail and to piece together all the evidence that is found.

As the earth is removed from a site, the archaeologist will watch for two things: the existence and position of any wall foundations, and the way in which the various levels or layers of earth change color and texture as the trenches are dug deeper. If one wall is built directly on top of another, it is reasonable to assume that the lower wall is from an earlier building.

Roman coins can usually be accurately dated because they have the emperors' heads and names stamped on them. If a coin of Nero is found in a layer, then the date of the layer can be no earlier than A.D. 54 since Nero was not emperor until then. If no coins of later emperors are found

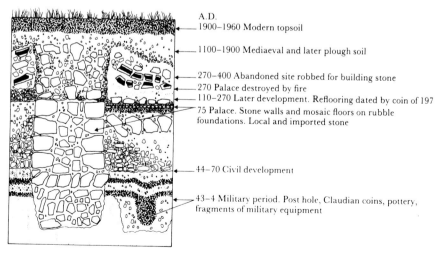

A.D.
1900–1960 Modern topsoil

1100–1900 Mediaeval and later plough soil

270–400 Abandoned site robbed for building stone
270 Palace destroyed by fire
110–270 Later development. Reflooring dated by coin of 197
75 Palace. Stone walls and mosaic floors on rubble foundations. Local and imported stone

44–70 Civil development

43–4 Military period. Post hole, Claudian coins, pottery, fragments of military equipment

Diagram showing layers of evidence for occupation at Fishbourne

in the layer, then it is reasonable to assume that the layer dates from Nero's reign (A.D. 54 to 68) or from the short period afterwards during which coins of Nero's reign continued to circulate.

Fairly accurate dates are also obtainable from a study of the styles and patterns of pottery found on a site. Large quantities have survived, as pottery is a durable material which does not rot, and broken pieces (shards) are found in very large numbers on many sites. All kinds of pottery were used throughout the Roman world and the presence on a British site of pottery which has come from Italy or Gaul shows that the owner was wealthy enough to pay for imported material. In ways such as this the archaeologist can begin to assemble information about the people who occupied the site.

Layers of ash, charred pottery, and other burnt objects will indicate a destruction by fire; a mass of broken rubble may suggest that a building was demolished, perhaps to make way for a larger, better one. Many sites in Britain show a gradual development from a simple timber-framed farmhouse building, which was replaced by a larger stone house, to a grander, multi-roomed mansion with baths, mosaic pavements, and colonnades.

By such painstaking processes archaeologists have been able to reconstruct a remarkably detailed picture of the Roman occupation of Britain. The fact that most of the Romano-British villas were sited in the southeast, whereas the military fortresses were established in the north and west, suggests that Britain at this period was largely peaceful and prosperous in the southeast but still troubled by the threat of hostile tribes in the northwest. Traces of a vast network of Roman roads have been found, showing just how numerous and effective communications must have been. Parts of many Romano-British towns have been excavated, revealing how advanced urban life was. It is not uncommon to find the remains of an extensive forum, carefully laid out grids of streets, the foundations of many large buildings including temples with altars and inscriptions, sometimes a theater and an amphitheater, and substantial city walls.

The excavation of military sites, such as forts, marching camps, and legionary fortresses, has shown how important the army was in maintaining peace and protection for Roman Britain. It has also shown very clearly the movements of the legions around the country and added considerably to our knowledge of the Roman army.

Inscriptional Evidence

Some important evidence about the Roman occupation of Britain comes from inscriptions, particularly on the tombstones of soldiers. Here is the inscription on the tombstone of a soldier who was buried at Chester.

D M

L LICINIUS L F

TER VALENS

ARE VETERAN

LEG XX VV AN VL

H S E

At first sight, this looks difficult to decipher. The task, however, is made easier by the fact that most of these inscriptions follow a standard pattern. The items are usually arranged in the following order:

(1) The dedication at the top of the stone—D M—abbreviation for "Dīs Mānibus," for the spirits of the departed.

(2) The praenomen. This is first of a citizen's three names and is usually abbreviated to a single letter, as here—L for "Lūcius."

(3) The nomen. Always given in full, as here—"Licinius."

(4) The father's name. It is usually only the father's praenomen that is given, and this can be recognized in abbreviated form by the single letter which comes before an F representing "fīlius." The son often had the same praenomen as his father, as here—L F for "Lūciī fīlius."

(5) Tribe. Roman soldiers were Roman citizens and were therefore enrolled in one of the thirty-five Roman tribes. The name of the tribe is abbreviated, as here—TER for "Teretīna."

(6) The cognomen. This is the last of the three names, usually placed after the father's name and the Roman tribe in which the soldier was enrolled. It is always given in full, as here—"Valēns." Three names were a mark of Roman citizenship and therefore an important indication of status.

(7) Birthplace. This can usually be identified as a town in the Roman empire, thus ARE for "Arelātē" (modern Arles in the south of France).

(8) Rank and legion. They are usually both abbreviated—VETERAN for "veterānus"; LEG XX VV for "legiōnis XX Valeriae Victrīcis."

(9) Age. This is represented by AN or ANN for "annōrum," followed by a number. This number is in most cases rounded off to a multiple of 5. Sometimes VIX ("vīxit" = lived) is placed before AN.

(10) Length of service (not included in the inscription above). This is represented by STIP followed by a number, e.g. STIP X for "stipendia X" (ten years' service).

(11) The final statement. This is abbreviated, and usually takes the form of H S E for "hīc situs est" (is buried here) or H F C for "hērēs faciendum cūrāvit" (his heir had this stone set up).

The Chester inscription can therefore be interpreted as follows:

D(IS) M(ANIBUS)
L(UCIUS) LICINIUS L(UCII) F(ILIUS)
TER(ETINA) VALENS
ARE(LATE) VETERAN(US)
LEG(IONIS) XX V(ALERIAE) V(ICTRICIS) AN(NORUM)
V L
H(IC) S(ITUS) E(ST)

This stone is dedicated to the spirits of the departed. Lucius Licinius Valens, son of Lucius, of the Teretine tribe, from Arelate, veteran of the Twentieth Legion Valeria Victrix, aged 45, is buried here.

On the opposite page is the inscription on another soldier's tombstone, also found at Chester.

Try to find out from it the following information:

1 The soldier's name   4 His age at death
2 His rank   5 The length of his service
3 His legion

D M

CÆCILIVS·AVIT
VS·EMER·AVG
OPTIO LEG XX
VV STP·XV·VIX.
AN.XXXIIII
H F C

In the same way, find as much information as you can from the following inscription:

Words and Phrases Checklist

ac	*and*
arrogantia, arrogantiae	*arrogance, gall*
atque	*and*
beneficium, beneficiī	*act of kindness, favor*
cōnstituō, cōnstituere, cōnstituī, cōnstitūtus	*decide*
corpus, corporis	*body*
dīligō, dīligere, dīlēxī, dīlēctus	*be fond of*
doleō, dolēre, doluī	*hurt, be in pain*
gemitus, gemitūs	*groan*
hērēs, hērēdis	*heir*
īra, īrae	*anger*
lingua, linguae	*tongue*
malus, mala, malum	*evil, bad*
mandō, mandāre, mandāvī, mandātus	*order, entrust, hand over*
metus, metūs	*fear*

mīlle	*a thousand*
mīlia	*thousands*
multō	*much*
occīdō, occīdere, occīdī, occīsus	*kill*
opēs, opum	*money, wealth*
pallidus, pallida, pallidum	*pale*
praeficiō, praeficere, praefēcī, praefectus	*put in charge*
quicquam (*also spelled* quidquam)	*anything*
sīc	*thus, in this way*
solvō, solvere, solvī, solūtus	*loosen, untie*
spēs, speī	*hope*
suspicātus, suspicāta, suspicātum	*having suspected*
testāmentum, testāmentī	*will*
ut	*as*
ventus, ventī	*wind*

ūnus	*one*
duo	*two*
trēs	*three*
quattuor	*four*
quīnque	*five*
sex	*six*
septem	*seven*
octō	*eight*
novem	*nine*
decem	*ten*
vīgintī	*twenty*
trīgintā	*thirty*
quadrāgintā	*forty*
quīnquāgintā	*fifty*
sexāgintā	*sixty*
septuāgintā	*seventy*
octōgintā	*eighty*
nōnāgintā	*ninety*
centum	*a hundred*
ducentī	*two hundred*

Word Search

beneficial, dissolve, doleful, incorporeal, malice, opulent, ventilate

1 . . . . .: melancholy, sad
2 . . . . .: helpful, advantageous
3 . . . . .: to supply with fresh air
4 . . . . .: rich, affluent
5 . . . . .: lacking material form or substance
6 . . . . .: to melt
7 . . . . .: harmful intent

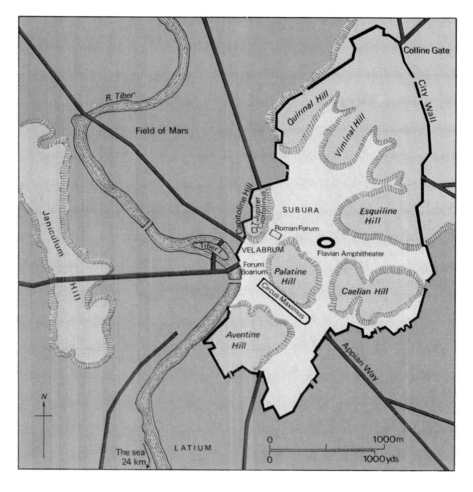

Map of Rome, showing the seven hills.

Stage 29

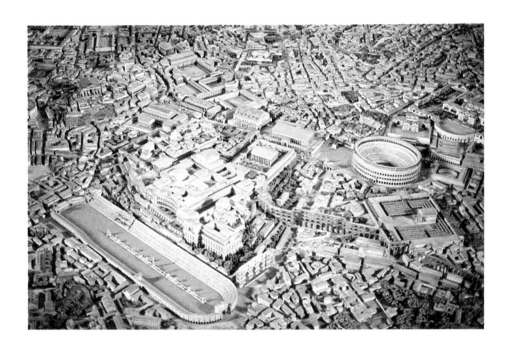

Rōma

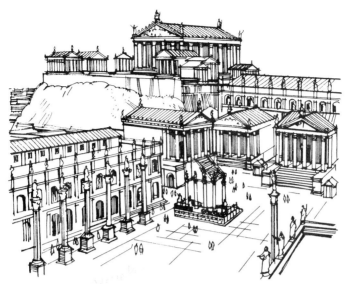

in mediā Rōmā est mōns nōtissimus, quī Capitōlium appellātur.
in summō Capitōliō stat templum, ubi deus Iuppiter adōrātur.

deus Iuppiter *Jupiter (god of the sky, greatest of Roman gods)*

sub Capitōliō iacet Forum Rōmānum.
forum ab ingentī multitūdine cīvium cotīdiē complētur.
aliī negōtium agunt; aliī in porticibus stant et ab amīcīs
salūtantur; aliī per forum in lectīcīs feruntur. ubīque magnus
strepitus audītur.

aliquandō pompae splendidae
per forum dūcuntur.

prope medium forum est
templum Vestae, ubi ignis
sacer ā Virginibus
Vestālibus cūrātur.

Vestae: Vesta   *Roman goddess of the hearth and the home*
Virginibus Vestālibus: Virginēs Vestālēs *the vestal Virgins, priestesses of Vesta*

in extrēmō forō stant Rōstra,
ubi contiōnēs apud populum
habentur.

prope Rōstra est carcer, ubi
captīvī populī Rōmānī
custōdiuntur.

nox

nox erat. lūna stēllaeque in caelō serēnō fulgēbant. tempus erat quō
hominēs quiēscere solent. Rōmae tamen nūlla erat quiēs, nūllum
silentium.

magnīs in domibus, ubi dīvitēs habitābant, cēnae splendidae
cōnsūmēbantur. cibus sūmptuōsus ā servīs offerēbātur; vīnum   5
optimum ab ancillīs fundēbātur; carmina ā citharoedīs perītissimīs
cantābantur.

in altīs autem īnsulīs, nūllae cēnae splendidae cōnsūmēbantur,
nūllī citharoedī audiēbantur. ibi pauperēs, famē paene cōnfectī,
vītam miserrimam agēbant. aliī ad patrōnōs epistulās scrībēbant ut   10
auxilium eōrum peterent, aliī scelera ac fūrta committere parābant.

prope forum magnus strepitus audiēbātur. nam arcus magnificus
in Viā Sacrā exstruēbātur. ingēns polyspaston arcuī imminēbat.
fabrī, quī arcum exstruēbant, dīligentissimē labōrābant. aliī figūrās

serēnō: serēnus	calm, clear	patrōnōs: patrōnus	patron
altīs: altus	high	arcus	arch
īnsulīs: īnsula	apartment building	polyspaston	crane
famē: famēs	hunger	figūrās: figūra	figure, shape
cōnfectī: cōnfectus	worn out, exhausted		

in arcū sculpēbant; aliī titulum in fronte arcūs īnscrībēbant; aliī
marmor ad summum arcum tollēbant. omnēs strēnuē labōrābant ut
arcum ante lūcem perficerent. nam Imperātor Domitiānus hunc
arcum frātrī Titō postrīdiē dēdicāre volēbat. Titum vīvum ōderat;
mortuum tamen eum honōrāre cupiēbat. Domitiānus enim favōrem
populī Rōmānī, quī Titum maximē dīlēxerat, nunc sibi conciliāre
volēbat.

praeerat huic operī Quīntus Haterius Latrōniānus, redēmptor
nōtissimus. eā nocte ipse fabrōs furēns incitābat. aderat quoque
Gāius Salvius Līberālis, Hateriī patrōnus, quī eum invicem
flāgitābat ut opus ante lūcem perficeret. anxius enim erat Salvius
quod Imperātōrī persuāserat ut Haterium operī praeficeret. ille
igitur fabrīs, quamquam omnīnō dēfessī erant, identidem imperāvit
nē labōre dēsisterent.

Glitus, magister fabrōrum, Haterium lēnīre temptābat.
"ecce, domine!" inquit. "fabrī iam arcum paene perfēcērunt.
ultimae litterae titulī nunc īnscrībuntur; ultimae figūrae
sculpuntur; ultimae marmoris massae ad summum arcum
tolluntur."

paulō ante hōram prīmam, fabrī arcum tandem perfēcērunt;
abiērunt omnēs ut quiēscerent. paulīsper urbs silēbat.

ūnus faber tamen, domum per forum rediēns, subitō trīstēs
fēminārum duārum clāmōrēs audīvit. duae enim captīvae, magnō
dolōre affectae, in carcere cantābant:

"mī Deus! mī Deus! respice mē! quārē mē dēseruistī?"

sculpēbant: sculpere	*carve, sculpt*	dēfessī: dēfessus	*exhausted, tired out*
titulum: titulus	*inscription*	identidem	*repeatedly*
fronte: frōns	*front*	ultimae: ultimus	*last*
īnscrībēbant: īnscrībere	*write, inscribe*	litterae: littera	*letter*
marmor	*marble*	massae: massa	*block*
lūcem: lūx	*light, daylight*	silēbat: silēre	*be silent*
perficerent: perficere	*finish*	dolōre: dolor	*grief*
dēdicāre	*dedicate*	affectae: affectus	*overcome*
operī: opus	*work, construction*	respice: respicere	*look at, look upon*
redēmptor	*contractor, builder*	quārē?	*why?*
flāgitābat: flāgitāre	*nag at, put pressure on*		

Rōmae	*in Rome*
Viā Sacrā: Via Sacra	*the Sacred Way (road running through forum)*
Titō: Titus	*Emperor of Rome, A.D.79–81*

SENATVS
POPVLVSQVEROMANV
DIVOTITODIVIVESPAS
VESPASIANOAVGVST

The rock of Masada.

Artist's impression of the hanging palace of Herod at Masada, with the snake path clearly visible to the left.

When you have read section I of this story, answer the questions at the
end of the section.

Masada

I

ex carcere obscūrō, ubi captīvī custōdiēbantur, trīstēs clāmōrēs
tollēbantur. duae enim fēminae Iūdaeae, superstitēs eōrum quī
contrā Rōmānōs rebellāverant, fortūnam suam lūgēbant. altera
erat anus septuāgintā annōrum, altera mātrōna trīgintā annōs nāta.
ūnā cum eīs in carcere erant quīnque līberī, quōrum Simōn nātū   5
maximus sōlācium mātrī et aviae ferre temptābat.

"māter, nōlī dolōrī indulgēre! decōrum est Iūdaeīs fortitūdinem
in rēbus adversīs praestāre."

māter fīlium amplexa,

"melius erat," inquit, "cum patre vestrō perīre abhinc annōs   10
novem. cūr tum ā morte abhorruī? cūr vōs servāvī?"

Simōn, hīs verbīs commōtus, mātrem rogāvit quō modō periisset
pater atque quārē rem prius nōn nārrāvisset. eam ōrāvit ut omnia
explicāret. sed tantus erat dolor mātris ut prīmō nihil dīcere posset.
mox, cum sē collēgisset, ad fīliōs conversa,   15

"dē morte patris vestrī," inquit, "prius nārrāre nōlēbam nē vōs
quoque perīrētis, exemplum eius imitātī. nunc tamen audeō vōbīs
tōtam rem patefacere quod nōs omnēs crās moritūrī sumus.

"nōs Iūdaeī contrā Rōmānōs trēs annōs ācriter rebellāvimus.
annō quārtō iste Beelzebub, Titus, urbem Ierosolymam   20
expugnāvit. numquam ego spectāculum terribilius vīdī: ubīque
aedificia flammīs cōnsūmēbantur; ubīque virī, fēminae, līberī

superstitēs: superstes	*survivor*	rēbus adversīs: rēs adversae	*misfortune*
rebellāverant: rebellāre	*rebel, revolt*	amplexa: amplexus	*having embraced*
lūgēbant: lūgēre	*lament, mourn*	abhinc	*ago*
altera . . . altera	*one . . . the other*	abhorruī: abhorrēre	*shrink (from)*
. . . annōs nāta	*. . . years old*	exemplum	*example*
ūnā cum	*together with*	imitātī: imitātus	*having imitated*
nātū maximus	*eldest*	crās	*tomorrow*
aviae: avia	*grandmother*	expugnāvit: expugnāre	*storm, take by storm*
indulgēre	*give way*	ubīque	*everywhere*
Iudaeae: Iudaea	*Jewish*	Ierosolymam: Ierosolyma	*Jerusalem*
Beelzebub	*Beelzebub, devil*		

occīdēbantur; Templum ipsum ā mīlitibus dīripiēbātur; tōta urbs
ēvertēbātur. in illā clāde periērunt multa mīlia Iūdaeōrum; sed
circiter mīlle superstitēs, duce Eleazārō, rūpem Masadam   25
occupāvērunt. tū, Simōn, illō tempore vix quīnque annōs nātus
erās.

"rūpēs Masada est alta et undique praerupta, prope lacum
Asphaltītēn sita. ibi nōs, mūnītiōnibus validīs dēfēnsī, Rōmānīs diū
resistēbāmus. intereā dux hostium, Lūcius Flāvius Silva, rūpem   30
castellīs multīs circumvēnit. tum mīlitēs, iussū Silvae, ingentem
aggerem usque ad summam rūpem exstrūxērunt. deinde aggerem
ascendērunt, magnamque partem mūnītiōnum ignī dēlēvērunt.
simulatque hoc effēcērunt, Silva mīlitēs ad castra redūxit ut
proximum diem victōriamque exspectārent."   35

circiter	*about*	castellīs: castellum	*fort*
duce: dux	*leader*	iussū Silvae	*at Silva's order*
rūpem: rūpēs	*rock, crag*	aggerem: agger	*ramp, mound of earth*
undique	*on all sides*	usque ad	*right up to*
mūnītiōnibus: mūnītiō	*defense, fortification*	ignī: ignis	*fire*
validīs: validus	*strong*		

lacum Asphaltītēn: lacus Asphaltītēs *Lake Asphaltites (the Dead Sea)*

1 How old were the two women? How many children were with them in
the prison? How were the children related to the two women?

2 How many years previously had the children's father died?

3 What two questions did Simon ask? What was his mother's answer to
his second question?

4 What disaster had happened to the Jews in the fourth year of their
revolt against the Romans?

5 What action was taken by a thousand Jewish survivors? Who was their
leader?

6 Judging from lines 28–9, and the picture on page 156, why do you
think the Jews at Masada were able to hold out for so long against the
Romans?

7 Who was the Roman general at Masada? What method did he use to
get his men to the top of the rock? Identify it in the picture.

II

"illā nocte Eleazārus, dē rērum statū dēspērāns, Iūdaeīs cōnsilium
dīrum prōposuit.

"'magnō in discrīmine sumus,' inquit. 'nōs Iūdaeī, Deō cōnfīsī,

---

Rōmānīs adhūc resistimus; nunc illī nōs in servitūtem trahere
parant. nūlla spēs salūtis nōbīs ostenditur. nōnne melius est perīre   5
quam Rōmānīs cēdere? ego ipse mortem meā manū īnflīctam
accipiō, servitūtem spernō.'

   "hīs verbīs Eleazārus Iūdaeīs persuāsit ut mortem sibi
cōnscīscerent. tantum ardōrem in eīs excitāvit ut, simulac fīnem
ōrātiōnī fēcit, ad exitium statim festīnārent. virī uxōrēs līberōsque   10
amplexī occīdērunt. cum hanc dīram et saevam rem cōnfēcissent,
decem eōrum sorte ductī cēterōs interfēcērunt. tum ūnus ex illīs,
sorte invicem ductus, postquam novem reliquōs mortī dedit, sē
ipsum ferrō trānsfīxit."

   "quō modō nōs ipsī effūgimus?" rogāvit Simōn.   15

   "ego Eleazārō pārēre nōn potuī," respondit māter. "vōbīscum in
specū latēbam."

   "ignāva!" clāmāvit Simōn. "ego mortem haudquāquam timeō.
ego, patris exemplī memor, eandem fortitūdinem praestāre volō."

rērum statū: rērum status	*situation, state of affairs*	ardōrem: ardor	*spirit, enthusiasm*
		sorte ductī	*chosen by lot*
discrīmine: discrīmen	*crisis*	reliquōs: reliquus	*remaining*
cōnfīsī: cōnfīsus	*having trusted, having put trust in*	ferrō: ferrum	*sword*
		specū: specus	*cave*
servitūtem: servitūs	*slavery*	memor	*remembering, mindful of*
īnflīctam: īnflīgere	*inflict*		
mortem sibi cōnscīscerent: mortem sibi cōnscīscere	*commit suicide*	eandem	*the same*

About the Language

1 In Unit 1, you met sentences like these:

   puer clāmōrem **audit**.   *A boy hears the shout.*
   ancilla vīnum **fundēbat**.   *A slave-girl was pouring wine.*

   The words in boldface are *active* forms of the verb.

2 In Stage 29, you have met sentences like these:

   clāmor ā puerō **audītur**.   *The shout **is heard** by a boy.*
   vīnum ab ancillā **fundēbātur**. *Wine **was being poured** by a
                                     slave-girl.*

   The words in boldface are *passive* forms of the verb.

3 Compare the following active and passive forms:

PRESENT TENSE

PRESENT ACTIVE	PRESENT PASSIVE
portat	portātur
he carries	*he is carried,* or *he is being carried*
portant	portantur
they carry	*they are carried,* or *they are being carried*

IMPERFECT TENSE

IMPERFECT ACTIVE	IMPERFECT PASSIVE
portābat	portābātur
he was carrying	*he was being carried*
portābant	portābantur
they were carrying	*they were being carried*

4 Further examples of the present passive:

1 cēna nostra ā coquō nunc parātur. (Compare this with the active form: coquus cēnam nostram nunc parat.)

2 multa scelera in hāc urbe cotīdiē committuntur.

3 laudantur; dūcitur; rogātur; mittuntur.

Further examples of the imperfect passive:

4 candidātī ab amīcīs salūtābantur.
   (Compare: amīcī candidātōs salūtābant.)

5 fābula ab āctōribus in theātrō agēbātur.

6 audiēbantur; laudābātur; necābantur; tenēbātur.

arcus Titī

I

postrīdiē māne ingēns Rōmānōrum multitūdō ad arcum Titī conveniēbat. diēs fēstus ab omnibus cīvibus celebrābātur. Imperātor Domitiānus, quod eō diē frātrī Titō arcum dēdicātūrus erat, pompam magnificam nūntiāverat. clāmōrēs virōrum fēminārumque undique tollēbantur. spectātōrum tanta erat 5 multitūdō ut eī quī tardius advēnērunt nūllum locum prope arcum invenīre possent. eīs cōnsistendum erat procul ab arcū vel in forō vel in viīs. nam iussū Imperātōris pompa tōtam per urbem dūcēbātur.

multae sellae ā servīs prope arcum pōnēbantur. illūc multī senātōrēs, spē favōris Domitiānī, conveniēbant. inter eōs Salvius, togam splendidam gerēns, locum quaerēbat ubi cōnspicuus esset. inter equitēs, quī post senātōrēs stābant, aderat Haterius ipse. favōrem Imperātōris avidē spērābat, et in animō volvēbat quandō ā Salviō praemium prōmissum acceptūrus esset.

āra ingēns, prō arcū exstrūcta, ā servīs flōribus ōrnābātur. vīgintī sacerdōtēs, togās praetextās gerentēs, circum āram stābant. haruspicēs quoque aderant quī exta victimārum īnspicerent. avium cursus ab auguribus dīligenter notābātur.

10

15

dēdicātūrus	*going to dedicate*
tardius	*too late*
vel . . . vel	*either . . . or*
cōnspicuus	*conspicuous, easily seen*
equitēs	*equites (wealthy men ranking below senators)*
quandō	*when*
acceptūrus	*going to receive*
exta	*entrails*
avium: avis	*bird*
cursus	*flight*
auguribus: augur	*augur*
notābātur: notāre	*note, observe*

II

intereā pompa lentē per Viam Sacram dūcēbātur. prīmā in parte incēdēbant tubicinēs tubās īnflantēs. post eōs vēnērunt iuvenēs quī trīgintā taurōs corōnīs ōrnātōs ad sacrificium dūcēbant. tum multī servī, quī gāzam Iūdaeōrum portābant, prīmam pompae partem claudēbant. huius gāzae pars pretiōsissima erat mēnsa sacra, tubae, candēlābrum, quae omnia aurea erant.

5

gāzam: gāza	*treasure*	claudēbant: claudere	*conclude, complete*

septem captīvī Iūdaeī, quī mediā in pompā incēdēbant, ā
spectātōribus vehementer dērīdēbantur. quīnque puerī, serēnō
vultū incēdentēs, clāmōrēs et contumēliās neglegēbant, sed duae
fēminae plūrimīs lacrimīs spectātōrēs ōrābant ut līberīs parcerent.   10

post captīvōs vēnit Domitiānus ipse, currū magnificō vectus. quia
Pontifex Maximus erat, togam praetextam gerēbat. post
Imperātōrem ambō ībant cōnsulēs, quōrum alter erat L. Flāvius
Silva. cōnsulēs et magistrātūs nōbilissimī effigiem Titī in umerīs
portābant. ā mīlitibus pompa claudēbātur.   15

ad arcum pompa pervēnit. Domitiānus ē currū ēgressus ut
sacrificium faceret, senātōrēs magistrātūsque salūtāvit. tum oculōs
in arcum ipsum convertit. admīrātiōne affectus, Imperātor Salvium
ad sē arcessītum maximē laudāvit. eī imperāvit ut Hateriō grātiās
ageret. inde ad āram prōgressus, cultrum cēpit quō victimam   20
sacrificāret. servus eī iugulum taurī obtulit. deinde Domitiānus,
victimam sacrificāns, frātrī Titō precēs adhibuit:

"tibi, dīve Tite, haec victima nunc sacrificātur; tibi hic arcus
dēdicātur; tibi precēs populī Rōmānī adhibentur."

subitō, dum Rōmānī oculōs in sacrificium intentē dēfīgunt,   25
Simōn occāsiōnem nactus prōsiluit. mediōs in sacerdōtēs irrūpit;
cultrum rapuit. omnēs spectātōrēs immōtī stābant, audāciā eius
attonitī. Domitiānus, pavōre commōtus, pedem rettulit. nōn
Imperātōrem tamen, sed mātrem, aviam, frātrēs Simōn petīvit.
cultrum in manū tenēns clāmāvit,   30

"nōs, quī superstitēs Iūdaeōrum rebellantium sumus, Rōmānīs
servīre nōlumus. mortem obīre mālumus."

haec locūtus, facinus dīrum commīsit. mātrem et aviam
amplexus cultrō statim occīdit. tum frātrēs, haudquāquam
resistentēs, eōdem modō interfēcit. postrēmō magnā vōce populum   35
Rōmānum dētestātus sē ipsum cultrō trānsfīxit.

vultū: vultus	*expression, face*	inde	*then*
currū: currus	*chariot*	cultrum: culter	*knife*
vectus: vehere	*carry*	dīve: dīvus	*god*
quia	*because*	dum	*while*
Pontifex Maximus	*Chief Priest*	dēfīgunt: dēfīgere	*fix*
cōnsulēs: cōnsul	*consul (senior magistrate)*	nactus	*having seized*
magistrātūs:		pedem rettulit:	
magistrātus	*magistrate (elected official*	pedem referre	*step back*
	of Roman government)	mālumus: mālle	*prefer*
admīrātiōne: admīrātiō	*admiration*	eōdem modō	*in the same way*

About the Language

1 In Stage 26, you met purpose clauses used with **ut**:

senex īnsidiās īnstrūxit ut fūrēs caperet.
The old man set a trap in order that he might catch the thieves.
   or, in more natural English:
The old man set a trap to catch the thieves.

2 In Stage 29, you have met purpose clauses used with forms of the relative pronoun **quī**:

fēmina servum mīsit quī cibum emeret.
The woman sent a slave who was to buy food.
   or, in more natural English:
The woman sent a slave to buy food.

You have also met purpose clauses used with **ubi**:

locum quaerēbāmus ubi stārēmus.
We were looking for a place where we might stand.
   or, in more natural English:
We were looking for a place to stand.

3 Further examples:

  1 sacerdōs haruspicem arcessīvit quī exta īnspiceret.
  2 senātor gemmam pretiōsam quaerēbat quam uxōrī daret.
  3 Haterius quīnque fabrōs ēlēgit quī figūrās in arcū sculperent.
  4 domum emere volēbam ubi fīlius meus habitāret.

Practicing the Language

1 Study the way in which the following verbs are formed, and give the meanings of the untranslated ones:

currere	dēcurrere	excurrere	recurrere
run	*run down*	*run out*	*run back*
iacere	dēicere	ēicere	reicere
throw			*throw back*
trahere	dētrahere	extrahere	retrahere
pull, drag	*pull down*		
salīre	dēsilīre	exsilīre	resilīre
jump		*jump out*	
cadere	dēcidere	excidere	recidere
fall		*fall out*	

The verbs in the second, third, and fourth columns are known as *compound verbs*.

Give the meaning of each of the following compound verbs:

exīre, ēmittere, expellere, ērumpere, effundere;
dēmittere, dēpōnere, dēspicere;
redūcere, remittere, redīre, respicere, repōnere, referre, revenīre, recipere, revocāre

2 Complete each sentence with the right form of the imperfect subjunctive, using the verb in parentheses, then translate.

For example: equitēs īnsidiās parāvērunt ut ducem hostium ...... (capere)

Answer: equitēs īnsidiās parāvērunt ut ducem hostium caperent.
The cavalry prepared a trap in order to catch the leader of the enemy.

The forms of the imperfect subjunctive are given on page 279 of the Review Grammar.

1 fabrī strēnuē labōrāvērunt ut arcum ...... (perficere)
2 Domitiānus ad āram prōcessit ut victimam ...... (sacrificāre)
3 ad forum contendēbāmus ut pompam ...... (spectāre)

4 barbarī facēs in manibus tenēbant ut templum . . . . . . (incendere)
5 extrā carcerem stābam ut captīvōs . . . . . . (custōdīre)

3 Complete each sentence with the most suitable participle from the lists below, using the correct form, and then translate. Do not use any participle more than once.

dūcēns	labōrāns	sedēns	incēdēns	clāmāns
dūcentem	labōrantem	sedentem	incēdentem	clāmantem
dūcentēs	labōrantēs	sedentēs	incēdentēs	clāmantēs

1 videō Salvium prope arcum . . . . . .
2 fabrī, in Viā Sacrā . . . . ., valdē dēfessī erant.
3 nōnne audīs puerōs . . . . .?
4 iuvenis, victimam . . . . ., ad āram prōcessit.
5 spectātōrēs captīvōs, per viās . . . . ., dērīdēbant.

4 Translate each English sentence into Latin by selecting correctly from the list of Latin words.

1 *The citizens, having been delighted by the show, applauded.*

| cīvis | spectāculum | dēlectātus | plaudunt |
| cīvēs | spectāculō | dēlectātī | plausērunt |

2 *I recognized the slave-girl who was pouring the wine.*

| ancilla | quī | vīnum | fundēbat | agnōvī |
| ancillam | quae | vīnō | fundēbant | agnōvit |

3 *Having returned to the bank of the river, the soldiers halted.*

| ad rīpam | flūmine | regressī | mīlitēs | cōnstitērunt |
| ad rīpās | flūminis | regressōs | mīlitum | cōnstiterant |

4 *The woman, sitting in prison, told a sad story.*

| fēmina | in carcerem | sedēns | fābulam | trīstis | nārrat |
| fēminae | in carcere | sedentem | fābulae | trīstem | nārrāvit |

5 *We saw the altar, decorated with flowers.*

| āram | flōrī | ōrnāta | vīdī |
| ārās | flōribus | ōrnātam | vīdimus |

6 *They killed the sleeping prisoners with swords.*

| captīvī | dormientem | gladiōs | occīdērunt |
| captīvōs | dormientēs | gladiīs | occīdit |

The Roman Forum

The forum of Rome (**forum Rōmānum**) was not only the social and commercial center of the city; it was the center of the whole empire. To symbolize this, the Emperor Augustus placed a golden milestone (**mīliārium aureum**) in the forum to mark the starting-point of the roads that radiated from the city to all the corners of the empire.

The ordinary people of Rome came in great numbers to the forum, sometimes to visit its temples and public buildings, sometimes to listen to speeches or watch a procession, and sometimes just to meet their friends and stroll idly about, pausing at times to gossip, listen to an argument, or bargain with a passing street-vendor.

In the great halls (**basilicae**), lawyers pleaded their cases in front of large and often noisy audiences, and merchants and bankers negotiated their business deals. Senators made their way to the senate-house (**cūria**) to conduct the affairs of government under the leadership of the emperor. Sometimes a funeral procession wound its way through the forum, accompanied by noisy lamentations and loud music; sometimes the crowd was forced to make way for a wealthy noble, who was carried through the forum in a sedan-chair by his slaves and escorted by a long line of citizens.

The forum lay on low ground between two of Rome's hills, the Capitol and the Palatine. On the Capitol at the western end of the forum stood the temple of Jupiter Optimus Maximus, the center of the Roman state religion. This was where the emperor came to pray for the continued safety of the Roman people; and this was where the consuls took their solemn vows on January 1st each year at the beginning of their consulship. On the Palatine stood the emperor's residence. In the time of Augustus, this had been a small and simple house; later emperors built palaces of steadily increasing splendor.

Near the foot of the Capitol stood the Rostra, a platform from which public speeches were made to the people. It took its name from the **rōstra** (*ships' prows*, which had been captured in a sea battle early in Rome's history) which were used to decorate it. One of the most famous speeches made from the Rostra was Mark Antony's speech over the body of Julius Caesar in 44 B.C. The listening crowds were so carried away by Antony's words and so angry at Caesar's murder that they rioted, seized the body, and burned it in the forum. A temple was later built in Caesar's memory

House of
Vestal
Virgins

Temple of
Julius
Caesar

Arch of
Titus

Via
Sacra

Temple of
Castor and
Pollux

Statues

Temple
of Vesta

Basilica
Aemilia

Forum
Romanum

Basilica Iulia

Temple of
Saturn

Temple of
Vespasian

at the eastern end of the forum, on the spot where his body had been
burned.

Not far from the Rostra was the prison. Prisoners of war, like the seven
Jews in the stories of this Stage, were held in the prison before being led in
a triumphal procession through the streets of Rome. Afterwards they
were taken back to the prison and killed.

Just outside the forum, near the temple of Julius Caesar, was a small
round building with a cone-shaped roof. This was the temple of Vesta,
where the Vestal Virgins tended the sacred flame of the city so that it
would burn forever.

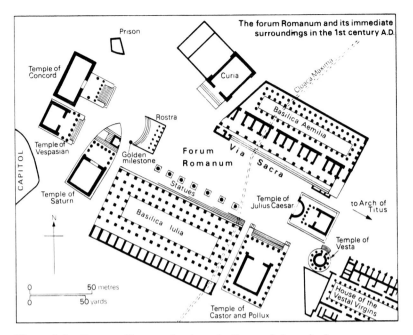

Plan of the Roman Forum during the Imperial period.

Through the forum ran the Sacred Way (**Via Sacra**), which provided an avenue for religious or triumphal processions. When the Romans celebrated a victory in war, the triumphal procession passed through the city and ended by traveling along the Sacred Way towards the temple of Jupiter on the Capitol, where the victorious general gave thanks. The story on pp. 160–163 describes a rather similar occasion: the dedication of the arch of Titus by the Emperor Domitian in A.D. 81. On this occasion, the procession would have followed the Sacred Way eastwards out of the forum, up a gentle slope to the site of the arch itself. The arch commemorated the victory of Domitian's brother Titus over the Jewish people. The Jews' last stand at Masada, their fortress near the Dead Sea, is described in the story on pp. 157–159.

The forum Romanum was not the only forum in the city. By the time of the events of this Stage, two other forums had been built by Julius Caesar and Augustus; later, two more were added by the Emperors Nerva and Trajan. The most splendid of these was Trajan's forum, which contained the famous column commemorating Trajan's victories over the Dacians. But none of these other forums replaced the forum Romanum as the political, religious, and social heart of the city. If one Roman said to another, "I'll meet you in the forum," he or she meant the Forum Romanum.

Words and Phrases Checklist

aliī . . . aliī	*some . . . others*
aliquandō	*sometimes*
amplexus, amplexa, amplexum	*having embraced*
audācia, audāciae	*boldness, audacity*
carmen, carminis	*song*
circumveniō, circumvenīre, circumvēnī, circumventus	*surround*
corōna, corōnae	*garland, wreath*
cursus, cursūs	*course, flight*
dēfessus, dēfessa, dēfessum	*exhausted, tired out*
dolor, dolōris	*grief, pain*
ferrum, ferrī	*iron, sword*
incēdō, incēdere, incessī	*march, stride*
līberī, līberōrum	*children*
lūx, lūcis	*light, daylight*
mālō, mālle, māluī	*prefer*
obscūrus, obscūra, obscūrum	*dark, gloomy*
ōdī	*I hate*
perficiō, perficere, perfēcī, perfectus	*finish*
populus, populī	*people*
prius	*earlier*
quiēs, quiētis	*rest*
redūcō, redūcere, redūxī, reductus	*lead back*
salūs, salūtis	*safety, health*
scelus, sceleris	*crime*
serviō, servīre, servīvī	*serve (as a slave)*
sors, sortis	*lot*
spernō, spernere, sprēvī, sprētus	*despise, reject*
undique	*on all sides*
vester, vestra, vestrum	*your (plural)*
vīvus, vīva, vīvum	*alive, living*

Word Search

audacious, coronation, obscurity, populous, salutary, servile, revive

1 . . . . .: slavish in manner
2 . . . . .: the act or ceremony of crowning a monarch
3 . . . . .: daring
4 . . . . .: to restore to life or consciousness
5 . . . . .: beneficial; healthful
6 . . . . .: thickly settled, densely inhabited
7 . . . . .: the condition of being unknown or unnoticed

Haterius

Haterius: quam fēlīx sum!
heri arcus meus ab Imperātōre dēdicātus est.
heri praemium ingēns mihi ā Salviō prōmissum est.
hodiē praemium exspectō . . .

Haterius: anxius sum.
arcus meus nūper ab Imperātōre laudātus est.
nūllum tamen praemium adhūc mihi ā Salviō missum est.
num ego ā Salviō dēceptus sum?
minimē! Salvius vir probus est . . .

When you have read this story, answer the questions at the end.

dignitās

cīvēs Rōmānī, postquam arcus ab Imperātōre dēdicātus est,
quattuor diēs fēstōs celebrāvērunt. templa vīsitābant ut dīs grātiās
agerent; Circum Maximum cotīdiē complēbant ut lūdōs magnificōs
ā cōnsulibus ēditōs spectārent; ad arcum ipsum conveniēbant ut
figūrās in eō sculptās īnspicerent. plūrimī clientēs domum Salviī   5
veniēbant quī grātulātiōnēs eī facerent. Salvius ipse summō gaudiō
affectus est quod Imperātor arcum Hateriī valdē laudāverat.

apud Haterium tamen nūllae grātulantium vōcēs audītae sunt.
neque clientēs neque amīcī ab eō admissī sunt. Haterius, īrā
commōtus, sōlus domī manēbat. adeō saeviēbat ut dormīre nōn   10
posset. quattuor diēs noctēsque vigilābat. quīntō diē uxor, Vitellia
nōmine, quae nesciēbat quārē Haterius adeō īrātus esset, eum
mollīre temptābat. ingressa hortum, ubi Haterius hūc illūc
ambulābat, eum anxia interrogāvit.

dīs = deīs: deus	*god*	grātulantium: grātulāns	*congratulating*
ēditōs: ēdere	*put on, present*	vigilābat: vigilāre	*stay awake*
clientēs: cliēns	*client*	quīntō: quīntus	*fifth*
grātulātiōnēs: grātulātiō	*congratulation*	hūc illūc	*here and there,*
gaudiō: gaudium	*joy*		*up and down*

Circum Maximum: Circus Maximus *the Circus Maximus (stadium for chariot-racing)*

Busts from the tomb of the Haterii, Rome, possibly Haterius and Vitellia.

Vitellia: cūr tam vehementer saevīs, mī Haterī? et amīcōs et   15
clientēs, quī vēnērunt ut tē salūtārent, domō abēgistī.
neque ūnum verbum mihi hōs quattuor diēs dīxistī. sine
dubiō, ut istum arcum cōnficerēs, nimis labōrāvistī,
neglegēns valētūdinis tuae. nōnne melius est tibi ad
vīllam rūsticam mēcum abīre? nam rūrī, cūrārum oblītus,   20
quiēscere potes.

Haterius: quō modō ego, tantam iniūriam passus, quiēscere
possum?

Vitellia: verba tua nōn intellegō. quis tibi iniūriam intulit?

Haterius: ego ā Salviō, quī mihi favēre solēbat, omnīnō dēceptus   25
sum. prō omnibus meīs labōribus ingēns praemium mihi
ā Salviō prōmissum est. nūllum praemium tamen, nē
grātiās quidem, accēpī.

Vitellia: contentus estō, mī Haterī! redēmptor nōtissimus es, cuius
arcus ab Imperātōre ipsō nūper laudātus est. multa   30
aedificia pūblica exstrūxistī, unde magnās dīvitiās
comparāvistī.

Haterius: dīvitiās floccī nōn faciō. in hāc urbe sunt plūrimī
redēmptōrēs quī opēs maximās comparāvērunt. mihi
autem nōn dīvitiae sed dignitās est cūrae.   35

Vitellia: dignitās tua amplissima est. nam nōn modo dītissimus es
sed etiam uxōrem nōbilissimā gente nātam habēs. Rūfilla,
soror mea, uxor est Salviī quī tibi semper fāvit et saepe tē
Imperātōrī commendāvit. quid aliud ā Salviō accipere
cupis?   40

Haterius: volō ad summōs honōrēs pervenīre, sīcut illī Hateriī quī
abhinc multōs annōs cōnsulēs factī sunt. praesertim
sacerdōs esse cupiō; multī enim virī, sacerdōtēs ab
Imperātōre creātī, posteā ad cōnsulātum pervēnērunt.
sed Salvius, quamquam sacerdōtium mihi identidem   45
prōmīsit, fidem nōn servāvit.

Vitellia: nōlī dēspērāre, mī Haterī! melius est tibi ad Salvium īre
blandīsque verbīs ab eō hunc honōrem repetere.

Haterius: mihi, quī redēmptor optimus sum, nōn decōrum est
honōrēs ita quaerere.   50

Vitellia: cōnsilium optimum habeō. invītā Salvium ad āream
tuam! ostentā eī polyspaston tuum! nihil maius nec
mīrābilius umquam anteā factum est. deinde Salvium
admīrātiōne affectum rogā dē sacerdōtiō.

abēgistī: abigere	*drive away*	dītissimus: dīves	*rich*
valētūdinis: valētūdō	*health*	commendāvit:	
rūrī	*in the country*	commendāre	*recommend*
oblītus	*having forgotten*	cōnsulātum:	
nē . . . quidem	*not even*	cōnsulātus	*consulship (rank of consul)*
estō!	*be!*	sacerdōtium	*priesthood*
pūblica: pūblicus	*public*	fidem . . . servāvit:	
dīvitiās: dīvitiae	*riches*	fidem servāre	*keep a promise, keep faith*
est cūrae	*is a matter of concern*	āream: ārea	*construction site*
amplissima:		ostentā: ostentāre	*show off, display*
amplissimus	*very great*	nec	*nor*

Vitellia *Haterius' wife, and sister of Salvius' wife, Rufilla*

1 How long was the holiday which followed the dedication of the arch? During this holiday, what happened (*a*) in the temples, (*b*) at the Circus Maximus, (*c*) at the arch itself?

2 Why did Salvius' clients come to his house? What happened to the clients of Haterius?

3 What does Vitellia at first think is the matter with Haterius? What action does she suggest?

4 In what way does Haterius consider he has been badly treated?

5 Explain Haterius' reason for saying "dīvitiās floccī nōn faciō" (line 33).

6 What honor does Haterius want to receive in the near future? What does he hope this will lead to?

7 Why does Haterius reject the advice given by Vitellia in lines 47–8? Explain what Haterius means by "ita" (line 50).

8 What suggestion does Vitellia make in lines 51–2? How does she think this will help Haterius to get what he wants?

About the Language

1 In this Stage, you have met the *perfect passive*. Compare it with the perfect active:

PERFECT ACTIVE

senex fūrem **accūsāvit**. *The old man **has accused** the thief.*
                            *or, The old man **accused** the thief.*

Rōmānī hostēs   *The Romans **have overcome** the enemy.*
superāvērunt.   *or, The Romans **overcame** the enemy.*

PERFECT PASSIVE

fūr ā sene **accūsātus est**. *The thief **has been accused** by the old*
                               man.
                               *or, The thief **was accused** by the old man.*

hostēs ā Rōmānīs   *The enemy **have been overcome** by the*
superātī sunt.   *Romans.*
                          *or, The enemy **were overcome** by the*
                          Romans.

2 The forms of the perfect passive are as follows:

portātus sum   *I have been carried*, or *I was carried*
portātus es   *you* (s.) *have been carried*, or *you were carried*
portātus est   *he has been carried*, or *he was carried*
portātī sumus   *we have been carried*, or *we were carried*
portātī estis   *you* (pl.) *have been carried*, or *you were carried*
portātī sunt   *they have been carried*, or *they were carried*

3 Notice that each form of the perfect passive is made up of two words:

  1 a perfect passive participle (e.g. **portātus**) in either a singular or a plural form,
  2 a form of the present tense of **sum**.

4 Further examples:

  1 arcus ab Imperātōre dēdicātus est.
    (Compare: Imperātor arcum dēdicāvit.)
  2 multī nūntiī ad urbem missī sunt.
  3 dux hostium ā mīlitibus captus est.
  4 audītus est; invītātī sunt; dēceptī sumus; laudātus es.

---

polyspaston

postrīdiē Haterius Salvium ad āream suam dūxit ut polyspaston eī
ostentāret. ibi sedēbat ōtiōsus Glitus magister fabrōrum. quī cum
dominum appropinquantem cōnspexisset, celeriter surrēxit
fabrōsque dīligentius labōrāre iussit.

tōta ārea strepitū labōrantium plēna erat. columnae ex marmore   5
pretiōsissimō secābantur; laterēs in āream portābantur; ingentēs
marmoris massae in plaustra pōnēbantur. Haterius, cum fabrōs
labōre occupātōs vīdisset, Salvium ad aliam āreae partem dūxit. ibi
stābat ingēns polyspaston quod ā fabrīs parātum erat. in tignō
polyspastī sēdēs fīxa erat. tum Haterius ad Salvium versus,   10

"mī Salvī," inquit, "nōnne mīrābile est hoc polyspaston? fabrī
meī id exstrūxērunt ut marmor ad summum arcum tollerent. nunc
autem tibi tālem urbis prōspectum praestāre volō quālem paucī
umquam vīdērunt. placetne tibi?"

laterēs: later	*brick*
tignō: tignum	*beam*
sēdēs	*seat*
fīxa erat: fīgere	*fix, fasten*
tālem . . . quālem	*such . . . as*
prōspectum:	
prōspectus	*view*

**Relief of a crane on the
tomb of the Haterii.**

Salvius, ubi sēdem in tignō fīxam vīdit, palluit. sed, quod fabrī 15
oculōs in eum dēfīxōs habēbant, timōrem dissimulāns in sēdem
cōnsēdit. iuxtā eum Haterius quoque cōnsēdit. tum fabrīs imperāvit
ut fūnēs, quī ad tignum adligātī erant, summīs vīribus traherent.
deinde tignum lentē ad caelum tollēbātur. Salvius pavōre paene
cōnfectus clausīs oculīs ad sēdem haerēbat. ubi tandem oculōs 20
aperuit, spectāculō attonitus,

"dī immortālēs!" inquit. "tōtam urbem vidēre possum. ecce
templum Iovis! ecce flūmen! ecce Amphitheātrum Flāvium et arcus
novus! quam in sōle fulget! Imperātor, simulatque illum arcum
vīdit, summā admīrātiōne affectus est. mihi imperāvit ut grātiās 25
suās tibi agerem."

cui respondit Haterius,

"maximē gaudeō quod opus meum ab Imperātōre laudātum est.
sed praemium illud quod tū mihi prōmīsistī nōndum accēpī."

Salvius tamen vōce blandā, 30

"dē sacerdōtiō tuō," inquit, "Imperātōrem iam saepe cōnsuluī, et
respōnsum eius etiam nunc exspectō. aliquid tamen tibi intereā
offerre possum. agellum quendam possideō, quī prope sepulcra
Metellōrum et Scīpiōnum situs est. tūne hunc agellum emere velīs?"

quae cum audīvisset, Haterius tantō gaudiō affectus est ut dē 35
tignō paene dēcideret.

"ita vērō," inquit, "in illō agellō, prope sepulcra gentium
nōbilissimārum, ego quoque sepulcrum splendidum mihi meīsque
exstruere velim, figūrīs operum meōrum ōrnātum; ita enim nōmen
factaque mea posterīs trādere possum. prō agellō tuō igitur 40
sēstertium vīciēns tibi offerō."

Salvius sibi rīsit; agellus enim eī grātīs ab Imperātōre datus erat.

"agellus multō plūris est," inquit, "sed quod patrōnus sum tuus
tibi faveō. mē iuvat igitur sēstertium tantum trīciēns ā tē accipere.
placetne tibi?" 45

Haterius libenter cōnsēnsit. tum fabrīs imperāvit ut tignum lentē
dēmitterent. itaque ambō domum rediērunt, alter spē
immortālitātis ēlātus, alter praesentī pecūniā contentus.

timōrem: timor	*fear*	nōndum	*not yet*
dissimulāns: dissimulāre	*conceal, hide*	blandā: blandus	*flattering, charming*
iuxtā	*next to*	agellum: agellus	*small plot of land*
fūnēs: fūnis	*rope*	quendam: quīdam	*one, a certain*
adligātī erant: adligāre	*tie*	sepulcra: sepulcrum	*tomb*
vīribus: vīrēs	*strength*	meīs: meī	*my family*

facta: factum	*deed, achievement*	humum	*to the ground*
posterīs: posterī	*future generations, posterity*	immortālitātis:	
sēstertium vīciēns	*two million sesterces*	immortālitās	*immortality*
multō plūris est	*is worth much more*	ēlātus	*thrilled, excited*
mē iuvat	*it pleases me*	praesentī: praesēns	*present, ready*
sēstertium . . . trīciēns	*three million sesterces*		

Iovis	*genitive of* Iuppiter
Amphitheātrum Flāvium	*Flavian Amphitheater (now known as Colosseum)*
Metellōrum: Metellī	*the Metelli (famous Roman family)*
Scīpiōnum: Scīpiōnēs	*the Scipiones (famous Roman family)*

About the Language

1 You have now met the *pluperfect passive*. Compare it with the pluperfect active:

PLUPERFECT ACTIVE
servus dominum **vulnerāverat**.   *A slave **had wounded** the master.*

PLUPERFECT PASSIVE
dominus ā servō **vulnerātus erat**.   *The master **had been wounded** by a slave.*

2 The forms of the pluperfect passive are as follows:

portātus eram	*I had been carried*
portātus erās	*you* (s.) *had been carried*
portātus erat	*he had been carried*
portātī erāmus	*we had been carried*
portātī erātis	*you* (pl.) *had been carried*
portātī erant	*they had been carried*

Each form of the pluperfect passive is made up of a perfect passive participle (e.g. **portātus**) and a form of the imperfect tense of **sum** (e.g. **erat**).

3 Further examples:

1 Simōn ā mātre servātus erat.
  (Compare: māter Simōnem servāverat.)
2 custōdēs prope arcum positī erant.
3 fabrī dīligenter labōrāre iussī erant.
4 Haterius ā Salviō dēceptus erat.
5 pūnītī erant; missus erat; audītus eram.

Practicing the Language

1 Study the forms and meanings of the following adjectives and nouns, and give the meanings of the untranslated words:

benignus	kind	benignitās	kindness
īnfirmus	weak	īnfirmitās	weakness
suāvis	sweet	suāvitās	
probus	honest	probitās	
līber		lībertās	freedom
avidus		aviditās	eagerness, greed
immortālis		immortālitās	
gravis	heavy, serious	gravitās	
sevērus		sevēritās	
celer		celeritās	speed
līberālis		līberālitās	generosity

Give the meaning of each of the following nouns:

crūdēlitās, tranquillitās, calliditās, ūtilitās, paupertās, caecitās, fēlīcitās

2 Translate each sentence; then, with the help of the table of nouns on pages 262–63 of the Review Grammar, change the words in boldface from singular to plural, and translate again.

1 mīles perfidus **amīcum** dēseruit.
2 dux virtūtem **legiōnis** laudāvit.
3 Imperātor multōs honōrēs **lībertō** dedit.
4 iūdex epistulam **testī** trādidit.
5 hostēs in **silvā** latēbant.
6 puella, **flōre** dēlectāta, suāviter rīsit.
7 barbarī **vīllam agricolae** incendērunt.
8 rēx pecūniam **mātrī puerī** reddidit.

3 Complete each sentence with the right word and then translate.

1 mercātor, ē carcere . . . . ., dīs grātiās ēgit. (līberātus, līberātī)
2 māter, verbīs Eleazārī . . . . ., cum līberīs in specum fūgit. (territus, territa)
3 Salvius epistulam, ab Imperātōre . . . . ., legēbat. (scrīpta, scrīptam)
4 nāvēs, tempestāte paene . . . . ., tandem ad portum revēnērunt. (dēlētus, dēlēta, dēlētae)

5 centuriō septem mīlitēs, gladiīs . . . . ., sēcum dūxit. (armātī, armātōs, armātīs)

4 Translate each pair of sentences, then link them together, using **cum** and the pluperfect subjunctive, and translate again.

For example: hospitēs advēnērunt. coquus cēnam intulit.
This becomes: cum hospitēs advēnissent, coquus cēnam intulit.
            When the guests had arrived, the cook brought the dinner in.

The forms of the pluperfect subjunctive are given on page 000 of the Review Grammar.

1 barbarī fūgērunt. mīlitēs ad castra revēnērunt.
2 servus iānuam aperuit. senex intrāvit.
3 Imperātor arcum dēdicāvit. senātōrēs populusque plausērunt.
4 fabrī polyspaston parāvērunt. Haterius Salvium ad āream dūxit.
5 rem perfēcimus. domum rediimus.

Roman Builders

The various carvings on the family tomb of the Haterii, especially the crane, suggest that at least one member of the family was a prosperous building contractor. His personal names are unknown but in the stories we have called him Quintus Haterius Latronianus. One of his contracts was for a magnificent arch to commemorate the popular Emperor Titus

The Ponte Rotto *(Broken Bridge)*, Rome—the remains of the Pons Aemilius, showing the construction of arch.

who died after only a short reign (A.D. 79–81). In Stage 29, Haterius is imagined as anxiously trying to complete it during the night before its dedication by the new emperor, Domitian, and in this Stage he is seeking his reward.

Helped by an architect who provided the design and technical advice Haterius would have employed sub-contractors to supply the materials and engage the workmen. Most of these were slaves and poor free men working as unskilled, occasional labor, but there were also craftsmen such as carpenters and stonemasons. It was the job of the carpenters to put up a timber framework to give shape and temporary support to the arches as they were being built (see diagram below). They also erected the scaffolding and made the timber molds for shaping concrete. The masons were responsible for the quarrying of the stone and its transport, often by barge up the river Tiber, to the building-site in the city before carving the elaborate decoration and preparing the blocks to be lifted into position. The richly carved panels on Titus' arch showed the triumphal procession with prisoners and treasure captured at the sack of Jerusalem in A.D. 70.

Many of our modern handtools have been inherited almost unchanged from those used by Roman craftsmen (for instance, mallets, chisels, crowbars, trowels, saws, and planes), but with the important difference that the Romans did not have the small electric motor that makes the modern power tool so much quicker and less laborious to use.

The blocks of dressed stone were lifted by man-powered cranes. The picture of Haterius' crane on page 177 shows it from the side and

Reliefs of buildings on the tomb of the Haterii. On the left the Flavian Amphitheater, in the center a triumphal arch, on the right the Arch of Titus.

therefore not all the details of its design are visible. It consisted of two wooden uprights, forming the jib, fastened together at the top and splayed apart at the feet. The hoisting rope ran around two pulleys, one at the top of the jib and one at the point where the load was fastened to the rope. After passing around the pulleys, the rope led down to a winding drum, which was turned by a treadmill fixed to the side of the crane and operated by two or three men inside. Smaller cranes had, instead of the treadmill, a capstan with projecting spokes to be turned by hand. This arrangement of pulleys and ropes multiplied the force exerted by human muscles so that a small crew could raise loads weighing up to eight or nine tons. To prevent the crane from toppling over, stayropes were stretched out from the jib, also with the help of pulleys, and firmly anchored to the ground. These machines were certainly cumbersome, slow, and liable to accidents, but they worked.

Another aid to building was good quality cement. The main ingredients of this versatile and easily produced material were (1) lime mortar, made by heating pieces of limestone to a high temperature and then crushing them to a powder, (2) fine sand, (3) clay. These were combined with water to make a smooth paste. In this form the cement was an excellent adhesive which could be spread in a thin layer between bricks or stones, as we do today, and when dry it held them firmly together.

The Romans also mixed cement with rubble, such as stone chips, broken bricks, and pieces of tile, to form the inner core of a wall, sandwiched between the two faces. The advantage of this was that the more expensive material, good quality stone or brick, could be reserved for the outer faces; these were often then covered with plaster and painted in bright colors. Marble, too, in thinly cut plates, was used as a facing material where cost was no object.

Another more novel use of concrete, that is cement mixed with rubble, was as a substitute for stone in the building of arches and vaulted ceilings. For the Romans found that concrete, when shaped into arches,

Interior of the Pantheon in Rome. The shaft of light from the skylight opening is clearly visible. The building now serves as the Christian church of Santa Maria dei Martiri.

was strong enough to span large spaces without any additional support from pillars, and that it could carry the weight of a heavy superstructure. The Romans were not the first people to make concrete but they improved its quality and applied it on a grand, revolutionary scale. They used it, for instance, on the aqueducts that supplied Rome with millions of gallons of fresh water daily, on the Pantheon, a temple whose domed concrete and brick roof (still in good condition today) has a span of 140 feet (43 meters) and rises to the same height above the floor. They also used it on the huge Flavian Amphitheater (known from medieval times as the Colosseum), which could hold up to 50,000 spectators, and is another of Haterius' surviving buildings (see p. 241).

Not all buildings, of course, were constructed so sturdily. The inhabitants of Rome in the first century A.D. were housed in a vast number of dwellings, many of them apartment buildings (**insulae**) which were built much more cheaply, mainly of brick and timber. They had a reputation for being rickety and liable to catch fire. To reduce the danger the Emperor Augustus fixed a limit of 70 feet (21 meters) in height for these insulae and organized fire brigades.

Nevertheless, serious fires did break out from time to time. One occurred in A.D. 80 and when Domitian became emperor in the following year he continued the program of repair that Titus had begun. He restored the spectacular temple of Jupiter Optimus Maximus on the Capitol which had been badly burned in the fire. He built more temples, a stadium, a concert hall, and even an artificial lake for sea fights, all no doubt to enhance the influence and majesty of the emperor.

The boast of Augustus, "urbem latericiam accepi, marmoream reliqui"—"I found Rome built of brick and left it made of marble," was certainly an exaggeration. For the spaces between the marble-faced public libraries, baths, and temples were crammed with the homes of ordinary people. Many builders must have spent most of their time working on these dwellings, described by the poet Juvenal as "propped up with sticks." But given the opportunity of a large contract and a technical challenge, Roman builders made adventurous use of concrete, cranes, and arches; and Domitian, who was determined to add to the splendors of his capital city, kept architects and builders very busy throughout most of his reign.

Words and Phrases Checklist

adhūc	*until now*
afficiō, afficere, affēcī, affectus	*affect, overcome*
ambō, ambae, ambō	*both*
cōnsulō, cōnsulere, cōnsuluī, cōnsultus	*consult*
creō, creāre, creāvī, creātus	*make, create*
dēmittō, dēmittere, dēmīsī, dēmissus	*let down, lower*
dīves, *gen.* dīvitis	*rich*
dīvitiae, dīvitiārum	*riches*
dubium, dubiī	*doubt*
exstruō, exstruere, exstrūxī, exstrūctus	*build*
fēstus, fēsta, fēstum	*festival, holiday*
iniūria, iniūriae	*injustice, injury*
lūdus, lūdī	*game*
magister, magistrī	*master, foreman*
nātus, nāta, nātum	*born*
nimis	*too*
omnīnō	*completely*
opus, operis	*work, construction*
pallēscō, pallēscere, palluī	*grow pale*
pavor, pavōris	*panic, terror*
praestō, praestāre, praestitī	*show, display*
praetereā	*besides*
quārē?	*why?*
sēdēs, sēdis	*seat*
sepulcrum, sepulcrī	*tomb*
sōl, sōlis	*sun*
soror, sorōris	*sister*
strepitus, strepitūs	*noise, din*
tempestās, tempestātis	*storm*
timor, timōris	*fear*

Word Search

affection, indubitably, ludicrous, magisterial, operate, sororal, tempestuous

1 . . . . .: laughable, ridiculous
2 . . . . .: fondness
3 . . . . .: sisterly
4 . . . . .: unquestionably
5 . . . . .: to function effectively
6 . . . . .: tumultuous, stormy
7 . . . . .: authoritative

Stage 31

in urbe

diēs illūcēscēbat.

diē illūcēscente, multī saccāriī in
rīpā flūminis labōrābant.

saccāriīs labōrantibus, advēnit
nāvis. nautae nāvem
dēligāvērunt.

nāve dēligātā, saccāriī
frūmentum expōnere coepērunt.

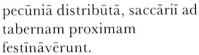

frūmentō expositō, magister
nāvis pecūniam saccāriīs
distribuit.

pecūniā distribūtā, saccāriī ad
tabernam proximam
festīnāvērunt.

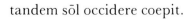

tandem sōl occidere coepit.

sōle occidente, saccāriī ā tabernā
ēbriī discessērunt, omnī pecūniā
cōnsūmptā.

adventus

diē illūcēscente, ingēns Rōmānōrum multitūdō viās urbis complēbat. pauperēs ex īnsulīs exībant ut aquam ē fontibus pūblicīs traherent. senātōrēs ad forum lectīcīs vehēbantur. in rīpīs flūminis Tiberis, ubi multa horrea sita erant, frūmentum ē nāvibus ā saccāriīs expōnēbātur. servī, quī ā vēnālīciīs ex Āfricā importātī   5
erant, ē nāvibus dūcēbantur, catēnīs gravibus vīnctī.

ex ūnā nāvium, quae modo ā Graeciā advēnerat, puella pulcherrima exiit. epistulam ad Haterium scrīptam manū tenēbat. sarcinae eius ā servō portābantur, virō quadrāgintā annōrum. tot tantaeque erant sarcinae ut servus eās ferre vix posset.   10

sōle ortō, puella ad Subūram advēnit. multitūdine clāmōribusque hominum valdē obstupefacta est. tanta erat multitūdō ut puella cum summā difficultāte prōcēderet. mendīcī, quī ad compita sedēbant, manūs ad praetereuntēs porrigēbant. ubīque sonitus labōrantium audiēbātur: ā crepidāriīs calceī   15
reficiēbantur; ā ferrāriīs gladiī excūdēbantur; ā fabrīs tigna secābantur. fabrī, puellā vīsā, clāmāre coepērunt; puellam verbīs procācibus appellāvērunt. quae tamen, clāmōribus fabrōrum neglēctīs, vultū serēnō celeriter praeteriit. servum iussit festīnāre nē domum Haterii tardius pervenīrent.   20

eōdem tempore multī clientēs per viās contendēbant ut patrōnōs salūtārent. aliī, scissīs togīs ruptīsque calceīs, per lutum lentē ībant. eīs difficile erat festīnāre quod lutum erat altum, viae angustae, multitūdō dēnsa. aliī, quī nōbilī gente nātī sunt, celeriter prōcēdēbant quod servī multitūdinem fūstibus dēmovēbant.   25
clientēs, quī sīcut unda per viās ruēbant, puellae prōcēdentī obstābant.

illūcēscente: illūcēscere	*dawn, grow bright*	mendīcī: mendīcus	*beggar*
lectīcīs: lectīca	*sedan-chair*	compita: compitum	*crossroads*
saccāriīs: saccārius	*docker, dock-worker*	porrigēbant: porrigere	*stretch out*
expōnēbātur: expōnere	*unload*	crepidāriīs: crepidārius	*shoemaker*
catēnīs: catēna	*chain*	ferrāriīs: ferrārius	*blacksmith*
modo	*just*	excūdēbantur: excūdere	*forge, hammer out*
sarcinae	*bags, luggage*	fabrīs: faber	*carpenter, workman*
ortō: ortus	*having risen*	procācibus: procāx	*impudent, impolite*
obstupefacta est:		appellāvērunt: appellāre	*call out to*
obstupefacere	*amaze, stun*	ruptīs: rumpere	*break, split*

lutum	*mud*	dēmovēbant: dēmovēre	*move out of the way*

Tiberis   *river Tiber*
Subūram: Subūra   *the Subura (noisy and crowded district north of forum)*

When you have read section I of this story, answer the questions at the end of the section.

salūtātiō

I

prīmā hōrā clientēs ante domum Hateriī conveniēbant. omnēs, oculīs in iānuam dēfīxīs, patrōnī favōrem exspectābant. aliī beneficium, aliī sportulam spērābant. puella, servō adstante, in extrēmā parte multitūdinis cōnstitit; ignāra mōrum Rōmānōrum, in animō volvēbat cūr tot hominēs illā hōrā ibi stārent.

iānuā subitō apertā, in līmine appāruit praecō. corpus eius erat

5

salūtātiō	*the morning visit (paid by clients to patron)*
sportulam: sportula	*handout (gift of food or money)*
extrēmā parte: extrēma pars	*edge*
līmine: līmen	*threshold, doorway*
praecō	*herald*

ingēns et obēsum, vultus superbus, oculī malignī. clientēs, praecōne
vīsō, clāmāre statim coepērunt. eum ōrāvērunt ut sē ad patrōnum
admitteret. ille tamen superbē circumspectāvit neque quicquam
prīmō dīxit.   10

omnibus tandem silentibus, praecō ita coepit:

"dominus noster, Quīntus Haterius Latrōniānus, ratiōnēs suās
subdūcit. iubet igitur trēs cīvēs ratiōnibus testēs subscrībere. cēdite
C. Iūliō Alexandrō, C. Memmiō Prīmō, L. Venūlēiō Aprōniānō."

quī igitur, audītīs nōminibus suīs, alacriter prōgressī domum   15
intrāvērunt. cēterī autem, oculīs in vultum praecōnis dēfīxīs, spē
favōris manēbant.

"ad cēnam," inquit praecō, "Haterius invītat L. Volusium
Maeciānum et M. Licinium Prīvātum. Maeciānus et Prīvātus
decimā hōrā redīre iubentur. nunc autem cēdite aliīs! cēdite   20
architectō C. Rabīriō Maximō! cēdite T. Claudiō Papīriō!"

dum illī per iānuam intrant, cēterīs nūntiāvit praecō:

"vōs omnēs iubet Haterius tertiā hōrā sē ad forum dēdūcere."

hīs verbīs dictīs, paucōs dēnāriōs in turbam sparsit. clientēs, nē
sportulam āmitterent, dēnāriōs rapere temptāvērunt. inter sē   25
vehementer certābant. intereā puella immōta stābat, hōc
spectāculō attonita.

malignī: malignus	*spiteful*		
superbē	*arrogantly*	subscrībere	*sign*
ratiōnēs . . . subdūcit:		alacriter	*eagerly*
ratiōnēs subdūcere	*draw up accounts, write up accounts*	dēdūcere	*escort*

House of Diana at Ostia, port city at the mouth of the Tiber.

1 At what time of day did these events take place?
2 Where did the girl stand? What puzzled her?
3 Who was seen on the threshold when the door opened? Describe him. What did the clients do when they caught sight of him?
4 Why do you think the herald remained silent at first?
5 How can we tell that all the clients mentioned in line 14 are Roman citizens? How can we tell that none of them is a freedman of Haterius?
6 What is the effect of the word order in lines 18–19 ("ad cēnam . . . Haterius invītat . . . et M. Licinium Prīvātum")?
7 In the herald's announcements, find two examples of small tasks that clients have to perform for their patrons, and one example of a favor granted by patrons to clients.
8 Why do you think the herald scattered the coins among the crowd (line 24) rather than handing the money over in any other way?

II

iānuā tandem clausā, abīre clientēs coepērunt. aliī dēnāriīs collēctīs abiērunt ut cibum sibi suīsque emerent; aliī spē pecūniae dēiectī invītī discessērunt. Haterium praecōnemque vituperābant.

deinde servō puella imperāvit ut iānuam pulsāret. praecōnī   5
regressō servus,

"ecce!" inquit. "domina mea, Euphrosynē, adest."

"abī, sceleste! nēmō alius hodiē admittitur," respondit praecō superbā vōce.

"sed domina mea est philosopha Graeca doctissima," inquit servus. "hūc missa est ā Quīntō Hateriō Chrȳsogonō ipsō, Hateriī   10
lībertō, quī Athēnīs habitat."

"īnsānīvit igitur Chrȳsogonus," respondit praecō. "odiō sunt omnēs philosophī Hateriō! redeundum vōbīs est Athēnās unde missī estis."

servus arrogantiā praecōnis īrātus, nihilōminus perstitit.   15

suīs: suī	*their families*	redeundum vōbīs est	*you must return*
spē . . . dēiectī	*disappointed in their hope*	nihilōminus	*nevertheless*
philosopha	*(female) philosopher*	perstitit: perstāre	*persist*
odiō sunt: odiō esse	*be hateful*		

Quīntō Hateriō Chrȳsogonō: *a Greek-born freedman who returned to Greece*
  Quintus Haterius Chrȳsogonus   *after he was freed by Haterius*
Athēnīs   *in Athens*

"sed Eryllus," inquit, "quī est Hateriō arbiter ēlegantiae, epistulam ad Chrȳsogonum scrīpsit in quā eum rogāvit ut philosopham hūc mitteret. ergō adsumus!" 20

hīs verbīs audītīs, praecō, quī Eryllum haudquāquam amābat, magnā vōce,

"Eryllus!" inquit. "quis est Eryllus? meus dominus Haterius est, nōn Eryllus! abī!" 25

haec locūtus servum in lutum dēpulit, iānuamque clausit. Euphrosynē, simulatque servum humī iacentem vīdit, eius īram lēnīre temptāvit.

"nōlī," inquit, "mentem tuam vexāre. nōs decet rēs adversās aequō animō ferre. nōbīs crās reveniendum est."

arbiter	*expert, judge*	dēpulit: dēpellere	*push down*
ēlegantiae: ēlegantia	*good taste*	mentem: mēns	*mind*
ergō	*therefore*	aequō animō	*calmly, in a calm spirit*

About the Language

1 Study the following pair of sentences:

mīlitēs discessērunt.
The soldiers departed.

urbe captā, mīlitēs discessērunt.
With the city having been captured, *the soldiers departed.*

The phrase in boldface is made up of a noun (**urbe**) and participle (**captā**) in the *ablative* case. Phrases of this kind are known as *ablative absolute* phrases, and are very common in Latin.

2 Ablative absolute phrases can be translated in many different ways. For instance, the example in paragraph 1 might be translated:

When the city had been captured, the soldiers departed.
or, *After the city was captured, the soldiers departed.*

3 Further examples:

1 arcū dēdicātō, cīvēs domum rediērunt.
2 pecūniā āmissā, ancilla lacrimāre coepit.
3 victimīs sacrificātīs, haruspex ōmina nūntiāvit.
4 duce interfectō, hostēs dēspērābant.
5 mercātor, clāmōribus audītīs, ē lectō perterritus surrēxit.
6 senātor, hāc sententiā dictā, cōnsēdit.

4 In each of the examples above, the participle in the ablative absolute phrase is a perfect passive participle. Ablative absolute phrases can also be formed with present participles. For example:

omnibus tacentibus, lībertus nōmina recitāvit.
With everyone being quiet, *the freedman read out the names.*
   or, in more natural English:
When everyone was quiet, *the freedman read out the names.*

Further examples:

1 custōdibus dormientibus, captīvī effūgērunt.
2 pompā per viās prōcēdente, spectātōrēs vehementer plausērunt.
3 Imperātor, sacerdōtibus adstantibus, precēs dīvō Titō obtulit.

Ablative absolute phrases can also be formed with perfect active participles. For example:

dominō ēgressō, servī garrīre coepērunt.
With the master having gone out, *the slaves began to chatter.*

or, in more natural English:

After the master had gone out, *the slaves began to chatter.*

Further examples:

4 mercātōre profectō, rēs dīra accidit.
5 nūntiīs ā Britanniā regressīs, imperātor senātōrēs arcessīvit.
6 cōnsule haec locūtō, omnēs cīvēs attonitī erant.

Emperor Titus, from the Vatican Museum.

Practicing the Language

1 Study the way in which the following verbs are formed, and give the meanings of the untranslated ones:

īre	abīre	circumīre	inīre
go		*go around*	
dūcere	abdūcere	circumdūcere	indūcere
lead			*lead in*
ferre	auferre	circumferre	īnferre
carry, bring	*carry away*		

Give the meaning of each of the following compound verbs:

abicere, āvertere, abesse;
circumstāre, circumvenīre, circumspectāre, circumpōnere;
inesse, inicere, īnsilīre, īnfundere, incurrere, immittere, irrumpere.

2 Complete each sentence with the right word and then translate.

1 multī leōnēs in Āfricā quotannīs . . . . . . (capitur, capiuntur)
2 ecce! ille senex ā latrōnibus . . . . . . (petitur, petuntur)
3 Haterius ā clientibus nunc . . . . . . (salūtātur, salūtantur)
4 mīlitēs in ōrdinēs longōs ā centuriōnibus . . . . . . (īnstruēbātur, īnstruēbantur)
5 oppidum ā barbarīs ferōcibus . . . . . . (oppugnābātur, oppugnābantur)
6 victimae ā sacerdōte . . . . . . (ēligēbātur, ēligēbantur)

3 Complete each sentence with the most suitable word from the list below, and then translate.

portābantur, fraude, vītārent, adeptī, morbō, abēgisset

1 puerī in fossam dēsiluērunt ut perīculum . . . . . .
2 Haterius, ... Salviī dēceptus, cōnsēnsit.
3 multae amphorae in triclīnium . . . . . .
4 senex, ... gravī afflīctus, medicum arcessīvit.
5 praecō, cum Euphrosynēn servumque . . . . ., iānuam clausit.
6 clientēs, sportulam . . . . ., abiērunt.

About the Language

1 In Stage 27, you met examples of indirect commands used with **ut**:

imperāvit nūntiīs ut redīrent.
He ordered the messengers that they should return.
  or, in more natural English:
He ordered the messengers to return.

2 From Stage 29 onwards, you have met examples of indirect commands used with the word **nē**:

imperāvit nūntiīs nē redīrent.
He ordered the messengers that they should not return.
  or, in more natural English:
He ordered the messengers not to return.

Further examples:

1 haruspex iuvenem monuit nē nāvigāret.
2 fēminae mīlitēs ōrāvērunt nē līberōs interficerent.
3 mercātor amīcō persuāsit nē vīllam vēnderet.

3 You have also met sentences in which **nē** is used with a purpose clause:

senex pecūniam cēlāvit nē fūrēs eam invenīrent.
The old man hid the money so that the thieves would not find it.
or, *The old man hid the money lest the thieves should find it.*

Further examples:

1 per viās celeriter contendēbāmus nē tardī ad arcum advenīrēmus.
2 in fossā latēbam nē hostēs mē cōnspicerent.
3 imperātor multum frūmentum ab Aegyptō importāvit nē cīvēs famē perīrent.

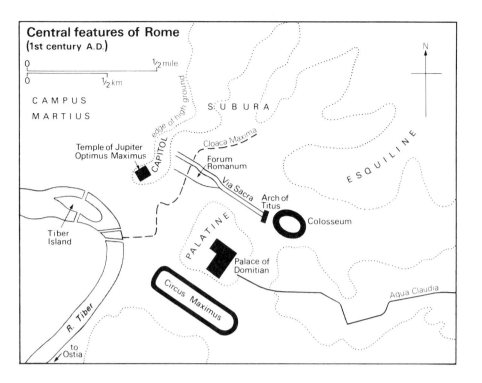

Central features of Rome
(1st century A.D.)

0 .... ½ mile
0 .... ½ km

N

CAMPUS MARTIUS

SUBURA

edge of high ground

Temple of Jupiter Optimus Maximus

CAPITOL

Cloaca Maxima

Forum Romanum

Via Sacra

Arch of Titus

ESQUILINE

Colosseum

Tiber Island

PALATINE

Palace of Domitian

Circus Maximus

R. Tiber

Aqua Claudia

to Ostia

The City of Rome

The city of Rome grew up in a very unplanned and unsystematic way, quite different from the neat grid-pattern of other Roman towns. It was also an extremely crowded city, as can be seen by comparing its approximate area and population with those of two modern metropolitan districts in America and Britain:

	population	*area (sq. miles)*
Los Angeles	2,970,000	465
Greater Manchester	2,595,000	497
Rome (1st century A.D.)	1,000,000 *approx.*	8

The city was bounded on the western side by the river Tiber. Ships brought goods up the Tiber from the coastal port of Ostia to the docks and riverside markets. Further upstream, beyond the wharves and warehouses, the river was divided for a short stretch by the Tiber Island (**īnsula Tiberīna**). This elongated island, shown in the picture on p.187, had been built up to look like a ship sailing the river, complete with an ornamental prow (**rōstrum**); it contained a temple of Aesculapius, the god of healing, to which many invalids came in the hope of a cure.

In the story on p.190, Euphrosyne and her slave disembark near the Tiber Island and then move off northeastwards. Their route could have taken them around the lower slopes of the Capitol and through the forum Romanum (described in Stage 29), passing the Palatine hill where the Emperor Domitian had his palace.

Euphrosyne and the slave would then have continued through the Subura, a densely populated district north of the forum, full of stores and large apartment buildings (**īnsulae**). Its inhabitants were mostly poor and some very poor indeed; they included barbers, shoemakers, butchers, weavers, blacksmiths, vegetable sellers, prostitutes, and thieves. Several Roman writers refer to the Subura, and give a vivid impression of its noise, its dirt, and its crowds. The following passage from Juvenal describes a street which might easily be in the Subura:

Tenements in the Via Biberatica, Rome.

We hurry on, but the way's blocked; there's a tidal wave of people in front, and we're pushed and prodded from behind. One man digs me with his elbow, another with the pole of a sedan-chair; somebody catches me on the head with a plank, and somebody else with a wine-barrel. My legs are plastered with mud, my feet are stepped on by all and sundry, and a soldier is sticking the nail of his boot in my toe.

Many rich and aristocratic Romans settled in the district of the Esquiline hill, which lay to the east of the Subura. Here they could enjoy peace and seclusion in huge mansions, surrounded by colonnaded gardens and landscaped parks which contrasted very sharply with the Subura's slums and crowded tenement blocks. In the stories of Unit 3, Stages 29–34, Haterius' house, where Euphrosyne's journey ended, is imagined as being on the Esquiline.

Among the well known landmarks of Rome were the Circus Maximus (south of the Palatine), where chariot races were held, the Colosseum (see p. 241), which lay between the Esquiline and the eastern end of the Sacred Way, and the Campus Martius on the western side of the city, formerly an army training area, which now provided some much-needed open space for the general population.

Crossing the city in various directions were the aqueducts, which brought water into the city at the rate of 200 million gallons (900 million liters) a day. The houses of the rich citizens were usually connected to this supply by means of pipes which brought water directly into their storage tanks; the poorer people had to collect their fresh water from public fountains on street corners. The city also possessed a very advanced system of drains and sewers: a complicated network of underground channels carried sewage and waste water from the larger private houses, public baths, fountains, and lavatories to the central drain (**Cloāca Maxima**), which emptied into the Tiber.

There were many hazards and discomforts for the inhabitants of Rome. As we have seen in Stage 30 (page 185), fires were frequent and the insulae in the slums were often jerry-built and liable to collapse. The overcrowding and congestion in the streets have already been mentioned above; wheeled traffic was banned from the city center during the hours of daylight, but blockages were still caused by the wagons of builders like Haterius, which were exempt from the ban. Disease was an ever-present danger in the overcrowded poorer quarters; crime and violence were commonplace in the unlit streets at night. Rome was a city of contrasts, in which splendor and squalor were often found side by side; it could be both an exciting and an unpleasant place to live.

Patronage

The story on pages 191–194 shows one aspect of Roman society known as patronage, in which a patron (**patrōnus**) gave help and protection to others less rich or powerful than himself, who performed various services for him in return.

There were many different types of patronage, but all were based on the same principle, namely that the patron gave assistance and received service. If the emperor nominated a senator to be one of the next year's consuls, this would be an example of patronage. A merchant might be introduced by his patron to some useful business contacts; a poet's patron might arrange for the poet to recite his work to an audience, or provide him with money or presents, sometimes on a very generous scale. In each case, the patron would expect not only gratitude but favors in return. A poet, for example, would praise the patron in his poetry; the Romans would regard this not as sickly flattery, but as a normal and proper thing to do.

The letters written by Pliny often give us glimpses of patronage in operation. Once, when Pliny was asked to speak in a case in court, he agreed on condition that a young friend of his, who had plenty of ability but had not yet had any chance to show how good he was, should be allowed to make a speech too. And when Pliny's friend Erucius stood as an election candidate, Pliny wrote to an influential ex-consul (and no doubt to other people too), asking him to support Erucius and persuade others to do the same. Pliny was also a patron of his hometown Comum in north Italy, and of the little town of Tifernum-on-Tiber. He gave generous gifts of buildings and money to both places.

But the commonest type of patronage was the type illustrated on pages 191–194, in which the patron looked after a number of poorer people who depended heavily on him for support, employment or even survival. They were known as clients (**clientēs**). A client was expected to present himself at his patron's house each day for the early morning ceremony of greeting (**salūtātiō**), at which he received a gift known as the **sportula**. In the past, the sportula had consisted of a little basket of food, but by Domitian's time it was normally money; the standard amount was fixed by custom at 6¼ sesterces. A client was expected to dress formally in a toga for the salutatio. He also had to address his patron as "**domine**";

the poet Martial complains that when he once forgot to do this, the patron punished him by giving him no sportula.

In addition to the sportula, the client might receive help of other kinds from his patron. His patron might advise him if he was in trouble, give him occasional presents, perhaps find him employment, or speak on his behalf in court. Once in a while, clients might be invited to dinner at their patron's house. At these dinners, as we know from the angry comments of several Roman writers, some patrons served two different qualities of food and wine: a superior quality for themselves and their close friends, and a poor one for the clients. Some patrons did this to save money, others to make it clear that they regarded their clients as inferiors.

In return for his help a patron would expect his clients not only to attend the salutatio, but also to perform various tasks and errands for him. For example, he might require some of them to escort him when he went to the forum on official business, or to witness the signing of a legal document, or to lead the applause if he made a public speech in court or elsewhere, or to help him at election time. It seems likely that for many clients their duties were not difficult, but could be boring and time-consuming.

Both patrons and clients had something to gain from the system. The government did not provide any state assistance or relief for the poor, apart from distributions of free grain or occasionally money, and so a patron might be a client's chief means of support. The main advantage for the patron was that he was able to call on the services of his clients when he needed them; and to have a large number of clients was good for his prestige and status.

One special type of patron—client relationship (which we shall see more of in Stage 34) should be mentioned: the relationship between an ex-master and his former slave. When a slave was set free, he automatically became a client of his ex-master, and his ex-master became his patron. The word **patrōnus** is sometimes used with the meaning *ex-master* as well as the meaning *patron*.

One man could be the patron of another who in turn was the patron of somebody else. The following diagram shows how several people could be linked by patronage:

EMPEROR nominates SALVIUS to an important priesthood
↓
SALVIUS obtains building contract for HATERIUS
↓
HATERIUS orders distribution of sportula to CLIENTS

The emperor has no patron. He is the most powerful patron of all.

Words and Phrases Checklist

altus, alta, altum	*high, deep*
angustus, angusta, angustum	*narrow*
ante	*before, in front of*
catēna, catēnae	*chain*
cliēns, clientis	*client*
dux, ducis	*leader*
favor, favōris	*favor*
fraus, fraudis	*trick*
haudquāquam	*not at all*
īdem, eadem, idem	*the same*
mōs, mōris	*custom*
neglegō, neglegere, neglēxī, neglēctus	*neglect*
ōrō, ōrāre, ōrāvī	*beg*
patrōnus, patrōnī	*patron*
praecō, praecōnis	*herald*
praetereō, praeterīre, praeteriī	*pass by, go past*
prōgressus, prōgressa, prōgressum	*having advanced*
pūblicus, pūblica, pūblicum	*public*
ratiōnēs, ratiōnum	*accounts*
reficiō, reficere, refēcī, refectus	*repair*
secō, secāre, secuī, sectus	*cut*
serēnus, serēna, serēnum	*calm, clear*
spērō, spērāre, spērāvī	*hope, expect*
superbus, superba, superbum	*arrogant, proud*
tempus, temporis	*time*
ubīque	*everywhere*
vehō, vehere, vexī, vectus	*carry*
vinciō, vincīre, vīnxī, vīnctus	*bind, tie up*
volvō, volvere, volvī, volūtus	*turn*
in animō volvere	*wonder, turn over in the mind*
vultus, vultūs	*expression, face*

Word Search

altitude, concatenate, extemporaneous, fraudulent, patronize, progressive, ubiquitous

1 . . . . .: found everywhere, omnipresent
2 . . . . .: to support; to go to regularly as a customer
3 . . . . .: elevation
4 . . . . .: impromptu
5 . . . . .: favoring reform; liberal
6 . . . . .: deceitful, false
7 . . . . .: to connect or link in a series

Stage 32

Euphrosynē

Euphrosynē revocāta

postrīdiē Eyphrosynē domum
Hateriī regressa est. iterum tamen
praecō eam verbīs dūrīs abēgit.

servus eam hortātus est ut praecōnem
dōnīs corrumperet; sed Euphrosynē   5
ab eiusmodī ambitiōne abhorruit.

septem continuōs diēs ā praecōne
abācta, Euphrosynē dēnique in
Graeciam redīre cōnstituit. hōc
cōnsiliō captō, ad flūmen Tiberim   10
ut nāvem cōnscenderet profecta est.

eōdem diē quō Euphrosynē discēdere
cōnstituit, celebrābat Haterius diem
nātālem. grātulātiōnibus clientium
acceptīs, ōtiōsus in hortō sedēbat, in   15
umbrā ingentis laurī. subitō Eryllus
hortum ingressus est.

revocāta: revocāre	*recall, call back*	abācta: abigere	*drive away*
regressa est	*returned*	profecta est	*set out*
hortātus est	*urged*	laurī: laurus	*laurel tree*
eiusmodī	*of that kind*	ingressus est	*entered*
ambitiōne: ambitiō	*bribery, corruption*		

Eryllus:	domine! omnia quae mandāvistī parāta sunt. centum amīcī et clientēs ad cēnam invītātī sunt. iussī coquum cibum sūmptuōsum parāre, cellāriumque vīnum Falernum veterrimum dēprōmere. nihil neglēctum est.	20
Haterius:	nōnne petauristāriōs condūxistī? hercle! quam mē dēlectant petauristāriī!	
Eryllus:	quid dīcis, domine? hominēs eiusmodī cīvibus urbānīs nōn placent. nunc philosophīs favet optimus quisque.	25
Haterius:	īnsānīs, Erylle! nam philosophī sunt senēs sevērī. neque saltāre neque circulōs trānsilīre possunt.	
Eryllus:	at domine, aliquid melius quam philosophum adeptus sum. mē enim auctōre, philosopha quaedam, puella pulcherrima, hūc invītāta est. ā Chrȳsogonō Athēnīs missa est.	30
Haterius:	philosopham mīsit Chrȳsogonus? optimē fēcistī, Erylle! philosopham nē Imperātor quidem habet. sed ubi est haec philosopha quam adeptus es?	35
Eryllus:	iamdūdum eam anxius exspectō. fortasse iste praecō, homō summae stultitiae, eam nōn admīsit.	
Haterius:	arcesse hūc praecōnem!	

ubi praecō ingressus est, Haterius rogāvit utrum philosopham
abēgisset necne. poenās maximās eī minātus est. praecō, verbīs   40
dominī perterritus, palluit; tōtā rē nārrātā, veniam ōrāvit.

praecō:	domine, ignōsce mihi! nesciēbam quantum tū philosophīs favērēs. illa philosopha, quam ignārus abēgī, ad flūmen profecta est ut nāvem cōnscenderet.	
Haterius:	abī statim, caudex! festīnā ad Tiberim! nōlī umquam revenīre nisi cum philosophā!	45

domō ēgressus, praecō per viās contendit. ad flūmen cum
advēnisset, Euphrosynēn in nāvem cōnscēnsūram cōnspexit.
magnā vōce eam appellāvit. Euphrosynē, nōmine audītō, conversa
est.   50

praecō:	ignōsce mihi, Euphrosynē doctissima! nōlī discēdere! necesse est tibi domum Hateriī mēcum prōcēdere.	
Euphrosynē:	cūr mē revocās? odiō sunt omnēs philosophī Hateriō, ut tū ipse dīxistī. Athēnās igitur nunc redeō. valē!	

deinde praecō, effūsīs lacrimīs, eam identidem ōrāvit nē discēderet.   55 diū Euphrosynē perstitit; dēnique, precibus lacrimīsque eius permōta, domum Hateriī regressa est.

veterrimum: vetus	*old*	mē . . . auctōre	*at my suggestion*
dēprōmere	*bring out*	quaedam: quīdam	*a certain*
petauristāriōs:		iamdūdum	*for a long time*
petauristārius	*acrobat*	utrum . . . necne	*whether . . . or not*
optimus quisque	*all the best people*	minātus est	*threatened*
sevērī: sevērus	*severe, strict*	ignōsce: ignōscere	*forgive*
circulōs: circulus	*hoop*	cōnscēnsūram:	
trānsilīre	*jump through*	cōnscēnsūrus	*about to go on board*
at	*but*	effūsīs lacrimīs	*bursting into tears*
adeptus sum	*I have obtained*		

Euphrosynēn	*Greek accusative of* Euphrosynē
vīnum Falernum	*a famous wine from an area in Campania, south of Rome*

cēna Hateriī

nōnā hōrā amīcī clientēsque, quōs Haterius invītāverat ut sēcum diem nātālem celebrārent, triclīnium ingrediēbantur. inter eōs aderant fīliī lībertōrum quī humilī locō nātī magnās opēs adeptī erant. aderant quoque nōnnūllī senātōrēs quī inopiā oppressī favōrem Hateriī conciliāre cōnābantur. 5

proximus Haterium recumbēbat T. Flāvius Sabīnus cōnsul, vir summae auctōritātis. Haterius blandīs et mollibus verbīs Sabīnum adloquēbātur, ut favōrem eius conciliāret. ipse in prīmō locō recumbēbat. pulvīnīs Tyriīs innītēbātur; ānulōs gerēbat aureōs quī gemmīs fulgēbant; dentēs spīnā argenteā perfodiēbat. 10

intereā duo Aethiopes triclīnium ingrediēbantur. lancem

ingrediēbantur	*were entering*
inopiā: inopia	*poverty*
cōnābantur	*were trying*
proximus	*next to*
adloquēbātur	*was addressing*
pulvīnīs: pulvīnus	*cushion*
innītēbātur	*was leaning, was resting*
spīnā: spīna	*toothpick*
perfodiēbat:	
perfodere	*pick*
lancem: lānx	*dish*

Tyriīs: Tyrius *Tyrian (colored with dye from city of Tyre)*

ingentem ferēbant, in quā positus erat aper tōtus. statim coquus,
quī Aethiopas in triclīnium secūtus erat, ad lancem prōgressus est
ut aprum scinderet. aprō perītē scissō, multae avēs statim
ēvolāvērunt suāviter pīpiantēs. convīvae, cum vīdissent quid   15
coquus parāvisset, eius artem vehementer laudāvērunt. quā rē
dēlectātus, Haterius servīs imperāvit ut amphorās vīnī Falernī
īnferrent. amphorīs inlātīs, cellārius titulōs quī īnfīxī erant magnā
vōce recitāvit, "Falernum Hateriānum, vīnum centum annōrum!"
tum vīnum in pōcula servī īnfundere coepērunt.   20

convīvīs laetissimē bibentibus, poposcit Haterius silentium.
spectāculum novum pollicitus est. omnēs convīvae in animō
volvēbant quāle spectāculum Haterius ēditūrus esset. ille rīdēns
digitīs concrepuit. hōc signō datō, Eryllus ē triclīniō ēgressus est.

appāruērunt in līmine duo tubicinēs. tubās vehementer   25
īnflāvērunt. tum Eryllus Euphrosynēn in triclīnium dūxit.
convīvae, simulatque eam vīdērunt, fōrmam eius valdē admīrātī
sunt.

Haterius rīdēns Euphrosynēn rogāvit ut sēcum in lectō
cōnsīderet. deinde convīvās adlocūtus est.   30

"haec puella," inquit glōriāns, "est philosopha doctissima,

---

nōmine Euphrosynē. iussū meō hūc vēnit Athēnīs, ubi habitant
philosophī nōtissimī. illa nōbīs dīligenter audienda est."

tum ad eam versus,

"nōbīs placet, mea Euphrosynē," inquit, "ā tē aliquid 35
philosophiae discere."

scinderet: scindere	*carve, cut open*	ēditūrus	*going to put on, going*
pīpiantēs: pīpiāre	*chirp*		*to present*
convīvae: convīva	*guest*	digitīs: digitus	*finger*
titulōs: titulus	*label*	concrepuit: concrepāre	*snap*
īnfīxī erant: īnfīgere	*fasten onto*	fōrmam: fōrma	*beauty, appearance*
īnfundere	*pour into*	admīrātī sunt	*admired*
pollicitus est	*promised*	adlocūtus est	*addressed*
		glōriāns	*boasting, boastfully*

About the Language

1 Study the following examples:

clientēs pecūniam rapere **cōnābantur**.   *The clients were trying to grab the money.*

praecō tandem **locūtus est**.   *At last the herald spoke.*

Notice the forms and meanings of the words in boldface. Each verb has
a *passive ending* (**-bantur**, **-tus est**) but an *active meaning* (*they were trying*,
he spoke). Verbs of this kind are known as *deponent* verbs.

2 Study the following forms of two common deponent verbs:

PRESENT

cōnātur	*he tries*	loquitur	*he speaks*
cōnantur	*they try*	loquuntur	*they speak*

IMPERFECT

cōnābātur	*he was trying*	loquēbātur	*he was speaking*
cōnābantur	*they were trying*	loquēbantur	*they were speaking*

PERFECT

cōnātus est	*he (has) tried*	locūtus est	*he spoke, he has spoken*
cōnātī sunt	*they (have) tried*	locūtī sunt	*they spoke, they have spoken*

PLUPERFECT

cōnātus erat	*he had tried*	locūtus erat	*he had spoken*
cōnātī erant	*they had tried*	locūtī erant	*they had spoken*

3 Further examples:

1 spectātōrēs dē arcū novō loquēbantur.
2 captīvus effugere cōnātus est.
3 sacerdōs ē templō ēgrediēbātur.
4 fabrī puellam cōnspicātī sunt.
5 sequēbantur; ingressus est; precātur; regrediuntur;
profectī erant; suspicātus erat.

4 You have already met the *perfect participles* of several deponent verbs.
For example:

adeptus   *having obtained*
hortātus   *having encouraged*
regressus   *having returned*

Compare them with the perfect participles of some ordinary verbs (i.e.
verbs which are not deponent):

DEPONENT		ORDINARY	
adeptus	*having obtained*	dēceptus	*having been deceived*
hortātus	*having encouraged*	laudātus	*having been praised*
regressus	*having returned*	missus	*having been sent*

Notice that the perfect participle of a deponent verb has an *active*
meaning; the perfect participle of an ordinary verb has a *passive*
meaning.

5 Further examples of perfect participles of deponent and ordinary
verbs:

DEPONENT	ORDINARY
cōnspicātus	portātus
ingressus	iussus
profectus	afflīctus
locūtus	audītus
cōnātus	vulnerātus

**A pastoral scene from Pompeii,
showing a shepherd with his
animals among religious shrines.**

When you have read this story, answer the two questions at the end.

philosophia

Euphrosynē convīvās, quī avidē spectābant, sīc adlocūta est:

"prīmum, fābula brevis mihi nārranda est. ōlim fuit homō pauper."

"quid est pauper?" rogāvit cōnsul Sabīnus, quī mīlle servōs habēbat.   5

quibus verbīs audītīs, omnēs plausērunt, iocō dēlectātī. Euphrosynē autem, convīvīs tandem silentibus,

"hic pauper," inquit, "fundum parvum, uxōrem optimam, līberōs cārissimōs habēbat. strēnuē in fundō labōrāre solēbat ut sibi suīsque cibum praebēret."   10

"scīlicet īnsānus erat," exclāmāvit Apollōnius, quī erat homō ignāvissimus. "nēmō nisi īnsānus labōrat."

cui respondit Euphrosynē vōce serēnā,

"omnibus autem labōrandum est. etiam eī quī spē favōris cēnās magistrātibus dant, rē vērā labōrant."   15

philosophia	*philosophy*	scīlicet	*obviously*
suīs: suī	*his family*	rē vērā	*in fact, truly*

quō audītō, Haterius ērubuit; cēterī, verbīs Euphrosynēs obstupefactī, tacēbant. deinde Euphrosynē,

"pauper," inquit, "neque dīvitiās neque honōrēs cupiēbat. numquam nimium edēbat nec nimium bibēbat. in omnibus vītae partibus moderātus ac temperāns esse cōnābātur."   20

L. Baebius Crispus senātor exclāmāvit,

"scīlicet avārus erat! nōn laudandus est nōbīs sed culpandus. Haterius noster tamen maximē laudandus est quod amīcīs sūmptuōsās cēnās semper praebet."

huic Baebiī sententiae omnēs plausērunt. Haterius, plausū   25
audītō, oblītus philosophiae servīs imperāvit ut plūs vīnī convīvīs offerrent. Euphrosynē tamen haec addidit,

"at pauper multōs cāsūs passus est. līberōs enim et uxōrem āmīsit, ubi afflīxit eōs morbus gravissimus; fundum āmīsit, ubi mīlitēs eum dīripuērunt; lībertātem āmīsit, ubi ipse in servitūtem ā   30
mīlitibus vēnditus est. nihilōminus, quia Stōicus erat, rēs adversās semper aequō animō patiēbātur; neque deōs neque hominēs dētestābātur. dēnique senectūte labōribusque cōnfectus, tranquillē mortuus est. ille pauper, quem hominēs miserrimum exīstimābant, rē vērā fēlīx erat."   35

Haterius cachinnāns "num fēlīcem eum exīstimās," inquit, "quī tot cāsūs passus est?"

Hateriō hoc rogantī respondit Euphrosynē,

"id quod locūta sum nōn rēctē intellegis. alia igitur fābula mihi nārranda est. ōlim fuit homō dīves."   40

sed cōnsul Sabīnus, quem iam taedēbat fābulārum, exclāmāvit,

"satis philosophiae! age, mea Euphrosynē, dā mihi ōsculum, immo ōscula multa."

Rabīrius Maximus tamen, quī cum haec audīvisset ēbrius surrēxit,   45

"sceleste," inquit, "nōlī eam tangere!"

haec locūtus, pōculum vīnō plēnum in ōs Sabīnī iniēcit.

statim rēs ad pugnam vēnit. pōcula iaciēbantur; lectī ēvertēbantur; togae scindēbantur. aliī Sabīnō, aliī Rabīriō subveniēbant. Haterius hūc illūc currēbat; discordiam compōnere   50
cōnābātur. eum tamen currentem atque ōrantem nēmō animadvertit.

Euphrosynē autem, ad iānuam triclīniī vultū serēnō prōgressa, convīvās pugnantēs ita adlocūta est:

"ēn Rōmānī, dominī orbis terrārum, ventris Venerisque servī!"   55

---

quibus verbīs dictīs, ad flūmen Tiberim ut nāvem quaereret profecta est.

edēbat: edere	*eat*	exīstimābant:	
moderātus	*restrained, moderate*	exīstimāre	*think, consider*
temperāns	*temperate, self-controlled*	rēctē	*rightly, properly*
culpandus: culpāre	*blame*	immo	*or rather*
plausū: plausus	*applause*	compōnere	*settle*
cāsūs: cāsus	*misfortune*	animadvertit:	
patiēbātur	*suffered, endured*	animadvertere	*notice, take notice of*
senectūte: senectūs	*old age*	orbis terrārum	*world*
tranquillē	*peacefully*		

Euphrosynēs   *Greek genitive of* Euphrosynē
Stōicus   *Stoic (believer in Stoic philosophy)*
Veneris: Venus   *Venus (Roman goddess of love)*

1   Why was Euphrosyne's philosophy lecture a failure?
2   Look again at Euphrosyne's remark "ille pauper . . . rē vērā fēlīx erat" (lines 34–5). Was Haterius right to suggest that this is a stupid remark? Or does it have some point?

About the Language

1   In Stage 26, you met the gerundive used in sentences like this:

mihi currendum est.   *I must run.*

2   In Stage 32, you have met more sentences containing gerundives. For example:

mihi fābula nārranda est.   *I must tell a story.*

Compare this with another way of expressing the same idea:

necesse est mihi fābulam nārrāre.

3   Further examples:

   1   mihi epistula scrībenda est.
      (Compare: necesse est mihi epistulam scrībere.)
   2   tibi testāmentum faciendum est.
   3   nōbīs Haterius vīsitandus est.
   4   coquō cēna paranda est.
   5   tibi fidēs servanda est.

Practicing the Language

1 Study the forms and meanings of the following verbs and nouns, and give the meanings of the untranslated words:

advenīre	*arrive*	adventus	*arrival*
movēre	*move*	mōtus	*movement*
plaudere	*applaud*	plausus	
metuere	*be afraid*	metus	
cōnspicere		cōnspectus	*sight*
monēre		monitus	*warning*
rīdēre		rīsus	
gemere		gemitus	

Give the meaning of each of the following nouns:

reditus, sonitus, cantus, cōnsēnsus

2 Make up five Latin sentences using some of the words listed below. Write out each sentence and then translate it. Include at least one sentence which does not contain a nominative.

A genitive usually follows the noun it refers to. For example:

amīcī rēgis equum invēnērunt.   *The friends of the king found the horse.*
amīcī equum rēgis invēnērunt.   *The friends found the king's horse.*

NOMINATIVES	ACCUSATIVES	GENITIVES	VERBS
uxor	domōs	puerōrum	invēnit
servus	nāvēs	rēgis	invēnērunt
fīliī	equum	agricolae	custōdiēbat
clientēs	pecūniam	mīlitum	custōdiēbant
lībertus	librum	fēminārum	dēlēbat
amīcī	gemmās	captīvī	dēlēbant
hostēs	corpus	haruspicis	abstulit
dux	pontem	populī Rōmānī	abstulērunt

3 With the help of paragraphs 1 and 2 on page 265 of the Review Grammar, complete each sentence by describing the word in boldface with the correct form of the adjective in parentheses, and then translate.

For example: clientēs **patrōnum** . . . . . laudāvērunt. (līberālis)
Answer: clientēs patrōnum līberālem laudāvērunt.
               The clients praised their generous patron.

The gender of the word in boldface is given after each sentence.

1 nautae **nāvem** . . . . . comparāvērunt. (optimus) (f.)
2 coquus īram **dominī** . . . . . timēbat. (crūdēlis) (m.)
3 mercātor, **itinere** . . . . . dēfessus, in rīpā flūminis cōnsēdit.
(longus) (n.)
4 senex testāmentum **amīcō** . . . . . mandāvit. (fidēlis) (m.)
5 centuriō verba **uxōris** . . . . . neglēxit. (īrātus) (f.)
6 **saxa** . . . . . ad arcum ā fabrīs trahēbantur. (gravis) (n.)
7 subitō vōcēs **mīlitum** . . . . . audīvimus. (īnfestus) (m.)
8 Euphrosynē **convīvīs** . . . . . statim respondit. (īnsolēns) (m.)

4 In each pair of sentences, translate sentence *a*; then change it from a
direct command to an indirect command by completing sentence *b*
with an imperfect subjunctive, and translate again.

For example: a pontem incende!
                       b centuriō mīlitī imperāvit ut pontem incender... .
Translated and completed, this becomes:
   a pontem incende! *Burn the bridge down!*
   b centuriō mīlitī imperāvit ut pontem incenderet.
   The centurion ordered the soldier to burn the bridge down.

The forms of the imperfect subjunctive are given on page 279 of the
Review Grammar.

1a pecūniam cēlāte!
1b mercātor amīcōs monuit ut pecūniam cēlār... .
2a arcum mihi ostende!
2b puer patrem ōrāvit ut arcum sibi ostender... .
3a iānuam aperīte!
3b imperātor nōbīs imperāvit ut iānuam aperīr... .
4a nōlīte redīre!
4b fēmina barbarīs persuāsit nē redīr... .

In sentences 5 and 6, turn the direct command into an indirect
command by adding the necessary words to sentence b:

5a cēnam optimam parāte!
5b dominus servīs imperāvit ut . . . .
6a epistulam scrībe!
6b frāter mihi persuāsit . . . .

About the Language

1 Study the following examples:

nunc ego quoque **moritūrus** sum.
Now I, too, am about to die.

nēmō sciēbat quid Haterius **factūrus** esset.
Nobody knew what Haterius was going to do.

praecō puellam vīdit, nāvem **cōnscēnsūram**.
The herald saw the girl about to go on board ship.

The words in boldface are *future participles*.

2 Further examples:

1 nunc ego vōbīs cēnam splendidam datūrus sum.
2 mīlitēs in animō volvēbant quid centuriō dictūrus esset.
3 convīvae Haterium rogāvērunt num Euphrosynē saltātūra esset.

3 Compare the future participle with the perfect passive participle:

PERFECT PASSIVE PARTICIPLE	FUTURE PARTICIPLE
portātus *having been carried*	portātūrus *about to carry*
doctus *having been taught*	doctūrus *about to teach*
tractus *having been dragged*	tractūrus *about to drag*
audītus *having been heard*	audītūrus *about to hear*

Roman Society

The diagram opposite shows one way of dividing up Roman society. At the top of the pyramid is the emperor. Below him are the men of the senatorial class. Membership in this group was by inheritance (in other words, members' sons were automatically qualified to become members themselves); membership could also be given to an individual by the

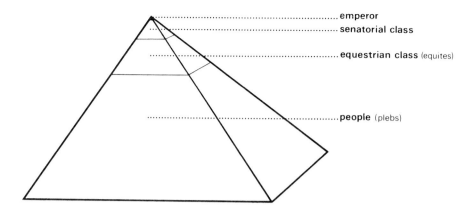

emperor as a special privilege. A man who was in the senatorial class had the opportunity to follow a political career which could lead (if he was good enough) to high positions such as the command of a legion, the consulship, or the governorship of a province. Both Agricola and Salvius are examples of men who reached high positions of this kind.

Members of the senatorial class also possessed various privileges to emphasize their status: they wore a broad purple stripe on their tunics, sat in special places reserved for them at public ceremonies and entertainments, and were eligible for certain priesthoods and similar honors. To retain their membership, however, men of the senatorial class had to possess 1,000,000 sesterces in money or property. It occasionally happened that a senatorial family's wealth dropped below the 1,000,000-sesterce line. When this happened, the members of the family, like the senators at the party on page 209, were in danger of being expelled from the senatorial class by the **censors**, who had the job of periodically bringing the membership list up to date.

Below the senatorial class are the men of equestrian class or **equitēs**. The qualification for membership of this class was 400,000 sesterces. The equites could follow a career in government if they wished, at a rather humbler level than the senatorial career; they might, for example, command an auxiliary unit in the army or supervise a province's financial affairs. If they were exceptionally able or lucky, they might rise to the highest positions in an equestrian career, such as the command of the praetorian guard or the governorship of Egypt. Signs of equestrian status included the wearing of a special gold ring, and a narrow stripe on the tunic. A number of equites, like Haterius in the stories in Unit 3, Stages 29–34, were extremely rich—richer in fact than many senators. Some were offered promotion by the emperor into the senatorial class, though not all of them chose to accept.

Below the equites are the ordinary people, or **plēbs**. As the diagram indicates, they formed the great mass of the Roman population. Some of them earned a reasonably comfortable living as craftsmen or storekeepers, or ran small businesses. Many depended on casual and irregular employment (as porters, for example, or as temporary laborers on building sites). Others lived in extreme poverty, with nothing to save them from starvation except the help of their patron or the public distribution of free grain made by the emperor's officials to Roman citizens. In general, the plebs were entirely excluded from positions of power and prestige. A few, however, through hard work or luck or their patron's assistance, succeeded in becoming equites or even (more rarely) reaching the senatorial class.

Astrology, Philosophy, and Other Beliefs

Many Romans were contented with the official state religion and its rituals of prayer, divination, and sacrifice, described in Stage 23. Some, however, found greater satisfaction in other forms of belief, including astrology, philosophy, and foreign cults. Many took part in both the state religion and some other kind of worship, without feeling that there was any conflict between the two.

One popular form of belief, which you met in Unit 2, was astrology. Astrologers claimed that the events in a person's life were controlled by the stars, and that it was possible to forecast the future by studying the positions and movements of stars and planets. The position of the stars at the time of a person's birth was known as a horoscope and regarded as particularly important. Astrology was officially disapproved of, especially if people used it to try to find out when their relatives or acquaintances were going to die, and from time to time all astrologers were banished from Rome. (They were always back again within a few months.) In particular, it was a serious offense to inquire about the horoscope of the emperor. Several emperors, however, were themselves firm believers in astrology and kept private astrologers of their own.

A few Romans, especially those who had come into contact with Greek ideas through education or travel, became interested in philosophy.

Philosophy was concerned with such questions as: "What is the world made of?" "What happens to us after we die?" "What is the right way to live?" In particular, a number of Romans were attracted by the philosophy of Stoicism. Stoics believed, like Euphrosyne in the story on pp. 213–215, that a man's aim in life should be Virtue (right behavior) rather than Pleasure. The philosopher Seneca, who taught the Emperor Nero, wrote: "Virtue stands tall and high like a king, invincible and untiring; Pleasure crawls and grovels like a beggar, weak and feeble. Virtue is found in temples, in the forum and the senate-house, defending the city walls, covered in dust, burnt by the sun, with hands hardened by toil; Pleasure is found skulking in the shadows, lurking in baths and brothels and places which fear the police, soft, flabby and gutless, soaked in scent and wine, with a face pale or painted with cosmetics."

At the time of the stories in Stage 32, the most important Stoic philosopher in Rome was a Greek named Epictetus. Epictetus had formerly been a slave; the lameness from which he suffered was said to have been caused by brutal treatment at the hands of his master (the Emperor's freedman, Epaphroditus). While still a slave, Epictetus was allowed to attend philosophy lectures, and when he was freed he became a philosophy teacher himself and attracted large audiences.

Stoics tended to disapprove of one-man rule, and to prefer the idea of a republic. They did not think supreme political power should be passed on by inheritance from one ruler to the next, and they thought a ruler should aim to benefit all his subjects, not just a few. As a result of this, at various times during the first century, a number of Roman Stoics challenged the power of the emperor, opposed him in the Senate, or even

Relief of Mithras killing the bull, surrounded by the signs of the zodiac.

plotted to kill him. Their efforts were unsuccessful, and they were punished by exile or death.

Some Romans became followers of foreign cults, especially those that involved dramatic initiation ceremonies or offered hope of life after death. One such cult was the religion of Isis, whose ritual was described in Stage 19. Another was Mithraism, or Mithras-worship. Mithras was a god of light and truth, who triumphed over the forces of evil, and promised life after death to his followers. His powers were summed up in the story of his chief exploit: the capture and killing of a mighty bull, whose blood had the power to give new life. There were seven grades of initiation into Mithraism, each with its own secret ceremony, involving tests and ordeals of various kinds. Lying in a pit formed part of one ceremony; branding may have formed part of another. Mithraism expected high standards of conduct from its followers; it laid great stress on courage and loyalty, and became popular in the army. Nevertheless, it was a rather expensive and exclusive religion; those who were initiated seem to have been mainly army officers (rather than ordinary legionaries) or wealthy businessmen. A number of Mithraic temples have been discovered, including one in London and another at Carrawburgh in Northumberland in northeast England, close to Hadrian's Wall.

Isis-worship and Mithraism both came to Rome from the east, Isis-worship from Egypt and Mithraism from Persia. From the east, too, came Christianity, which was at first disliked by the Romans and at times was fiercely attacked, but eventually became the official religion of the Roman empire. It will be described more fully in Stage 33.

Words and Phrases Checklist

addō, addere, addidī, additus	*add*
adversus, adversa, adversum	*hostile, unfavorable*
rēs adversae	*misfortune*
aequus, aequa, aequum	*fair, calm*
aequō animō	*calmly, in a calm spirit*
appellō, appellāre, appellāvī, appellātus	*call, call out to*
avis, avis	*bird*
cāsus, cāsūs	*misfortune*
compōnō, compōnere, composuī, compositus	*put together, arrange, settle*
cōnātus, cōnāta, cōnātum	*having tried*
condūcō, condūcere, condūxī, conductus	*hire*
convertō, convertere, convertī, conversus	*turn*
effundō, effundere, effūdī, effūsus	*pour out*
identidem	*repeatedly*
ignōscō, ignōscere, ignōvī	*forgive*
labor, labōris	*work*
lībertās, lībertātis	*freedom*
nē . . . quidem	*not even*
nihilōminus	*nevertheless*
opprimō, opprimere, oppressī, oppressus	*crush*
ōtiōsus, ōtiōsa, ōtiōsum	*at leisure, idle, on holiday, on vacation*
pauper, *gen.* pauperis	*poor*
permōtus, permōta, permōtum	*alarmed, disturbed*
profectus, profecta, profectum	*having set out*
quia	*because*
quīdam, quaedam, quoddam	*one, a certain*
scindō, scindere, scidī, scissus	*tear, tear up, cut up*
secūtus, secūta, secūtum	*having followed*
strēnuē	*hard, energetically*
subveniō, subvenīre, subvēnī	*help, come to help*
sūmptuōsus, sūmptuōsa, sūmptuōsum	*expensive, lavish, costly*
vērus, vēra, vērum	*true, real*
rē vērā	*in fact, truly, really*

Word Search

adversary, appellation, aviation, casualty, consecutive, conversely, effusive

1 . . . . .: an opponent
2 . . . . .: successive, occurring in series
3 . . . . .: on the contrary; the other way around
4 . . . . .: an unfortunate accident, especially one involving loss of life
5 . . . . .: unrestrained in emotional expression; gushy
6 . . . . .: the operation of aircraft
7 . . . . .: a name or title

Mosaic of two theatrical masks, from Musei Capitolini, Rome.

Stage 33

pantomīmus

praecō prīmus: fābula! fābula optima!
Paris, pantomīmus nōtissimus, in theātrō crās
fābulam aget.
Myropnous, tībīcen perītissimus, tībiīs cantābit.

praecō secundus: lūdī! lūdī magnificī!
duodecim aurīgae in Circō Maximō crās
certābunt.
Imperātor ipse victōrī praemium dabit.

praecō tertius: spectāculum! spectāculum splendidum!
quīnquāgintā gladiātōrēs in amphitheātrō Flāviō
crās pugnābunt.
multus sanguis fluet.

Tychicus

in hortō Hateriī, fābula agēbātur. Paris, pantomīmus nōtissimus,
mortem rēgīnae Dīdōnis imitābātur. aderant multī spectātōrēs quī
ad fābulam ā Vitelliā, uxōre Hateriī, invītātī erant. Haterius ipse
nōn aderat. labōribus cōnfectus atque spē sacerdōtiī dēiectus, ad
vīllam rūsticam abierat ut quiēsceret. 5

Paris mōtibus ēlegantissimīs aptissimīsque dolōrem rēgīnae
morientis imitābātur. cum dēnique quasi mortuus prōcubuisset,
omnēs spectātōrēs admīrātiōne affectī identidem plaudēbant. aliī
flōrēs iactābant; aliī Paridem deum appellābant. surrēxit Paris ut
plausum spectātōrum exciperet. 10

pantomīmus   *pantomime actor, dancer*   mōtibus: mōtus *movement*
imitābātur   *was imitating, was miming*   quasi   *as if*

Dīdōnis: Dīdō *queen of Carthage and lover of Aeneas in Vergil's epic poem, the Aeneid*

sed priusquam ille plūra ageret, vir quīdam statūrā brevī vultūque sevērō prōgressus magnā vōce silentium poposcit. oculīs in eum statim conversīs, spectātōrēs quis esset et quid vellet rogābant. paucī eum agnōvērunt. Iūdaeus erat, Tychicus nōmine, cliēns T. Flāviī Clēmentis. Paris ipse fābulā interruptā adeō 15 obstupefactus est ut stāret immōtus. omnīnō ignōrābat quid Tychicus factūrus esset.

"audīte, ō scelestī!" clāmāvit Tychicus. "vōs prāvī hunc hominem tamquam deum adōrātis. sunt tamen nūllī deī praeter ūnum! ūnus Deus sōlus adōrandus est! hunc Deum quem plērīque 20 vestrum ignōrant, oportet mē nunc vōbīs dēclārāre."

mussitāre coepērunt spectātōrēs. aliī rogāvērunt utrum Tychicus iocōs faceret an īnsānīret; aliī servōs arcessīvērunt quī eum ex hortō ēicerent. Tychicus autem perstitit.

"Deus, ut prophētae nostrī nōbīs praedīxērunt, homō factus est et 25 inter nōs habitāvit. aegrōs sānāvit; evangelium prōnūntiāvit; vītam aeternam nōbīs pollicitus est. tum in cruce suffīxus, mortuus est et in sepulcrō positus est. sed tertiō diē resurrēxit et vīvus ā discipulīs suīs vīsus est. deinde in caelum ascendit, ubi et nunc rēgnat et in perpetuum rēgnābit." 30

dum haec Tychicus dēclārat, servī Vitelliae signō datō eum comprehendērunt. domō eum trahēbant magnā vōce clāmantem:

"mox Dominus noster, rēx glōriae, ad nōs reveniet; ē caelō dēscendet cum sonitū tubārum, magnō numerō angelōrum comitante. et vīvōs et mortuōs iūdicābit. nōs Chrīstiānī, sī vītam pūram vīxerimus et eī crēdiderimus, ad caelum ascendēmus. ibi semper cum Dominō erimus. tū autem, Paris, fīlius diabolī, nisi vitiīs tuīs dēsīteris, poenās dabis. nūlla erit fuga. nam flammae, ē caelō missae, tē et omnēs scelestōs dēvorābunt."

35

quae cum prōnūntiāvisset, Tychicus multīs verberibus acceptīs domō ēiectus est. spectātōrum plūrimī eum vehementer dērīdēbant; paucī tamen, praesertim servī ac lībertī, tacēbant, quod Chrīstiānī erant ipsī.

40

priusquam	before
statūrā: statūra	height
interruptā: interrumpere	interrupt
praeter	except
plērīque vestrum	most of you
dēclārāre	declare, proclaim
mussitāre	murmur
prophētae: prophēta	prophet
praedīxērunt: praedīcere	foretell, predict
evangelium	good news, gospel
prōnūntiāvit: prōnūntiāre	proclaim, preach
aeternam: aeternus	eternal
cruce: crux	cross
suffīxus: suffīgere	nail, fasten
resurrēxit: resurgere	rise again
discipulīs: discipulus	disciple, follower
caelum	sky, heaven
rēgnat: rēgnāre	reign
in perpetuum	forever
glōriae: glōria	glory
angelōrum: angelus	angel
comitante: comitāns	accompanying
iūdicābit: iūdicāre	judge
pūram: pūrus	pure
erimus	shall be
diabolī: diabolus	devil
nisi	unless
vitiīs: vitium	sin
verberibus: verber	blow

When you have read section I of this story, answer the questions at the
end of the section.

in aulā Domitiānī   🔲

I

in scaenā parvā, quae in aulae Domitiānī ātriō exstrūcta erat, Paris
fābulam dē amōre Mārtis et Veneris agēbat. simul pūmiliō,
Myropnous nōmine, tībīcen atque amīcus Paridis, suāviter tībiīs
cantābat. nūllī aderant spectātōrēs nisi Domitia Augusta, uxor
Imperātōris Domitiānī, quae Paridem inter familiārissimōs suōs   5
habēbat. oculīs in eō fīxīs fābulam intentē spectābat. tam mīrābilis,
tam perīta ars eius erat ut lacrimās retinēre Domitia vix posset.

subitō servus, nōmine Olympus, quem Domitia iānuam ātriī
custōdīre iusserat, ingressus est.

"domina," inquit, "nōs Epaphrodītum, Augustī lībertum, modo   10
cōnspicātī sumus trānseuntem āream, decem mīlitibus comitantibus. mox hūc intrābit."

quibis verbīs audītīs, Paris ad Domitiam versus rīsit.

Paris: dēliciae meae! quam fortūnāta es! Epaphrodītus ipse,
           Augustī lībertus, tē vīsitāre cupit.   15
Domitia: (adventū Epaphrodītī commōta) mī Pari, tibi perīculōsum est
           hīc manēre. odiō es Epaphrodītō! sī tē apud mē ille
           invēnerit, poenās certē dabis. iubēbit mīlitēs in carcerem
           tē conicere. fuge!
Paris: cūr fugiendum est? illum psittacum Domitiānī floccī nōn   20
           faciō.
Domitia: at ego valdē timeō. nam mihi quoque Epaphrodītus est
           inimīcus. iussū eius conclāvia mea saepe īnspiciuntur;
           epistulae meae resignantur; ancillārum meārum fidēs ā
           ministrīs eius temptātur. potestās eius nōn minor est   25
           quam Imperātōris ipsīus.
Paris: mea columba, dēsine timēre! mē nōn capiet iste
           homunculus. paulīsper abībō.

haec locūtus, columnam proximam celeriter cōnscendit et per
compluvium ēgressus in tēctō sē cēlāvit. Myropnous quoque sē   30
cēlāre cōnstituit. post tapēte quod dē longuriō gravī pendēbat sē

collocāvit. Domitia contrā, quae quamquam perterrita erat in lectō manēbat vultū compositō, Olympō imperāvit ut aliquōs versūs recitāret.

simul	*at the same time*	ministrīs: minister	*servant, agent*
tībiīs cantābat:		temptātur:	
tībiīs cantāre	*play on the pipes*	temptāre	*put to the test*
familiārissimōs:		compluvium	*compluvium (opening in roof)*
familiāris	*close friend*	tapēte	*tapestry, wall-hanging*
certē	*certainly*	longuriō: longurius	*pole*
conclāvia: conclāve	*room*	contrā	*on the other hand*
īnspiciuntur: īnspicere	*search*	compositō:	
resignantur: resignāre	*open, unseal*	compositus	*composed, steady*

Augustī lībertum: Augustī lībertus *freedman of Augustus, freedman of the emperor*

1 Where in the palace did Paris' performance take place? What story was he performing? Who was supplying the musical accompaniment?
2 Who was the only spectator? What effect did Paris' skill have on her?
3 What had the slave Olympus been ordered to do? What news did he bring? What were Domitia's feelings on hearing this news?
4 Domitia mentions three ways in which Epaphroditus and his men are making life unpleasant for her. What are they?
5 Where did (*a*) Paris and (*b*) Myropnous hide?

6 While Paris and Myropnous were hiding, where was Domitia? In what ways did she try to pretend that everything was normal?

7 Judging from this story, especially lines 14–28, what impression do you have of Paris' personality?

Remains of Domitian's Palace, Rome, showing the impluvium.

II

Olympō suāviter recitante, ingressus est Epaphrodītus. decem mīlitēs eum comitābantur.

Epaphrodītus:	ubi est iste pantomīmus quem impudēns tū amās? ubi eum cēlāvistī?	
Domitia:	verba tua nōn intellegō. sōla sum, ut vidēs. hic servus mē versibus dēlectat, nōn Paris.	5
Epaphrodītus:	(*conversus ad mīlitēs*) quaerite Paridem! festīnāte! omnia īnspicite conclāvia!	

mīlitēs igitur conclāvia ācriter perscrūtātī sunt, sed frūstrā. Paridem nusquam invenīre poterant.   10

Epaphrodītus: caudicēs! sī Paris effūgerit, vōs poenās dabitis. cūr
                tēctum nōn perscrūtātī estis? ferte scālās!

quae cum audīvisset Domitia palluit. Myropnous tamen quī per
tapēte cautē prōspiciēbat sēcum rīsit; cōnsilium enim callidissimum
et audācissimum cēperat. tapēte lēniter manū movēre coepit. mox   15
Epaphrodītus, dum ātrium suspīciōsus circumspectat, mōtum
tapētis animadvertit.

Epaphrodītus: ecce! movētur tapēte! latebrās Paridis invēnī!
                nunc illum capiam.

quibus dictīs, Epaphrodītus ad tapēte cum magnō clāmōre sē   20
praecipitāvit. Myropnous haudquāquam perturbātus, ubi Epaphrodītus appropinquāvit, tapēte magnā vī dētrāxit. dēcidit tapēte,
dēcidit longurius. Epaphrodītus, tapētī convolūtus atque simul
longuriō percussus, prōcubuit exanimātus. magnopere cachinnāvit
Myropnous et exsultāns tībiīs cantāre coepit.   25
    Domitia, quae sē iam ex pavōre recēperat, ad mīlitēs in ātrium
cum scālīs regressōs conversa est. eōs iussit Epaphrodītum
extrahere. mīlitibus eum extrahentibus Myropnous assem in labra
eius quasi mortuī posuit. dēnique Paris per compluvium dēspexit et
Epaphrodītō ita valēdīxit: 30
    "hīc iacet Tiberius Claudius Epaphrodītus, Augustī lībertus,
longuriō gravī strātus."

impudēns	*shameless*	dētrāxit: dētrahere	*pull down*
perscrūtātī sunt	*examined*	convolūtus: convolvere	*entangle*
scālās: scālae	*ladders*	assem: as	*as (small coin)*
suspīciōsus	*suspicious*	dēspexit: dēspicere	*look down*
latebrās: latebrae	*hiding-place*	strātus: sternere	*lay low*
sē praecipitāvit: sē praecipitāre	*hurl oneself*		

About the Language

1 Study the following examples:

nōlī dēspērāre! amīcus meus tē **servābit**.
*Don't give up! My friend **will save** you.*

servī ad urbem heri iērunt; crās **revenient**.
*The slaves went to the city yesterday; they **will come back** tomorrow.*

The words in boldface are in the *future* tense.

2 The first and second conjugations form their future tense in the following way:

FIRST CONJUGATION		SECOND CONJUGATION	
portābō	*I shall carry*	docēbō	*I shall teach*
portābis	*you will carry*	docēbis	*you will teach*
portābit	*s/he, it will carry*	docēbit	*s/he, it will teach*
portābimus	*we shall carry*	docēbimus	*we will teach*
portābitis	*you will carry*	docēbitis	*you will teach*
portābunt	*they will carry*	docēbunt	*they will teach*

3 The third and fourth conjugations form their future tense in another way:

THIRD CONJUGATION		FOURTH CONJUGATION	
traham	*I shall drag*	audiam	*I shall hear*
trahēs	*you will drag*	audiēs	*you will hear*
trahet	*s/he, it will drag*	audiet	*s/he, it will hear*
trahēmus	*we shall drag*	audiēmus	*we will hear*
trahētis	*you will drag*	audiētis	*you will hear*
trahent	*they will drag*	audient	*they will hear*

4 Further examples:

1 crās ad Graeciam nāvigābimus.
2 ille mercātor est mendāx; tibi numquam pecūniam reddet.
3 fuge! mīlitēs tē in carcerem conicient!
4 dux noster est vir benignus, quī vōs omnēs līberābit.
5 "quid crās faciēs?" "ad theātrum ībō."
6 laudābō; respondēbit; appropinquābunt; rīdēbitis.
7 veniēmus; trādent; dīcam; dormiet.

5 The future tense of **sum** is as follows:

erō	*I shall be*	erimus	*we shall be*
eris	*you will be*	eritis	*you will be*
erit	*he will be*	erunt	*they will be*

Practicing the Language

1 Study the forms and meanings of the following nouns, and give the meanings of the untranslated ones:

homō	*man*	homunculus	*little man*
servus	*slave*	servulus	*little slave*
lagōna	*bottle*	laguncula	
corpus		corpusculum	*little body*
febris		febricula	*slight fever*
liber	*book*	libellus	
ager		agellus	
lapis		lapillus	
fīlia		fīliola	
mēnsa		mēnsula	

The nouns in the right-hand pair of columns are known as *diminutives*.

Give the meaning of each of the following diminutives:

vīllula, fīliolus, nāvicula, cēnula, ponticulus

Study the following nouns and their diminutives:

sporta		*basket*
sportula	(1)	*little basket*
	(2)	*gift for clients (named after the little basket in which it once used to be carried)*

cōdex (*often spelled* caudex)

	(1)	*piece of wood*
	(2)	*someone with no more sense than a piece of wood,* i.e. *fool, blockhead*

cōdicillī	(1)	*wooden writing-tablets*
	(2)	*codicil (written instructions added to a will)*

2 Complete each sentence with the right word and then translate.

1 hīs verbīs . . . . ., Paris aequō animō respondit. (audītīs, portātīs)
2 signō . . . . ., servī Tychicum ēiēcērunt. (victō, datō)
3 cēnā . . . . ., Haterius amīcōs in triclīnium dūxit. (cōnsūmptā, parātā)
4 nāve . . . . ., mercātor dēspērābat. (āmissā, refectā)
5 clientibus . . . . ., praecō iānuam clausit. (dīmissīs, dēpositīs)
6 tergīs . . . . ., hostēs fūgērunt. (īnstrūctīs, conversīs)

3 In each pair of sentences, translate sentence *a*; then, with the help of page 277 of the Review Grammar, express the same idea in a different way by completing sentence *b* with a passive form, and translate again.

For example: a tabernāriī cibum vēndēbant.
                           b cibus ā tabernāriīs . . . . . .

Translated and completed, this becomes:
   a tabernāriī cibum vēndēbant.
     The storekeepers were selling food.
   b cibus ā tabernāriīs vēndēbātur.
     Food was being sold by the storekeepers.

In sentences 1–3, the verbs are in the *imperfect* tense:

1a servī amphorās portābant.
1b amphorae ā servīs . . . . . .
2a Salvius Haterium dēcipiēbat.
2b Haterius ā Salviō . . . . . .
3a barbarī horreum oppugnābant.
3b horreum ā barbarīs . . . . . .

In sentences 4–6, the verbs are in the *present* tense:

4a rhētor puerōs docet.
4b puerī ā rhētore . . . . . .
5a aliquis iānuam aperit.
5b iānua ab aliquō . . . . . .
6a centuriō mīlitēs cōnsistere iubet.
6b mīlitēs ā centuriōne cōnsistere . . . . . .

About the Language

1 Study the following example:

sī tē audīverō, respondēbō.
If I hear you, I shall reply.

The replying takes place in the future, so Latin uses the future tense (**respondēbō**). The hearing also takes place in the future, but at a different time: hearing comes before replying. To indicate this difference in time, Latin uses an unusual tense known as the *future perfect* (**audīverō**).

2 The forms of the future perfect are as follows:

portāverō   portāverimus
portāveris   portāveritis
portāverit   portāverint

3 The future perfect is often translated by an English present tense, as in the example in paragraph 1.

4 Further examples:

  1   sī Epaphrodītus nōs cōnspexerit, mē interficiet.
  2   sī dīligenter quaesīveris, pecūniam inveniēs.
  3   sī servī bene labōrāverint, eīs praemium dabō.
  4   sī mīlitēs vīderō, fugiam.

Christianity

Christianity originated in the Roman province of Judaea, the central part of modern Israel, where Jesus Christ was crucified in about A.D.29. It may have reached Rome during the reign of the Emperor Claudius (A.D.41–54). Saint Paul, who was brought to Rome under arrest in about A.D.60, ends one of his letters from Rome by passing on messages of greeting from several Christians living in the city, including some who belong to "Caesar's house" (the household of the emperor).

Head of Christ from mosaic in Hinton St. Mary, southern England.

The early Christians believed that Jesus had not only risen from the dead and ascended into heaven, but would return again to earth in the fairly near future, in the way described by Tychicus on page 229. The message of Christianity appealed mainly to the poor and the downtrodden, although it also attracted a few of the wealthy and nobly born.

At first the Romans tended to confuse Christianity with Judaism. This is not surprising, since both religions came from Judaea, and both believed that there was only one God. Christians were generally disliked by the Romans; occasionally they were persecuted (hunted down and punished). The most famous persecution took place in A.D.64 under the Emperor Nero, who treated the Christians as scapegoats for the great fire of Rome. They were condemned to be torn to pieces by wild beasts, or set alight as human torches.

But persecutions like these were not common; the Roman government usually preferred to leave the Christians alone. When Pliny, the Roman governor of Bithynia, asked the Emperor Trajan how he ought to deal with people accused of Christianity, Trajan replied: "They are not to be hunted down: if they are brought before you and proved guilty, they must be punished, but if any one says that he is *not* a Christian and proves it by saying a prayer to our Roman gods, he must go free, even if his previous behavior has been very suspicious."

Entertainment

Throughout the first century A.D., the three theaters in Rome regularly provided popular entertainment at festival time. But there was a change in the kind of drama presented.

The traditional type of tragedy was losing its popularity and being replaced by pantomime. A pantomime had only one actor; he was known as a **pantomīmus** (meaning "acting everything") because he acted all the parts in the story, changing his mask as he changed characters. For example, a pantomime actor who was presenting the love affair of Mars and Venus would take the parts not only of Mars and Venus themselves but also of Helios the sun-god telling Venus' husband Vulcan about the affair, Vulcan setting a trap for the guilty pair, and the other gods coming one by one to look at Mars and Venus when they were caught in the act.

The pantomime actor did not speak, but danced and mimed rather in the manner of a modern ballet dancer, and was often accompanied by an orchestra and a chorus who sang the words of the story. The story itself was usually based on Greek myth but sometimes on history. The pantomime actor represented the story's action with graceful movements and gestures; he needed plenty of physical skill and stamina, as well as an attractive appearance and a wide knowledge of literature. One of the most famous of all pantomime actors was the dancer Paris, who appears in the stories of Stages 33 and 34.

In the same way that pantomimes were replacing tragedies, comedies were being replaced by mimes. A mime was a crude slapstick farce, usually on a theme taken from everyday life. The style of performance was generally obscene or grotesque or both.

The most popular form of public entertainment in Rome, however, was undoubtedly chariot-racing. Almost everybody, from the emperor downwards, took an interest in this sport. The Circus Maximus, where the most important chariot-racing took place, could hold 250,000 spectators—a far higher capacity than any modern football or baseball stadium. Much money changed hands in betting, and each of the rival chariot-teams was cheered on by its fans with passionate enthusiasm.

There were four teams (**factiōnēs**) competing regularly with each other: green, blue, red, and white. Each team consisted of one, two, or three chariots, and the commonest number of horses to a chariot was four. A day's program normally consisted of twenty-four races, each lasting seven laps (about 5 miles or 8 kilometers) and taking about a quarter of an hour to run. Seven huge eggs of marble or wood were hoisted high above the central platform (**spīna**), and every time the chariots completed a lap, one egg was lowered. The charioteer had to race at full speed down the length of the circus and then display his greatest skill at the turning-point (**mēta**); if he took the bend too slowly he would be overtaken, and if he took it too fast he might crash. He raced with the reins tied tightly around his body, and in his belt he carried a knife; if he crashed, his life might depend on how quickly he could cut himself free from the wreckage.

Another center of entertainment was the Flavian Amphitheater, later known as the Colosseum. Up to 50,000 spectators could watch the gladiatorial combats and beast-hunts that took place here. On occasion, the arena was filled with water for the representation of sea battles.

Study the photograph and answer the questions that follow it.

1 How many charioteers are shown? Whereabouts in the circus are they?
2 What are the three objects placed on conical pillars on the right?
3 It has been suggested that the charioteer on the left is reining in the inside horse. Why would he do this?
4 The charioteer on the right seems to be whipping up his team. Why can he now drive them faster?

The Colosseum (the Flavian amphitheater in Rome). Inaugurated AD 80.

Not all entertainment was public. Rich Romans enjoyed presenting private shows of various kinds, as in the story on pp. 227–29, where Paris performs in Haterius' garden for Vitellia and her friends. One elderly lady, Ummidia Quadratilla, kept her own private troupe of pantomimi. Often such entertainment would be presented at a dinner-party. This might consist of dancing-girls, freaks, actors, jugglers, acrobats, a band of musicians, a novelty like the philosopher Euphrosyne, or a trained slave reciting a poem or other literary work—possibly written by the host, which might sometimes be rather embarrassing for the guests. The more serious types of entertainment were often put on by highly educated hosts for equally cultivated and appreciative guests; but they might sometimes, like Euphrosyne's philosophy lecture, be presented by ignorant and uninterested hosts who merely wanted to be in the fashion or were trying to pass themselves off as persons of good taste and culture.

Words and Phrases Checklist

ācriter	*keenly, fiercely*
at	*but*
brevis, breve	*short, brief*
certō, certāre, certāvī	*compete*
coniciō, conicere, coniēcī, coniectus	*hurl, throw*
contrā	*against, on the other hand*

crās	*tomorrow*
ēiciō, ēicere, ēiēcī, ēiectus	*throw out*
et . . . et	*both . . . and*
excipiō, excipere, excēpī, exceptus	*receive*
fuga, fugae	*escape*
hīc	*here*
lēniter	*gently*
moveō, movēre, mōvī, mōtus	*move*
nisi	*except, unless*
obstupefaciō, obstupefacere, obstupefēcī, obstupefactus	*amaze, stun*
odiō sum, odiō esse	*be hateful*
potestās, potestātis	*power*
rēgīna, rēgīnae	*queen*
sevērus, sevēra, sevērum	*severe, strict*
tēctum, tēctī	*ceiling, roof*
utrum	*whether*

NUMBERS

ūnus	*one*	prīmus	*first*
duo	*two*	secundus	*second*
trēs	*three*	tertius	*third*
quattuor	*four*	quārtus	*fourth*
quīnque	*five*	quīntus	*fifth*
sex	*six*	sextus	*sixth*
septem	*seven*	septimus	*seventh*
octō	*eight*	octāvus	*eighth*
novem	*nine*	nōnus	*ninth*
decem	*ten*	decimus	*tenth*
vīgintī	*twenty*	septuāgintā	*seventy*
trīgintā	*thirty*	octōgintā	*eighty*
quadrāgintā	*forty*	nōnāgintā	*ninety*
quīnquāgintā	*fifty*	centum	*a hundred*
sexāgintā	*sixty*	ducentī	*two hundred*

Word Search

acrimony, brevity, centrifugal, concerted, contravene, procrastinate, stupefaction

1 . . . . .: bitterness or animosity
2 . . . . .: moving or directed away from a center
3 . . . . .: astonishment
4 . . . . .: undertaken or accomplished together
5 . . . . .: to act counter to, oppose
6 . . . . .: briefness of duration
7 . . . . .: to postpone or delay needlessly

lībertus

ultiō Epaphrodītī

Epaphrodītus, ā Paride atque Domitiā ēlūsus, eōs ulcīscī vehementissimē cupiēbat. Imperātor quoque, īrā et suspīciōne commōtus, Epaphrodītum saepe hortābātur ut Paridem Domitiamque pūnīret. Epaphrodītō tamen difficile erat Domitiam, uxōrem Imperātōris, et Paridem, pantomīmum nōtissimum, apertē   5
accūsāre. auxilium igitur ab amīcō C. Salviō Līberāle petīvit.

Epaphrodītus "nōn modo ego," inquit, "sed etiam Imperātor poenās Paridis Domitiaeque cupit. sī mē in hāc rē adiūveris, magnum praemium tibi dabitur."

Salvius, rē paulīsper cōgitātā, tranquillē respondit: 10

"cōnfīde mihi, amīce; ego tibi rem tōtam administrābō. īnsidiae parābuntur; Domitia et Paris in īnsidiās ēlicientur; ambō capientur et pūnientur."

"quid Domitiae accidet?" rogāvit Epaphrodītus.

"Domitia accūsābitur; damnābitur; fortasse relēgābitur."   15

"et Paris?"

Salvius rīsit.

"ēmovēbitur."

ēlūsus: ēlūdere	*trick, outwit*
ulcīscī	*to take revenge on*
suspīciōne: suspīciō	*suspicion*
ēlicientur: ēlicere	*lure, entice*
relēgābitur: relēgāre	*exile*

When you have read this story, answer the questions at the end.

īnsidiae

paucīs post diēbus Domitia ancillam, nōmine Chionēn, ad sē
vocāvit.

"epistulam," inquit, "ā Vitelliā, uxōre Hateriī, missam modo
accēpī. ēheu! Vitellia in morbum gravem incidit. statim mihi
vīsitanda est. tē volō omnia parāre."   5

tum Chionē, e cubiculō dominae ēgressa, iussit lectīcam parārī et
lectīcāriōs arcessī. medicum quoque nōmine Asclēpiadēn quaesīvit
quī medicāmenta quaedam Vitelliae parāret. inde Domitia lectīcā
vecta, comitantibus servīs, domum Hateriī profecta est. difficile erat
eīs per viās prōgredī, quod nox obscūra erat multumque pluēbat.   10

parārī   *to be prepared*
lectīcāriōs: lectīcārius   *chair-carrier, sedan-chair carrier*
arcessī   *to be summoned, to be sent for*
medicāmenta: medicāmentum   *medicine, drug*

Chionēn   *Greek accusative of* Chionē
Asclēpiadēn   *Greek accusative of* Asclēpiadēs

cum domum Haterii pervēnissent, iānuam apertam invēnērunt. servīs extrā iānuam relictīs, Domitia cum Chionē ingressa est. spectāculum inopīnātum eīs ingredientibus obiectum est. ātrium magnificē ōrnātum erat: ubīque lūcēbant lucernae, corōnae rosārum dē omnibus columnīs pendēbant. sed omnīnō dēsertum   15
erat ātrium. inde fēminae, triclīnium ingressae, id quoque dēsertum vīdērunt. in mediō tamen cēna sūmptuōsa posita erat: mēnsae epulīs exquīsītissimīs cumulātae erant, pōcula vīnō optimō plēna erant. quibus vīsīs, ancilla timidā vōce,
   "cavendum est nōbīs," inquit. "aliquid mīrī hīc agitur."   20
   "fortasse Vitellia morbō affecta est cum cēnāret. sine dubiō iam in cubiculō convalēscit," respondit Domitia, ignāra īnsidiārum quās Salvius parāverat.
   itaque per domum dēsertam, ancillā timidē sequente, Domitia prōgredī coepit. cum ad cubiculum ubi Vitellia dormīre solēbat   25
pervēnisset, in līmine cōnstitit. cubiculum erat obscūrum. Chionēn ad triclīnium remīsit quae lucernam ferret. in silentiō noctis diū exspectābat dum redīret ancilla. haec tamen nōn rediit. tandem Domitia morae impatiēns in cubiculum irrūpit. vacuum erat. tum dēmum pavōre magnō perturbāta est. tenebrae, silentium, ancillae   30
absentia, haec omnia perīculī indicia esse vidēbantur. scīlicet falsa fuerat epistula, mendāx nūntius morbī!
   Domitia ad aulam quam celerrimē regredī cōnstituit priusquam aliquid malī sibi accideret. dum per vacua conclāvia fugit, vōce hominis subitō perterrita est.   35
   "dēliciae meae, salvē! tūne quoque ad cēnam invītāta es?"
   tum vōcem agnōvit.
   "mī Pari," inquit, "īnsidiae, nōn cēna, nōbīs parātae sunt. etfugiendum nōbīs est, dum possumus."

inopīnātum: inopīnātus	*unexpected*
obiectum est	*met, was presented*
epulīs: epulae	*dishes*
cumulātae erant: cumulāre	*heap*
cavendum est: cavēre	*beware*
mīrī: mīrus	*extraordinary, strange*
remīsit: remittere	*send back*
dum	*until*
vacuum: vacuus	*empty*
tum dēmum	*then at last, only then*
absentia	*absence*
vidēbantur: vidērī	*seem*
nūntius	*message, news*

1 What message about Vitellia did Domitia receive? What did she decide to do immediately?
2 What preparations did Chione make?
3 Why was the journey difficult?
4 What did Domitia and Chione discover (*a*) at the entrance to the house, (*b*) in the atrium, (*c*) in the triclinium?
5 What explanation of the situation does Domitia give Chione in lines 21–2?
6 Where did Domitia and Chione go next? Why did Domitia send Chione back?
7 "haec tamen nōn rediit" (line 28). Suggest an explanation for this.
8 What did Domitia at last realize? What made her realize this?
9 Who is the speaker in line 36? How has he been lured to the house? Now that he and Domitia are at the house, what do you suppose will be the next step in Salvius' plan?

exitium

I

Domitiā haec dīcente, Myropnous, quī dominum comitābātur, ad iānuam contendit. cautē prōspexit. ecce! via tōta mīlitibus praetōriānīs plēna erat. neque lectīca, neque medicus, neque servī usquam vidērī poterant.

ad ātrium reversus Myropnous "āctum est dē nōbīs!" exclāmāvit. 5
"appropinquant praetōriānī! mox hūc ingredientur!"

hōc tamen cognitō, Paris "nōlī dēspērāre," inquit. "cōnsilium habeō. Myropnū, tibi iānua custōdienda est. prohibē mīlitēs ingredī. sī mē vel Domitiam hōc locō cēperint, certē nōs interficient. cōnandum est nōbīs per postīcum ēlābī." 10

Myropnous igitur iānuam claudere contendit. quō factō ad triclīnium reversus lectōs mēnsāsque raptim in faucēs trahere

praetōriānīs: praetōriānus	*praetorian (member of emperor's bodyguard)*
usquam	*anywhere*
revērsus: revertī	*return*
āctum est dē nōbīs	*it's all over with us*
postīcum	*back gate*
ēlābī	*escape*
faucēs	*passage, entrance-way*

coepit. sellās quoque ex ātriō, lectōs ē cubiculīs proximīs collēctōs in
cumulum imposuit. brevī ingēns pyra in faucibus exstrūcta est.

    mīlitēs praetōriānī, cum iānuam clausam cōnspexissent,   15
haesitantēs cōnstitērunt. sed tribūnus, nē Paris et Domitia
effūgerent, iānuam effringī iussit. statim iānua secūribus
pulsābātur. Myropnous ubi strepitum pulsantium audīvit pyram
incendit. amphoram oleī ē culīnā portāvit quā flammās augēret.
tum pyrā flagrante, amīcōs sequī contendit.   20

imposuit: impōnere	*put onto*
pyra	*pyre*
secūribus: secūris	*axe*
flagrante: flagrāre	*blaze*

II

Paris et Domitia, ubi ad postīcum pervēnērunt, duōs mīlitēs ibi
positōs invēnērunt. quōs cum vīdissent, quamquam Domitia
omnīnō dē salūte dēspērābat, Paris in hōc discrīmine audācissimum
atque callidissimum sē praestitit. nam cēlātā haud procul Domitiā,
ipse per postīcum audācter prōgressus sē mīlitibus ostendit. tum   5
quasi fugiēns, retrō in hortum cucurrit.

   statim clāmāvērunt mīlitēs: "ecce Paris! Paris effugere cōnātur!"

   mīlitibus sequentibus, Paris per hortum modo hūc modo illūc
ruēbat. post statuās sē cēlābat mīlitēsque vōce blandā dērīdēbat. illī
incertī ubi esset pantomīmus, vōcem Paridis circā hortum   10
sequēbantur.

   tandem audīvit Paris strepitum cēterōrum mīlitum domum
irrumpentium. brevī tōta domus mīlitibus plēna erat. tribūnus aliōs
iussit aquam ferre ut flammās exstinguerent, aliōs gladiīs dēstrictīs
omnēs domūs partēs perscrūtārī ut Paridem invenīrent. hic bene   15
intellēxit quantō in perīculō esset sed etiam tum haudquāquam
dēspērāvit.

   mediō in hortō stābat laurus veterrima, quae tēctō domūs
imminēbat. simulatque intrāvērunt mīlitēs hortum, laurum Paris
cōnscendit. hinc prōsilīre in tēctum cōnātus est. prōsiluit, sed   20
tēgulae tēctī lūbricae erant. paulīsper in margine tēctī stetit; deinde
praeceps humum lāpsus est.

   intereā Domitia, quae per postīcum nūllō vidente ēgressa erat,
haud procul exspectābat dum Paris ad sē venīret. lāpsō tamen
corpore eius, tantus erat fragor ut etiam ad aurēs Domitiae   25
advenīret. quae metū āmēns vītaeque suae neglegēns in hortum
reversa est. ubi corpus Paridis humī iacēns vīdit, dolōre cōnfecta sē
in eum coniēcit eīque ōscula multa dedit.

   "valē, dēliciae meae, valē!"

   adiit tribūnus. Domitiam ad aulam dēdūcī iussit. ipse caput   30
pantomīmī amputātum ad Epaphrodītum rettulit.

retrō	*back*	lūbricae: lūbricus	*slippery*
modo . . . modo	*now . . . now*	margine: margō	*edge*
circā	*around*	nūllō *(used as ablative of* nēmō*)*	*no one*
exstinguerent:		fragor	*crash*
exstinguere	*put out*	āmēns	*out of her mind,*
dēstrictīs: dēstringere	*draw, unsheathe*		*in a frenzy*
prōsilīre	*jump*	cōnfecta: cōnfectus	*overcome*
tēgulae: tēgula	*tile*	amputātum: amputāre	*cut off*

About the Language

1 In Stage 13, you met sentences containing infinitives:

currere volō.   *I want **to run***.
servī **labōrāre** nōn possunt.   *The slaves are not able **to work***.

This kind of infinitive is known in full as the *present active infinitive*.

2 In Stage 34, you have met another kind of infinitive:

volō epistulam **recitārī**.   *I want the letter **to be read out***.
Paris **invenīrī** nōn poterat.   *Paris was unable **to be found***.

This infinitive is known as the *present passive infinitive*.

3 Compare the following examples of present active and present passive infinitives:

PRESENT ACTIVE		PRESENT PASSIVE	
portāre	*to carry*	portārī	*to be carried*
docēre	*to teach*	docērī	*to be taught*
trahere	*to drag*	trahī	*to be dragged*
audīre	*to hear*	audīrī	*to be heard*

4 Further examples of the present passive infinitive:

1 volō iānuam aperīrī.
2 neque Vitellia neque ancilla vidērī poterant.
3 fūr capī nōlēbat.
4 dux iussit captīvum līberārī.

5 Notice how deponent verbs form their infinitive:

cōnārī   *to try*
pollicērī   *to promise*
ingredī   *to enter*
orīrī   *to rise*

Further examples:

1 lībertus iussit mīlitēs pantomīmum sequī.
2 aegrōtī deam precārī volēbant.
3 nūntius tandem proficīscī cōnstituit.
4 puerī tam perterritī erant ut loquī nōn possent.

honōrēs

Salviō aulam intrantī obviam iit Epaphrodītus. cōmiter excēpit.

Epaphrodītus: mī Salvī, quālis artifex es! tuā arte iste pantomīmus
occīsus est. tuā arte Domitia ex Ītaliā relēgāta est.
Imperātor, summō gaudiō affectus, spectāculum
splendidissimum in amphitheātrō Flāviō darī iussit.   5
crās diēs fēstus ab omnibus cīvibus celebrābitur;
puerī puellaeque deōrum effigiēs corōnīs flōrum
ōrnābunt; sacerdōtēs sacrificia offerent; ingēns
cīvium multitūdō Imperātōrem ad templum Iovis
comitābitur, ubi ille dīs immortālibus grātiās aget.   10
mox senātōrēs ad cūriam fēstīs vestīmentīs
prōgredientur et Domitiānō grātulābuntur. venī
mēcum! nōn morandum est nōbīs. Imperātor enim
nōs exspectat. mihi ōrnāmenta praetōria, tibi
cōnsulātum prōmīsit.   15

Salvius: cōnsulātum mihi prōmīsit? quam fortūnātus sum!

Epaphrodītus: venī! oportet nōs Imperātōrī grātiās agere.

Epaphrodītō et Salviō ēgressīs ut Domitiānum salūtārent, ē latebrīs
rēpsit Myropnous. manifesta nunc omnia erant. nunc dēnique
intellēxit quis esset auctor exitiī Paridis. lacrimīs effūsīs, indignam   20
amīcī mortem lūgēbat. tum manibus ad caelum sublātīs nōmen
Salviī dētestātus est. tībiās āmēns frēgit. ultiōnem sibi hīs verbīs
prōmīsit:

"ego numquam iterum tībiīs cantābō priusquam pereat Salvius."

artifex	*artist*
cūriam: cūria	*senate-house*
morandum est: morārī	*delay*
ōrnāmenta praetōria	*honorary praetorship,*
	honorary rank of praetor
manifesta: manifestus	*clear*
auctor	*person responsible,*
	originator
indignam: indignus	*unworthy, undeserved*
sublātīs: tollere	*raise, lift up*
priusquam pereat	*until . . . perishes*

sella curūlis

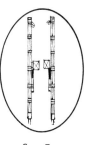

fascēs

About the Language

1 Study the following examples:

crās nūntiī ad rēgem **mittentur**.
*Tomorrow messengers **will be sent** to the king.*

cēna sūmptuōsa ā servīs **parābitur**.
*An expensive dinner **will be prepared** by the slaves.*

The words in boldface are *passive* forms of the *future* tense.

2 Compare the following active and passive forms:

FUTURE ACTIVE	FUTURE PASSIVE
portābit	portābitur
he will carry	*he will be carried*
portābunt	portābuntur
they will carry	*they will be carried*
trahet	trahētur
he will drag	*he will be dragged*
trahent	trahentur
they will drag	*they will be dragged*

3 Further examples:

1 ingēns praemium victōrī dabitur.
2 omnēs vīllae dēlēbuntur.
3 Paris mox capiētur.
4 illī custōdēs quī in statiōne dormīvērunt sevērissimē pūnientur.

4 Notice how the future tense of deponent verbs is formed:

cōnābitur   *he will try*
cōnābuntur   *they will try*

loquētur   *he will speak*
loquentur   *they will speak*

Further examples:

1 mīlitēs crās proficīscentur.
2 dominus meus, quī stultissimus est, nihil suspicābitur.
3 multī senātōrēs Domitiānum ad forum comitābuntur.
4 sī inimīcus tuus hoc venēnum cōnsūmpserit, moriētur.

Practicing the Language

1 Study the forms and meanings of the following verbs and nouns, and give the meanings of the untranslated words:

haesitāre	*hesitate*	haesitātiō	*hesitation*
nāvigāre	*sail*	nāvigātiō	*voyage*
coniūrāre	*conspire*	coniūrātiō	
mūtāre	*change, alter*	mūtātiō	
salūtāre		salūtātiō	
cōgitāre	*think*	cōgitātiō	
dubitāre		dubitātiō	

Match each of the following Latin nouns with the correct English translation:

Latin: rogātiō, festīnātiō, recūsātiō, hortātiō, recitātiō
English: *haste, encouragement, request, refusal, public reading*

2 Complete each sentence with the right word and then translate.

1 ego vōbīs rem tōtam . . . . . . (nārrābō, nārrābimus)
2 amīcī meī cibum vestīmentaque nōbīs . . . . . . (praebēbit, praebēbunt)
3 Imperātor spectāculum splendidum in amphitheātrō crās . . . . . . (dabunt, dabit)
4 vōs estis fortiōrēs quam illī barbarī; eōs facile . . . . . . (superābitis, superābis)
5 caudex! tū mē numquam . . . . . . (capiēs, capiētis)
6 tū in vīllā manē; nōs per postīcum . . . . . . (effugiam, effugiēmus)
7 ego sum probus; ego tibi pecūniam . . . . . . (reddēmus, reddam)
8 fugite! hostēs mox . . . . . . (aderunt, aderit)

3 Translate each English sentence into Latin by selecting correctly from the list of Latin words.

1 *Many flowers were being thrown by the spectators.*
  multa   flōris   ā spectātōribus   iactābant
  multī   flōrēs   inter spectātōrēs   iactābantur
2 *They warned my friend not to cross the bridge.*
  amīcum   meīs   monuerant   nē   pōns   trānsīret
  amīcōs   meum   monuērunt   ut   pontem   trānsībat

3 *Having been ordered by the leader, we carried out the body.*
   ad ducem   iussus   corpus   extulī
   ā duce   iussī   corporum   extulimus
4 *We saw the man whose brother you* (s.) *had arrested.*
   hominem   quī   frāter   comprehenderātis   vidēmus
   hominum   cuius   frātrem   comprehenderās   vīdimus
5 *When the soldiers had been drawn up* (two Latin words only), *I gave the centurion a sign.*
   mīlitibus   īnstrūctīs   centuriōnem   signum   dedī
   mīlitēs   īnstrūctōs   centuriōnī   signō   dedit

4 In each pair of sentences, translate sentence *a*; then, with the help of page 278 of the Review Grammar, express the same idea in a different way by completing sentence *b* with a passive form, and translate again.

For example: a centuriō fūrēs vulnerāverat.
              b fūrēs ā centuriōne . . . . . .
Translated and completed, this becomes:
a centuriō fūrēs vulnerāverat.
   The centurion had wounded the thieves.
b fūrēs ā centuriōne vulnerātī erant.
   The thieves had been wounded by the centurion.

The perfect and pluperfect tenses are both used in this exercise. The verbs in sentences 1–5 are all first conjugation like **portō**.

1a coquus cibum parāverat.
1b cibus ā coquō . . . . . .
2a mercātor latrōnēs superāverat.
2b latrōnēs ā mercātōre . . . . . .
3a dominī servōs laudāvērunt.
3b servī ā dominīs . . . . . .
4a clientēs patrōnum salūtāvērunt.
4b patrōnus ā clientibus . . . . . .
5a rēx mē ipsum accūsāvit.
5b ego ipse ā rēge . . . . . .
6a custōs magnum clāmōrem audīvit.
6b magnus clāmor ā custōde . . . . . .

Freedmen

When a slave was set free (manumitted), he ceased to be the property of his master and became a **lībertus** instead of a **servus**. He also, as we have seen (p.202), became a **cliēns** of his ex-master, and his ex-master was now his **patrōnus**.

In addition, a freedman became a Roman citizen. He now had three names, of which the first two came from the name of his ex-master. (For example, Tiro, the freedman of Marcus Tullius Cicero, became Marcus Tullius Tiro.) As a citizen, he now had the right to vote in elections, and to make a will or business agreement which would be valid in the eyes of the law. He could also get married. If he had been living in an unofficial marriage with a slave-woman, one of his first acts after manumission might be to save up enough money to buy her out of slavery and marry her legally.

There were some limits to the rights and privileges of a freedman, compared with other Roman citizens. He could not become a **senator** or an **eques**, except by special favor of the emperor (and a freedwoman could not become a senator's wife). He could not serve in the legions, or stand as a candidate in elections. One privilege, however, was available to freedmen and to no one else. A freedman could become one of the six priests (**sēvirī Augustālēs**) who were appointed in many Italian towns to look after the worship of the deified Emperor Augustus. Like all priesthoods, the priesthood of Augustus was a position of honor and prestige, and it was open to freedmen only.

The law laid down certain obligations which a freedman owed to his ex-master. For example, a freedman was supposed to leave money to his ex-master in his will (ex-masters did not often insist on this); he was forbidden to do anything that would bring harm to his ex-master; and he had to do a certain number of days' work for his ex-master every year, or pay him a sum of money instead. It is clear from this that it would often be financially worthwhile for a master to manumit a slave; he would still be able to make some use of the ex-slave's services, but would no longer have to provide and pay for his food, clothing, and shelter.

After manumission, a freedman had to put up with a certain amount of prejudice from those who despised him for having been a slave. He was also faced with the need to earn a living. His ex-master might help by providing money to start a small business, as Quintus did for Clemens in

Relief showing a manumission ceremony.

Stage 18, or introducing him to potential customers. Many highly skilled or educated freedmen were quickly able to earn a good living because they already possessed some special ability or experience; for example, a freedman might already be a skilled craftsman, teacher, musician, or secretary, or be experienced in accountancy, trade, or banking. Freedmen who had previously used these skills in their masters' service could now use them for their own benefit. There was plenty of demand for such services, and not much competition from freeborn Romans, who often lacked the necessary skills or regarded such work as below their dignity.

It is not surprising, therefore, that many freedmen became rich and successful, and a few freedmen became very rich indeed. The Vettii brothers, who set up their own business in Pompeii and eventually owned one of the most splendid houses in the town, are good examples of successful freedmen. But perhaps the most famous example of a wealthy freedman is a fictitious one: Trimalchio, the vulgar millionaire in Petronius' novel *Satyrica*. The story "cēna Hateriī" in Stage 32 is partly based on Petronius' account of Trimalchio's dinner party.

Some freedmen continued to live in their ex-master's household, doing the same work that they had done as slaves. One such man was Pliny's talented freedman Zosimus, who was equally skilled at reciting, lyre-playing, and comedy-acting. Pliny treated Zosimus with kindness and affection, and when Zosimus fell ill with tuberculosis, Pliny arranged a holiday abroad for him.

Further evidence of friendly relationships between ex-masters and freedmen comes from the large number of inscriptions, particularly on tombstones, that refer to freedmen and freedwomen. Sometimes, for example, freedmen set up tombstones in honor of their ex-masters:

D M
T. FLAVIO HOMERO T.
FLAVIVS HYACINTHVS
PATRONO BENE MERENTI

Sometimes ex-masters set up tombstones to their favorite freedmen:

D M
IVLIO VITALI
PATRONVS LIBERTO
BENE MERENTI

Some ex-masters allowed freedmen and freedwomen to be buried with them in their tombs:

D M
TITVS FLAVIVS EV
MOLPVS ET FLAVIA
QVINTA SIBI FECE
RVNT ET LIBERTIS LI
BERTABVSQVE POS
TERISQVE EORVM

An ex-master might marry his freedwoman:

D M
T. FLAVIVS CERIALIS
FLAVIAE PHILAENIDI
LIBERTAE IDEM
ET COIVGI
B M F

A small but very important group of freedmen worked as personal assistants to the emperor. As slaves, they had been known as **servī Caesaris**, and as freedmen they were known as **lībertī Augustī**. ("Caesar" and "Augustus" were both used as titles of the emperor.) One of these men was Epaphroditus, who worked first for Nero and later for Domitian. He eventually fell out of favor with Domitian and was executed in A.D.95 for having helped Nero to commit suicide twenty-seven years earlier.

Epaphroditus' official title was secretary **ā libellīs** (in charge of petitions—the word **ā** has an unusual meaning in this phrase), which means that he helped the emperor to deal with the various petitions or requests submitted to him by groups and individuals. The opportunities for bribery are obvious. Other freedmen of the emperor were in charge of correspondence (**ab epistulīs**) and accounts (**ā ratiōnibus**). They all worked closely with the emperor in the day-to-day running of government business.

Under some emperors, especially Claudius and Nero, these freedmen became immensely rich and powerful. They were often bitterly resented by the Roman nobles and senators. This resentment can be seen very plainly in two letters which Pliny wrote about Pallas, the secretary **ā ratiōnibus** of the Emperor Claudius. Pallas had been awarded the **ōrnāmenta praetōria** (*honorary praetorship*), like Epaphroditus in the story on page 251. This means he was given the various privileges normally possessed by a praetor: special dress, special seat at public ceremonies, special funeral after death, and so on. Pliny, having come across the inscription commemorating these honors, is furiously angry. He describes Pallas as a "furcifer," and much else besides. Even though the whole incident had happened fifty years previously, Pliny is boiling with indignation. He is particularly angry that the inscription praised Pallas for refusing a further gift of 15 million sesterces. In Pliny's opinion, Pallas was insulting the praetorian rank by refusing the money as excessive while accepting the privileges as if they meant less; besides he already had 300 million sesterces of his own. Pliny's outburst shows very clearly how much ill feeling could be caused by an emperor's use of ex-slaves as important and powerful assistants in running the empire.

Words and Phrases Checklist

auctor, auctōris	*creator, originator, person responsible*
mē auctōre	*at my suggestion*
cōnsulātus, cōnsulātūs	*consulship (rank of consul)*
damnō, damnāre, damnāvī, damnātus	*condemn*
dum	*while, until*
exstinguō, exstinguere, exstīnxī, exstīnctus	*extinguish, put out, destroy*
gaudium, gaudiī	*joy*

haud	*not*
immineō, imminēre, imminuī	*hang over*
impōnō, impōnere, imposuī, impositus	*impose, put into, put onto*
indicium, indiciī	*sign, evidence*
lectīca, lectīcae	*sedan-chair, carrying-chair*
modo	*just*
obviam eō, obviam īre, obviam iī	*meet, go to meet*
pendeō, pendēre, pependī	*hang*
priusquam	*before, until*
procul	*far*
quasi	*as if*
tenebrae, tenebrārum	*darkness*
ultiō, ultiōnis	*revenge*
vel	*or*
vestīmenta, vestīmentōrum	*clothes*

DEPONENT VERBS

adipīscor, adipīscī, adeptus sum	*obtain*
amplector, amplectī, amplexus sum	*embrace*
comitor, comitārī, comitātus sum	*accompany*
cōnor, cōnārī, cōnātus sum	*try*
cōnspicor, cōnspicārī, cōnspicātus sum	*catch sight of*
ēgredior, ēgredī, ēgressus sum	*go out*
hortor, hortārī, hortātus sum	*encourage, urge*
ingredior, ingredī, ingressus sum	*enter*
loquor, loquī, locūtus sum	*speak*
morior, morī, mortuus sum	*die*
nāscor, nāscī, nātus sum	*be born*
patior, patī, passus sum	*suffer*
precor, precārī, precātus sum	*pray (to)*
proficīscor, proficīscī, profectus sum	*set out*
prōgredior, prōgredī, prōgressus sum	*advance*
regredior, regredī, regressus sum	*go back, return*
revertor, revertī, reversus sum	*turn back, return*
sequor, sequī, secūtus sum	*follow*
suspicor, suspicārī, suspicātus sum	*suspect*

Word Search

compassion, exhort, extinct, imminent, loquacious, nascent, pendulous

1 . . . . .: coming into being; emerging
2 . . . . .: loosely suspended
3 . . . . .: no longer existing in living form
4 . . . . .: empathy, co-feeling; pity
5 . . . . .: talkative
6 . . . . .: to urge strongly
7 . . . . .: about to occur

Language
Information
Section

PART ONE: Review Grammar

Nouns

1 You have now met examples of all the declensions and all the cases. For the ways in which the different cases are used, see page 285.

	first declension	*second declension*			*third declension*
	f.	*m.*	*m.*	*n.*	*m.*
SINGULAR					
nominative and *vocative*	**puella**	**servus** (*voc.* **serve**)	**puer**	**templum**	**mercātor**
genitive	**puellae**	**servī**	**puerī**	**templī**	**mercātōris**
dative	**puellae**	**servō**	**puerō**	**templō**	**mercātōrī**
accusative	**puellam**	**servum**	**puerum**	**templum**	**mercātōrem**
ablative	**puellā**	**servō**	**puerō**	**templō**	**mercātōre**
PLURAL					
nominative and *vocative*	**puellae**	**servī**	**puerī**	**templa**	**mercātōrēs**
genitive	**puellārum**	**servōrum**	**puerōrum**	**templōrum**	**mercātōrum**
dative	**puellīs**	**servīs**	**puerīs**	**templīs**	**mercātōribus**
accusative	**puellās**	**servōs**	**puerōs**	**templa**	**mercātōrēs**
ablative	**puellīs**	**servīs**	**puerīs**	**templīs**	**mercātōribus**

	fourth declension		*fifth declension*	
	f.	*n.*	*m.*	*f.*
SINGULAR				
nominative and *vocative*	**manus**	**genū**	**diēs**	**rēs**
genitive	**manūs**	**genūs**	**diēī**	**reī**
dative	**manuī**	**genū**	**diēī**	**reī**
accusative	**manum**	**genū**	**diem**	**rem**
ablative	**manū**	**genū**	**diē**	**rē**
PLURAL				
nominative and *vocative*	**manūs**	**genua**	**diēs**	**rēs**
genitive	**manuum**	**genuum**	**diērum**	**rērum**
dative	**manibus**	**genibus**	**diēbus**	**rēbus**
accusative	**manūs**	**genua**	**diēs**	**rēs**
ablative	**manibus**	**genibus**	**diēbus**	**rēbus**

m.	m.f.	m.	f.	n.	n.	
						SINGULAR
leō	cīvis	rēx	urbs	nōmen	tempus	*nominative* and *vocative*
leōnis	cīvis	rēgis	urbis	nōminis	temporis	*genitive*
leōnī	cīvī	rēgī	urbī	nōminī	temporī	*dative*
leōnem	cīvem	rēgem	urbem	nōmen	tempus	*accusative*
leōne	cīve	rēge	urbe	nōmine	tempore	*ablative*
						PLURAL
leōnēs	cīvēs	rēgēs	urbēs	nōmina	tempora	*nominative* and *vocative*
leōnum	cīvium	rēgum	urbium	nōminum	temporum	*genitive*
leōnibus	cīvibus	rēgibus	urbibus	nōminibus	temporibus	*dative*
leōnēs	cīvēs	rēgēs	urbēs	nōmina	tempora	*accusative*
leōnibus	cīvibus	rēgibus	urbibus	nōminibus	temporibus	*ablative*

2 Translate each sentence, then change the words in boldface from singular to plural, and translate again.

1 ancilla **cīvī** aquam obtulit.
2 dominus **amīcō** cibum praebuit.
3 prīncipēs **nūntium rēgis** interfēcērunt.
4 amīcus noster **nāvem mercātōris** vīdit.
5 māter **pompam deae** laudāvit.
6 nūntius in **urbe** multōs mīlitēs invēnit.
7 prīncipēs, ā **mercātōre** dēceptī, testēs vocāvērunt.

3 Translate each sentence, then change the words in boldface from plural to singular, and translate again.

  1 senex **puellīs** sellam reddidit.
  2 rēgīna **uxōrēs cīvium** ad aulam vocāvit.
  3 medicus **oculōs mīlitum** īnspexit.
  4 gubernātor **nōmina nautārum** recitāvit.
  5 ancilla **manūs hostium** lāvit.
  6 sacerdōtēs in **templīs** deōs adōrant.
  7 bēstiāriī ā **leōnibus** necātī sunt.

4 Notice again the way in which the cases of third-declension nouns are formed. In particular, compare the nominative singular of **leō**, **rēx**, and **nōmen** with the genitive singular and other cases. Use the list on pp. 314–38 to find the genitive singular of the following nouns, and then use the table in paragraph 1 to find their ablative singular and plural:

dux; homō; pēs; difficultās; nox; iter.

5 With the help of paragraph 1, find the Latin for the words in boldface italics in the following sentences:

  1 Eight *days* had now passed.
  2 The priest raised his *hand*.
  3 The injured man's *knees* were very painful.
  4 The mother washed the child's *hands* and face.
  5 It was the sixth hour of the *day*.
  6 The senators voted with their upraised *hands*.
  7 The messenger set out on the third *day*.

Adjectives

1 The following adjectives belong to the 1st and 2nd declension:

	masculine (2nd)	feminine (1st)	neuter (2nd)	masculine (2nd)	feminine (1st)	neuter (2nd)
SINGULAR						
nominative and vocative	bonus (voc. bone)	bona	bonum	pulcher	pulchra	pulchrum
genitive	bonī	bonae	bonī	pulchrī	pulchrae	pulchrī
dative	bonō	bonae	bonō	pulchrō	pulchrae	pulchrō
accusative	bonum	bonam	bonum	pulchrum	pulchram	pulchrum
ablative	bonō	bonā	bonō	pulchrō	pulchrā	pulchrō
PLURAL						
nominative and vocative	bonī	bonae	bona	pulchrī	pulchrae	pulchra
genitive	bonōrum	bonārum	bonōrum	pulchrōrum	pulchrārum	pulchrōrum
dative	bonīs	bonīs	bonīs	pulchrīs	pulchrīs	pulchrīs
accusative	bonōs	bonās	bona	pulchrōs	pulchrās	pulchra
ablative	bonīs	bonīs	bonīs	pulchrīs	pulchrīs	pulchrīs

2 The following adjectives belong to the 3rd declension:

	masc. and fem.	neuter	masc. and fem.	neuter
SINGULAR				
nominative and vocative	fortis	forte	ingēns	ingēns
genitive	fortis	fortis	ingentis	ingentis
dative	fortī	fortī	ingentī	ingentī
accusative	fortem	forte	ingentem	ingēns
ablative	fortī	fortī	ingent-ī/-e	ingent-ī/-e
PLURAL				
nominative and vocative	fortēs	fortia	ingentēs	ingentia
genitive	fortium	fortium	ingentium	ingentium
dative	fortibus	fortibus	ingentibus	ingentibus
accusative	fortēs	fortia	ingentēs	ingentia
ablative	fortibus	fortibus	ingentibus	ingentibus

3 Compare the third-declension adjectives in paragraph 2 with the third-declension nouns on pp. 262–63. Notice in particular the possible different ending of the ablative singular. The **-ī** ending is generally used when the adjective modifies a stated noun, e.g. **ā servō ingentī** (*by the huge slave*). The **-e** ending is generally used when the adjective describes a noun not stated, but understood, e.g. **ab ingente** (*by the huge (person)*).

4 With the help of paragraphs 1 and 2 and (if necessary) the information about gender in the table of nouns on pages 262–63 find the Latin for the words in boldface italics in the following sentences:

1 The visitors admired the ***beautiful*** city.
2 The ***huge*** lions ran into the arena.
3 The magistrate praised the ***good*** merchants for their honesty.
4 The commander gave medals to the ***brave*** boys.
5 The ***beautiful*** temple stood in the middle of the city.
6 This is the house of a ***brave*** citizen.
7 The craftsmen built three ***huge*** temples.
8 They set up a statue to the ***good*** girl.
9 He was the son of a ***good king***.
10 The guests were attacked by a ***huge slave***.
11 We visited many ***beautiful cities***.
12 The robbers were driven off by the ***brave merchant***.
13 The walls of the ***huge temples*** were built slowly and carefully.
14 I took the ***brave girl*** to the centurion.

Comparison of Adjectives

1

	COMPARATIVE	SUPERLATIVE
longus	**longior**	**longissimus**
long	*longer*	*longest, very long*
pulcher	**pulchrior**	**pulcherrimus**
beautiful	*more beautiful*	*most beautiful, very beautiful*
fortis	**fortior**	**fortissimus**
brave	*braver*	*bravest, very brave*
fēlīx	**fēlīcior**	**fēlīcissimus**
lucky	*luckier*	*luckiest, very lucky*
prūdēns	**prūdentior**	**prūdentissimus**
shrewd	*shrewder*	*shrewdest, very shrewd*
facilis	**facilior**	**facillimus**
easy	*easier*	*easiest, very easy*

2 Irregular forms:

bonus	**melior**	**optimus**
good	*better*	*best, very good*
malus	**peior**	**pessimus**
bad	*worse*	*worst, very bad*
magnus	**maior**	**maximus**
big	*bigger*	*biggest, very big*
parvus	**minor**	**minimus**
small	*smaller*	*smallest, very small*
multus	**plūs**	**plūrimus**
much	*more*	*most, very much*
multī	**plūrēs**	**plūrimī**
many	*more*	*most, very many*

Note: **plūs**, the comparative form of **multus** above, is a neuter noun, e.g. **plūs pecūniae** "more (of) money."

3 Study the forms of the comparative adjective **longior** (*longer*) and the superlative adjective **longissimus** (*longest, very long*):

	masc. and fem.	neuter	masculine	feminine	neuter
SINGULAR					
nominative and *vocative*	longior	longius	longissimus (*voc.*longissime)	longissima	longissimum
genitive	longiōris	longiōris	longissimī	longissimae	longissimī
dative	longiōrī	longiōrī	longissimō	longissimae	longissimō
accusative	longiōrem	longius	longissimum	longissimam	longissimum
ablative	longiōre	longiōre	longissimō	longissimā	longissimō
PLURAL					
nominative and *vocative*	longiōrēs	longiōra	longissimī	longissimae	longissima
genitive	longiōrum	longiōrum	longissimōrum	longissimārum	longissimōrum
dative	longiōribus	longiōribus	longissimīs	longissimīs	longissimīs
accusative	longiōrēs	longiōra	longissimōs	longissimās	longissima
ablative	longiōribus	longiōribus	longissimīs	longissimīs	longissimīs

4 Translate the following examples:

1 "nēmō fortior est quam Modestus," inquit Vilbia.
2 longissima erat pompa, pulcherrima quoque.
3 peior es quam fūr!
4 Salviī vīlla erat minor quam aula Cogidubnī.
5 facillimum erat nōbīs urbem capere.
6 numquam tabernam meliōrem quam tuam vīsitāvī.
7 Memor ad maiōrēs honōrēs ascendere volēbat.
8 in mediō oppidō labōrābant plūrimī fabrī, quī templum maximum exstruēbant.

5 You have also met another way of translating the superlative:

Rūfe, prūdentissimus es omnium amīcōrum quōs habeō.
Rufus, you are the shrewdest of all the friends that I have.

The following examples can be translated in the same way:

1 Bregāns erat īnsolentissimus omnium servōrum quōs Salvius habēbat.
2 omnēs mīlitēs meī sunt fortēs; tū tamen fortissimus es.
3 postrēmō Athēnās vīsitāvimus, pulcherrimam omnium urbium.

6 With the help of paragraphs 1–3, and the table of nouns on pp. 262–63, find the Latin for the words in boldface italics in the following sentences:

1 I have never known a **shrewder merchant**.
2 She sent the **worst slaves** back to the slave-dealer.
3 **Better times** have come.
4 The **bravest citizens** were fighting in the front line.
5 We did not visit the **biggest temple**, as we had seen a **more beautiful temple** next to it.

Pronouns

1 ego, tū, nōs, and vōs (*I, you* (sg.), *we, you* (pl.))

	singular		*plural*	
nominative	ego	tū	nōs	vōs
genitive	meī	tuī	nostrum	vestrum
dative	mihi	tibi	nōbīs	vōbīs
accusative	mē	tē	nōs	vōs
ablative	mē	tē	nōbīs	vōbīs

mēcum, tēcum = *with me, with you* (singular)
nōbīscum, vōbīscum = *with us, with you* (plural)

2 sē (*herself, himself, itself, themselves,* etc.)

	singular	*plural*
nominative (no forms)		
genitive	suī	suī
dative	sibi	sibi
accusative	sē	sē
ablative	sē	sē

sēcum (*with himself, with herself,* etc.) is formed like **mēcum, tēcum**, etc.

Notice some of the ways it can be translated:

tribūnus multōs comitēs **sēcum** habēbat.
*The tribune had many companions **with him**.*

Rūfilla ancillās **sēcum** habēbat.
*Rufilla kept the slave-girls **with her**.*

vēnātōrēs canēs ferōcēs **sēcum** habēbant.
*The hunters had ferocious dogs **with them**.*

Agricola **sēcum** cōgitābat.
*Agricola thought **with himself**.*
   Or, in more natural English:
Agricola thought to himself.

3 **hic** (*this, these*, etc.)

	singular			plural		
	masculine	feminine	neuter	masculine	feminine	neuter
nominative	hic	haec	hoc	hī	hae	haec
genitive	huius	huius	huius	hōrum	hārum	hōrum
dative	huic	huic	huic	hīs	hīs	hīs
accusative	hunc	hanc	hoc	hōs	hās	haec
ablative	hōc	hāc	hōc	hīs	hīs	hīs

The various forms of **hic** can also be used to mean *he, she, they*, etc.:

hic tamen nihil dīcere poterat.
He, *however, could say nothing.*

hī tamen nihil dīcere poterant.
They, *however, could say nothing.*

4 **ille** (*that, those*, etc.; sometimes used with the meaning *he, she, it*, etc.)

	singular			plural		
	masculine	feminine	neuter	masculine	feminine	neuter
nominative	ille	illa	illud	illī	illae	illa
genitive	illīus	illīus	illīus	illōrum	illārum	illōrum
dative	illī	illī	illī	illīs	illīs	illīs
accusative	illum	illam	illud	illōs	illās	illa
ablative	illō	illā	illō	illīs	illīs	illīs

5 **ipse** (*myself, yourself, himself*, etc.)

	singular			plural		
	masculine	feminine	neuter	masculine	feminine	neuter
nominative	ipse	ipsa	ipsum	ipsī	ipsae	ipsa
genitive	ipsīus	ipsīus	ipsīus	ipsōrum	ipsārum	ipsōrum
dative	ipsī	ipsī	ipsī	ipsīs	ipsīs	ipsīs
accusative	ipsum	ipsam	ipsum	ipsōs	ipsās	ipsa
ablative	ipsō	ipsā	ipsō	ipsīs	ipsīs	ipsīs

sacerdōs **ipse** lacrimābat.
*The priest **himself** was weeping.*

dominus mē **ipsum** līberāvit, sed nōn līberōs meōs.
*The master freed me **myself**, but not my children.*

Further examples:

1 ego ipse servum pūnīvī.
2 ego ipsa marītum vocāvī.
3 nōs ipsī in templō aderāmus.
4 subitō ursam ipsam vīdimus.
5 templum ipsum nōn erat magnum.
6 Cogidubnum ipsum audīvimus.
7 dea ipsa mihi appāruit.

6 is (*he, she, it,* etc.)

	singular			*plural*		
	masculine	*feminine*	*neuter*	*masculine*	*feminine*	*neuter*
nominative	**is**	**ea**	**id**	**eī**	**eae**	**ea**
genitive	**eius**	**eius**	**eius**	**eōrum**	**eārum**	**eōrum**
dative	**eī**	**eī**	**eī**	**eīs**	**eīs**	**eīs**
accusative	**eum**	**eam**	**id**	**eōs**	**eās**	**ea**
ablative	**eō**	**eā**	**eō**	**eīs**	**eīs**	**eīs**

The forms of **is** can also be used to mean *that, those,* etc.:

eā nocte rediit dominus.   ***That*** *night, the master returned.*

7 From Stage 23 onwards, you have met various forms of the word **īdem**, meaning *the same (person)*:

	singular			*plural*		
	masculine	*feminine*	*neuter*	*masculine*	*feminine*	*neuter*
nominative	**īdem**	**eadem**	**idem**	**eīdem**	**eaedem**	**eadem**
genitive	**eiusdem**	**eiusdem**	**eiusdem**	**eōrundem**	**eārundem**	**eōrundem**
dative	**eīdem**	**eīdem**	**eīdem**	**eīsdem**	**eīsdem**	**eīsdem**
accusative	**eundem**	**eandem**	**idem**	**eōsdem**	**eāsdem**	**eadem**
ablative	**eōdem**	**eādem**	**eōdem**	**eīsdem**	**eīsdem**	**eīsdem**

Compare the forms of **īdem** with **is** in paragraph 6.

With the help of the table above, find the Latin for the words in boldface italics in the following sentences:

1 I heard ***the same*** boy again.   3 This is ***the same*** man's house.
2 ***The same*** women were there.   4 He saw ***the same*** girl.

8 With the help of paragraphs 3–7 and (if necessary) the gender information in the table of nouns on pages 262–63, find the Latin for the words in boldface italics in the following sentences.

1 I have never seen **that** girl before.
2 Guard **those** slaves!
3 **These** lions are dangerous.
4 I hate the noise of **this** city.
5 We shall give the prize to **this** citizen.
6 We soon found **him**.
7 Where are the cities? I want to see **them**.
8 Where is the temple? I want to see **it**.
9 Where is the king? I want to see **him**.
10 I hurried to **his** house.
11 We described the bear to **him**.
12 We gave **him** the bear.
13 You **yourself** (f.) were called by the Emperor's wife.
14 This is not the **same thing**.

9 Notice the genitive, dative, and ablative plural of the relative pronoun **quī**:

	singular			*plural*		
	masculine	*feminine*	*neuter*	*masculine*	*feminine*	*neuter*
nominative	**quī**	**quae**	**quod**	**quī**	**quae**	**quae**
genitive	**cuius**	**cuius**	**cuius**	**quōrum**	**quārum**	**quōrum**
dative	**cui**	**cui**	**cui**	**quibus**	**quibus**	**quibus**
accusative	**quem**	**quam**	**quod**	**quōs**	**quās**	**quae**
ablative	**quō**	**quā**	**quō**	**quibus**	**quibus**	**quibus**

Examples of sentences with relative pronouns:

senex **cuius** vīlla ardēbat magnōs clāmōrēs tollēbat.
*The old man **whose** house was on fire was raising great shouts.*

duōs servōs ēmī, **quōrum** alter Graecus, alter Aegyptius erat.
*I bought two slaves, one **of whom** was a Greek, the other an Egyptian.*

mercātor **cui** sellās mēnsāsque herī vēndidī hodiē revēnit.
*The merchant **to whom** I sold chairs and tables yesterday came back today.*

nūntiī **quibus** mandāta dedimus herī discessērunt.
*The messengers **to whom** we gave the instructions departed yesterday.*

Further examples of the various forms of **quī**:

1 mīlitēs quōs Salvius ēmīserat tandem rediērunt.
2 iuvenis, cuius nōmen erat Narcissus, sē in aquā vīdit.
3 centuriō custōdēs quī dormīverant sevērissimē pūnīvit.
4 servus, cui sacerdōs signum dederat, victimās ad āram dūxit.
5 templum, quod in mediō oppidō stābat, saepe vīsitābam.
6 epistulam, quam nūntius tulerat, celeriter lēgī.
7 agricolae, quōrum plaustrum servī Salviī frēgerant, in fossam cucurrērunt.
8 ancillae, quārum dominae aberant, nōn labōrāre voluerant.

10 Sometimes the relative pronoun is used at the *beginning* of a sentence. Study the different ways of translating it:

Salviī amīcī īnsidiās Belimicō parāvērunt. **quī**, nihil suspicātus, ad aulam libenter vēnit.
*Salvius' friends prepared a trap for Belimicus. **He**, having suspected nothing, came willingly to the palace.*

mīles pecūniam custōdiēbat. **quem** cum cōnspexissent, fūrēs fūgērunt.
*A soldier was guarding the money. When they caught sight of **him**, the thieves ran away.*

centuriō "ad carnificēs dūcite!" inquit. **quibus** verbīs perterritī, captīvī clāmāre ac lacrimāre coepērunt.
*"Take them to the executioners!" said the centurion. Terrified by **these** words, the prisoners began to shout and weep.*

Further examples:

1 "cur mihi nihil dās?" rogāvit Belimicus. quod cum audīvisset, Salvius īrātissimus erat.
2 domina ancillīs pecūniam trādidit. quae, postquam cibum vīnumque ēmērunt, ad vīllam revēnērunt.
3 deinde rēx Memorī signum dedit. quī, togam praetextam gerēns, ad āram sollemniter prōcessit.
4 multī mīlitēs iam aulam complēbant. quōs cum vīdissent, sacerdōtēs surrēxērunt.
5 tum pūmiliōnēs intrāvērunt. quōs cum vīdisset, puer rīsit.

11 From Stage 26 you have met the relative pronoun used with forms of the pronoun **is**:

fēcī **id** quod iussistī.
*I have done **that** which you ordered.*

Or, in more natural English, use the word *what* to translate both Latin words:

fēcī **id quod** iussistī.
*I have done **what** you ordered.*

Further examples:

1 id quod Salvius in epistulā scrīpsit falsum est.
2 nūntius ea patefēcit quae apud Britannōs audīverat.
3 id quod mihi dīxistī vix intellegere possum.
4 servus tamen, homō ignāvissimus, id quod dominus iusserat omnīnō neglēxit.

Regular Verbs

Indicative Active

1

first conjugation	*second conjugation*	*third conjugation*	*third "-iō" conjugation*	*fourth conjugation*
PRESENT *(I carry, etc.)*				
portō	**doceō**	**trahō**	**capiō**	**audiō**
portās	**docēs**	**trahis**	**capis**	**audīs**
portat	**docet**	**trahit**	**capit**	**audit**
portāmus	**docēmus**	**trahimus**	**capimus**	**audīmus**
portātis	**docētis**	**trahitis**	**capitis**	**audītis**
portant	**docent**	**trahunt**	**capiunt**	**audiunt**
IMPERFECT *(I was carrying, etc.)*				
portābam	**docēbam**	**trahēbam**	**capiēbam**	**audiēbam**
portābās	**docēbās**	**trahēbās**	**capiēbās**	**audiēbās**
portābat	**docēbat**	**trahēbat**	**capiēbat**	**audiēbat**
portābāmus	**docēbāmus**	**trahēbāmus**	**capiēbāmus**	**audiēbāmus**
portābātis	**docēbātis**	**trahēbātis**	**capiēbātis**	**audiēbātis**
portābant	**docēbant**	**trahēbant**	**capiēbant**	**audiēbant**

2 In Stage 33, you met the FUTURE tense (*I shall/will carry, etc.*):

portābō	**docēbō**	**traham**	**capiam**	**audiam**
portābis	**docēbis**	**trahēs**	**capiēs**	**audiēs**
portābit	**docēbit**	**trahet**	**capiet**	**audiet**
portābimus	**docēbimus**	**trahēmus**	**capiēmus**	**audiēmus**
portābitis	**docēbitis**	**trahētis**	**capiētis**	**audiētis**
portābunt	**docēbunt**	**trahent**	**capient**	**audient**

Notice again how the first and second conjugations form their future tense in one way, the third and third "-iō" and fourth conjugations in another.

3 In paragraph 2, find the Latin for:

they will carry; we shall/will take; you (sg.) will teach; he will take; she will hear; you (pl.) will drag; they will carry.

What would be the Latin for the following?

he will teach; we shall/will take; we shall/will hear; you (pl.) will teach.

4 Translate each word, then with the help of paragraph 2 change it into the future tense, keeping the same person and number (e.g. 1st person plural) and translate again. For example, **portāmus** ("we carry") would become **portābimus** ("we shall/will carry"):

portātis; docēbam; capiēbāmus; trahō; audīs; capit; audiēbat.

5

first conjugation	second conjugation	third conjugation	third "-iō" conjugation	fourth conjugation
PERFECT *(I have carried, I carried, etc.)*				
portāvī	docuī	trāxī	cēpī	audīvī
portāvistī	docuistī	trāxistī	cēpistī	audīvistī
portāvit	docuit	trāxit	cēpit	audīvit
portāvimus	docuimus	trāximus	cēpimus	audīvimus
portāvistis	docuistis	trāxistis	cēpistis	audīvistis
portāvērunt	docuērunt	trāxērunt	cēpērunt	audīvērunt
PLUPERFECT *(I had carried, etc.)*				
portāveram	docueram	trāxeram	cēperam	audīveram
portāverās	docuerās	trāxerās	cēperās	audīverās
portāverat	docuerat	trāxerat	cēperat	audīverat
portāverāmus	docuerāmus	trāxerāmus	cēperāmus	audīverāmus
portāverātis	docuerātis	trāxerātis	cēperātis	audīverātis
portāverant	docuerant	trāxerant	cēperant	audīverant

6 In Stage 33, you met the FUTURE PERFECT tense *(I shall/will have carried, etc.)*:

portāverō	docuerō	trāxerō	cēperō	audīverō
portāveris	docueris	trāxeris	cēperis	audīveris
portāverit	docuerit	trāxerit	cēperit	audīverit
portāverimus	docuerimus	trāxerimus	cēperimus	audīverimus
portāveritis	docueritis	trāxeritis	cēperitis	audīveritis
portāverint	docuerint	trāxerint	cēperint	audīverint

The future perfect is often translated by an English present tense:

sī **effūgerō**, iter ad vōs faciam.
*If **I escape**, I shall/will make my way to you.*

7 For passive and other forms of the verb, see pp. 277–80.

Indicative Passive

1 In Stage 29, you met the following forms of the *passive*:

first conjugation	second conjugation	third conjugation	third "-iō" conjugation	fourth conjugation
PRESENT				
portātur	**docētur**	**trahitur**	**capitur**	**audītur**
s/he, it is (being) carried	*s/he, it is (being) taught*	*s/he, it is (being) dragged*	*s/he, it is (being) taken*	*s/he, it is (being) heard*
portantur	**docentur**	**trahuntur**	**capiuntur**	**audiuntur**
they are (being) carried	*they are (being) taught*	*they are (being) dragged*	*they are (being) taken*	*they are (being) heard*
IMPERFECT				
portābātur	**docēbātur**	**trahēbātur**	**capiēbātur**	**audiēbātur**
s/he, it was being carried	*s/he, it was being taught*	*s/he, it was being dragged*	*s/he, it was being taken*	*s/he, it was being heard*
portābantur	**docēbantur**	**trahēbantur**	**capiēbantur**	**audiēbantur**
they were being carried	*they were being taught*	*they were being dragged*	*they were being taken*	*they were being heard*

2 Translate each word, then change it from singular to plural, so that it means *they . . .* instead of *s/he, it . . .*, and translate again:

audītur; trahēbātur; faciēbātur; laudātur; custōdiēbātur; dēlētur.

3 In Stage 34, you met the third-person forms of the *future* passive:

first conjugation	second conjugation	third conjugation	third "-iō" conjugation	fourth conjugation
FUTURE				
portābitur	**docēbitur**	**trahētur**	**capiētur**	**audiētur**
s/he, it will be carried	*s/he, it will be taught*	*s/he, it will be dragged*	*s/he, it will be taken*	*s/he, it will be heard*
portābuntur	**docēbuntur**	**trahentur**	**capientur**	**audientur**
they will be carried	*they will be taught*	*they will be dragged*	*they will be taken*	*they will be heard*

4 In Stage 30, you met the PERFECT and PLUPERFECT tenses of the passive:

first conjugation	second conjugation	third conjugation	third "-iō" conjugation	fourth conjugation
PERFECT *(I have been carried, I was carried, etc.)*				
portātus sum	doctus sum	tractus sum	captus sum	audītus sum
portātus es	doctus es	tractus es	captus es	audītus es
portātus est	doctus est	tractus est	captus est	audītus est
portātī sumus	doctī sumus	tractī sumus	captī sumus	audītī sumus
portātī estis	doctī estis	tractī estis	captī estis	audītī estis
portātī sunt	doctī sunt	tractī sunt	captī sunt	audītī sunt
PLUPERFECT *(I had been carried, etc.)*				
portātus eram	doctus eram	tractus eram	captus eram	audītus eram
portātus erās	doctus erās	tractus erās	captus erās	audītus erās
portātus erat	doctus erat	tractus erat	captus erat	audītus erat
portātī erāmus	doctī erāmus	tractī erāmus	captī erāmus	audītī erāmus
portātī erātis	doctī erātis	tractī erātis	captī erātis	audītī erātis
portātī erant	doctī erant	tractī erant	captī erant	audītī erant

5 Give the meaning of:

audītus eram; portātus erat; captī sunt; doctus sum; tractus es; portātī erāmus.

6 In paragraph 4, find the Latin for:

they had been carried; I have been dragged; you (sg.) have been taught; he was taken.

7 Notice again that the two tenses in paragraph 4 are formed with perfect passive participles, which change their endings to indicate *number* (singular or plural) and *gender* (masculine, feminine, or neuter). For example:

masculine singular:	puer ā mīlitibus **captus** est.
neuter singular:	templum ā mīlitibus **captum** est.
feminine singular:	urbs ā mīlitibus **capta** est.
feminine plural:	multae urbēs ā mīlitibus **captae** sunt.

What would be the Latin for the following?

she has been taught; it had been dragged; they [=the girls] were heard; it has been taken.

8 For subjunctive and other forms of the verb, see pp. 279–80.

Subjunctive Active

1

first conjugation	second conjugation	third conjugation	third "-iō" conjugation	fourth conjugation
IMPERFECT SUBJUNCTIVE				
portārem	docērem	traherem	caperem	audīrem
portārēs	docērēs	traherēs	caperēs	audīrēs
portāret	docēret	traheret	caperet	audīret
portārēmus	docērēmus	traherēmus	caperēmus	audīrēmus
portārētis	docērētis	traherētis	caperētis	audīrētis
portārent	docērent	traherent	caperent	audīrent
PLUPERFECT SUBJUNCTIVE				
portāvissem	docuissem	trāxissem	cēpissem	audīvissem
portāvissēs	docuissēs	trāxissēs	cēpissēs	audīvissēs
portāvisset	docuisset	trāxisset	cēpisset	audīvisset
portāvissēmus	docuissēmus	trāxissēmus	cēpissēmus	audīvissēmus
portāvissētis	docuissētis	trāxissētis	cēpissētis	audīvissētis
portāvissent	docuissent	trāxissent	cēpissent	audīvissent

There are various ways of translating the subjunctive, depending on the way it is being used in a particular sentence (see, in this section, pp. 290–93, Uses of the Subjunctive).

2 Complete each sentence with the correct word and then translate.

1 intellegere nōn poteram cūr cīvēs portum . . . . . . (peteret, peterent)
2 optiō in fossam dēsiluit ut hastās hostium . . . . . . (vītāret, vītārent)
3 senātor scīre voluit num pater meus . . . . . . (superfuisset, superfuissent)
4 cum senex tergum . . . . . , fūrēs per fenestram tacitē intrāvērunt. (vertisset, vertissent)
5 frātribus meīs tandem persuāsī ut ānulum aureum . . . . . . (redderet, redderent)
6 tanta erat nūbēs ut pāstōrēs sōlem vidēre nōn . . . . . . (posset, possent)

Other Forms of the Verb

1 ACTIVE INFINITIVE

portāre	**docēre**	**trahere**	**capere**	**audīre**
to carry	*to teach*	*to drag*	*to take*	*to hear*

PASSIVE INFINITIVE

portārī	**docērī**	**trahī**	**capī**	**audīrī**
to be carried	*to be taught*	*to be dragged*	*to be taken*	*to be heard*

2 IMPERATIVE

(sg.) **portā**	**docē**	**trahe**	**cape**	**audī**
(pl.) **portāte**	**docēte**	**trahite**	**capite**	**audīte**
carry!	*teach!*	*drag!*	*take!*	*hear!*

3 PRESENT ACTIVE PARTICIPLE

portāns	**docēns**	**trahēns**	**capiēns**	**audiēns**
carrying	*teaching*	*dragging*	*taking*	*hearing*

Study the forms of the present participle **portāns**:

	singular		*plural*	
	masc. and fem.	*neuter*	*masc. and fem.*	*neuter*
nominative and *vocative*	**portāns**	**portāns**	**portantēs**	**portantia**
genitive	**portantis**	**portantis**	**portantium**	**portantium**
dative	**portantī**	**portantī**	**portantibus**	**portantibus**
accusative	**portantem**	**portāns**	**portantēs**	**portantia**
ablative	**portant-ī/-e**	**portant-ī/-e**	**portantibus**	**portantibus**

4 PERFECT PASSIVE PARTICIPLE

first *conjugation*	*second* *conjugation*	*third* *conjugation*	*third "-iō"* *conjugation*	*fourth* *conjugation*
portātus	**doctus**	**tractus**	**captus**	**audītus**
having been carried	*having been taught*	*having been dragged*	*having been taken*	*having been heard*

Perfect passive participles change their endings in the same way as **bonus** (shown on p. 265).

For examples of perfect *active* participles, see Deponent Verbs, pp. 281–82.

For examples of ways in which participles are used, see pp. 286–89.

5 FUTURE ACTIVE PARTICIPLE

portātūrus	**doctūrus**	**tractūrus**	**captūrus**	**audītūrus**
about to carry	*about to teach*	*about to drag*	*about to take*	*about to hear*

Future participles change their endings in the same way as **bonus** (shown on p. 265).

6 GERUNDIVE

portandus	**docendus**	**trahendus**	**capiendus**	**audiendus**

Gerundives change their endings in the same way as **bonus**.

Notice again the way in which the gerundive is used:

nōbīs audiendum est.   mihi amphora portanda est.
We must listen.   *I must carry the wine-jar.*

Deponent Verbs

1 From Stage 32 onwards, you have met *deponent verbs*:

PRESENT				
cōnātur	*s/he, it tries*		**loquitur**	*s/he, it speaks*
cōnantur	*they try*		**loquuntur**	*they speak*
FUTURE				
cōnābitur	*s/he, it will try*		**loquētur**	*s/he, it will speak*
cōnābuntur	*they will try*		**loquentur**	*they will speak*
IMPERFECT				
cōnābātur	*s/he, it was trying*		**loquēbātur**	*s/he, it was speaking*
cōnābantur	*they were trying*		**loquēbantur**	*they were speaking*
PERFECT				
cōnātus sum	*I (have) tried*		**locūtus sum**	*I spoke, I have spoken*
cōnātus es	*you (have) tried*		**locūtus es**	*you spoke, you have spoken*
cōnātus est	*s/he, it (has) tried*		**locūtus est**	*s/he, it spoke, s/he, it has spoken*
cōnātī sumus	*we (have) tried*		**locūtī sumus**	*we spoke, we have spoken*
cōnātī estis	*you (have) tried*		**locūtī estis**	*you spoke, you have spoken*
cōnātī sunt	*they (have) tried*		**locūtī sunt**	*they spoke, they have spoken*
PLUPERFECT				
cōnātus eram	*I had tried*		**locūtus eram**	*I had spoken*
cōnātus erās	*you had tried*		**locūtus erās**	*you had spoken*
cōnātus erat	*s/he, it had tried*		**locūtus erat**	*s/he, it had spoken*
cōnātī erāmus	*we had tried*		**locūtī erāmus**	*we had spoken*
cōnātī erātis	*you had tried*		**locūtī erātis**	*you had spoken*
cōnātī erant	*they had tried*		**locūtī erant**	*they had spoken*
PERFECT ACTIVE PARTICIPLE				
cōnātus	*having tried*		**locūtus**	*having spoken*

Perfect active participles change their endings in the same way as **bonus** (shown on p. 265).

INFINITIVE				
cōnārī	*to try*		**loquī**	*to speak*

2 The present, imperfect, and future tenses are shown only in the form of the 3rd person singular and plural. You have not yet met the 1st and 2nd persons (*I try, you try*, etc.) in the stories in the Stages.

3 Give the meaning of:

cōnātus eram; locūtī sumus; ingressī sumus; ingressus erās; profectus es.

4 Translate each word (or pair of words), then change it from plural to singular, so that it means *s/he, it* . . . instead of *they* . . ., and translate again.

loquuntur; cōnātī sunt; profectī sunt; sequēbantur; ēgressī erant; hortantur.

5 Compare the two verbs in paragraph 1 with the passive forms of **portō** and **trahō** listed on pp. 277–78.

6 For further practice with deponent verbs, see paragraphs 7–8 on p. 313.

Irregular Verbs

1 INFINITIVE

esse	posse	īre	velle	nōlle	ferre
to be	*to be able*	*to go*	*to want*	*not to want*	*to bring*

PRESENT INDICATIVE *(I am, etc.)*

sum	possum	eō	volō	nōlō	ferō
es	potes	īs	vīs	nōn vīs	fers
est	potest	it	vult	nōn vult	fert
sumus	possumus	īmus	volumus	nōlumus	ferimus
estis	potestis	ītis	vultis	nōn vultis	fertis
sunt	possunt	eunt	volunt	nōlunt	ferunt

IMPERFECT INDICATIVE *(I was, etc.)*

eram	poteram	ībam	volēbam	nōlēbam	ferēbam
erās	poterās	ībās	volēbās	nōlēbās	ferēbās
erat	poterat	ībat	volēbat	nōlēbat	ferēbat
erāmus	poterāmus	ībāmus	volēbāmus	nōlēbāmus	ferēbāmus
erātis	poterātis	ībātis	volēbātis	nōlēbātis	ferēbātis
erant	poterant	ībant	volēbant	nōlēbant	ferēbant

2 Study the forms of the FUTURE tense *(I shall/will be, etc.)*; see Stage 33, p. 234:

erō	poterō	ībō	volam	nōlam	feram
eris	poteris	ībis	volēs	nōlēs	ferēs
erit	poterit	ībit	volet	nōlet	feret
erimus	poterimus	ībimus	volēmus	nōlēmus	ferēmus
eritis	poteritis	ībitis	volētis	nōlētis	ferētis
erunt	poterunt	ībunt	volent	nōlent	ferent

3 Translate each word, then change it into the future tense, keeping the same person and number (e.g. 3rd person singular), and translate again:

est; potestis; ībam; vīs; nōlunt; ferēbāmus.

---

4 PERFECT INDICATIVE *(I have been, I was, etc.)*

fuī	potuī	iī	voluī	nōluī	tulī
fuistī	potuistī	iistī	voluistī	nōluistī	tulistī
fuit	potuit	iit	voluit	nōluit	tulit
fuimus	potuimus	iimus	voluimus	nōluimus	tulimus
fuistis	potuistis	iistis	voluistis	nōluistis	tulistis
fuērunt	potuērunt	iērunt	voluērunt	nōluērunt	tulērunt

PLUPERFECT INDICATIVE *(I had been, etc.)*

fueram	potueram	ieram	volueram	nōlueram	tuleram
fuerās	potuerās	ierās	voluerās	nōluerās	tulerās
fuerat	potuerat	ierat	voluerat	nōluerat	tulerat
fuerāmus	potuerāmus	ierāmus	voluerāmus	nōluerāmus	tulerāmus
fuerātis	potuerātis	ierātis	voluerātis	nōluerātis	tulerātis
fuerant	potuerant	ierant	voluerant	nōluerant	tulerant

---

5 Translate the following:

1 potes; vult; eō; fers; nōlunt; fuī; potueram.
2 ībātis; poterant; tulistis; voluimus; fuerāmus; iistis.

---

6 IMPERFECT SUBJUNCTIVE

essem	possem	īrem	vellem	nōllem	ferrem
essēs	possēs	īrēs	vellēs	nōllēs	ferrēs
esset	posset	īret	vellet	nōllet	ferret
essēmus	possēmus	īrēmus	vellēmus	nōllēmus	ferrēmus
essētis	possētis	īrētis	vellētis	nōllētis	ferrētis
essent	possent	īrent	vellent	nōllent	ferrent

PLUPERFECT SUBJUNCTIVE

fuissem	potuissem	iissem	voluissem	nōluissem	tulissem
fuissēs	potuissēs	iissēs	voluissēs	nōluissēs	tulissēs
fuisset	potuisset	iisset	voluisset	nōluisset	tulisset
fuissēmus	potuissēmus	iissēmus	voluissēmus	nōluissēmus	tulissēmus
fuissētis	potuissētis	iissētis	voluissētis	nōluissētis	tulissētis
fuissent	potuissent	iissent	voluissent	nōluissent	tulissent

7 Study the following *passive* forms of **ferō**:

PRESENT		IMPERFECT	
fertur	*s/he, it is brought*	**ferēbātur**	*s/he, it was being brought*
feruntur	*they are brought*	**ferēbantur**	*they were being brought*
PERFECT		PLUPERFECT	
lātus sum	*I have been brought, I was brought*	**lātus eram**	*I had been brought*
lātus es	*you have been brought, you were brought*	**lātus erās**	*you had been brought*
lātus est	*s/he, it has been brought, s/he, it was brought*	**lātus erat**	*s/he, it had been brought*
lātī sumus	*we have been brought, we were brought*	**lātī erāmus**	*we had been brought*
lātī estis	*you have been brought, you were brought*	**lātī erātis**	*you had been brought*
lātī sunt	*they have been brought, they were brought*	**lātī erant**	*they had been brought*

PERFECT PASSIVE PARTICIPLE
lātus   *having been brought*

8 What would be the Latin for the following?

he had been brought; he has been brought; we have been brought; he was brought.

Uses of the Cases

1 *nominative*

    captīvus clāmābat.   *The prisoner was shouting.*

2 *vocative*

    valē, **domine**!   *Good-by, master!*

3 *genitive*

    3a māter **puerōrum**   *the mother of the boys*
    3b plūs **pecūniae**   *more money*
    3c vir **maximae virtūtis**   *a man of very great courage*

4 *dative*

    4a **mīlitibus** cibum dedimus.   *We gave food to the soldiers.*
    4b **vestrō candidātō** nōn faveō.   *I do not support your candidate.*

5 *accusative*

    5a **pontem** trānsiimus.   *We crossed the bridge.*
    5b **trēs hōrās** labōrābam.   *I was working for three hours. (Compare 6d)*
    5c per **agrōs**; ad **vīllam**   *through the fields; to the house (Compare 6e)*

6 *ablative* (learned in Stage 28)

    6a **spectāculō** attonitus   *astonished by the sight*
    6b senex **longā barbā**   *an old man with a long beard*
    6c **nōbilī gente** nātus   *born from a noble family*
    6d **quārtō diē** revēnit.   *He came back on the fourth day. (Compare 5b)*
    6e cum **amīcīs**; ē **tabernā**   *with friends; from the inn (Compare 5c)*

For examples of the "ablative absolute," see paragraph 11 on p. 289.

7 Further examples of some of the uses listed above:

    1 Vitellia erat fēmina summae prūdentiae.
    2 sextā hōrā discessimus.
    3 uxor imperātōris in cubiculō Paridem exspectābat.
    4 Haterius, verbīs Salviī dēceptus, cōnsēnsit.
    5 multōs annōs ibi habitābam.
    6 cūr cōnsiliīs meīs obstās?
    7 satis vīnī bibistī?

Uses of the Participle

1 In Stage 20 you met the *present active participle:*

canis dominum **intrantem** vīdit.
*The dog saw his master **entering**.*

2 In Stage 21, you met the *perfect passive participle:*

servus, graviter **vulnerātus**, sub plaustrō iacēbat.
*The slave, **(having been)** seriously **wounded**, was lying under the cart.*

3 In Stage 22, you met the *perfect active participle* (also known as the *deponent participle*):

aegrōtī, deam **precātī,** remedium mīrābile spērābant.
*The invalids, **having prayed** to the goddess, were hoping for a remarkable cure.*

4 Translate the following examples. Find the participle in each sentence and say whether it is present, perfect passive, or perfect active (= deponent):

1 Latrō, prope iānuam tabernae stāns, pugnam spectābat.
2 Vilbia, ē tabernā ēgressa, sorōrem statim quaesīvit.
3 fūrēs, ad iūdicem ductī, veniam petīvērunt.
4 centuriō, amphoram vīnī optimī adeptus, ad amīcōs celeriter rediit.
5 subitō equōs appropinquantēs audīvimus.
6 iuvenis callidus pecūniam, in terrā cēlātam, invēnit.

A participle is used to describe a noun. For example, in sentence 1 above, **stāns** (*standing*) describes **Latrō**. Find the nouns described by the participles in sentences 2–6.

5 A participle agrees with the noun it describes in three ways: in case, number, and gender. For example:

nominative:	**rēx**, in mediā turbā **sedēns**, dōna accipiēbat.
accusative:	Quīntus **rēgem**, in mediā turbā **sedentem**, agnōvit.
singular:	**lēgātus**, ad carcerem **regressus**, nēminem ibi invēnit.
plural:	**custōdēs**, ad carcerem **regressī**, nēminem ibi invēnērunt.
masculine:	**nūntius**, statim **profectus**, ad fundum contendit.
feminine:	**uxor**, statim **profecta**, ad fundum contendit.

6 You have met the following forms of the *present participle:*

	singular		plural	
	masc. and fem.	neuter	masc. and fem.	neuter
nominative and *vocative*	**trahēns**	**trahēns**	**trahentēs**	**trahentia**
genitive	**trahentis**	**trahentis**	**trahentium**	**trahentium**
dative	**trahentī**	**trahentī**	**trahentibus**	**trahentibus**
accusative	**trahentem**	**trahēns**	**trahentēs**	**trahentia**
ablative	**trahent-ī/-e**	**trahent-ī/-e**	**trahentibus**	**trahentibus**

Compare the endings of **trahēns** with the endings of the adjective **ingēns** ("huge"), on p. 265.

7 You have met the following forms of the *perfect passive participle:*

	singular			plural		
	masculine	feminine	neuter	masculine	feminine	neuter
nominative and *vocative*	**portātus (portāte)**	**portāta**	**portātum**	**portātī**	**portātae**	**portāta**
genitive	**portātī**	**portātae**	**portātī**	**portātōrum**	**portātārum**	**portātōrum**
dative	**portātō**	**portātae**	**portātō**	**portātīs**	**portātīs**	**portātīs**
accusative	**portātum**	**portātam**	**portātum**	**portātōs**	**portātās**	**portāta**
ablative	**portātō**	**portātā**	**portātō**	**portātīs**	**portātīs**	**portātīs**

You have met the following forms of the *perfect active participle:*

	singular			plural		
	masculine	feminine	neuter	masculine	feminine	neuter
nominative and *vocative*	**ingressus (ingresse)**	**ingressa**	**ingressum**	**ingressī**	**ingressae**	**ingressa**
genitive	**ingressī**	**ingressae**	**ingressī**	**ingressōrum**	**ingressārum**	**ingressōrum**
dative	**ingressō**	**ingressae**	**ingressō**	**ingressīs**	**ingressīs**	**ingressīs**
accusative	**ingressum**	**ingressam**	**ingressum**	**ingressōs**	**ingressās**	**ingressa**
ablative	**ingressō**	**ingressā**	**ingressō**	**ingressīs**	**ingressīs**	**ingressīs**

Compare the endings of **portātus** and **ingressus** with the endings of the adjective **bonus** ("good"), on p. 265.

8 With the help of paragraphs 6 and 7 above, find the Latin words for the participles in the following sentences:

1 I saw the soldiers **dragging** the slave to prison.
2 The goddess, **having been carried** in procession, watched her sacred boat.
3 The king, **having entered**, greeted the chieftains.

9 Notice that a Latin participle can be translated various ways. For example:

nūntius, aulam ingressus, rēgem quaesīvit.
The messenger, having entered the palace, looked for the king.
After the messenger had entered the palace, he looked for the king.
On entering the palace, the messenger looked for the king.
The messenger entered the palace and looked for the king.

10 Translate the following examples and pick out the participle in each sentence:

1 ingēns multitūdō lūdōs, ab imperātōre ēditōs, spectābat.
2 custōdēs captīvō dormientī appropinquāvērunt.
3 mīlitēs, ā centuriōnibus īnstrūctī, in longīs ōrdinibus stābant.
4 mercātor amīcum, ā Graeciā regressum, ad cēnam sūmptuōsam invītāvit.

Find the nouns described by the participles in the sentences above, and say whether each noun-and-participle pair is nominative, dative, or accusative.

11 In Stage 31, you met examples of the *ablative absolute*, consisting of a noun and participle in the ablative case:

bellō cōnfectō, Agricola ad Ītaliam rediit.
With the war having been finished, Agricola returned to Italy.
    Or, in more natural English:
When the war had been finished, Agricola returned to Italy, or
After finishing the war, Agricola returned to Italy.

Further examples:

1 ponte dēlētō, nēmō flūmen trānsīre poterat.
2 hīs verbīs audītīs, cīvēs plausērunt.
3 nāve refectā, mercātor ā Britanniā discessit.
4 iuvenēs, togīs dēpositīs, balneum intrāvērunt.
5 cōnsule ingressō, omnēs senātōrēs surrēxērunt.
6 fēle absente, mūrēs semper lūdunt.

12 From Stage 31 onwards, you have met examples in which a noun and participle in the *dative* case are placed at the beginning of the sentence:

amīcō auxilium petentī multam pecūniam obtulī.
To a friend asking for help I offered a lot of money.
    Or, in more natural English:
When my friend asked for help I offered him a lot of money.

Further examples:

1 servō haesitantī Vitellia "intrā!" inquit.
2 Hateriō haec rogantī Salvius nihil respondit.
3 praecōnī regressō senex epistulam trādidit.
4 puellae prōcēdentī obstābat ingēns multitūdō clientium.

Uses of the Subjunctive

1 *With* **cum** *(meaning "when")*

Iūdaeī, cum cōnsilium Eleazārī audīvissent, libenter cōnsēnsērunt.
When the Jews had heard Eleazar's plan, they willingly agreed.

Further examples:
1 Agricola, cum legiōnem īnspexisset, mīlitēs centuriōnēsque laudāvit.
2 cum haruspex in templō cēnāret, rēx ipse appropinquābat.
3 fabri, cum pecūniam accēpissent, abiērunt.

2 *Indirect Question*

cōnsul nesciēbat quis arcum novum aedificāvisset.
The consul did not know who had built the new arch.

mē rogāvērunt num satis pecūniae habērem.
They asked me whether I had enough money.

From Stage 28 onwards, you have met the words **utrum** and **an** in indirect questions:

incertī erant utrum dux mortuus an vīvus esset.
They were unsure whether their leader was dead or alive.

Further examples:
1 incertus eram quam longum esset flūmen.
  (Compare this with the direct question: "quam longum est flūmen?")
2 cognōscere voluimus cūr multitūdō convēnisset.
  (Compare this with the direct question: "cūr multitūdō convēnit?")
3 equitēs fēminās rogāvērunt num fugitīvōs vīdissent.
  (Compare this with the direct question: "fugitīvōsne vīdistis?")
4 nēmō sciēbat num Memor lībertō venēnum praebuisset.
5 Rōmānī nesciēbant quot hostēs in castrīs manērent.
6 mē rogāvit num māter mea vīveret.

3 *Purpose Clause*

ad urbem iter fēcimus ut amphitheātrum vīsitārēmus.
We traveled to the city in order to visit the amphitheater.

Further examples:

1 amīcī ad urbem festīnāvērunt ut auxilium cīvibus ferrent.
2 epistulam scrīpsī ut lēgātum dē perīculō monērem.
3 senātor mē arcessīvit ut rem hospitibus nārrārem.

In Stage 29, you met purpose clauses used with the relative pronoun
quī:

nūntiōs ēmīsit quī prīncipēs ad aulam arcesserent.
He sent out messengers who were to summon the chieftains to the palace.
   Or, in more natural English:
He sent out messengers to summon the chieftains to the palace.

From Stage 29 onwards, you have met purpose clauses used with **nē**:

centuriō omnēs portās clausit nē captīvī effugerent.
The centurion shut all the gates so that the prisoners would not escape.

4 *Indirect Command*

Domitiānus Salviō imperāverat ut rēgnum Cogidubnī occupāret.
Domitian had ordered Salvius to seize Cogidubnus' kingdom.

Further examples:

1 nūntius Britannīs persuāsit ut dōna ad aulam ferrent.
   (Compare the direct command: "dōna ad aulam ferte!")
2 dominus nōbīs imperāvit ut sellās lectōsque emerēmus.
   (Compare this with the direct command: "sellās lectōsque emite!").
3 senex deam Sūlem ōrāvit ut morbum sānāret.

   In Stage 29, you met indirect commands introduced by **nē**:

   puer agricolam ōrāvit nē equum occīderet.
   The boy begged the farmer not to kill the horse.

Haterius ab amīcīs monitus est nē Salviō cōnfīderet.
Haterius was warned by friends not to trust Salvius.

5 *Result Clause*

tam perītus erat tībīcen ut omnēs eum laudārent.
The pipe player was so skillful that everyone praised him.

Further examples:

1 tam dīligenter carcerem custōdīvī ut lēgātus ipse mē laudāret.
2 mercātor tot vīllās habēbat ut eās numerāre nōn posset.
3 tantus erat timor iuvenum ut astrologō crēderent.

6 If you want to understand why a subjunctive is being used in a particular sentence, you must look at the whole sentence, not just the subjunctive by itself.

For example, study these two sentences; one contains a *purpose* clause, and the other contains a *result* clause:

1 tam īrātus erat Agricola ut dormīre nōn posset.
   Agricola was so angry that he could not sleep.
2 Salvius mīlitēs ēmīsit ut Quīntum invenīrent.
   Salvius sent out the soldiers to find Quintus.

Sentence 1 clearly contains the result clause; Agricola's failure to sleep was the *result* of his anger. The word **tam** (*so*) is a further clue; it is often followed by a result clause later in the sentence. Other words like **tam** (*so*) are **tantus** (*so great*), **tot**(*so many*), and **adeō** (*so* or *so much*).

Sentence 2 clearly contains the purpose clause; finding Quintus was Salvius' *purpose* in sending out the soldiers.

7 Translate the following examples:

1 lībertus, cum venēnum bibisset, mortuus prōcubuit.
2 tot hostēs castra nostra oppugnābant ut dē vītā dēspērārēmus.
3 prīncipēs mē rogāvērunt cūr pontem trānsīre vellem.
4 Gutta sub mēnsā sē cēlāvit ut perīculum vītāret.
5 centuriōnēs mīlitibus imperāvērunt ut plaustra reficerent.
6 cum ancillae pōcula lavārent, quattuor equitēs ad tabernam advēnērunt.
7 adeō attonitus erat fīlius meus ut diū immōtus stāret.
8 portas cellārum aperuimus ut amīcōs nostrōs līberārēmus.
9 amīcus mē monuit ut latērem.
10 Modestus explicāre nōn poterat quō modō captīvī effūgissent.
11 cum servī vīnum intulissent, Haterius silentium poposcit.
12 tanta erat fortitūdō Iūdaeōrum ut perīre potius quam cēdere māllent.
13 nēmō sciēbat utrum Haterius an Salvius rem administrāvisset.
14 uxor mihi persuāsit nē hoc susciperem.
15 extrā carcerem stābant decem mīlitēs quī captīvōs custōdīrent.

In each sentence, find the reason why a subjunctive is being used.

From Stage 33 onwards, you have met the subjunctive used with **priusquam** (meaning *before*) and **dum** (meaning *until*):

Myropnous iānuam clausit priusquam mīlitēs intrārent.
Myropnous shut the door before the soldiers could enter.

exspectābam dum amīcus advenīret.
I was waiting until my friend should arrive.
  Or, in more natural English:
I was waiting for my friend to arrive.

Word Order

1 In Unit 1, you met the following word order:

dēspērābat senex.   *The old man was in despair.*

Further examples:
1 fūgit Modestus.   2 revēnērunt mercātōrēs.

2 From Stage 21 onwards, you have met the following word order:

dedit signum haruspex.   *The soothsayer gave the signal.*

Further examples:
1 rapuērunt pecūniam fūrēs.   2 īnspiciēbat mīlitēs Agricola.

3 From Stage 23 onwards, you have met the following word order:

ēmīsit Salvius equitēs.   *Salvius sent out horsemen.*

Further examples:
1 tenēbat Cephalus pōculum.   2 posuērunt cīvēs statuam.

4 Further examples of all three types of word order:

1 discessit nūntius.   4 poposcit captīvus lībertātem.
2 fēcērunt hostēs impetum.   5 vexābant mē puerī.
3 reficiēbat mūrum faber.   6 periērunt īnfantēs.

5 Study the word order in the following examples:

in hāc prōvinciā   ad nostrum patrem
in this province   *to our father*

From Stage 24 onwards, you have met a different word order:

mediīs in undīs   hanc ad tabernam
in the middle of the waves *to this shop*

Further examples:
1 hāc in urbe   4 omnibus cum legiōnibus
2 multīs cum mīlitibus   5 tōtam per noctem
3 parvum ad oppidum   6 mediō in flūmine

Longer Sentences

1 Study the following groups of sentences:

1a puerī timēbant.
   The boys were afraid.

1b puerī timēbant quod prope iānuam iacēbat ingēns canis.
   The boys were afraid because near the door was lying a huge dog.

1c puerī timēbant quod prope iānuam iacēbat ingēns canis, vehementer lātrāns.
   The boys were afraid because near the door was lying a huge dog, barking loudly.

2a Strȳthiōnem cōnspexit.
   He caught sight of Strythio.

2b ubi ā culīnā redībat, Strȳthiōnem cōnspexit.
   When he was returning from the kitchen, he caught sight of Strythio.

2c ubi ā culīnā in quā cēnāverat redībat, Strȳthiōnem cōnspexit.
   When he was returning from the kitchen in which he had been dining, he caught sight of Strythio.

3a Salvius incertus erat.
   Salvius was uncertain.

3b Salvius incertus erat quō fūgisset Dumnorix.
   Salvius was uncertain where Dumnorix had fled to.

3c Salvius incertus erat quō fūgisset Dumnorix, cūr abesset Quīntus.
   Salvius was uncertain where Dumnorix had fled to, and why Quintus was missing.

2 Further examples:

4a centuriō immōtus manēbat.

4b centuriō immōtus manēbat, quamquam appropinquābant hostēs.

4c centuriō immōtus manēbat, quamquam appropinquābant hostēs, quī hastās vibrābant.

5a omnēs cīvēs plausērunt.

5b ubi puellae cantāre coepērunt, omnēs cīvēs plausērunt.

5c ubi puellae quae prō pompā ambulābant cantāre coepērunt, omnēs cīvēs plausērunt.

6a nūntius prīncipia petīvit.

6b nūntius quī epistulam ferēbat prīncipia petīvit.

6c nūntius quī epistulam ferēbat, simulac ad castra advēnit, prīncipia petīvit.

3 Further examples of the longer (c) type of sentences:

7 tantae erant flammae ut vīllam magnam dēlērent, quam architectus clārus aedificāverat.

8 lībertus cubiculum intrāre nōlēbat quod Memor, quī multum vīnum biberat, graviter iam dormiēbat.

9 Salvius, Belimicō diffīsus, tribūnum arcessīvit ut vērum cognōsceret.

10 postquam ad forum vēnimus, ubi mercātōrēs negōtium agere solēbant, rem mīrābilem vīdimus.

11 pater, cum fīliōs pōcula hauriēntēs cōnspexisset, vehementer saeviēbat.

12 explōrātōrēs mox cognōvērunt ubi hostēs castra posuissent, quot mīlitēs in castrīs essent, quis mīlitibus praeesset.

4 Study each sentence and answer the questions that follow it:

1 postquam Haterius fabrōs, quī labōrābant in āreā, dīmīsit, Salvius negōtium agere coepit.
   Where were the craftsmen working? What did Haterius do to them? What did Salvius then do? Translate the sentence.

2 spectātōrēs, cum candēlābrum aureum ē templō Iūdaeōrum raptum cōnspexissent, iterum iterumque plausērunt.
   What did the spectators catch sight of? Where had it been seized? What was the reaction of the spectators? Translate the sentence.

3 fūr, cum verba centuriōnis audīvisset, tantō metū poenārum affectus est ut pecūniam quam ē tabernā abstulerat, statim abicere cōnstitueret.
   What did the thief hear? What were his feelings? What did he decide to do? Where had the money come from? Translate the sentence.

5 Further examples for study and translation:

1 ancillae, quod dominam vehementer clāmantem audīvērunt, cubiculum eius quam celerrimē petīvērunt.

2 equitēs adeō pugnāre cupiēbant ut, simulac dux signum dedit, ē portīs castrōrum ērumperent.

3 postquam cōnsul hanc sententiam dīxit, Domitiānus servō adstantī imperāvit ut epistulam ab Agricolā nūper missam recitāret.

PART TWO: Reference Grammar

(Including some forms introduced later in the course.)

I Nouns

See Review Grammar, pp.262–63, for complete tables of nouns of all five declensions.

II Adjectives

See Review Grammar, pp.265–67, for tables of adjectives and their comparative forms.

III Pronouns

See Review Grammar, pp.269–72, for tables of personal and reflexive pronouns, and also **hic, ille, ipse, is, īdem,** and **quī**.

IV Regular Verbs

See Review Grammar, pp.275–80, for complete tables of active forms of regular verbs, including participles, infinitives, and gerundives.

INDICATIVE PASSIVE

PRESENT *(I am carried, I am being carried, etc.)*

portor	doceor	trahor	capior	audior
portāris	docēris	traheris	caperis	audīris
portātur	docētur	trahitur	capitur	audītur
portāmur	docēmur	trahimur	capimur	audīmur
portāminī	docēminī	trahiminī	capiminī	audīminī
portantur	docentur	trahuntur	capiuntur	audiuntur

FUTURE *(I shall/will be carried, etc.)*

portābor	docēbor	trahar	capiar	audiar
portāberis	docēberis	trahēris	capiēris	audiēris
portābitur	docēbitur	trahētur	capiētur	audiētur
portābimur	docēbimur	trahēmur	capiēmur	audiēmur
portābiminī	docēbiminī	trahēminī	capiēminī	audiēminī
portābuntur	docēbuntur	trahentur	capientur	audientur

IMPERFECT *(I was being carried, etc.)*

portābar	docēbar	trahēbar	capiēbar	audiēbar
portābāris	docēbāris	trahēbāris	capiēbāris	audiēbāris
portābātur	docēbātur	trahēbātur	capiēbātur	audiēbātur
portābāmur	docēbāmur	trahēbāmur	capiēbāmur	audiēbāmur
portābāminī	docēbāminī	trahēbāminī	capiēbāminī	audiēbāminī
portābantur	docēbantur	trahēbantur	capiēbantur	audiēbantur

PERFECT *(I have been carried, I was carried, etc.)*

portātus sum	doctus sum	tractus sum	captus sum	audītus sum
portātus es	doctus es	tractus es	captus es	audītus es
portātus est	doctus est	tractus est	captus est	audītus est
portātī sumus	doctī sumus	tractī sumus	captī sumus	audītī sumus
portātī estis	doctī estis	tractī estis	captī estis	audītī estis
portātī sunt	doctī sunt	tractī sunt	captī sunt	audītī sunt

FUTURE PERFECT *(I shall/will have been carried, etc.; but often translated as an English present tense: I am carried, etc.)*

portātus erō	doctus erō	tractus erō	captus erō	audītus erō
portātus eris	doctus eris	tractus eris	captus eris	audītus eris
portātus erit	doctus erit	tractus erit	captus erit	audītus erit
portātī erimus	doctī erimus	tractī erimus	captī erimus	audītī erimus
portātī eritis	doctī eritis	tractī eritis	captī eritis	audītī eritis
portātī erunt	doctī erunt	tractī erunt	captī erunt	audītī erunt

PLUPERFECT *(I had been carried, etc.)*

portātus eram	doctus eram	tractus eram	captus eram	audītus eram
portātus erās	doctus erās	tractus erās	captus erās	audītus erās
portātus erat	doctus erat	tractus erat	captus erat	audītus erat
portātī erāmus	doctī erāmus	tractī erāmus	captī erāmus	audītī erāmus
portātī erātis	doctī erātis	tractī erātis	captī erātis	audītī erātis
portātī erant	doctī erant	tractī erant	captī erant	audītī erant

V Deponent Verbs

DEPONENT INDICATIVE

	first conjugation	*second conjugation*	*third conjugation*	*third "-iō" conjugation*	*fourth conjugation*
PRESENT					
I try	cōnor	vereor	loquor	ingredior	mentior
you try	cōnāris	verēris	loqueris	ingrederis	mentīris
s/he, it tries	cōnātur	verētur	loquitur	ingreditur	mentītur
we try	cōnāmur	verēmur	loquimur	ingredimur	mentīmur
you try	cōnāminī	verēminī	loquiminī	ingrediminī	mentīminī
they try	cōnantur	verentur	loquuntur	ingrediuntur	mentiuntur
FUTURE					
I shall/will try	cōnābor	verēbor	loquar	ingrediar	mentiar
you will try	cōnāberis	verēberis	loquēris	ingrediēris	mentiēris
s/he, it will try	cōnābitur	verēbitur	loquētur	ingrediētur	mentiētur
we shall/will try	cōnābimur	verēbimur	loquēmur	ingrediēmur	mentiēmur
you will try	cōnābiminī	verēbiminī	loquēminī	ingrediēminī	mentiēminī
they will try	cōnābuntur	verēbuntur	loquentur	ingredientur	mentientur
IMPERFECT					
I was trying	cōnābar	verēbar	loquēbar	ingrediēbar	mentiēbar
you were trying	cōnābāris	verēbāris	loquēbāris	ingrediēbāris	mentiēbāris
s/he, it was trying	cōnābātur	verēbātur	loquēbātur	ingrediēbātur	mentiēbātur
we were trying	cōnābāmur	verēbāmur	loquēbāmur	ingrediēbāmur	mentiēbāmur
you were trying	cōnābāminī	verēbāminī	loquēbāminī	ingrediēbāminī	mentiēbāminī
they were trying	cōnābantur	verēbantur	loquēbantur	ingrediēbantur	mentiēbantur
PERFECT					
I (have) tried	cōnātus sum	veritus sum	locūtus sum	ingressus sum	mentītus sum
you (have) tried	cōnātus es	veritus es	locūtus es	ingressus es	mentītus es
s/he, it (has) tried	cōnātus est	veritus est	locūtus est	ingressus est	mentītus est
we (have) tried	cōnātī sumus	veritī sumus	locūtī sumus	ingressī sumus	mentītī sumus
you (have) tried	cōnātī estis	veritī estis	locūtī estis	ingressī estis	mentītī estis
they (have) tried	cōnātī sunt	veritī sunt	locūtī sunt	ingressī sunt	mentītī sunt
FUTURE PERFECT					
I shall/will have tried	cōnātus erō	veritus erō	locūtus erō	ingressus erō	mentītus erō
you will have tried	cōnātus eris	veritus eris	locūtus eris	ingressus eris	mentītus eris
s/he, it will have tried	cōnātus erit	veritus erit	locūtus erit	ingressus erit	mentītus erit
we shall/will have tried	cōnātī erimus	veritī erimus	locūtī erimus	ingressī erimus	mentītī erimus
you will have tried	cōnātī eritis	veritī eritis	locūtī eritis	ingressī eritis	mentītī eritis
they will have tried	cōnātī erunt	veritī erunt	locūtī erunt	ingressī erunt	mentītī erunt
PLUPERFECT					
I had tried	cōnātus eram	veritus eram	locūtus eram	ingressus eram	mentītus eram
you had tried	cōnātus erās	veritus erās	locūtus erās	ingressus erās	mentītus erās
s/he, it had tried	cōnātus erat	veritus erat	locūtus erat	ingressus erat	mentītus erat
we had tried	cōnātī erāmus	veritī erāmus	locūtī erāmus	ingressī erāmus	mentītī erāmus
you had tried	cōnātī erātis	veritī erātis	locūtī erātis	ingressī erātis	mentītī erātis
they had tried	cōnātī erant	veritī erant	locūtī erant	ingressī erant	mentītī erant

VI Irregular Verbs

1 FUTURE PERFECT

FUTURE PERFECT ("I shall/will have been," also often translated as "I am," etc.)

esse	posse	īre	velle	nōlle	ferre
fuerō	potuerō	ierō	voluerō	nōluerō	tulerō
fueris	potueris	ieris	volueris	nōlueris	tuleris
fuerit	potuerit	ierit	voluerit	nōluerit	tulerit
fuerimus	potuerimus	ierimus	voluerimus	nōluerimus	tulerimus
fueritis	potueritis	ieritis	volueritis	nōlueritis	tuleritis
fuerint	potuerint	ierint	voluerint	nōluerint	tulerint

See Review Grammar, pp.282–84, for other forms of these irregular verbs.

2 PASSIVE INDICATIVE of ferō, ferre, tulī, lātus (*to bring*)

PRESENT

feror	*I am (being) brought*
ferris	*you are (being) brought*
fertur	*s/he, it is (being) brought*
ferimur	*we are (being) brought*
feriminī	*you are (being) brought*
feruntur	*they are (being) brought*

FUTURE

ferar	*I shall/will be brought*
ferēris	*you will be brought*
ferētur	*s/he, it will be brought*
ferēmur	*we shall/will be brought*
ferēminī	*you will be brought*
ferentur	*they will be brought*

IMPERFECT

ferēbar	*I was being brought*
ferēbāris	*you were being brought*
ferēbātur	*s/he, it was being brought*
ferēbāmur	*we were being brought*
ferēbāminī	*you were being brought*
ferēbantur	*they were being brought*

PERFECT

lātus sum	*I have been/was brought*
lātus es	*you have been/were brought*
lātus est	*s/he, it has been/was brought*
lātī sumus	*we have been/were brought*
lātī estis	*you have been/were brought*
lātī sunt	*they have been/were brought*

FUTURE PERFECT

lātus erō	*I shall/will have been brought*
lātus eris	*you will have been brought*
lātus erit	*s/he, it will have been brought*
lātī erimus	*we shall/will have been brought*
lātī eritis	*you will have been brought*
lātī erunt	*they will have been brought*

PLUPERFECT

lātus eram	*I had been brought*
lātus erās	*you had been brought*
lātus erat	*s/he, it had been brought*
lātī erāmus	*we had been brought*
lātī erātis	*you had been brought*
lātī erant	*they had been brought*

PERFECT PASSIVE PARTICIPLE	
lātus	*having been brought*

3 IRREGULAR PASSIVE of faciō, facere, fēcī, factus *(to do, to make)*: fīō, fierī, factus sum *(to become)*

PRESENT	
fīō	*I become (= I am being made)*
fīs	*you become*
fit	*s/he, it becomes*
fīunt	*they become*

FUTURE	
fīam	*I shall/will become (= I shall be made)*
fīēs	*you will become*
fīet	*s/he, it will become*
fīēmus	*we shall/will become*
fīētis	*you will become*
fīent	*they will become*

IMPERFECT	
fīēbam	*I was becoming (= I was being made)*
fīēbās	*you were becoming*
fīēbat	*s/he, it was becoming*
fīēbāmus	*we were becoming*
fīēbātis	*you were becoming*
fīēbant	*they were becoming*

PERFECT	
factus sum	*I have become, I became (= I was made)*
factus es	*you have become, you became*
factus est	*s/he, it has become, he became*
factī sumus	*we have become, we became*
factī estis	*you have become, you became*
factī sunt	*they have become, they became*

FUTURE PERFECT	
factus erō	*I shall/will have become*
factus eris	*you will have become*
factus erit	*s/he, it will have become*
factī erimus	*we shall/will have become*
factī eritis	*you will have become*
factī erunt	*they will have become*

PLUPERFECT	
factus eram	*I had become (= I had been made)*
factus erās	*you had become*
factus erat	*s/he, it had become*
factī erāmus	*we had become*
factī erātis	*you had become*
factī erant	*they had become*

PRESENT PASSIVE INFINITIVE	
fierī	*to become, to be made*

PERFECT PASSIVE PARTICIPLE	
factus	*having become, having been made*

VII Subordinate Clauses

In Unit 2, you learned a type of subordinate clause called a *relative clause*, which performs an adjectival function in a sentence (see Unit 2 Reference Grammar, § VII, "Relative Clauses"). In Unit 3, you have met a variant of the relative clause (see § VII.3.C, "Relative Purpose Clauses," below). In addition, you have been introduced to several other new types of subordinate clauses, which can be loosely classified as *adverb clauses* and *noun clauses*. That is, certain kinds of subordinate clause have the function of an adverb, and others have the function of a noun, in the same way that relative clauses have the function of an adjective.

An *adverb clause*, like an adverb, generally describes when, where, how, or why an event (e.g. the action described by the main verb of a sentence) takes place. For example, study the following pair of English sentences:

a.   Yesterday the merchant examined the jewels.
b.   When the merchant had examined all the jewels, he chose the best ones.

In sentence (a), the adverb "yesterday" modifies the verb "examined": it describes *when* the merchant examined the jewels. In sentence (b), the adverb clause "When the merchant had examined the jewels" modifies the main verb of the sentence "chose": it tells *when* the merchant chose the best jewels.

A *noun clause* replaces a noun (usually the direct object) in a sentence. Consider the following pair of English sentences:

a.   The manager demanded an investigation.
b.   The manager demanded that an investigation be carried out.

In sentence (a), the noun "investigation" is the direct object of the verb "demanded." In sentence (b), the noun clause "that an investigation be carried out" takes the place of the direct object in the sentence, as the receiver of the action of the main verb "demanded."

Most of the subordinate clauses introduced in Unit 3 contain a verb in the subjunctive.

1. **cum**-clauses

In Stage 24, you encountered a type of adverb clause known as a **cum**-clause, which is introduced by **cum** (= *when* or *while*), and contains a verb in the subjunctive. Study the following example:

cum lēgātus adventum Agricolae nūntiāvisset, mīlitēs plausērunt.
When the commander had announced the arrival of Agricola, the soldiers applauded.

Notice that the main verb **plausērunt** is perfect indicative, and that the verb in the **cum**-clause **nūntiāvisset** is pluperfect subjunctive. A **cum**-clause can also contain a verb in the imperfect subjunctive:

cum poēta nōbīs recitāret, ego tranquillē dormiēbam.
While the poet was reciting for us, I was sleeping peacefully.

In this sentence, the main verb **dormiēbam** is imperfect indicative, and the verb in the **cum**-clause **recitāret** is imperfect subjunctive. When the main verb is in the imperfect or perfect indicative, a *pluperfect* subjunctive verb in the **cum**-clause denotes action *prior to* that of the main verb, while an *imperfect* subjunctive verb in the **cum**-clause denotes action occurring *at the same time as* that of the main verb.

---

2. **dum**-clauses

Like **cum**-clauses, **dum**-clauses are adverbial. You have met two kinds of **dum**-clause:

A. **dum** + present indicative verb (**dum** = *while*)
You met this type of clause in Stage 29. Study the following example:

omnēs servī, dum dominus crūdēlis in urbe abest, ē fundō fūgērunt.
While the cruel master was away in the city, all the slaves fled from the farm.

Note that, although the main verb of this sentence, **fūgērunt**, is in the perfect tense, the verb in the **dum**-clause, **abest**, is in the present tense. When the **dum**-clause refers to a period of time during which an event in the main clause happens, the verb in the **dum**-clause is regularly in the present tense. Both the main verb and the verb in the **dum**-clause are indicative, in this type of sentence.

B. **dum** + subjunctive verb (**dum** = *until*)
This kind of **dum**-clause first appeared in Stage 34. Study the following example:

exspectābāmus dum ex oppidō sine perīculō discēderēmus.
We were waiting until we could leave the town without danger.

Observe that the verb in the **dum**-clause is imperfect subjunctive. When **dum** is used to mean *until*, in a sentence where there is an idea of purpose or intention, the verb in the **dum**-clause is imperfect subjunctive. Here is an additional example:

quiēverāmus dum prōgredī possēmus.
We had rested until we were able to go on.

3. Purpose Clauses

You have learned three kinds of purpose clause: the **ut**-clause of purpose, introduced by the particle **ut** (first met in Stage 26); the negative purpose clause introduced by **nē** (of which the first example appears in Stage 29, the language note in Stage 31); and the relative purpose clause, introduced by a form of the relative pronoun **quī** or by the relative adverb **ubi** (Stage 29).

A. **ut**-clauses of Purpose
This kind of purpose clause is introduced by the particle **ut**, and explains the purpose for some action usually expressed by the main verb of a sentence. Consider the following example:

domina ancillās saepe laudābat, ut sibi fidēlēs manērent.
The mistress often praised the slave-girls, so that they would remain loyal to her.

An **ut**-clause of purpose can sometimes be translated with "to" or "in order to," as in the following sentence:

lucernam tulī, ut melius vidērem.
I brought a lamp, (in order) to see better.

When a sentence whose main verb is in the imperfect, perfect, or pluperfect tense contains a purpose clause, the verb in the purpose clause is in the imperfect subjunctive. This is true of all three types of purpose clause that you have met (see § VII. 3.B and C below).

B. Negative Purpose Clauses with **nē**

This type of purpose clause indicates an intention to *prevent* something happening; *ne* is used instead of *ut* to introduce the clause, as in the following example:

fēmina fortis fūrem dēligāverat, nē ē vīllā effugeret.
The brave woman had tied up the thief, so that he would not escape from the house.

C. Relative Purpose Clauses with **quī** and **ubi**

Certain kinds of sentences may contain a special type of purpose clause that is introduced by a relative pronoun or adverb. Like some **ut**- clauses, relative purpose clauses can often be translated with "to."

Study the following examples:

a. **prīnceps nūntium arcessīvit quī epistulam ad rēgem ferret.**
The chieftain summoned a messenger who might bring a letter to the king.
or *The chieftain summoned a messenger to bring a letter to the king.*

b. **māter locum quaerēbat ubi līberōs cēlāret.**
The mother was seeking a place where she might hide her children.
or *The mother was seeking a place to hide her children.*

Note that purpose clauses with **ut** and **nē** are adverbial, in that they describe *why* something happens; relative purpose clauses, on the other hand, although they may be translated in much the same way as **ut**-clauses of purpose, are technically adjectival, just like ordinary relative clauses, because they actually describe a noun. In sentence (a) above, the relative purpose clause **quī epistulam ad rēgem ferret** describes the noun **nūntium**, and in sentence (b), the relative purpose clause **ubi līberōs cēlāret** describes the noun **locum**.

4. Result Clauses

In Stage 27, you learned about result clauses, which are introduced by the particle **ut**, and contain a verb in the subjunctive. A result clause describes the result or effect of some action or situation usually stated in the main clause. Consider the following examples:

tot librōs ēmistī, ut vix eōs portāre possēs.
You bought so many books that you could scarcely carry them.
tam fessus erat iuvenis, ut graviter dormīret.
The young man was so tired that he slept soundly.

In a sentence containing a result clause, when the main verb is in the imperfect, perfect, or pluperfect tense, the verb in the result clause is most commonly imperfect subjunctive. Frequently, although not invariably, a word such as **tot, tantum, tam**, or **adeō** prepares us for the result clause.

Notice how negative clauses are formed:

tantum cibī iam cōnsūmpserat puer, ut cēnam suam nōn cuperet.
The boy had already eaten so much food that he did not want his dinner.
adeō attonitus eram, ut nihil prīmō dīcerem.
I was so astonished that at first I said nothing.

A negative result clause is introduced by **ut**, which is followed either by **nōn** or by another negative word such as **nihil, nūllus, nēmō,** or **numquam**.

The result clauses that you have seen are adverbial, in that they answer a theoretical question that asks "how?" or "to what extent?" For example, the question, "How angry were you?" in Latin would be "quam īrātus erās?" The answer to this question, in Latin, might be:

tam īrātus eram, ut omnēs amīcōs saeviēns dīmitterem.
I was so angry that, in a rage, I sent away all my friends.

5. Indirect Questions

In Stage 25, you met indirect questions, a type of noun clause normally adopting the function of a direct object: it can be the object of the main verb of a sentence, of an infinitive dependent on the main verb, or of a participle.

An indirect question generally begins with an interrogative pronoun, adjective, or adverb, or with the interrogative particles **num** (*whether*) or **utrum** . . . **an** (*whether . . . or*). The verb in the indirect question is subjunctive. Study the following examples:

a. **nēmō sciēbat quis pecūniam cēpisset.**
   No one knew who had taken the money.
b. **rogāvimus num cīvibus auxilium ferre dēbērēmus.**
   We asked whether we ought to bring help to the citizens.
c. **cognōscere volēbam utrum ille amīcus an inimīcus esset.**
   I wanted to find out whether he was a friend or an enemy.

Observe that in sentence (a) the verb in the indirect question is pluperfect subjunctive, but in sentences (b) and (c) the verb in the indirect question is imperfect subjunctive. In a sentence containing an indirect question, when the main verb is in the imperfect, perfect, or pluperfect tense, a *pluperfect* subjunctive in the indirect question denotes action *prior to* that of the main verb, while an *imperfect* subjunctive verb denotes action occurring *at the same time as* that of the main verb.

Verbs that have to do with asking, knowing or not knowing, finding out, etc., lead naturally into indirect questions: **rogāre, scīre, nescīre,** and **cognōscere** are some examples of verbs that may frequently appear in the main clause of sentences containing indirect questions.

6. Indirect Commands

You learned about indirect commands, another type of noun clause, in Stage 27. Indirect commands function as objects in the same way that indirect questions do (see § VII. 5, above), and they also contain a verb in the subjunctive. Indirect commands are introduced by the particle **ut**. Study the following examples:

Agricola Salviō imperāvit ut omnia explicāret.
Agricola ordered Salvius that he explain everything.
or *Agricola ordered Salvius to explain everything.*
Vilbia Modestum ōrāverat ut Bulbō parceret.
Vilbia had begged Modestus that he spare Bulbus.
or *Vilbia had begged Modestus to spare Bulbus.*

In a sentence containing an indirect command, when the main verb is in the imperfect, perfect, or pluperfect tense, the verb in the indirect command is imperfect subjunctive. Verbs having to do with ordering, advising, begging, etc., tend to prepare us for indirect commands: **imperāre, monēre,** and **ōrāre** are some examples.

A negative indirect command is introduced by the particle **nē**, which replaces **ut**, as in the following example:

pater saepe mē monēbat nē mīlitibus crēderem.
My father often warned me that I should not trust soldiers.
or *My father often warned me not to trust soldiers.*

Note, in the preceding examples, that indirect commands are often best translated with "to" or "not to," rather than with "that" or "that . . . not."

VIII Participles

In Unit 2, you met *present active participles* (e.g. **portāns** *carrying*).
In Unit 3, you have learned two new kinds of participles: the *perfect passive participle* (e.g. **portātus** *having been carried*) and the *perfect active participle* (**locūtus** *having spoken*).

1. Perfect Passive Participles
The perfect passive participle, which you learned in Stage 21, is the fourth principal part of a verb. When the perfect passive participle is used, like an adjective, to describe a noun, it reflects some action that has been performed on the noun. For example, the perfect passive participle **captus** (fourth principal part of **capiō, capere** *to catch* or *to capture*) means *having been captured* or simply *captured*. For example:

canis **verberātus** ululāvit.
The dog, beaten, howled. Or *The dog howled when he was beaten.*

nūntius **captus** epistulam trādidit.
The messenger, having been captured, handed over the letter.
or *When he was captured the messenger handed over the letter.*

līberī dōnīs **dēlectātī** mātrī grātiās ēgērunt.
The children, delighted by the gifts, thanked their mother.
or *The children thanked their mother because they were delighted by the gifts.*

Note that certain linking or intransitive verbs, such as **esse, īre, venīre, ambulāre,** and **dormīre**, do not have perfect passive participles.

2. Perfect Active Participles
In Stage 22, you met the perfect active participle, which comes from a special class of verbs known as *deponent verbs*, which are distinctive because they are passive in form, but active in meaning. Likewise, the perfect active participle is formed like a perfect passive participle, but is not translated in the same way. When used to describe a noun, a perfect active participle reflects some action that the noun has performed. For example, the perfect active participle **profectus** (from **proficīscor, proficīscī** *to set out*) means *having set out* as in "the leader, having set out": **dux profectus**. Some further examples are illustrated by the following sentences:

servī, multa tormenta **passī**, tōtam rem tandem nārrāvērunt.
The slaves, having suffered many tortures, finally told the whole story.
or *The slaves, because they had suffered many tortures, finally told the whole story.*

mercātōrēs, multam pecūniam **adeptī**, nōn erant laetī.
The merchants, having obtained a lot of money, were not happy.
or *The merchants, although they had obtained a lot of money, were not happy.*

māter, īnfantem **amplexa**, valedīxit.
The mother, having embraced her baby, said good-by.
or *The mother, when she had embraced her baby, said good-by.*

---

3. Most of the participles in paragraphs 1 and 2 above appear in phrases, i.e. **dōnīs dēlectātī, multa tormenta passī, multam pecūniam adeptī, īnfantem amplexa**. These phrases are participial phrases using perfect participles. There will be some further examples of participial phrases using perfect participles in § IX.3 below, "The Ablative Absolute." You met participial phrases using the present active participle in Unit 2 (see Unit 2 Reference Grammar, § VIII, "Participial Phrases").

IX The Ablative Case

In Stage 28, you learned about the ablative case of the noun. You have seen the ablative case used with and without a preposition.

1. The Ablative with a Preposition

A. Certain prepositions always govern the ablative case. The most important of these are **ā/ab, cum** (= *with*), **dē, ē/ex, prō,** and **sine**. The preposition **in** takes either the ablative or the accusative case: **in** means *in* or *on* with the ablative case, and *into* or *onto* with the accusative case. For example:

Rūfilla **in vīllā** est.
*Rufilla is **in the house**.*

Rūfilla **in vīllam** ambulat.
*Rufilla walks **into the house**.*

B. Frequently, with passive verbs and participles, the ablative of nouns indicating persons is found with the preposition **ā/ab**, e.g. **ā prīncipe** arcessēbātur, or "he was being summoned by the chieftain." This kind of ablative is often called the *ablative of agent*, because it normally refers to a person (or possibly an animal) perceived as acting as an agent, or doer of the action. Further examples:

fēminā aegra **ā medicō** sānāta erat.
*The sick woman had been cured **by the doctor**.*

bēstiārius **ā leōne** petēbātur.
*The gladiator was being attacked **by the lion**.*

2. The Ablative Without a Preposition
The ablative is also used without a preposition, in a context with passive verbs or participles, when it refers to a thing or an abstract quality (not a person). For example:

mīles, **hastā** vulnerātus, ad terram dēcidit.
*The soldier, wounded **by a spear,** fell to the ground.*

horreum **flammīs** dēlētum est, ubi hostēs id incendērunt.
*The granary was destroyed **by flames** when the enemy set it alight.*

timor puellae tandem **amōre** iuvenis victus erat.
*The girl's fear had at last been conquered **by** the young man's **love**.*

frūmentum **plaustrō** vehēbātur.
*The grain was being carried **in a wagon**.*

clāmōribus puerōrum perturbātī erāmus.
*We had been disturbed **by the shouting** of the boys.*

---

3. The Ablative Absolute

The ablative absolute, which you met in Stage 31, is a special kind of adverbial phrase that describes under what circumstances an event takes place or a situation exists. Study the following sentences, in which the ablative absolutes are in boldface:

a. **frātre adiuvante**, iuvenis iānuam frāctam reficiēbat.
    With his brother assisting, the young man was repairing the broken door.

b. **iānuā refectā**, iuvenis ēgressus est.
    The door having been repaired, the young man went out.

c. **iuvene ēgressō**, amīcus frātrem vīsitāvit.
    The young man having gone out, a friend visited the brother.

Observe that, in each sentence, the ablative absolute consists of a noun and a participle, both in the ablative case. This is the basic form of an ablative absolute (although it can take other forms as well, e.g. a noun plus a pronoun: **vōbīs ducibus** *with you as the leaders*). In sentence (a), the ablative absolute contains a *present* participle, **adiuvante** *assisting*. A *present* participle in the ablative absolute denotes action occurring *at the same time as* that of the main verb, no matter what tense the main verb is in. So in sentence (a), the brother was helping the young man while the young man was repairing (**reficiēbat**) the door. Sentence (a) could also be translated: *The young man was repairing the broken door, while his brother helped.* In sentences (b) and (c), the ablative absolutes contain *perfect* participles: **refectō** *having been repaired* (perfect passive), and **ēgressō** *having gone out* (perfect active), respectively. A *perfect* participle in the ablative absolute denotes action *prior to* that of the main verb. Thus, in sentence (b), the young man went out after the door had been repaired, and in sentence (c), a friend visited the brother after the young man had gone out. Sentences (b) and (c) could also be translated as follows:

b. *After the door had been repaired, the young man went out.*
c. *After the young man had gone out, a friend visited the brother.*

Notice that in each of the preceding examples, the noun in the ablative absolute and the subject of the sentence are not the same. In a sentence containing an ablative absolute, the noun in the ablative absolute can never be the subject or object of the main clause. Here are some additional sentences using the ablative absolute. Note the possible variations in translation:

servīs ē vīllā ēlāpsīs, dominus valdē saeviēbat.
The slaves having escaped from the house, the master was very much enraged.
Also possible:
Because the slaves had escaped from the house, the master was very much enraged.

cibō parātō, hospes convīvās ad cēnam vocāvit.
The food having been prepared, the host called his guests to dinner.
or *When the food had been prepared, the host called his guests to dinner.*

fīliā parvā tandem dormiente, māter tacitē ē cubiculō exiit.
Her little daughter sleeping at last, the mother quietly left the bedroom.
or *Since her little daughter was sleeping at last, the mother quietly left the bedroom.*

There are many different ways of translating the ablative absolute; the context in which it appears will determine the most suitable translation.

X Gerundive of Obligation

In Stage 24, you met a form of the verb called the *gerundive*, which appeared in such expressions as:

mihi fugiendum est.
I must flee.

nōbīs cēnandum est.
We must dine.

The gerundive of the verb, like the perfect participle, is declined in the same way as adjectives of the type **bonus, bona, bonum** (p.265 above). The form of the gerundive is distinguished by the **-nd-** which precedes the ending **-us**, **-a**, or **-um**. When the gerundive appears in the neuter singular with **est** (or the 3rd person singular of **esse** in some other tense), as in the examples above, it expresses necessity or obligation. Note that the examples provided each include a pronoun in the dative case, which refers to the person or persons for whom it is necessary to carry out the action implied by the gerundive.

You have also encountered the gerundive of obligation in expressions like the following:

a. **mihi fābula nārranda est.**
    I must tell a story.

b. **nōbīs cibus comparandus est.**
    We must obtain food.

In this form, the gerundive of obligation has an explicit subject, which was not true of the previous examples. In sentence (a), the subject is **fābula** *story*, and in sentence (b), the subject is **cibus** *food*. When a subject is expressed in a gerundive of obligation, the gerundive must agree with that subject in gender, number, and case (usually nominative), just as an adjective must agree with the noun it describes. For example, consider the following sentences:

a. **illī sorōrēs cūrandae sunt.**
    He must take care of his sisters.

b. **nōbīs templa aedificanda sunt.**
    We must build temples.

In sentence (a), the subject, **sorōrēs** *sisters* is feminine plural, so the gerundive **cūrandae** is also feminine plural to agree with it, and the verb **sunt** is plural, to agree with the subject. In sentence (b), the subject, **templa** *temples*, is neuter nominative plural, so the gerundive **aedificanda** is also neuter nominative plural, to agree with it, and the verb **sunt**, again, is plural, to agree with the subject.

XI Sentence Patterns

Below are some of the most important sentence patterns which you have learned in
Unit 3. The patterns are shown on the left, with examples given on the right.
Key: NOM = nominative; ACC = accusative; DAT = dative; GEN = genitive; ABL
= ablative; V = verb; N = noun; ADJ = adjective.

PATTERNS		EXAMPLES
XI.1	participial phrase + preposition	saxum, ā puerō ēmissum, in aquam dēcidit. *The rock, thrown by the boy, fell into the water.* mīlitēs, ad castra profectī, arma sēcum portābant. *The soldiers, having set out for the camp, were carrying their weapons with them.*
XI.2	participial phrase + accusative	coquus, culīnam ingressus, cibum parāre coepit. *The cook, having entered the kitchen, began to prepare the food.*
XI.3	V + NOM + ACC	fēcit faber statuam. *A craftsman made the statue.*
XI.4	ADJ + preposition + N	fēmina summā cum cūrā flōrēs in āram posuit. *The woman placed the flowers on the altar with the utmost care.*
XI.5	extended participial phrase + preposition	captīvus, ē tenebrīs carceris ēgressus, anxius circumspectāvit. *The prisoner, having emerged from the darkness of the prison, looked around anxiously.*
XI.6	postponement of subordinating conjunction	hanc fābulam cum nārrāvisset, māter līberōs dīmīsit. *When she had told this story, the mother sent the children away.*
XI.7	DAT + NOM + ACC + V	lībertīs multīs fortūna potestātem offert. *Fortune offers power to many freedmen.*
XI.8	ABL + V	cīvēs Imperātōrem magnō clāmōre salūtāvērunt. *The citizens greeted the Emperor with a great cheer.*
XI.9	increased complexity of subordinate clauses: "nesting" and combination of "nesting"and"stringing"	dīvitum tantus erat numerus ut pauper, quī numquam in illā parte urbis prius fuerat, valdē attonitus erat et pedem subitō rettulit. *So great was the number of rich men, that the poor man, who had never been in that part of the city before, was very much astonished, and stepped back suddenly.*
XI.10	increased variety in word order in sentences using passive voice	ā fēminīs librī scrībēbantur. *The books were being written by women.*

PART THREE: Complete Vocabulary

1 Nouns and adjectives are listed as in the Unit 2 Language Information Section.

2 Prepositions used with the ablative, such as **ex**, are marked +*abl.*; those used with the accusative, such as **per**, are marked +*acc.*

3 Verbs are usually listed in the following way:

the 1st person singular of the present tense, e.g. pōnō (*I place*);
the infinitive, e.g. pōnere (*to place*);
the 1st person singular of the perfect tense, e.g. posuī (*I placed*);
the perfect passive participle, e.g. positus (*having been placed*);
the meaning.

4 Study the following examples of verbs. They are listed in the way described in paragraph 3. Notice particularly the usual ways in which the different conjugations form their perfect tense and perfect passive participle.

1st conjugation
amō, amāre, amāvī, amātus *love, like*
laudō, laudāre, laudāvī, laudātus *praise*

2nd conjugation
moneō, monēre, monuī, monitus *warn*
praebeō, praebēre, praebuī, praebitus *provide*

3rd conjugation
Verbs of the 3rd conjugation form their perfect tense and perfect passive participle in several different ways that are not always predictable. Here are some of the ways:

claudō, claudere, clausī, clausus *shut, close*
dūcō, dūcere, dūxī, ductus *lead*
frangō, frangere, frēgī, frāctus *break*

3rd conjugation ("-iō")
faciō, facere, fēcī, factus *do, make*
rapiō, rapere, rapuī, raptus *seize*

4th conjugation
custōdiō, custōdīre, custōdīvī, custōdītus *guard*
impediō, impedīre, impedīvī, impedītus *hinder*

5 Use paragraph 4 to find the meaning of:

amāvī; laudātus; monēre; praebitus; dūxī; frēgī; frāctūs; facere; rapiō; custōdīre; impedītus.

6 Deponent verbs (met and explained in Stage 32) are listed in the following way:

The 1st person singular of the present tense. This always ends in -or, e.g. cōnor (*I try*);
the infinitive. This always ends in -ī, e.g. cōnārī (*to try*);
the 1st person singular of the perfect tense, e.g. cōnātus sum (*I tried*);
the meaning.

So, if the following forms are given:

loquor, loquī, locūtus sum *speak*

loquor means *I speak*, **loquī** means *to speak*, **locūtus sum** means *I spoke*.

7 Study the following deponent verbs, listed in the way described in paragraph 6:

cōnspicor, cōnspicārī, cōnspicātus sum *catch sight of*
ingredior, ingredī, ingressus sum *enter*
lābor, lābī, lāpsus sum *fall*

Give the meaning of:

cōnspicor, ingredī, lāpsus sum, ingredior, cōnspicātus sum, lābī.

8 Use the list on pages 314–38 to find the meaning of:

ēgredior, hortātus sum, pollicērī, sequor, minārī, adeptus sum.

9 All words which are given in the "Words and Phrases Checklists" for Stages 1–34 are marked with an asterisk.

a

*ā, ab +*abl.* *from; by*
abdūcō, abdūcere, abdūxī, abductus
   lead away
*abeō, abīre, abiī *go away*
abhinc *ago*
abhorreō, abhorrēre, abhorruī *shrink
   (from)*
abigō, abigere, abēgī, abāctus *drive
   away*
absēns, *gen.* absentis *absent*
absentia, absentiae, f. *absence*
abstulī *see* auferō
*absum, abesse, āfuī *be out, be absent, be
   away*
absurdus, absurda, absurdum *absurd*
*ac *and*
*accidō, accidere, accidī *happen*
*accipiō, accipere, accēpī, acceptus
   accept, take in, receive
accurrō, accurrere, accurrī *run up*
*accūsō, accūsāre, accūsāvī, accūsātus
   accuse
*ācriter *keenly, eagerly, fiercely*
āctus *see* agō
*ad +*acc.* *to, at*
*addō, addere, addidī, additus *add*
addūcō, addūcere, addūxī, adductus
   lead, lead on, encourage
*adeō, adīre, adiī *approach, go up to*
*adeō *so much, so greatly*
adeptus *see* adipīscor
adest *see* adsum
adhibeō, adhibēre, adhibuī, adhibitus
   use, apply
   precēs adhibēre *offer prayers to*
*adhūc *until now*
*adipīscor, adipīscī, adeptus sum
   receive, obtain
*aditus, aditūs, m. *entrance*
*adiuvō, adiuvāre, adiūvī *help*
adligō, adligāre, adligāvī, adligātus
   tie
adloquor, adloquī, adlocūtus sum
   speak to, address
*administrō, administrāre,
   administrāvī, administrātus
   look after, manage
admīrātiō, admīrātiōnis, f. *admiration*
admīror, admīrārī, admīrātus sum
   admire

admittō, admittere, admīsī, admissus
   admit, let in
adōrō, adōrāre, adōrāvī, adōrātus
   worship
*adstō, adstāre, adstitī *stand by*
*adsum, adesse, adfuī *be here, be present*
*adveniō, advenīre, advēnī *arrive*
*adventus, adventūs, m. *arrival*
*adversus, adversa, adversum *hostile,
   unfavorable*
* rēs adversae *misfortune*
advesperāscit, advesperāscere,
   advesperāvit *get dark, become dark*
*aedificium, aedificiī, n. *building*
*aedificō, aedificāre, aedificāvī,
   aedificātus *build*
*aeger, aegra, aegrum *sick, ill*
aegrōtus, aegrōtī, m. *invalid*
Aegyptius, Aegyptia, Aegyptium
   Egyptian
Aegyptus, Aegyptī, f. *Egypt*
*aequus, aequa, aequum *fair, calm*
* aequō animō *calmly, in a calm spirit*
aeternus, aeterna, aeternum *eternal*
Aethiopes, Aethiopum, m.pl.
   Ethiopians
afferō, afferre, attulī, adlātus *bring*
*afficiō, afficere, affēcī, affectus *affect*
   affectus, affecta, affectum *overcome,
   struck*
afflīgō, afflīgere, afflīxī, afflīctus *afflict,
   hurt*
agellus, agellī, m. *small plot of land*
ager, agrī, m. *field*
agger, aggeris, m. *ramp, mound of
   earth*
*agitō, agitāre, agitāvī, agitātus *chase,
   hunt*
*agmen, agminis, n. *column (of people),
   procession*
agna, agnae, f. *lamb*
*agnōscō, agnōscere, agnōvī, agnitus
   recognize
*agō, agere, ēgī, āctus *do, act*
   āctum est dē nōbīs *it's all over with us*
   age! *come on!*
* fābulam agere *act in a play*
* grātiās agere *thank, give thanks*
* negōtium agere *do business, work*
   officium agere *do one's duty*
   persōnam agere *play a part*
   vītam agere *lead a life*

*agricola, agricolae, m. *farmer*
alacriter *eagerly*
ālea, āleae, f. *dice*
*aliquandō *sometimes*
aliquī, aliqua, aliquod *some*
*aliquis, aliquid *someone, something*
aliquid mīrī *something extraordinary*
*alius, alia, aliud *other, another, else*
* aliī . . . aliī *some . . . others*
*alter, altera, alterum *the other, another, a*
   second, the second
   alter . . . alter *one . . . the other*
*altus, alta, altum *high, deep*
amārus, amāra, amārum *bitter*
ambitiō, ambitiōnis, f. *bribery,*
   corruption
*ambō, ambae, ambō *both*
*ambulō, ambulāre, ambulāvī *walk*
āmēns, *gen.* āmentis *out of one's mind, in*
   a frenzy
amīcitia, amīcitiae, f. *friendship*
*amīcus, amīcī, m. *friend*
*āmittō, āmittere, āmīsī, āmissus *lose*
*amō, amāre, amāvī, amātus *love, like*
*amor, amōris, m. *love*
amphitheātrum, amphitheātrī, n.
   amphitheater
amphora, amphorae, f. *wine-jar*
*amplector, amplectī, amplexus sum
   embrace
amplissimus, amplissima,
   amplissimum *very great*
amputō, amputāre, amputāvī,
   amputātus *cut off*
amulētum, amulētī, n. *amulet, lucky*
   charm
*ancilla, ancillae, f. *slave-girl, slave-woman*
angelus, angelī, m. *angel*
angulus, angulī, m. *corner*
*angustus, angusta, angustum *narrow*
animadvertō, animadvertere,
   animadvertī, animadversus *notice,*
   take notice of
*animus, animī, m. *spirit, soul, mind*
* aequō animō *calmly, in a calm spirit*
* in animō volvere *wonder, turn over in the*
   mind
*annus, annī, m. *year*
*ante +acc. *before, in front of*
*anteā *before*
*antīquus, antīqua, antīquum *old,*
   ancient

*ānulus, ānulī, m. *ring*
anus, anūs, f. *old woman*
anxius, anxia, anxium *anxious*
aper, aprī, m. *boar*
*aperiō, aperīre, aperuī, apertus *open*
apertē *openly*
apodytērium, apodytēriī, n. *changing-*
   room
*appāreō, appārēre, appāruī *appear*
*appellō, appellāre, appellāvī,
   appellātus *call, call out to*
*appropinquō, appropinquāre,
   appropinquāvī *approach, come near to*
aptus, apta, aptum *suitable*
*apud +acc. *among, at the house of*
*aqua, aquae, f. *water*
Aquae Sūlis, Aquārum Sūlis, f.pl. *Bath*
   (city in England)
*āra, ārae, f. *altar*
arānea, arāneae, f. *spider, spider's web*
arbiter, arbitrī, m. *expert, judge*
arca, arcae, f. *strong-box, chest*
*accessō, accessere, accessīvī, accessītus
   summon, send for
architectus, architectī, m. *builder,*
   architect
arcus, arcūs, m. *arch*
*ardeō, ardēre, arsī *burn, be on fire*
ardor, ardōris, m. *spirit, enthusiasm*
ārea, āreae, f. *courtyard, construction site*
*argenteus, argentea, argenteum *made*
   of silver
arma, armōrum, n.pl. *arms, weapons*
armārium, armāriī, n. *chest, cupboard*
armātus, armāta, armātum *armed*
*arrogantia, arrogantiae, f. *arrogance,*
   gall
*ars, artis, f. *art, skill*
artifex, artificis, m. *artist, craftsman*
as, assis, m. *as (small coin)*
*ascendō, ascendere, ascendī *climb,*
   rise
asinus, asinī, m. *ass, donkey*
aspiciō, aspicere, aspexī *look towards*
astrologus, astrologī, m. *astrologer*
*at *but*
Athēnae, Athēnārum, f.pl. *Athens*
Athēnīs *at Athens*
*atque *and*
*ātrium, ātriī, n. *atrium, reception hall*
*attonitus, attonita, attonitum
   astonished

*auctor, auctōris, m. *creator, originator, person responsible*
* mē auctōre *at my suggestion*
*auctōritās, auctōritātis, f. *authority*
auctus *see* augeō
*audācia, audāciae, f. *boldness, audacity*
audācter *boldly*
*audāx, *gen.* audācis *bold, daring*
*audeō, audēre *dare*
ausim *I would dare*
*audiō, audīre, audīvī, audītus *hear, listen to*
*auferō, auferre, abstulī, ablātus *take away, steal*
augeō, augēre, auxī, auctus *increase*
augur, auguris, m. *augur*
*aula, aulae, f. *palace*
*aureus, aurea, aureum *golden, made of gold*
aurīga, aurīgae, m. *charioteer*
*auris, auris, f. *ear*
*autem *but*
*auxilium, auxiliī, n. *help*
avāritia, avāritiae, f. *greed*
*avārus, avārī, m. *miser*
avē atque valē *hail and farewell*
avia, aviae, f. *grandmother*
*avidē *eagerly*
avidus, avida, avidum *eager*
*avis, avis, f. *bird*

b

balneum, balneī, n. *bath*
barba, barbae, f. *beard*
barbarus, barbara, barbarum *barbarian*
*barbarus, barbarī, m. *barbarian*
*bellum, bellī, n. *war*
* bellum gerere *wage war, campaign*
*bene *well*
* optimē *very well*
*beneficium, beneficiī, n. *act of kindness, favor*
benignē *kindly*
*benignus, benigna, benignum *kind*
bēstia, bēstiae, f. *wild animal, beast*
*bibō, bibere, bibī *drink*
blanditiae, blanditiārum, f.pl. *flatteries*
blandus, blanda, blandum *flattering, charming*
*bonus, bona, bonum *good*

bona, bonōrum, n.pl. *goods*
* melior, melius *better*
melius est *it would be better*
* optimus, optima, optimum *very good, excellent, best*
bracchium, bracchiī, n. *arm*
brevī *in a short time*
*brevis, breve *short, brief*
Britannī, Britannōrum, m.pl. *Britons*
Britannia, Britanniae, f. *Britain*
Britannicus, Britannica, Britannicum *British*

c

C. = Gāius
cachinnō, cachinnāre, cachinnāvī *laugh, cackle*
cadō, cadere, cecidī *fall*
caecus, caeca, caecum *blind*
*caedō, caedere, cecīdī, caesus *kill*
*caelum, caelī, n. *sky, heaven*
calceus, calceī, m. *shoe*
Calēdonia, Calēdoniae, f. *Scotland*
calliditās, calliditātis, f. *cleverness, shrewdness*
*callidus, callida, callidum *clever, smart*
candēlābrum, candēlābrī, n. *lamp-stand, candelabrum*
candidātus, candidātī, m. *candidate*
*canis, canis, m. *dog*
*cantō, cantāre, cantāvī *sing, chant*
tībiīs cantāre *play on the pipes*
capillī, capillōrum, m.pl. *hair*
*capiō, capere, cēpī, captus *take, catch, capture*
cōnsilium capere *make a plan, have an idea*
Capitōlium, Capitōliī, n. *Capitol*
captīva, captīvae, f. *(female) prisoner, captive*
*captīvus, captīvī, m. *prisoner, captive*
*caput, capitis, n. *head*
*carcer, carceris, m. *prison*
*carmen, carminis, n. *song*
carnifex, carnificis, m. *executioner*
*cārus, cāra, cārum *dear*
casa, casae, f. *small house, cottage*
castellum, castellī, n. *fort*
*castīgō, castīgāre, castīgāvī, castīgātus *scold, nag*
*castra, castrōrum, n.pl. *military camp*
*cāsus, cāsūs, m. *misfortune*

*catēna, catēnae, f. *chain*
caudex, caudicis, m. *blockhead, idiot*
caupō, caupōnis, m. *innkeeper*
causa, causae, f. *reason, cause*
*cautē *cautiously*
caveō, cavēre, cāvī *beware*
cecidī *see* cadō
*cēdō, cēdere, cessī *give in, yield*
*celebrō, celebrāre, celebrāvī,
    celebrātus *celebrate*
celer, celeris, celere *quick, fast*
    celerrimus, celerrima, celerrimum
    very fast
*celeriter *quickly, fast*
    celerrimē *very quickly, very fast*
    quam celerrimē *as quickly as possible*
cella, cellae, f. *cell, sanctuary*
cellārius, cellāriī, m. *(house) steward*
*cēlō, cēlāre, cēlāvī, cēlātus *hide*
*cēna, cēnae, f. *dinner*
*cēnō, cēnāre, cēnāvī *eat dinner, dine*
*centum *a hundred*
*centuriō, centuriōnis, m. *centurion*
cēpī *see* capiō
*cēra, cērae, f. *wax, wax tablet*
*certāmen, certāminis, n. *struggle,
    contest, fight*
certē *certainly*
*certō, certāre, certāvī *compete*
certus, certa, certum *certain, infallible*
    prō certō habēre *know for certain*
cessī *see* cēdō
*cēterī, cēterae, cētera *the others, the rest*
Chrīstiānī, Chrīstiānōrum, m.pl.
    Christians
*cibus, cibī, m. *food*
*cinis, cineris, m. *ash*
circā +*acc. around*
circiter +*acc. about*
circulus, circulī, m. *hoop*
*circum +*acc. around*
*circumspectō, circumspectāre,
    circumspectāvī *look around*
*circumveniō, circumvenīre,
    circumvēnī, circumventus *surround*
circus, circī, m. *circus, stadium*
citharoedus, citharoedī, m. *cithara
    player*
*cīvis, cīvis, m.f. *citizen*
clādēs, clādis, f. *disaster*
clam *secretly, in private*
*clāmō, clāmāre, clāmāvī *shout*

*clāmor, clāmōris, m. *shout, uproar,
    racket*
*clārus, clāra, clārum *famous,
    distinguished*
*claudō, claudere, clausī, clausus *shut,
    close, block, conclude, complete*
clēmēns, gen. clēmentis *merciful*
*cliēns, clientis, m. *client*
Cn. = Gnaeus
*coepī *I began*
*cōgitō, cōgitāre, cōgitāvī *think, consider*
    sēcum cōgitāre *consider to oneself*
*cognōscō, cognōscere, cognōvī,
    cognitus *find out, get to know*
*cōgō, cōgere, coēgī, coāctus *force,
    compel*
*cohors, cohortis, f. *cohort*
*colligō, colligere, collēgī, collēctus
    gather, collect, assemble
*collocō, collocāre, collocāvī,
    collocātus *place, put*
*colloquium, colloquiī, n. *talk, chat*
colō, colere, coluī, cultus *seek favor of,
    make friends with*
columba, columbae, f. *dove, pigeon*
columna, columnae, f. *pillar*
*comes, comitis, m.f. *comrade, companion*
cōmiter *politely, courteously*
*comitor, comitārī, comitātus sum
    accompany
    comitāns, gen. comitantis
    accompanying
commeātus, commeātūs, m. *(military)
    leave*
*commemorō, commemorāre,
    commemorāvī, commemorātus
    talk about, mention, recall
commendō, commendāre,
    commendāvī, commendātus
    recommend
committō, committere, commīsī,
    commissus *commit, begin*
*commodus, commoda, commodum
    convenient
*commōtus, commōta, commōtum
    *moved, upset, affected, alarmed, excited,
    distressed, overcome*
*comparō, comparāre, comparāvī,
    comparātus *obtain*
compitum, compitī, n. *crossroads*
*compleō, complēre, complēvī,
    complētus *fill*

---

compluvium, compluviī, n. *compluvium (opening in roof of atrium)*

*compōnō, compōnere, composuī, compositus *put together, arrange, settle, mix, make up*
compositus, composita, compositum *composed, steady*

*comprehendō, comprehendere, comprehendī, comprehēnsus *arrest*

cōnātus *see* cōnor

conciliō, conciliāre, conciliāvī, conciliātus *win over, gain*

conclāve, conclāvis, n. *room*

concrepō, concrepāre, concrepuī *snap*

*condūcō, condūcere, condūxī, conductus *hire*

*cōnficiō, cōnficere, cōnfēcī, cōnfectus *finish*
cōnfectus, cōnfecta, cōnfectum *worn out, exhausted, overcome*

*cōnfīdō, cōnfīdere *trust, put trust*
cōnfīsus, cōnfīsa, cōnfīsum *having trusted, having put trust*

*coniciō, conicere, coniēcī, coniectus *hurl, throw*

*coniūrātiō, coniūrātiōnis, f. *plot, conspiracy*

coniūrō, coniūrāre, coniūrāvī *plot, conspire*

*cōnor, cōnārī, cōnātus sum *try*

*cōnscendō, cōnscendere, cōnscendī *climb on, embark on, go on board, mount*

cōnscīscō, cōnscīscere, cōnscīvī *inflict*
mortem sibi cōnscīscere *commit suicide*

*cōnsentiō, cōnsentīre, cōnsēnsī *agree*

cōnsīdō, cōnsīdere, cōnsēdī *sit down*

*cōnsilium, cōnsiliī, n. *plan, idea, advice*
cōnsilium capere *make a plan, have an idea*

*cōnsistō, cōnsistere, cōnstitī *stand one's ground, stand firm, halt, stop*

cōnspectus, cōnspectūs, m. *sight*

cōnspicātus *see* cōnspicor

*cōnspiciō, cōnspicere, cōnspexī, cōnspectus *catch sight of*

*cōnspicor, cōnspicārī, cōnspicātus sum *catch sight of*

cōnspicuus, cōnspicua, cōnspicuum *conspicuous, easily seen*

*cōnstituō, cōnstituere, cōnstituī, cōnstitūtus *decide*

cōnsul, cōnsulis, m. *consul (highest elected official of Roman government)*

*cōnsulātus, cōnsulātūs, m. *the office of consul*

*cōnsulō, cōnsulere, cōnsuluī, cōnsultus *consult*

*cōnsūmō, cōnsūmere, cōnsūmpsī, cōnsūmptus *eat*

*contemnō, contemnere, contempsī, contemptus *reject, despise*

*contendō, contendere, contendī *hurry*

contentiō, contentiōnis, f. *argument*

*contentus, contenta, contentum *satisfied*

contineō, continēre, continuī *contain*

continuus, continua, continuum *continuous, on end*

contiō, contiōnis, f. *speech*

*contrā (1) +acc. *against*
(2) *on the other hand*

contrārius, contrāria, contrārium *opposite*

contumēlia, contumēliae, f. *insult, abuse*

convalēscō, convalēscere, convaluī *get better, recover*

*conveniō, convenīre, convēnī *come together, gather, meet*

conversus *see* convertor

*convertō, convertere, convertī, conversus *turn*

convertor, convertī, conversus sum *turn*

convīva, convīvae, m. *guest*

convolvō, convolvere, convolvī, convolūtus *entangle*

*coquō, coquere, coxī, coctus *cook*

*coquus, coquī, m. *cook*

*corōna, corōnae, f. *garland, wreath*

*corpus, corporis, n. *body*

corrumpō, corrumpere, corrūpī, corruptus *corrupt*
dōnīs corrumpere *bribe*

*cotīdiē *every day*

*crās *tomorrow*

*crēdō, crēdere, crēdidī *trust, believe, have faith in*

cremō, cremāre, cremāvī, cremātus *cremate*

*creō, creāre, creāvī, creātus *make, create*

crepidārius, crepidāriī, m. *shoemaker*

crīmen, crīminis, n. *charge*

*crūdēlis, crūdēle *cruel*
cruentus, cruenta, cruentum *covered with blood, bloody*
crux, crucis, f. *cross*
*cubiculum, cubiculī, n. *bedroom*
cucurrī *see* currō
cui, cuius *see* quī
culīna, culīnae, f. *kitchen*
culpō, culpāre, culpāvī *blame*
culter, cultrī, m. *knife*
*cum (1) *when*
*cum (2) +abl. *with*
cumulō, cumulāre, cumulāvī, cumulātus *heap*
cumulus, cumulī, m. *pile, heap*
*cupiō, cupere, cupīvī *want*
*cūr? *why?*
*cūra, cūrae, f. *care*
cūrae esse *be a matter of concern*
cūria, cūriae, f. *senate-house*
*cūrō, cūrāre, cūrāvī *take care of, supervise*
*currō, currere, cucurrī *run*
currus, currūs, m. *chariot*
*cursus, cursūs, m. *course, flight*
*custōdiō, custōdīre, custōdīvī, custōdītus *guard*
*custōs, custōdis, m. *guard*

d

*damnō, damnāre, damnāvī, damnātus *condemn*
dare *see* dō
*dē +abl. *from, down from; about*
*dea, deae, f. *goddess*
*dēbeō, dēbēre, dēbuī, dēbitus *owe; ought, should, must*
*decem *ten*
*decet, decēre, decuit *be proper*
nōs decet *we ought*
*dēcidō, dēcidere, dēcidī *fall down*
*decimus, decima, decimum *tenth*
*dēcipiō, dēcipere, dēcēpī, dēceptus *deceive, trick*
dēclārō, dēclārāre, dēclārāvī, dēclārātus *declare, proclaim*
*decōrus, decōra, decōrum *right, proper*
dedī *see* dō
dēdicō, dēdicāre, dēdicāvī, dēdicātus *dedicate*

dēdūcō, dēdūcere, dēdūxī, dēductus *escort*
*dēfendō, dēfendere, dēfendī, dēfēnsus *defend*
*dēfessus, dēfessa, dēfessum *exhausted, tired out*
dēfīgō, dēfīgere, dēfīxī, dēfīxus *fix*
dēfīxiō, dēfīxiōnis, f. *curse*
*dēiciō, dēicere, dēiēcī, dēiectus *throw down, throw*
dēiectus, dēiecta, dēiectum *disappointed, downcast*
*deinde *then*
*dēlectō, dēlectāre, dēlectāvī, dēlectātus *delight, please*
*dēleō, dēlēre, dēlēvī, dēlētus *destroy*
dēliciae, dēliciārum, f.pl. *darling*
dēligō, dēligāre, dēligāvī, dēligātus *bind, tie, tie up, moor*
*dēmittō, dēmittere, dēmīsī, dēmissus *let down, lower*
*dēmōnstrō, dēmōnstrāre, dēmōnstrāvī, dēmōnstrātus *point out, show*
dēmoveō, dēmovēre, dēmōvī, dēmōtus *dismiss, move out of*
dēmum *at last*
tum dēmum *then at last, only then*
dēnārius, dēnāriī, m. *denarius (a small coin worth four sesterces)*
*dēnique *at last, finally*
dēns, dentis, m. *tooth, tusk*
*dēnsus, dēnsa, dēnsum *thick*
dēnūntiō, dēnūntiāre, dēnūntiāvī, dēnūntiātus *denounce, reveal*
dēpellō, dēpellere, dēpulī, dēpulsus *drive off, push down*
*dēpōnō, dēpōnere, dēposuī, dēpositus *put down, take off*
dēprōmō, dēprōmere, dēprōmpsī, dēprōmptus *bring out*
*dērīdeō, dērīdēre, dērīsī, dērīsus *mock, make fun of*
*dēscendō, dēscendere, dēscendī *go down, come down*
*dēserō, dēserere, dēseruī, dēsertus *desert*
*dēsiliō, dēsilīre, dēsiluī *jump down*
*dēsinō, dēsinere *end, cease*
dēsistō, dēsistere, dēstitī *stop*
*dēspērō, dēspērāre, dēspērāvī *despair, give up*

dēspiciō, dēspicere, dēspexī *look down*

dēstinō, dēstināre, dēstināvī,
dēstinātus *intend*

dēstringō, dēstringere, dēstrīnxī,
dēstrictus *draw out, draw (a sword),
pull out*

dētestātus *see* dētestor

dētestor, dētestārī, dētestātus sum
curse

dētrahō, dētrahere, dētrāxī, dētractus
pull down

*deus, deī, m. *god*

* dī immortālēs! *heavens above!*

Dēva, Dēvae, f. *Chester*

dēvorō, dēvorāre, dēvorāvī,
dēvorātus *devour, eat up*

dī *see* deus

diabolus, diabolī, m. *devil*

*dīcō, dīcere, dīxī, dictus *say*

*dictō, dictāre, dictāvī, dictātus
dictate

*diēs, diēī, m. *day*
    diēs fēstus, diēī fēstī, m. *festival,
    holiday*

* diēs nātālis, diēī nātālis, m. *birthday*

*difficilis, difficile *difficult*
    difficillimus, difficillima,
    difficillimum *very difficult*

difficultās, difficultātis, f. *difficulty*

diffīsus, diffīsa, diffīsum *having
distrusted*

digitus, digitī, m. *finger*

*dignitās, dignitātis, f. *dignity,
importance, honor, prestige*

dignus, digna, dignum *worthy,
appropriate*

dīlaniō, dīlaniāre, dīlaniāvī, dīlaniātus
tear to pieces

*dīligenter *carefully*

*dīligentia, dīligentiae, f. *industry,
hard work*

*dīligō, dīligere, dīlēxī *be fond of*

*dīmittō, dīmittere, dīmīsī, dīmissus
send away, dismiss

dīrigō, dīrigere, dīrēxī, dīrēctus *steer*

dīripiō, dīripere, dīripuī, dīreptus
tear apart, ransack

*dīrus, dīra, dīrum *dreadful, awful*

dīs *see* deus

*discēdō, discēdere, discessī *depart,
leave*

disciplīna, disciplīnae, f. *discipline,
orderliness*

discipulus, discipulī, m. *disciple,
follower*

discō, discere, didicī *learn*

discordia, discordiae, f. *strife*

discrīmen, discrīminis, n. *crisis*

*dissentiō, dissentīre, dissēnsī
disagree, argue

dissimulō, dissimulāre, dissimulāvī,
dissimulātus *conceal, hide*

distribuō, distribuere, distribuī,
distribūtus *distribute*

*diū *for a long time*

diūtius *for a longer time*

*dīves, *gen.* dīvitis *rich*
    dītissimus, dītissima, dītissimum *very
    rich*

*dīvitiae, dīvitiārum, f.pl. *riches*

dīvus, dīvī, m. *god*

dīxī *see* dīcō

*dō, dare, dedī, datus *give*

* poenās dare *pay the penalty, be punished*

*doceō, docēre, docuī, doctus *teach*

* doctus, docta, doctum *educated,
learned, skillful*

*doleō, dolēre, doluī *hurt, be in pain*

*dolor, dolōris, m. *pain, grief*

dolus, dolī, m. *trickery*

*domina, dominae, f. *lady (of the house),
mistress*

*dominus, dominī, m. *master (of the
house)*

*domus, domūs, f. *home*
    domī *at home*
    domum redīre *return home*

*dōnum, dōnī, n. *present, gift*
    dōnīs corrumpere *bribe*

*dormiō, dormīre, dormīvī *sleep*

*dubium, dubiī, n. *doubt*

*ducentī, ducentae, ducenta *two hundred*

*dūcō, dūcere, dūxī, ductus *lead*
    sorte ductus *chosen by lot*

*dulcis, dulce *sweet*

*dum *while, until*

*duo, duae, duo *two*

duodecim *twelve*

*dūrus, dūra, dūrum *harsh, hard*

*dux, ducis, m. *leader*

dūxī *see* dūcō

---

e

*ē, ex +*abl. from, out of*
ea, eā, eam *see* is
eādem, eandem *the same*
eās *see* is
ēbrius, ēbria, ēbrium *drunk*
*ecce! *see! look!*
edō, edere, ēdī, ēsus *eat*
ēdō, ēdere, ēdidī, ēditus *put on, present*
efferō, efferre, extulī, ēlātus *bring
    out, carry out*
ēlātus, ēlāta, ēlātum *thrilled, excited*
*efficiō, efficere, effēcī, effectus *carry
    out, accomplish*
*effigiēs, effigiēī, f. *image, statue*
effringō, effringere, effrēgī, effrāctus
    break down
*effugiō, effugere, effūgī *escape*
*effundō, effundere, effūdī, effūsus
    pour out
effūsīs lacrimīs *bursting into tears*
ēgī *see* agō
*ego, meī *I, me*
mēcum *with me*
*ēgredior, ēgredī, ēgressus sum *go out*
ēgressus *see* ēgredior
*ēheu! *alas! oh dear!*
eī *see* is
*ēiciō, ēicere, ēiēcī, ēiectus *throw out*
eīs, eius *see* is
eiusmodī *of that kind*
ēlābor, ēlābī, ēlāpsus sum *escape*
ēlāpsus *see* ēlābor
ēlātus *see* efferō
ēlegāns, *gen.* ēlegantis *tasteful, elegant*
ēlegantia, ēlegantiae, f. *good taste,
    elegance*
ēliciō, ēlicere, ēlicuī, ēlicitus *lure, entice*
*ēligō, ēligere, ēlēgī, ēlēctus *choose*
ēlūdō, ēlūdere, ēlūdī, ēlūsus *slip past,
    trick, outwit*
*ēmittō, ēmittere, ēmīsī, ēmissus *throw,
    send out*
*emō, emere, ēmī, ēmptus *buy*
ēmoveō, ēmovēre, ēmōvī, ēmōtus *move,
    clear away, remove*
ēn! *look!*
ēn iūstitia! *so this is justice!*
ēn Rōmānī! *so these are the Romans!*
*enim *for*

*eō, īre, iī *go*
obviam īre *meet, go to meet*
eō *see* is
eōdem *the same*
eōrum, eōs *see* is
*epistula, epistulae, f. *letter*
epulae, epulārum, f.pl. *dishes*
*eques, equitis, m. *horseman; man of
    equestrian rank*
*equitō, equitāre, equitāvī *ride a horse*
*equus, equī, m. *horse*
eram *see* sum
ergō *therefore*
ēripiō, ēripere, ēripuī, ēreptus *snatch, tear*
*errō, errāre, errāvī *make a mistake*
ērubēscō, ērubēscere, ērubuī *blush*
ērumpō, ērumpere, ērūpī *break away,
    break out*
est, estō *see* sum
ēsuriō, ēsurīre *be hungry*
*et *and*
* et ... et *both ... and*
*etiam *even, also*
nōn modo ... sed etiam *not only ... but
    also*
*euge! *hurrah!*
eum *see* is
evangelium, evangeliī, n. *good news,
    gospel*
ēvertō, ēvertere, ēvertī, ēversus *overturn*
ēvolō, ēvolāre, ēvolāvī *fly out*
*ex, ē +*abl. from, out of*
*exanimātus, exanimāta, exanimātum
    unconscious
*excipiō, excipere, excēpī, exceptus
    receive
*excitō, excitāre, excitāvī, excitātus
    arouse, wake up, awaken
*exclāmō, exclāmāre, exclāmāvī
    exclaim, shout
excruciō, excruciāre, excruciāvī,
    excruciātus *torture, torment*
excūdō, excūdere, excūdī, excūsus
    forge, hammer out
exemplum, exemplī, n. *example*
*exeō, exīre, exiī *go out*
*exerceō, exercēre, exercuī, exercitus
    exercise
exilium, exiliī, n. *exile*
exīstimō, exīstimāre, exīstimāvī,
    exīstimātus *think, consider*

*exitium, exitiī, n. *ruin, destruction*
expello, expellere, expulī, expulsus *drive out*
*explicō, explicāre, explicāvī, explicātus
  explain
explōrātor, explōrātōris, m. *scout, spy*
expōnō, expōnere, exposuī, expositus
  unload
expugnō, expugnāre, expugnāvī,
  expugnātus *storm, take by storm*
exquīsītus, exquīsīta, exquīsītum *special*
*exspectō, exspectāre, exspectāvī,
  exspectātus *wait for*
*exstinguō, exstinguere, exstīnxī,
  exstīnctus *extinguish, put out, destroy*
*exstruō, exstruere, exstrūxī,
  exstrūctus *build*
exsultō, exsultāre, exsultāvī *exult, be
  triumphant*
exta, extōrum, n.pl. *entrails*
extorqueō, extorquēre, extorsī, extortus
  take by force, extort
*extrā *outside*
*extrahō, extrahere, extrāxī, extractus
  drag out, pull out, take out
extrēmus, extrēma, extrēmum *furthest*
  extrēma pars *edge*
extulī *see* efferō
exuō, exuere, exuī, exūtus *take off*

f

*faber, fabrī, m. *craftsman, carpenter,
  workman*
*fābula, fābulae, f. *play, story*
* fābulam agere *act in a play*
facēs *see* fax
*facile *easily*
*facilis, facile *easy*
*facinus, facinoris, n. *crime*
*faciō, facere, fēcī, factus *make, do*
  floccī nōn faciō *I don't give a hoot about*
  impetum facere *charge, make an attack*
  sēditiōnem facere *revolt*
factum, factī, n. *deed, achievement*
factus *see* fīō
fallō, fallere, fefellī, falsus *deceive*
falsum, falsī, n. *lie*
*falsus, falsa, falsum *false, untrue,
  dishonest*
famēs, famis, f. *hunger*
*familiāris, familiāris, m. *relative,
  relation, close friend*

faucēs, faucium, f.pl. *passage, entrance-
  way*
*faveō, favēre, fāvī *favor, support*
*favor, favōris, m. *favor*
*fax, facis, f. *torch*
fēcī *see* faciō
fefellī *see* fallō
fēlēs, fēlis, f. *cat*
fēlīx, *gen.* fēlīcis *lucky, happy*
*fēmina, fēminae, f. *woman*
fenestra, fenestrae, f. *window*
*ferō, ferre, tulī, lātus *bring, carry*
  graviter ferre *take badly*
*ferōciter *fiercely*
*ferōx, *gen.* ferōcis *fierce, ferocious*
ferrārius, ferrāriī, m. *blacksmith*
*ferrum, ferrī, n. *iron, sword*
*fessus, fessa, fessum *tired*
*festīnō, festīnāre, festīnāvī *hurry*
*fēstus, fēsta, fēstum *festival, holiday*
fibula, fibulae, f. *brooch*
*fidēlis, fidēle *faithful, loyal*
*fidēs, fideī, f. *loyalty, trustworthiness*
  fidem servāre *keep a promise, keep faith*
fīdus, fīda, fīdum *loyal, trustworthy*
fīgō, fīgere, fīxī, fīxus *fix, fasten*
figūra, figūrae, f. *figure, shape*
*fīlia, fīliae, f. *daughter*
*fīlius, fīliī, m. *son*
fingō, fingere, fīnxī, fictus *invent, pretend*
fīnis, fīnis, m. *end*
fīō *I become*
  factus sum *I became*
fīxus *see* fīgō
flāgitō, flāgitāre, flāgitāvī *nag at, put
  pressure on*
flagrō, flagrāre, flagrāvī *blaze*
*flamma, flammae, f. *flame*
floccī nōn faciō *I don't give a hoot about*
*flōs, flōris, m. *flower*
*flūmen, flūminis, n. *river*
*fluō, fluere, flūxī *flow*
*fōns, fontis, m. *fountain, spring*
fōrma, fōrmae, f. *beauty, shape*
*fortasse *perhaps*
*forte *by chance*
*fortis, forte *brave, strong*
*fortiter *bravely*
fortitūdō, fortitūdinis, f. *courage*
*fortūna, fortūnae, f. *fortune, luck*
fortūnātus, fortūnāta, fortūnātum *lucky*
*forum, forī, n. *forum, business center*

---

*fossa, fossae, f. *ditch*
fragor, fragōris, m. *crash*
*frangō, frangere, frēgī, frāctus
    break
*frāter, frātris, m. *brother*
*fraus, fraudis, f. *trick*
frōns, frontis, f. *front*
*frūmentum, frūmentī, n. *grain*
*frūstrā *in vain*
*fuga, fugae, f. *escape*
*fugiō, fugere, fūgī *run away,
    flee (from)*
fugitīvus, fugitīvī, m. *fugitive, runaway*
fuī *see* sum
*fulgeō, fulgēre, fulsī *shine, glitter*
*fundō, fundere, fūdī, fūsus *pour*
*fundus, fundī, m. *farm*
fūnis, fūnis, m. *rope*
fūnus, fūneris, n. *funeral*
*fūr, fūris, m. *thief*
furcifer, furciferī, m. *scoundrel, crook*
*furēns, *gen.* furentis *furious, in a rage*
fūrtum, fūrtī, n. *theft, robbery*
fūstis, fūstis, m. *club, stick*

g

garriō, garrīre, garrīvī *chatter, gossip*
garum, garī, n. *sauce*
*gaudeō, gaudēre *be pleased, rejoice*
*gaudium, gaudiī, n. *joy*
gāza, gāzae, f. *treasure*
*geminī, geminōrum, m.pl. *twins*
*gemitus, gemitūs, m. *groan*
*gemma, gemmae, f. *jewel, gem*
*gēns, gentis, f. *family, tribe*
    ubi gentium? *where in the world?*
genū, genūs, n. *knee*
*gerō, gerere, gessī, gestus *wear*
* bellum gerere *wage war, campaign*
gladiātor, gladiātōris, m. *gladiator*
*gladius, gladiī, m. *sword*
glōria, glōriae, f. *glory*
glōriāns, *gen.* glōriantis *boasting,
    boastfully*
Graecia, Graeciae, f. *Greece*
Graecus, Graeca, Graecum *Greek*
grānum, grānī, n. *grain*
grātiae, grātiārum, f.pl. *thanks*
* grātiās agere *thank, give thanks*
grātīs *free*

grātulātiō, grātulātiōnis, f. *congratulation*
grātulor, grātulārī, grātulātus sum
    congratulate
grātulāns, *gen.* grātulantis
    congratulating
*gravis, grave *heavy, serious*
*graviter *heavily, soundly, seriously*
    graviter dolēre *be extremely painful*
    graviter ferre *take badly*
gubernātor, gubernātōris, m. *helmsman*
*gustō, gustāre, gustāvī *taste*
guttur, gutturis, n. *throat*

h

*habeō, habēre, habuī, habitus *have*
    in memoriā habēre *keep in mind,
        remember*
    minōris pretiī habēre *care less about*
    prō certō habēre *know for certain*
    prō hostibus habēre *consider as enemies*
    sermōnem habēre *have a conversation,
        talk*
*habitō, habitāre, habitāvī *live*
hāc, hae, haec *see* hic
*haereō, haerēre, haesī *stick, cling*
*haesitō, haesitāre, haesitāvī *hesitate*
hanc *see* hic
*haruspex, haruspicis, m. *diviner,
    soothsayer*
hās *see* hic
*hasta, hastae, f. *spear*
*haud *not*
*haudquāquam *not at all*
*hauriō, haurīre, hausī, haustus *drain,
    drink up*
*hercle! *by Hercules!*
*hērēs, hērēdis, m.f. *heir*
*herī *yesterday*
heus! *hey!*
*hic, haec, hoc *this*
*hīc *here*
*hiems, hiemis, f. *winter*
hilare *cheerfully*
hinc *from here*
Hispānia, Hispāniae, f. *Spain*
hoc, hōc, *see* hic
*hodiē *today*
*homō, hominis, m. *person, man*
homunculus, homunculī, m. *little man,
    pip-squeak*
*honor, honōris, m. *honor, official position*

*honōrō, honōrāre, honōrāvī,
   honōrātus *honor*
*hōra, hōrae, f. *hour*
*horreum, horreī, n. *barn, granary*
hortātus *see* hortor
*hortor, hortārī, hortātus sum *encourage,
   urge*
*hortus, hortī, m. *garden*
hōrum *see* hic
*hospes, hospitis, m. *guest, host*
*hostis, hostis, m.f. *enemy*
*hūc *here, to this place*
   hūc illūc *here and there, up and down*
huic, huius *see* hic
humilis, humile *low-born, of low class*
humus, humī, f. *ground*
* humī *on the ground*
   humum *to the ground*
   hunc *see* hic

i

*iaceō, iacēre, iacuī *lie, rest*
*iaciō, iacere, iēcī, iactus *throw*
*iactō, iactāre, iactāvī, iactātus *throw*
*iam *now, already*
iamdūdum *for a long time*
*iānua, iānuae, f. *door*
   ībam *see* eō
*ibi *there*
   id *see* is
*īdem, eadem, idem *the same*
*identidem *repeatedly*
iecur, iecoris, n. *liver*
Ierosolyma, Ierosolymae, f. *Jerusalem*
*igitur *therefore, and so*
*ignārus, ignāra, ignārum *not knowing,
   unaware*
*ignāvus, ignāva, ignāvum *cowardly, lazy*
ignis, ignis, m. *fire*
ignōrō, ignōrāre, ignōrāvī *not know
   about*
*ignōscō, ignōscere, ignōvī *forgive*
ignōtus, ignōta, ignōtum *unknown*
ii *see* eō
*ille, illa, illud *that, he, she*
*illūc *there, to that place*
   hūc illūc *here and there, up and down*
illūcēscō, illūcēscere, illūxī *dawn, grow
   bright*
imitor, imitārī, imitātus sum *imitate,
   mime*

*immemor, *gen.* immemoris *forgetful*
*immineō, imminēre, imminuī *hang over*
immo *or rather*
*immortālis, immortāle *immortal*
* dī immortālēs! *heavens above!*
immortālitās, immortālitātis, f.
   immortality
*immōtus, immōta, immōtum *still,
   motionless*
impatiēns, *gen.* impatientis *impatient*
*impediō, impedīre, impedīvī,
   impedītus *delay, hinder*
impellō, impellere, impulī, impulsus
   push, force
*imperātor, imperātōris, m. *emperor*
*imperium, imperiī, n. *empire*
*imperō, imperāre, imperāvī *order,
   command*
*impetus, impetūs, m. *attack*
   impetum facere *charge, make an attack*
*impōnō, impōnere, imposuī, impositus
   impose, put into, put onto
importō, importāre, importāvī,
   importātus *import*
imprecātiō, imprecātiōnis, f. *curse*
impudēns, *gen.* impudentis *shameless*
impulī *see* impellō
*in (1) + *acc.* *into, onto*
   (2) +*abl.* *in, on*
inānis, ināne *empty, meaningless*
*incēdō, incēdere, incessī *march, stride*
*incendō, incendere, incendī, incēnsus
   burn, set fire to
incēnsus, incēnsa, incēnsum *inflamed,
   angered*
incertus, incerta, incertum *uncertain*
*incidō, incidere, incidī *fall*
*incipiō, incipere, incēpī, inceptus *begin*
*incitō, incitāre, incitāvī, incitātus *urge
   on, encourage*
inclūsus, inclūsa, inclūsum *shut up,
   imprisoned, trapped*
incurrō, incurrere, incurrī *run onto,
   collide with, bump into*
inde *then*
*indicium, indiciī, n. *sign, evidence*
indignus, indigna, indignum *unworthy,
   undeserved*
indulgeō, indulgēre, indulsī *give way*
*induō, induere, induī, indūtus *put on*
inest *see* īnsum
*īnfāns, īnfantis, m. *baby, child*

*īnfēlīx, *gen.* īnfēlīcis *unlucky*
*īnferō, īnferre, intulī, inlātus *bring in, bring on, bring against*
  iniūriam īnferre *do an injustice to, bring injury to*
*īnfestus, īnfesta, īnfestum *hostile, dangerous*
  īnfīgō, īnfīgere, īnfīxī, īnfīxus *fasten onto*
  īnflīgō, īnflīgere, īnflīxī, īnflīctus *inflict*
  īnflō, īnflāre, īnflāvī *blow*
  īnfundō, īnfundere, īnfūdī, īnfūsus *pour into*
*ingenium, ingeniī, n. *character*
*ingēns, *gen.* ingentis *huge*
  ingravēscō, ingravēscere *grow worse*
*ingredior, ingredī, ingressus sum *enter*
  ingressus *see* ingredior
*iniciō, inicere, iniēcī, iniectus *throw in*
  inimīcitia, inimīcitiae, f. *feud, dispute*
*inimīcus, inimīcī, m. *enemy*
*iniūria, iniūriae, f. *injustice, injury*
  iniūriam īnferre *do an injustice to, bring injury to*
  inlātus *see* īnferō
  innītor, innītī, innīxus sum *lean, rest*
  innīxus *see* innītor
  innocēns, *gen.* innocentis *innocent*
  inopia, inopiae, f. *poverty*
  inopīnātus, inopīnāta, inopīnātum *unexpected*
*inquit *says, said*
  inquam *I said*
  īnsānia, īnsāniae, f. *insanity*
  īnsāniō, īnsānīre, īnsānīvī *be crazy, be insane*
*īnsānus, īnsāna, īnsānum *crazy, insane*
  īnscrībō, īnscrībere, īnscrīpsī, īnscrīptus *write, inscribe*
*īnsidiae, īnsidiārum, f.pl. *trap, ambush*
  īnsolēns, *gen.* īnsolentis *rude, insolent*
  īnsolenter *rudely, insolently*
*īnspiciō, īnspicere, īnspexī, īnspectus *look at, inspect, examine, search*
*īnstruō, īnstruere, īnstrūxī, īnstrūctus *draw up, set up*
*īnsula, īnsulae, f. *island; apartment building*
  īnsum, inesse, īnfuī *be inside*
*intellegō, intellegere, intellēxī, intellēctus *understand*
*intentē *intently*
*inter +*acc.* among, between*

inter sē *among themselves, with each other*
*intereā *meanwhile*
*interficiō, interficere, interfēcī, interfectus *kill*
  interrogō, interrogāre, interrogāvī, interrogātus *question*
  interrumpō, interrumpere, interrūpī, interruptus *interrupt*
*intrō, intrāre, intrāvī *enter*
  intulī *see* īnferō
  intus *inside*
  inultus, inulta, inultum *unavenged*
*inveniō, invenīre, invēnī, inventus *find*
  invicem *in turn*
*invītō, invītāre, invītāvī, invītātus *invite*
*invītus, invīta, invītum *unwilling, reluctant*
  iō! *hurrah!*
*iocus, iocī, m. *joke*
  Iovis *see* Iuppiter
*ipse, ipsa, ipsum *himself, herself, itself*
*īra, īrae, f. *anger*
*īrātus, īrāta, īrātum *angry*
  īre *see* eō
*irrumpō, irrumpere, irrūpī *burst in, burst into*
*is, ea, id *he, she, it*
*iste, ista, istud *that*
*ita *in this way*
*ita vērō *yes*
  Ītalia, Ītaliae, f. *Italy*
*itaque *and so*
*iter, itineris, n. *journey, trip, progress*
*iterum *again*
*iubeō, iubēre, iussī, iussus *order*
  Iūdaeī, Iūdaeōrum, m.pl. *Jews*
  Iūdaeus, Iūdaea, Iūdaeum *Jewish*
*iūdex, iūdicis, m. *judge*
  iūdicō, iūdicāre, iūdicāvī, iūdicātus *judge*
  iugulum, iugulī, n. *throat*
  Iuppiter, Iovis, m. *Jupiter (god of the sky, greatest of Roman gods)*
  iussī *see* iubeō
*iussum, iussī, n. *order, instruction*
  iussū Silvae *at Silva's order*
  iūstitia, iūstitiae, f. *justice*
  iuvat, iuvāre *please*
  mē iuvat *it pleases me*
*iuvenis, iuvenis, m. *young man*
  iuxtā +*acc.* next to*

l

L. = Lūcius

labefaciō, labefacere, labefēcī, labefactus *weaken*

lābor, lābī, lāpsus sum *fall*

*labor, labōris, m. *work*

*labōrō, labōrāre, labōrāvī *work*

labrum, labrī, n. *lip*

lacertus, lacertī, m. *muscle*

*lacrima, lacrimae, f. *tear*

lacrimīs effūsīs *bursting into tears*

*lacrimō, lacrimāre, lacrimāvī *cry, weep*

lacus, lacūs, m. *lake*

*laedō, laedere, laesī, laesus *harm*

laetē *happily*

*laetus, laeta, laetum *happy*

lānx, lancis, f. *dish*

lāpsus *see* lābor

latebrae, latebrārum, f.pl. *hiding-place*

*lateō, latēre, latuī *lie hidden*

later, lateris, m. *brick*

*latrō, latrōnis, m. *robber*

*lātus, lāta, lātum *wide*

*laudō, laudāre, laudāvī, laudātus *praise*

laurus, laurī, f. *laurel tree*

*lavō, lavāre, lāvī, lautus *wash*

*lectīca, lectīcae, f. *sedan-chair, carrying-chair*

lectīcārius, lectīcāriī, m. *chair-carrier, sedan-chair carrier*

*lectus, lectī, m. *couch, bed*

*lēgātus, lēgātī, m. *commander*

lēgibus *see* lēx

*legiō, legiōnis, f. *legion*

lēgō, lēgāre, lēgāvī, lēgātus *bequeath*

*legō, legere, lēgī, lēctus *read*

lēniō, lēnīre, lēnīvī, lēnītus *soothe, calm down*

*lēniter *gently*

*lentē *slowly*

*leō, leōnis, m. *lion*

leviter *lightly, slightly*

lēx, lēgis, f. *law*

libellus, libellī, m. *little book*

*libenter *gladly*

*liber, librī, m. *book*

*līberālis, līberāle *generous*

*līberī, līberōrum, m.pl. *children*

*līberō, līberāre, līberāvī, līberātus *free, set free*

*lībertās, lībertātis, f. *freedom*

*lībertus, lībertī, m. *freedman, ex-slave*

Augustī lībertus *freedman of Augustus, freedman of the emperor*

librōs *see* liber

librum *see* liber

līmen, līminis, n. *threshold, doorway*

*lingua, linguae, f. *tongue*

littera, litterae, f. *letter*

*lītus, lītoris, n. *seashore, shore*

līvidus, līvida, līvidum *lead-colored*

*locus, locī, m. *place*

locūtus *see* loquor

longē *far*

longē errāre *make a big mistake*

longurius, longuriī, m. *pole*

*longus, longa, longum *long*

loquāx, *gen.* loquācis *talkative*

*loquor, loquī, locūtus sum *speak*

lūbricus, lūbrica, lūbricum *slippery*

lūcem *see* lūx

lūceō, lūcēre, lūxī *shine*

lucerna, lucernae, f. *lamp*

lūdō, lūdere, lūsī *play*

*lūdus, lūdī, m. *game*

lūgeō, lūgēre, lūxī *lament, mourn*

*lūna, lūnae, f. *moon*

lutum, lutī, n. *mud*

*lūx, lūcis, f. *light, daylight*

m

M. = Marcus

madidus, madida, madidum *soaked through, drenched*

magicus, magica, magicum *magic*

*magister, magistrī, m. *master, foreman*

magistrātus, magistrātūs, m. *public official*

magnificē *splendidly, magnificently*

magnificus, magnifica, magnificum *splendid, magnificent*

*magnopere *greatly*

* maximē *very greatly, very much, most of all*

*magnus, magna, magnum *big, large, great*

maior, *gen.* maiōris *bigger, larger, greater*

* maximus, maxima, maximum *very big, very large, very great, greatest*

Pontifex Maximus *Chief Priest*

maiestās, maiestātis, f. *treason*

malignus, maligna, malignum *spiteful*

*mālō, mālle, māluī *prefer*
  mālim *I would prefer*

*malus, mala, malum *evil, bad*
  peior, *gen.* peiōris *worse*

* pessimus, pessima, pessimum *very
  bad, worst*

*mandātum, mandātī, n. *instruction,
  order*

*mandō, mandāre, mandāvī,
  mandātus *order, entrust, hand over*

*māne *in the morning*

*maneō, manēre, mānsī *remain, stay*

  manifestus, manifesta, manifestum
  clear

*manus, manūs, f. *hand; band*

*mare, maris, n. *sea*

  margō, marginis, m. *edge*

*marītus, marītī, m. *husband*

  marmor, marmoris, n. *marble*

  Mārs, Mārtis, m. *Mars (god of war)*

  massa, massae, f. *block*

*māter, mātris, f. *mother*

  mātrimōnium, mātrimōniī, n. *marriage*

  mātrōna, mātrōnae, f. *lady*

  maximē *see* magnopere

  maximus *see* magnus

  mē *see* ego

  medicāmentum, medicāmentī, n.
  ointment, medicine, drug

*medicus, medicī, m. *doctor*

*medius, media, medium *middle*

  melior *see* bonus

  melius est *see* bonus

  memor, *gen.* memoris *remembering,
  mindful of*

  memoria, memoriae, f. *memory*
  in memoriā habēre *keep in mind,
  remember*

*mendāx, mendācis, m. *liar*

  mendāx, *gen.* mendācis *lying, deceitful*

  mendīcus, mendīcī, m. *beggar*

  mēns, mentis, f. *mind*

*mēnsa, mēnsae, f. *table*

  mēnsis, mēnsis, m. *month*

*mercātor, mercātōris, m. *merchant*

  meritus, merita, meritum *well-deserved*

*metus, metūs, m. *fear*

*meus, mea, meum *my, mine*
  meī, meōrum, m.pl. *my family*
  mī Haterī *my dear Haterius*

mī Quīnte *my dear Quintus*

mihi *see* ego

*mīles, mīlitis, m. *soldier*

  mīlitō, mīlitāre, mīlitāvī *be a soldier*

*mīlle *a thousand*

* mīlia *thousands*

*minimē *no, least, very little*

  minimus *see* parvus

  minister, ministrī, m. *servant, agent*

  minor *see* parvus

  minor, minārī, minātus sum *threaten*

*mīrābilis, mīrābile *marvelous, strange,
  wonderful*

  mīrus, mīra, mīrum *extraordinary*

  misceō, miscēre, miscuī, mixtus *mix*

*miser, misera, miserum *miserable,
  wretched, sad*
  o mē miserum! *oh wretched me!*

*mittō, mittere, mīsī, missus *send*

  moderātus, moderāta, moderātum
  restrained, moderate

*modo *just, now, only*
  modo . . . modo *now . . . now*
  nōn modo . . . sed etiam *not only
  . . . but also*

*modus, modī, m. *manner, way, kind*

* quō modō? *how? in what way?*
  rēs huius modī *a thing of this kind*

*molestus, molesta, molestum
  troublesome

  molliō, mollīre, mollīvī, mollītus *soothe*

  mollis, molle *soft, gentle*

  mōmentum, mōmentī, n. *importance*

*moneō, monēre, monuī, monitus *warn,
  advise*

*mōns, montis, m. *mountain*

  mora, morae, f. *delay*

*morbus, morbī, m. *illness*

*morior, morī, mortuus sum *die*
  (eī) moriendum est *(he) must die*
  moriēns, *gen.* morientis *dying*

* mortuus, mortua, mortuum *dead*

  moror, morārī, morātus sum *delay*

*mors, mortis, f. *death*
  mortem sibi cōnscīscere *commit suicide*

  mortuus *see* morior

*mōs, mōris, m. *custom*

  mōtus, mōtūs, m. *movement*

*moveō, movēre, mōvī, mōtus *move*

*mox *soon*

*multitūdō, multitūdinis, f. *crowd*

*multō *much*

multum *much*
*multus, multa, multum *much*
* multī *many*
* plūrimī, plūrimae, plūrima *very many*
* plūrimus, plūrima, plūrimum *very much, most*
plūris est *is worth more*
* plūs, *gen.* plūris *more*
plūs vīnī *more wine*
mūnītiō, mūnītiōnis, f. *defense, fortification*
*mūrus, mūrī, m. *wall*
mūs, mūris, m.f. *mouse*
mussitō, mussitāre, mussitāvī *murmur*

n

nactus, nacta, nactum *having seized*
*nam *for*
*nārrō, nārrāre, nārrāvī, nārrātus *tell, relate*
*nāscor, nāscī, nātus sum *be born*
nātū maximus *eldest*
trīgintā annōs nātus *thirty years old*
nāsus, nāsī, m. *nose*
*(diēs) nātālis, (diēī) nātālis, m. *birthday*
nātus *see* nāscor
*nauta, nautae, m. *sailor*
*nāvigō, nāvigāre, nāvigāvī *sail*
*nāvis, nāvis, f. *ship*
nē *that . . . not, so that . . . not*
* nē . . . quidem *not even*
nec *and not, nor*
*necesse *necessary*
*necō, necāre, necāvī, necātus *kill*
*neglegēns, *gen.* neglegentis *careless*
*neglegō, neglegere, neglēxī, neglēctus *neglect*
*negōtium, negōtiī, n. *business*
* negōtium agere *do business, work*
*nēmō *no one, nobody*
neque *and not, nor*
* neque . . . neque *neither . . . nor*
*nescio, nescīre, nescīvī *not know*
niger, nigra, nigrum *black*
*nihil *nothing*
*nihilōminus *nevertheless*
*nimis *too*
*nimium *too much*
*nisi *except, unless*
*nōbilis, nōbile *noble, of noble birth*

nōbīs *see* nōs
nocēns, *gen.* nocentis *guilty*
*noceō, nocēre, nocuī *hurt*
noctis *see* nox
noctū *see* nox
*nōlō, nōlle, nōluī *not want*
nōlī, nōlīte *do not, don't*
*nōmen, nōminis, n. *name*
*nōn *not*
*nōnāgintā *ninety*
nōndum *not yet*
*nōnne? *surely?*
*nōnnūllī, nōnnūllae, nōnnūlla *some, several*
*nōnus, nōna, nōnum *ninth*
*nōs *we, us*
*noster, nostra, nostrum *our*
notō, notāre, notāvī, notātus *note, observe*
*nōtus, nōta, nōtum *known, well-known, famous*
*novem *nine*
*nōvī *I know*
*novus, nova, novum *new*
*nox, noctis, f. *night*
noctū *by night*
*nūbēs, nūbis, f. *cloud*
*nūllus, nūlla, nūllum *not any, no*
*num? *(1) surely . . . not?*
*num *(2) whether*
*numerō, numerāre, numerāvī, numerātus *count*
*numerus, numerī, m. *number*
*numquam *never*
*nunc *now*
*nūntiō, nūntiāre, nūntiāvī, nūntiātus *announce*
*nūntius, nūntiī, m. *messenger, message, news*
*nūper *recently*
*nusquam *nowhere*

o

obdormiō, obdormīre, obdormīvī *fall asleep*
obeō, obīre, obiī *meet, go to meet*
obēsus, obēsa, obēsum *fat*
obiciō, obicere, obiēcī, obiectus *present*
oblītus, oblīta, oblītum *having forgotten*
*obscūrus, obscūra, obscūrum *dark, gloomy*

obstinātus, obstināta, obstinātum
  stubborn
*obstō, obstāre, obstitī *obstruct, block the
  way*
*obstupefaciō, obstupefacere,
  obstupefēcī, obstupefactus *amaze,
  stun*
obtulī *see* offerō
*obviam eō, obviam īre, obviam iī *meet,
  go to meet*
occāsiō, occāsiōnis, f. *opportunity*
*occīdō, occīdere, occīdī, occīsus *kill*
occidō, occidere, occidī *set*
*occupātus, occupāta, occupātum *busy*
*occupō, occupāre, occupāvī,
  occupātus *seize, take over*
*occurrō, occurrere, occurrī *meet*
*octāvus, octāva, octāvum *eighth*
*octō *eight*
*octōgintā *eighty*
*oculus, oculī, m. *eye*
*ōdī *I hate*
*odiō sum, odiō esse *be hateful*
*offerō, offerre, obtulī, oblātus *offer*
officium, officiī, n. *duty*
  officium agere *do one's duty*
oleum, oleī, n. *oil*
*ōlim *once, some time ago*
ōmen, ōminis, n. *omen (sign from the
  gods)*
omittō, omittere, omīsī, omissus *drop,
  leave out, omit*
*omnīnō *completely*
*omnis, omne *all*
  omnia *all, everything*
*opēs, opum, f.pl. *money, wealth*
*oportet, oportēre, oportuit *be right*
  mē oportet *I must*
*oppidum, oppidī, n. *town*
*opprimō, opprimere, oppressī,
  oppressus *crush*
*oppugnō, oppugnāre, oppugnāvī,
  oppugnātus *attack*
optimē *see* bene
optimus *see* bonus
optiō, optiōnis, m. *optio (military officer
  ranking below centurion)*
*opus, operis, n. *work, construction*
ōrātiō, ōrātiōnis, f. *speech*
orbis, orbis, m. *globe*
  orbis terrārum *world*
*ōrdō, ōrdinis, m. *row, line*

orior, orīrī, ortus sum *rise*
ōrnāmentum, ōrnāmentī, n. *ornament,
  decoration*
  ōrnāmenta praetōria *the honorary
  rank and privileges of a praetor*
ōrnātus, ōrnāta, ōrnātum *decorated,
  elaborately furnished*
*ōrnō, ōrnāre, ōrnāvī, ōrnātus *decorate*
*ōrō, ōrāre, ōrāvī *beg*
ortus *see* orior
*ōs, ōris, n. *face*
*ōsculum, ōsculī, n. *kiss*
*ostendō, ostendere, ostendī, ostentus
  show
ostentō, ostentāre, ostentāvī,
  ostentātus *show off, display*
*ōtiōsus, ōtiōsa, ōtiōsum *at leisure, with
  time off, idle, on vacation*

p

*paene *nearly, almost*
*pallēscō, pallēscere, palluī *grow pale*
*pallidus, pallida, pallidum *pale*
pallium, palliī, n. *cloak*
pālus, pālī, m. *stake, post*
pantomīmus, pantomīmī, m.
  pantomime actor, dancer
*parātus, parāta, parātum *ready,
  prepared*
*parcō, parcere, pepercī *spare*
*parēns, parentis, m.f. *parent*
*pāreō, pārēre, pāruī *obey*
*parō, parāre, parāvī, parātus *prepare*
*pars, partis, f. *part*
  extrēma pars *edge*
  in prīmā parte *in the forefront*
*parvus, parva, parvum *small*
  minor, *gen.* minōris *less, smaller*
* minimus, minima, minimum *very
  little, least*
passus *see* patior
pāstor, pāstōris, m. *shepherd*
*patefaciō, patefacere, patefēcī,
  patefactus *reveal*
*pater, patris, m. *father*
patera, paterae, f. *bowl*
patientia, patientiae, f. *patience*
*patior, patī, passus sum *suffer, endure*
*patrōnus, patrōnī, m. *patron*
*paucī, paucae, pauca *few, a few*
*paulīsper *for a short time*

paulō *a little*
*pauper, *gen.* pauperis *poor*
*pavor, pavōris, m. *panic*
*pāx, pācis, f. *peace*
*pecūnia, pecūniae, f. *money*
pedem *see* pēs
peior *see* malus
*pendeō, pendēre, pependī *hang*
*per +*acc.* *through, along*
percutiō, percutere, percussī,
    percussus *strike*
perdomitus, perdomita, perdomitum
    conquered
*pereō, perīre, periī *die, perish*
*perficiō, perficere, perfēcī, perfectus
    finish
*perfidia, perfidiae, f. *treachery*
*perfidus, perfida, perfidum *treacherous,
    untrustworthy*
perfodiō, perfodere, perfōdī,
    perfossus *pick (teeth)*
perfuga, perfugae, m. *deserter*
*perīculōsus, perīculōsa, perīculōsum
    dangerous
*perīculum, perīculī, n. *danger*
periī *see* pereō
perītē *skillfully*
*perītus, perīta, perītum *skillful*
*permōtus, permōta, permōtum
    alarmed, disturbed
perpetuus, perpetua, perpetuum
    perpetual
 in perpetuum *forever*
perrumpō, perrumpere, perrūpī,
    perruptus *burst through, burst in*
perscrūtor, perscrūtārī, perscrūtātus
    sum *examine*
persecūtus, persecūta, persecūtum
    having pursued
persōna, persōnae, f. *character*
    personam agere *play a part*
perstō, perstāre, perstitī *persist*
*persuādeō, persuādēre, persuāsī,
    persuade
perterreō, perterrēre, perterruī,
    perterritus *terrify*
*perterritus, perterrita, perterritum
    terrified
perturbō, perturbāre, perturbāvī,
    perturbātus *disturb, alarm*

*perveniō, pervenīre, pervēnī *reach,
    arrive at*
*pēs, pedis, m. *foot, paw*
pedem referre *step back*
pessimē *very badly*
pessimus *see* malus
*pestis, pestis, f. *pest, rascal*
petauristārius, petauristāriī, m. *acrobat*
*petō, petere, petīvī, petītus *head for,
    attack; seek, beg for, ask for*
philosopha, philosophae, f. *(female)
    philosopher*
philosophia, philosophiae, f. *philosophy*
philosophus, philosophī, m. *philosopher*
pīpiō, pīpiāre, pīpiāvī *chirp, peep*
*placet, placēre, placuit *please, suit*
*plaudō, plaudere, plausī, plausus
    applaud, clap
*plaustrum, plaustrī, n. *wagon, cart*
plausus, plausūs, m. *applause*
*plēnus, plēna, plēnum *full*
plērīque, plēraeque, plēraque *most*
pluit, pluere, pluit *rain*
plūrimus, plūs *see* multus
*pōculum, pōculī, n. *cup (often for wine)*
*poena, poenae, f. *punishment*
* poenās dare *pay the penalty, be punished*
*poēta, poētae, m. *poet*
poliō, polīre, polīvī, polītus *polish*
polliceor, pollicērī, pollicitus sum *promise*
polyspaston, polyspastī, n. *crane*
*pompa, pompae, f. *procession*
Pompēiānus, Pompēiāna,
    Pompēiānum *Pompeian*
*pōnō, pōnere, posuī, positus *put, place,
    put up*
*pōns, pontis, m. *bridge*
pontifex, pontificis, m. *priest*
    Pontifex Maximus *Chief Priest*
poposcī *see* poscō
*populus, populī, m. *people*
porrigō, porrigere, porrēxī, porrēctus
    stretch out
porrō *what's more, furthermore*
*porta, portae, f. *gate*
porticus, porticūs, f. *colonnade*
*portō, portāre, portāvī, portātus *carry*
*portus, portūs, m. *harbor*
*poscō, poscere, poposcī *demand, ask for*
positus *see* pōnō

possideō, possidēre, possēdī,
  possessus *possess*
*possum, posse, potuī *can, be able*
*post +*acc. after, behind*
*posteā *afterwards*
posterī, posterōrum, m.pl. *future
  generations, posterity*
postīcum, postīcī, n. *back gate*
*postquam *after, when*
*postrēmō *finally, lastly*
*postrīdiē *(on) the next day*
*postulō, postulāre, postulāvī,
  postulātus *demand*
posuī *see* pōnō
*potēns, *gen.* potentis *powerful*
potentia, potentiae, f. *power*
potes *see* possum
*potestās, potestātis, f. *power*
potius *rather*
potuī *see* possum
*praebeō, praebēre, praebuī,
  praebitus *provide*
*praeceps, *gen.* praecipitis *headlong*
praecipitō, praecipitāre, praecipitāvī
  hurl
*praecō, praecōnis, m. *herald, announcer*
praeda, praedae, f. *booty, plunder, loot*
praedīcō, praedīcere, praedīxī,
  praedictus *foretell, predict*
praefectus, praefectī, m. *commander*
*praeficiō, praeficere, praefēcī,
  praefectus *put in charge*
*praemium, praemiī, n. *prize, reward,
  profit*
praeruptus, praerupta, praeruptum
  sheer, steep
praesēns, *gen.* praesentis *present, ready*
praesertim *especially*
*praesidium, praesidiī, n. *protection*
*praestō, praestāre, praestitī *show,
  display*
*praesum, praeesse, praefuī *be in charge
  of*
praeter +*acc. except*
*praetereā *besides*
*praetereō, praeterīre, praeteriī *pass
  by, go past*
praetextus, praetexta, praetextum
  with a purple border
praetōriānus, praetōriānī, m.
  *praetorian (member of emperor's
  bodyguard)*

praetōrius, praetōria, praetōrium
  praetorian
ōrnāmenta praetōria *honorary
  praetorship, honorary rank of praetor*
*prāvus, prāva, prāvum *evil*
precātus *see* precor
*precēs, precum, f.pl. *prayers*
*precor, precārī, precātus sum *pray (to)*
prēnsō, prēnsāre, prēnsāvī, prēnsātus
  take hold of, clutch
*pretiōsus, pretiōsa, pretiōsum
  expensive, precious
*pretium, pretiī, n. *price*
minōris pretiī habēre *care less about*
prīmō *at first*
prīmum *first*
*prīmus, prīma, prīmum *first*
in prīmā parte *in the forefront*
in prīmīs *in particular*
*prīnceps, prīncipis, m. *chief, chieftain*
*prīncipia, prīncipiōrum, n.pl.
  headquarters
*prior *first, in front*
*prius *earlier*
*priusquam *before, until*
*prō +*abl. in front of, for, in return for*
prō certō habēre *know for certain*
prō hostibus habēre *reckon as enemies*
probus, proba, probum *honest*
procāx, *gen.* procācis *impudent, impolite*
*prōcēdō, prōcēdere, prōcessī *advance,
  proceed*
*procul *far off*
*prōcumbō, prōcumbere, prōcubuī *fall
  down*
prōcūrātor, prōcūrātōris, m. *manager·*
prōdō, prōdere, prōdidī, prōditus
  betray
profectus *see* proficīscor
*proficīscor, proficīscī, profectus sum
  set out
(tibi) proficīscendum est *(you) must set
  out*
*prōgredior, prōgredī, prōgressus sum
  advance
prōgressus *see* prōgredior
prohibeō, prohibēre, prohibuī,
  prohibitus *prevent*
*prōmittō, prōmittere, prōmīsī,
  prōmissus *promise*
prōmoveō, prōmovēre, prōmōvī,
  prōmōtus *promote*

prōnūntiō, prōnūntiāre, prōnūntiāvī,
 prōnūntiātus *proclaim, preach*
*prope *near*
prophēta, prophētae, m. *prophet*
prōpōnō, prōpōnere, prōposuī,
 prōpositus *propose, put forward*
prōsiliō, prōsilīre, prōsiluī *leap forward,
 jump*
prōspectus, prōspectūs, m. *view*
prōspiciō, prōspicere, prōspexī *look out*
*prōvincia, prōvinciae, f. *province*
*proximus, proxima, proximum *nearest,
 next to*
prūdēns, *gen.* prūdentis *shrewd,
 intelligent, sensible*
*prūdentia, prūdentiae, f. *prudence, good
 sense, shrewdness*
psittacus, psittacī, m. *parrot*
*pūblicus, pūblica, pūblicum *public*
*puella, puellae, f. *girl*
*puer, puerī, m. *boy*
pugiō, pugiōnis, m. *dagger*
*pugna, pugnae, f. *fight*
*pugnō, pugnāre, pugnāvī *fight*
*pulcher, pulchra, pulchrum *beautiful*
*pulsō, pulsāre, pulsāvī, pulsātus *hit,
 knock on, whack, punch*
pulvīnus, pulvīnī, m. *cushion*
pūmiliō, pūmiliōnis, m. *dwarf*
*pūniō, pūnīre, pūnīvī, pūnītus *punish*
pūrgō, pūrgāre, pūrgāvī, pūrgātus
 clean
pūrus, pūra, pūrum *pure, clean, spotless*
pyra, pyrae, f. *pyre*

q

quā *see* quī
*quadrāgintā *forty*
'quae *see* quī
quaedam *see* quīdam
*quaerō, quaerere, quaesīvī, quaesītus
 search for, look for, inquire
*quālis, quāle *what sort of*
 tālis . . . quālis *such . . . as*
*quam (1) *how*
 quam celerrimē *as quickly as possible*
*quam (2) *than*
 quam (3) *see* quī
*quamquam *although*
 quandō *when*
*quantus, quanta, quantum *how big*

*quārē? *why?*
*quārtus, quārta, quārtum *fourth*
*quasi *as if*
*quattuor *four*
*-que *and*
 quendam *see* quīdam
 quī, quae, quod *who, which*
*quia *because*
*quicquam (*also spelled* quidquam)
 anything
 quid? *see* quis?
 quid vīs *see* quis?
*quīdam, quaedam, quoddam *one, a
 certain*
 quidem *indeed*
 nē . . . quidem *not even*
*quiēs, quiētis, f. *rest*
 quiēscō, quiēscere, quiēvī *rest*
 quiētus, quiēta, quiētum *quiet*
 quīngentī, quīngentae, quīngenta *five
 hundred*
*quīnquāgintā *fifty*
*quīnque *five*
*quīntus, quīnta, quīntum *fifth*
*quis? quid? *who? what?*
 quid vīs? *what do you want?*
 quisque, quaeque, quidque *each one*
 optimus quisque *all the best people*
*quō? (1) *where? where to?*
 quō (2) *see* quī
*quō modō? *how? in what way?*
*quod (1) *because*
 quod (2) *see* quī
*quondam *one day, once*
*quoque *also, too*
 quōs *see* quī
*quot? *how many?*
 quotannīs *every year*
 quotiēns *whenever*

r

rādō, rādere, rāsī, rāsus
 scratch, scrape
*rapiō, rapere, rapuī, raptus *seize, grab*
 raptim *hastily, quickly*
*ratiōnēs, ratiōnum, f.pl. *accounts*
 ratiōnēs subdūcere *write up accounts*
 raucus, rauca, raucum *harsh*
 rē *see* rēs
 rebellō, rebellāre, rebellāvī *rebel, revolt*
 rēbus *see* rēs

*recipiō, recipere, recēpī, receptus *recover, take back*
  sē recipere *recover*
  recitō, recitāre, recitāvī, recitātus *recite, read out*
  rēctē *rightly, properly*
*recumbō, recumbere, recubuī *lie down, recline*
*recūsō, recūsāre, recūsāvī, recūsātus *refuse*
*reddō, reddere, reddidī, redditus *give back, make*
  redēmptor, redēmptōris, m. *contractor, builder*
*redeō, redīre, rediī *return, go back, come back*
  redeundum est vōbīs *you must return*
  reditus, reditūs, m. *return*
*redūcō, redūcere, redūxī, reductus *lead back*
*referō, referre, rettulī, relātus *bring back, carry, deliver, tell, report*
  pedem referre *step back*
*reficiō, reficere, refēcī, refectus *repair*
*rēgīna, rēgīnae, f. *queen*
  rēgnō, rēgnāre, rēgnāvī *reign*
*rēgnum, rēgnī, n. *kingdom*
*regredior, regredī, regressus sum *go back, return*
  regressus *see* regredior
  relēgō, relēgāre, relēgāvī, relēgātus *exile*
*relinquō, relinquere, relīquī, relictus *leave*
  reliquus, reliqua, reliquum *remaining*
  rem *see* rēs
*remedium, remediī, n. *cure*
  remittō, remittere, remīsī, remissus *send back*
  renovō, renovāre, renovāvī, renovātus *restore, renew, repeat*
  repetō, repetere, repetīvī, repetītus *claim*
  rēpō, rēpere, rēpsī *crawl*
*rēs, reī, f. *thing, business, affair*
* rē vērā *in fact, truly, really*
  rem administrāre *manage the task*
  rem cōgitāre *consider the problem*
  rem cōnficere *finish the job*
  rem intellegere *understand the truth*
  rem nārrāre *tell the story*
  rem perficere *finish the job*

  rem suscipere *undertake the task*
  rērum status *situation, state of affairs*
* rēs adversae *misfortune*
  rēs contrāria *the opposite*
  resignō, resignāre, resignāvī, resignātus *open, unseal*
*resistō, resistere, restitī *resist*
  respiciō, respicere, respexī *look at, look upon*
*respondeō, respondēre, respondī *reply*
  respōnsum, respōnsī, n. *answer*
  resurgō, resurgere, resurrēxī *rise again*
*retineō, retinēre, retinuī, retentus *keep, hold back*
  retrō *back*
  rettulī *see* referō
*reveniō, revenīre, revēnī *come back, return*
*revertor, revertī, reversus sum *turn back, return*
  revocō, revocāre, revocāvī, revocātus *recall, call back*
*rēx, rēgis, m. *king*
  rhētor, rhētoris, m. *teacher*
*rīdeō, rīdēre, rīsī *laugh, smile*
  rīdiculus, rīdicula, rīdiculum *ridiculous, silly*
  rīma, rīmae, f. *crack, chink*
*rīpa, rīpae, f. *river bank*
  rīsus, rīsūs, m. *smile*
*rogō, rogāre, rogāvī, rogātus *ask*
  Rōma, Rōmae, f. *Rome*
   Rōmae *at Rome*
  Rōmānī, Rōmānōrum, m.pl. *Romans*
  Rōmānus, Rōmāna, Rōmānum *Roman*
  rosa, rosae, f. *rose*
  rumpō, rumpere, rūpī, ruptus *break, split*
*ruō, ruere, ruī *rush*
  rūpēs, rūpis, f. *rock, crag*
  rūrī *in the country*
*rūrsus *again*
  rūsticus, rūstica, rūsticum *country, in the country*
  vīlla rūstica *house in the country*

S

  saccārius, saccāriī, m. *stevedore, dock-worker*
  saccus, saccī, m. *bag, purse*
*sacer, sacra, sacrum *sacred*

*sacerdōs, sacerdōtis, m. *priest*
sacerdōtium, sacerdōtiī, n. *priesthood*
sacrificium, sacrificiī, n. *offering,*
   sacrifice
sacrificō, sacrificāre, sacrificāvī,
   sacrificātus *sacrifice*
*saepe *often*
*saeviō, saevīre, saeviī *be in a rage*
*saevus, saeva, saevum *savage, cruel*
saltātrīx, saltātrīcis, f. *dancing-girl*
*saltō, saltāre, saltāvī *dance*
*salūs, salūtis, f. *safety, health*
salūtem plūrimam dīcit *sends his best*
   wishes
salūtātiō, salūtātiōnis, f. *the morning*
   visit
*salūtō, salūtāre, salūtāvī, salūtātus
   greet
*salvē! *hello!*
*sānē *obviously*
*sanguis, sanguinis, m. *blood*
sānō, sānāre, sānāvī, sānātus *heal, cure,*
   treat
sānus, sāna, sānum *well, healthy*
*sapiēns, *gen.* sapientis *wise*
sarcinae, sarcinārum, f.pl. *bags,*
   luggage
*satis *enough*
*saxum, saxī, n. *rock*
scaena, scaenae, f. *stage, scene*
scālae, scālārum, f.pl. *ladders*
*scelestus, scelesta, scelestum *wicked*
*scelus, sceleris, n. *crime*
scīlicet *obviously*
*scindō, scindere, scidī, scissus *tear, tear*
   up, cut up, cut open, carve
*sciō, scīre, scīvī *know*
scrība, scrībae, m. *secretary*
*scrībō, scrībere, scrīpsī, scrīptus *write*
sculpō, sculpere, sculpsī, sculptus
   sculpt, carve
scurrīlis, scurrīle *obscene, dirty*
*sē *himself, herself, themselves*
sēcum *with him, with her, with them*
sēcum cōgitāre *consider to oneself*
*secō, secāre, secuī, sectus *cut*
sēcrētus, sēcrēta, sēcrētum *secret*
*secundus, secunda, secundum *second*
secūris, secūris, f. *axe*
secūtus *see* sequor
*sed *but*
*sedeō, sedēre, sēdī *sit*

*sēdēs, sēdis, f. *seat*
sēditiō, sēditiōnis, f. *rebellion*
sēditiōnem facere *revolt*
*sella, sellae, f. *chair*
*semper *always*
*senātor, senātōris, m. *senator*
senectūs, senectūtis, f. *old age*
*senex, senis, m. *old man*
*sententia, sententiae, f. *opinion*
*sentiō, sentīre, sēnsī, sēnsus *feel, notice*
sepeliō, sepelīre, sepelīvī, sepultus *bury*
*septem *seven*
*septimus, septima, septimum *seventh*
*septuāgintā *seventy*
*sepulcrum, sepulcrī, n. *tomb*
*sequor, sequī, secūtus sum *follow*
sequēns, *gen.* sequentis *following*
*serēnus, serēna, serēnum *calm, clear*
*sermō, sermōnis, m. *conversation*
sermōnem habēre *have a conversation,*
   talk
*serviō, servīre, servīvī *serve (as a slave)*
servitūs, servitūtis, f. *slavery*
*servō, servāre, servāvī, servātus *save,*
   protect
fidem servāre *keep a promise, keep faith*
*servus, servī, m. *slave*
sēstertius, sēstertiī, m. *sesterce (coin)*
sēstertium vīciēns *two million sesterces*
sevērē *severely*
*sevērus, sevēra, sevērum *severe, strict*
*sex *six*
*sexāgintā *sixty*
*sextus, sexta, sextum *sixth*
*sī *if*
sibi *see* sē
*sīc *thus, in this way*
siccō, siccāre, siccāvī, siccātus *dry*
*sīcut *like*
significō, significāre, significāvī,
   significātus *mean, indicate*
signō, signāre, signāvī, signātus *sign,*
   seal
*signum, signī, n. *seal, signal*
*silentium, silentiī, n. *silence*
sileō, silēre, siluī *be silent*
*silva, silvae, f. *woods, forest*
simul *at the same time*
*simulac, simulatque *as soon as*
*sine +abl. *without*
situs, sita, situm *situated*
*sōl, sōlis, m. *sun*

sōlācium, sōlāciī, n. *comfort*
*soleō, solēre *be accustomed*
sollemniter *solemnly*
*sollicitus, sollicita, sollicitum *worried,*
anxious
sōlum *only*
   nōn sōlum . . . sed etiam *not only . . .*
but also
*sōlus, sōla, sōlum *alone, lonely, only, on*
one's own
solūtus, solūta, solūtum *relaxed*
*solvō, solvere, solvī, solūtus *loosen,*
untie, cast off
*sonitus, sonitūs, m. *sound*
*sordidus, sordida, sordidum *dirty*
*soror, sorōris, f. *sister*
*sors, sortis, f. *lot*
   sorte ductus *chosen by lot*
spargō, spargere, sparsī, sparsus *scatter*
*spectāculum, spectāculī, n. *show,*
spectacle
spectātor, spectātōris, m. *spectator*
spectō, spectāre, spectāvī, spectātus
look at, watch
specus, specūs, m. *cave*
spernō, spernere, sprēvī, sprētus
despise, reject
*spērō, spērāre, spērāvī *hope, expect*
*spēs, speī, f. *hope*
spīna, spīnae, f. *thorn, toothpick*
splendidus, splendida, splendidum
splendid, impressive
sportula, sportulae, f. *handout*
squālidus, squālida, squālidum *covered*
with dirt, filthy
stābam *see* stō
*statim *at once*
*statiō, statiōnis, f. *post*
statua, statuae, f. *statue*
statūra, statūrae, f. *height*
status, statūs, m. *state*
   rērum status *situation, state of affairs*
stēlla, stēllae, f. *star*
sternō, sternere, strāvī, strātus *lay low*
stilus, stilī, m. *pen, stick*
*stō, stāre, stetī *stand, lie at anchor*
Stōicus, Stōicī, m. *Stoic (believer in Stoic*
philosophy)
*stola, stolae, f. *(long) dress*
*strēnuē *hard, energetically*
*strepitus, strepitūs, m. *noise, din*

studium, studiī, n. *enthusiasm, zeal*
stultitia, stultitiae, f. *stupidity,*
foolishness
*stultus, stulta, stultum *stupid, foolish*
*suāvis, suāve *sweet*
*suāviter *sweetly*
*sub +abl. *under, beneath*
subdūcō, subdūcere, subdūxī,
   subductus *draw up*
   ratiōnēs subdūcere *draw up accounts,*
write up accounts
*subitō *suddenly*
sublātus *see* tollō
subscrībō, subscrībere, subscrīpsī,
   subscrīptus *sign*
*subveniō, subvenīre, subvēnī *help, come*
to help
sūdō, sūdāre, sūdāvī *sweat*
suffīgō, suffīgere, suffīxī, suffīxus *nail,*
fasten
*sum, esse, fuī *be*
   estō! *be!*
*summus, summa, summum *highest,*
greatest, top
sūmptuōsē *lavishly*
sūmptuōsus, sūmptuōsa,
   sūmptuōsum *expensive, lavish, costly*
superbē *arrogantly*
*superbus, superba, superbum *arrogant,*
proud
superō, superāre, superāvī, superātus
overcome, overpower
superstes, superstitis, m. *survivor*
*supersum, superesse, superfuī *survive*
*surgō, surgere, surrēxī *get up, stand up,*
rise
suscipiō, suscipere, suscēpī,
   susceptus *undertake, take on*
suspicātus *see* suspicor
suspiciō, suspiciōnis, f. *suspicion*
suspiciōsus, suspiciōsa,
   suspiciōsum *suspicious*
suspicor, suspicārī, suspicātus sum
suspect
suspīrium, suspīriī, n. *heart-throb*
sustulī *see* tollō
susurrō, susurrāre, susurrāvī *whisper,*
mumble
*suus, sua, suum *his, her, their, his own*
   suī, suōrum, m.pl. *his men, his family,*
their families

t

T. = Titus

*taberna, tabernae, f. *store, shop, inn*

tabernārius, tabernāriī, m. *store-owner, storekeeper*

tabula, tabulae, f. *tablet, writing- tablet*

*taceō, tacēre, tacuī *be silent, be quiet*
  tacē! *shut up! be quiet!*

*tacitē *quietly, silently*

*tacitus, tacita, tacitum *quiet, silent, in silence*

*taedet, taedēre *be tiring*
  mē taedet *I am tired, I am bored*

*tālis, tāle *such*
  tālis . . . quālis *such . . . as*

*tam *so*

*tamen *however*

*tamquam *as, like*

*tandem *at last*

tangō, tangere, tetigī, tāctus *touch*

*tantum *only*

*tantus, tanta, tantum *so great, such a great*

tapēte, tapētis, n. *tapestry, wall-hanging*
tardē *late*
  tardius *too late*

*tardus, tarda, tardum *late*

taurus, taurī, m. *bull*
tē *see* tū

*tēctum, tēctī, n. *ceiling, roof*

tēgula, tēgulae, f. *tile*

temperāns, *gen.* temperantis *temperate, self-controlled*

*tempestās, tempestātis, f. *storm*

*templum, templī, n. *temple*

*temptō, temptāre, temptāvī, temptātus *try, put to the test*

*tempus, temporis, n. *time*

*tenebrae, tenebrārum, f.pl. *darkness*

*teneō, tenēre, tenuī, tentus *hold, own*

*tergum, tergī, n. *back*

terō, terere, trīvī, trītus *waste (time)*

*terra, terrae, f. *ground, land*
  orbis terrārum *world*

*terreō, terrēre, terruī, territus *frighten*

terribilis, terribile *terrible*

*tertius, tertia, tertium *third*

*testāmentum, testāmentī, n. *will*

*testis, testis, m.f. *witness*

theātrum, theātrī, n. *theater*

thermae, thermārum, f. pl. *baths*

Tiberis, Tiberis, m. *river Tiber*

tibi *see* tū

tībia, tībiae, f. *pipe*
  tībiīs cantāre *play on the pipes*

tībīcen, tībīcinis, m. *pipe player*

tignum, tignī, n. *beam*

*timeō, timēre, timuī *be afraid, fear*

timidē *fearfully*

timidus, timida, timidum *fearful, frightened*

*timor, timōris, m. *fear*

tintinnō, tintinnāre, tintinnāvī *ring*

titulus, titulī, m. *advertisement, slogan, inscription, label*

toga, togae, f. *toga*

*tollō, tollere, sustulī, sublātus *raise, lift up, hold up*

tormentum, tormentī, n. *torture*

torqueō torquēre, torsī, tortus *torture, twist*

*tot *so many*

*tōtus, tōta, tōtum *whole*

*trādō, trādere, trādidī, trāditus *hand over*

*trahō, trahere, trāxī, tractus *drag*

tranquillē *peacefully*

trāns *across*

trānscendō, trānscendere, trānscendī *climb over*

*trānseō, trānsīre, trānsiī *cross*

trānsfīgō, trānsfīgere, trānsfīxī, trānsfīxus *pierce, stab*

trānsiliō, trānsilīre, trānsiluī *jump through*

tremō, tremere, tremuī *tremble, shake*

*trēs, tria *three*

tribūnal, tribūnālis, n. *platform*

*tribūnus, tribūnī, m. *tribune (high-ranking officer)*

trīciēns sēstertium *three million sesterces*

triclīnium, triclīniī, n. *dining-room*

*trīgintā *thirty*

tripodes, tripodum, m.pl. *tripods*

*trīstis, trīste *sad*

*tū, tuī *you (singular)*
  tēcum *with you (singular)*

*tuba, tubae, f. *trumpet*

tubicen, tubicinis, m. *trumpeter*

*tum *then*
  tum dēmum *then at last, only then*

tunica, tunicae, f. *tunic*

*turba, turbae, f. *crowd*
*tūtus, tūta, tūtum *safe*
  tūtius est *it would be safer*
*tuus, tua, tuum *your (singular), yours*
  Tyrius, Tyria, Tyrium *Tyrian*
    (colored with dye from city of Tyre)

u

*ubi *where, when*
*ubīque *everywhere*
  ulcīscor, ulcīscī, ultus sum *take revenge*
    on
  ūllus, ūlla, ūllum *any*
*ultimus, ultima, ultimum *furthest, last*
*ultiō, ultiōnis, f. *revenge*
  ululō, ululāre, ululāvī *howl*
*umbra, umbrae, f. *shadow, ghost*
*umerus, umerī, m. *shoulder*
*umquam *ever*
  ūnā cum +*abl. *together with*
*unda, undae, f. *wave*
*unde *from where*
*undique *on all sides*
  unguō, unguere, ūnxī, ūnctus *anoint,*
    smear
*ūnus, ūna, ūnum *one*
  urbānus, urbāna, urbānum *fashionable,*
    sophisticated
*urbs, urbis, f. *city*
  ursa, ursae, f. *bear*
  usquam *anywhere*
  usque ad +*acc. *right up to*
*ut (1) *as*
*ut (2) *that, so that, in order that*
*ūtilis, ūtile *useful*
*utrum *whether*
  utrum . . . an *whether . . . or*
  utrum . . . necne *whether . . . or not*
*uxor, uxōris, f. *wife*

v

  vacuus, vacua, vacuum *empty*
  vah! *ugh*
*valdē *very much, very*
*valē *good-by, farewell*
  valedīcō, valedīcere, valedīxī *say*
    good-by
  valētūdō, valētūdinis, f. *health*
  validus, valida, validum *strong*
  vallum, vallī, n. *embankment, rampart*

  varius, varia, varium *different*
*vehementer *violently, loudly*
*vehō, vehere, vexī, vectus *carry*
*vel *or*
  vel . . . vel *either . . . or*
  velim, vellem *see* volō
  vēnālīcius, vēnālīciī, m. *slave-dealer*
*vēnātiō, vēnātiōnis, f. *hunt*
*vēndō, vēndere, vēndidī, vēnditus *sell*
  venēnātus, venēnāta, venēnātum
    poisoned
*venēnum, venēnī, n. *poison*
*venia, veniae, f. *mercy*
*veniō, venīre, vēnī *come*
  venter, ventris, m. *stomach*
*ventus, ventī, m. *wind*
  Venus, Veneris, f. *Venus (goddess of love)*
  vēr, vēris, n. *spring*
  verber, verberis, n. *blow*
*verberō, verberāre, verberāvī,
  verberātus *strike, beat*
*verbum, verbī, n. *word*
  versus, versa, versum *having turned*
  versus, versūs, m. *verse, line of poetry*
*vertō, vertere, vertī, versus *turn*
  sē vertere *turn around*
*vērum, vērī, n. *truth*
*vērus, vēra, vērum *true, real*
* rē vērā *in fact, truly, really*
*vester, vestra, vestrum *your (plural)*
*vestīmenta, vestīmentōrum, n.pl.
  clothes
  vestrum *see* vōs
  vetus, *gen.* veteris *old*
*vexō, vexāre, vexāvī, vexātus *annoy*
  vī *see* vīs
*via, viae, f. *street, way*
  vibrō, vibrāre, vibrāvī, vibrātus *wave,*
    brandish
  vīciēns sēstertium *two million sesterces*
  victī *see* vincō
  victima, victimae, f. *victim*
*victor, victōris, m. *victor, winner*
  victōria, victōriae, f. *victory*
  victus *see* vincere
  vīcus, vīcī, m. *town, village, settlement*
*videō, vidēre, vīdī, vīsus *see*
  videor, vidērī, vīsus sum *seem*
  vigilō, vigilāre, vigilāvī *stay awake*
*vīgintī *twenty*
*vīlla, vīllae, f. *villa, (large) house*

*vinciō, vincīre, vīnxī, vīnctus *bind, tie up*

*vincō, vincere, vīcī, victus *conquer, win, be victorious*
  victī, victōrum, m.pl. *the conquered*
*vīnum, vīnī, n. *wine*
*vir, virī, m. *man*
  vīrēs, vīrium, f.pl *strength*
  virgō, virginis, f. *virgin*
*virtūs, virtūtis, f. *courage*
  vīs, f. *force, violence*
  vīs *see* volō
  vīsitō, vīsitāre, vīsitāvī, vīsitātus *visit*
  vīsus *see* videō
*vīta, vītae, f. *life*
  vītam agere *lead a life*
  vitium, vitiī, n. *sin*
*vītō, vītāre, vītāvī, vītātus *avoid*
*vituperō, vituperāre, vituperāvī, vituperātus *find fault with, tell off, curse*

*vīvō, vīvere, vīxī *live, be alive*
*vīvus, vīva, vīvum *alive, living*
*vix *hardly, scarcely, with difficulty*
  vōbīs *see* vōs
  vōcem *see* vōx
*vocō, vocāre, vocāvī, vocātus *call*
*volō, velle, voluī *want*
  quid vīs? *what do you want?*
  velim *I would like*
*volvō, volvere, volvī, volūtus *turn*
* in animō volvere *wonder, turn over in the mind*
*vōs *you (plural)*
  vōbīscum *with you (plural)*
*vōx, vōcis, f. *voice*
*vulnerō, vulnerāre, vulnerāvī, vulnerātus *wound, injure*
*vulnus, vulneris, n. *wound*
  vult *see* volō
*vultus, vultūs, m. *expression, face*

Guide to Characters and Places

(The numeral in parenthesis identifies the Stage in which the person(s) or place is/are first featured.)

Gnaeus Iūlius AGRICOLA (24): Roman governor of Britain in A.D. 78–84; disapproved of Salvius' plot (although this was supposedly endorsed by the Emperor Domitian) to remove King Cogidubnus.

Gāius Iūlius ALEXANDER (31): witness to patron Haterius' accounts (see also "Aprōniānus" and "Prīmus").

Apollōnius (32): a lazy man; guest at Haterius' birthday dinner-party (see also "Crispus," "Maximus," and "Sabīnus").

Lūcius Venūlēius APRŌNIĀNUS (31): witness to patron Haterius' accounts (see also "Alexander" and "Prīmus").

Aquae Sūlis (21): town in Roman Britain famous for its hot-water springs; modern Bath, in the county of Avon.

Asclēpiadēs (34): Greek-born doctor; accompanied Empress Domitia on false call to Haterius' house (see also "Chionē" below), supposedly to cure Vitellia; disappeared before the ambush there by praetorian guards.

Athēnae (31): Athens.

Aulus (27): invited (along with Publicus) by his friend Modestus to a clandestine party under a granary in the fortress at Deva (see "Strȳthiō" below).

Belimicus (24): native chieftain loyal to Salvius; his men killed Dumnorix and wounded Quintus; he falsely accused Cogidubnus to Agricola; was poisoned by Salvius. (He was the loser of the boat-race in Stage 15 and had the mishap with the bear in Stage 16.)

Bulbus (22): the rejected suitor of Vilbia; pushed Modestus into the sacred spring and won Vilbia back (see "Gutta" below).

Gāius Iūlius CAESAR (28): Roman general who in 55 and 54 B.C.—over a century before the events of Unit 3—had transported Roman soldiers to southeastern Britain in order to reconnoiter and to intimidate the native peoples.

Calēdonia (26): the far north of Scotland.

Celts (23): the comprehensive name for the tribal peoples of Indo-European origin who had settled and were living in Britain when the Romans occupied it in A.D.43.

Cephalus (21): freedman of Memor; though ordered by Memor to give Cogidubnus a poisoned cup, was forced to drink it himself; revealed, by posthumous letter, Salvius' and Memor's plot to kill Cogidubnus.

Chionē (34): slave-girl of Empress Domitia; accompanied her and the doctor Asclepiades (see "Asclēpiadēs" above), supposedly to help Vitellia; disappeared before the ambush there by praetorian guards.

Quīntus Haterius CHRȲSOGONUS (31): a Greek-born freedman, freed by Haterius (see "Haterius" below) and consequently sharing his first two names; returned, after manumission, to live in Athens; sent Euphrosyne to entertain Haterius and his guests in Rome (see "Euphrosynē" below).

Claudius (23): Roman emperor (A.D. 41–54) who conquered Britain in A.D. 43; temple built to him at Camulodunum, modern Colchester, in Essex.

Titus Flāvius CLĒMĒNS (33): a senator, married to Emperor Domitian's niece, Flavia Domitilla; possibly converted to Christianity; patron of Tychicus (see "Tychicus" below).

Tiberius Claudius COGIDUBNUS (21): native king of the Regnenses and client of the Roman emperor, already met in Unit 2; sought cure for serious illness at Aquae Sulis, where he was almost poisoned in a plot laid by Salvius and Memor; later regretted his loyalty to Rome and died a prisoner of Salvius.

Lūcius Baebius CRISPUS (32): a senator; guest at Haterius' birthday dinner-party (see also "Apollōnius," "Maximus," and "Sabīnus").

Deceanglī (25): native tribe that lived in the northern parts of what are now Clwyd and Gwynedd in northeastern Wales.

Dēva (24): northwestern British town with a fortress where a Roman legion was stationed; modern Chester, in Cheshire.

Dīdō (33): legendary queen of Carthage; killed herself when abandoned by Aeneas; her story was danced by Paris in Haterius' garden as entertainment.

DOMITIA Augusta (33): wife of Domitian and Empress of Rome; later sent away because of her affair with Paris (see also "Epaphrodītus," "Paris," and "Salvius").

Titus Flavius DOMITIĀNUS, or DOMITIAN (23): Emperor of Rome (A.D. 81–96); son of Emperor Vespasian and younger brother of Emperor Titus (see "Titus" below); according to Salvius, secretly charged the latter with the responsibility for terminating the nominally independent rule of Cogidubnus. In A.D. 81 commissioned an arch to honor the memory of his brother.

Dumnorix (23): native chieftain loyal to Cogidubnus; forced Cephalus to drink his own poisoned cup; later persuaded Quintus to intercede for Cogidubnus with the governor Agricola; murdered by Belimicus' henchmen. (He was the winner of the boat-race in Stage 15.)

Eborācum (27): northeastern British town with a fortress where a Roman legion was stationed; modern York, in the heart of Yorkshire.

Eleazārus (29): Eleazar, leader, after the fall of Jerusalem, of the Jewish last-stand at Masada (see "Masada" below); in A.D. 73 instigated the mass suicide rather than surrender to Silva and the Tenth Legion (see "Silva" below).

Claudius EPAPHRODĪTUS (33): freedman of Emperor Nero; later powerful secretary to Emperor Domitian; when played for a fool by Paris and Myropnous (see "Paris" and "Myropnous" below), he plotted with Salvius to entrap Empress Domitia and kill Paris.

Eryllus (31): slave of Haterius and his resident expert on questions of taste; sent letter to Chrysogonus inviting him to send Euphrosyne to Rome (see also "Chrȳsogonus" and "Euphrosynē").

Euphrosynē (31): young Greek woman and believer in Stoic philosophy; sent from Athens by Chrysogonus to entertain Haterius and his guests (see "Chrȳsogonus" above).

Falernus ager (32): an area in Campania, southeast of Rome; famous for its wine.

Glitus (29): foreman on Haterius' arch-construction project.

Graecia (31): Greece

Gutta (22): bribed by his friend Bulbus into impersonating the girl Vilbia and thus luring Modestus by night into the spring-house of Sulis (see "Bulbus" above).

Quīntus HATERIUS Latrōniānus (29): wealthy, ambitious contractor who arranged for construction of the Arch of Titus; son of a freedman of the noble Haterii; client and brother-in-law of Salvius (see "Salvius" below); allowed Salvius to use his house as ambush for Empress Domitia and the dancer Paris.

Hispānia (28): Latin name for modern Spain; source of the "garum" ("fish-sauce") which Salvius adulterated in order to poison Belimicus.

Ierosolyma (29): Jerusalem, capital of Judaea; captured by Titus and his Roman legions in A.D. 70 (see also "Eleazārus" and "Titus").

Iūdaeī (29): the Jewish people.

Latrō (22): innkeeper in Aquae Sulis; father of Rubria and Vilbia.

Legiō II Adiūtrīx (25): the Second Legion, the "Helper," stationed in the fortress at Deva until A.D. 87.

Legiō XX Valeria Vīctrīx (26): the Twentieth Legion, the "Valerian Victorious," stationed after A.D. 87 in the fortress at Deva.

Lūcius Volusius MAECIĀNUS (31): client-visitor of Haterius; ordered to return later in the day (for dinner) (see also "Prīvātus").

Mārs (22): god of war; had affair with goddess Venus (see also "Olympus" and "Venus").

Masada (29): a Jewish fortress atop a cliff overlooking the Dead Sea

Gāius Rabīrius MAXIMUS (31): architect and client visitor of Haterius; at Haterius' birthday dinner-party, defended Euphrosyne against the advances of Sabinus (see "Sabīnus" below).

Lūcius Marcius MEMOR (21): a professional haruspex, or diviner, who foretold the future by interpreting animal entrails and other natural phenomena; acted as Roman administrator of the temple precinct and sacred spring at Aquae Sulis.

Metellī (30): long line of senators and generals called Metellus, whose tombs were located near Haterius' dearly-bought burial plot (see also "Scīpiōnēs" below).

Minerva (21): Roman goddess (see "Sūlis" below).

Modestus (22): Roman soldier in the Second Legion, friend of Strythio; when wounded, took cure at Aquae Sulis, where he had an affair with Vilbia; later, in the fortress at Deva, allowed—through negligence resulting from gluttony—the prisoner Vercobrix to escape, went A.W.O.L., but eventually recaptured Vercobrix under a granary.

Myropnous (33): a dwarf slave; accompanist, on double-flute, to Paris; managed to knock Epaphroditus unconscious (see "Epaphrodītus" above); later tried but failed to save Paris from the praetorian guards sent by Epaphroditus and Salvius; vowed vengeance against Salvius.

Nerō (28): Roman emperor in A.D. 54–68.

Nigrīna (27): dancer invited to Modestus' clandestine party (see "Strȳthiō" below).

Olympus (33): slave of Empress Domitia; guarded atrium-door of palace while Paris was performing "The Love of Mars and Venus" (see "Mārs" and "Venus").

Titus Claudius PAPĪRIUS (31): client-visitor of Haterius.

Paris (33): a "pantomīmus," or dancer; lover of Empress Domitia; died in ambush set by Salvius at client Haterius' house (see also "Epaphrodītus" and "Salvius").

Gāius Memmius PRĪMUS (31): witness to patron Haterius' accounts (see also "Alexander" and "Aprōniānus").

Marcus Licinius PRĪVĀTUS (31): client-visitor of Haterius; ordered to return later in the day (for dinner) (see also "Maeciānus").

Pūblicus (27): invited (along with Aulus) by his friend Modestus to a clandestine party (see "Strȳthiō" below).

QUĪNTUS Caecilius Iūcundus (21): son of the Pompeian banker Caecilius (see Unit 1); spent the winter in Britain as the guest of Salvius and his wife Rufilla, a distant relative of Quintus (see Unit 2); frequently visited Cogidubnus; alerted Cogidubnus to the plot of the poisoned cup; was wounded (see "Belimicus" above) during his escape from Salvius northward to Agricola at Deva, but managed to reach the governor and to disclose Salvius' machinations.

Rubria (22): daughter of Latro and sister of Vilbia.

Rūfus (26): "tribūnus mīlitum," or high-ranking officer under Agricola; vouched for the good character of Quintus, on the basis of a letter from his father Barbillus, whose guest Quintus had been in Alexandria (see Unit 2).

Titus Flāvius SABĪNUS (32): consul in A.D. 82, and married to (previous) Emperor

Titus' daughter, Iulia; guest at Haterius' birthday dinner-party, where he tried to kiss Euphrosyne (see also "Euphrosynē" and "Maximus").

Gāius SALVIUS Līberālis (21): circuit judge in southern Britain (already met in Unit 2); supposedly on secret mission from Emperor Domitian to terminate the rule of Cogidubnus, plotted unsuccessfully with Memor to poison the king; later had Cogidubnus arrested and slandered him to Agricola. In Rome plotted, with encouragement from Epaphroditus, an ambush to entrap Empress Domitia and kill Paris; patron and brother-in-law of Haterius.

Scīpiōnēs (30): long line of senators and generals called Scipio (see also "Metellī").

Gāius Iūlius SĪLĀNUS (26): "lēgātus legiōnis," or commander of the Second Legion stationed at Deva.

Lūcius Flāvius SILVA (29): commander of the Tenth Legion which captured the Jewish fortress at Masada in A.D. 73; had laid siege to Masada and entered by massive dirt ramp.

Simōn (29): thirteen-year-old boy and oldest of five brothers who survived, together with their mother and grandmother, the mass suicide at Masada (see "Masada" above); on parade in Rome, stabbed all his family and himself.

Strȳthiō (22): Roman soldier of the Second Legion, friend of Modestus; alone, failed to guard Vercobrix in the fortress jail at Deva; hid under a granary with Modestus; went to invite guests to Modestus' party.

Sūlis (21): Celtic goddess, also known as Sul, whose cult flourished at Aquae Sulis; identified by the Romans with their own goddess Minerva.

Tacitus (26): Roman historian who wrote a *Life* of Agricola, who was his father-in-law.

Tiberis (31): the Tiber, river flowing through Rome to the Tyrrhenian Sea; thoroughfare for grain ships coming up from harbor at Ostia.

TITUS Flāvius Vespasiānus (29): older brother of Domitian (see "Domitiānus" above); Emperor of Rome (A.D. 79–81); declared a god after his death.

Tychicus (33): a Jewish-born convert to Christianity; client of Clemens (see "Clēmēns" above); interrupted Paris' performance of "Dido."

Valerius (25): centurion or captain of the "centuria" ("company") of the Second Legion in which Modestus and Strythio served.

Venus (33): goddess of love, and wife of god Vulcan; had adulterous affair with Mars (see "Mārs" above); the story was danced by Paris at palace for Empress Domitia's private entertainment.

Vercobrix (25): young chieftain of the tribe of Deceangli; escaped from the jail in the fortress at Deva; was unexpected "guest" at Modestus' party under a granary, where he was recaptured.

Verulāmium (26): Romano-British town; modern St. Albans, some twenty miles north of London, in Hertfordshire.

Vesta (23): Roman goddess of the hearth and home.

Vilbia (22): daughter of Latro and sister of Rubria; had brief affair with Roman soldier Modestus; betrothed to Bulbus.

Virginēs Vestālēs (29): Vestal Virgins, priestesses of Vesta.

Viroōnium (26): northwestern Romano-British town; modern Wroxeter, just south of Shrewsbury, in Shropshire.

Vitellia (30): noble-born wife of Haterius (see "Haterius" above); sister of Salvius' wife Rufilla (met in Unit 2, Stage 13).

Index of Cultural Topics

The page references are all to the background sections of the Stages. You will also find cultural information in the Latin stories.

Pliny the Younger 202, 238,
256, 258
Pontifex Maximus 50
praetorian guard 219
praetōrium 116
prīncipia 116

roads 64 ff., 138 (maps), 142
Romanization of Britain 19, 51,
102, 139
Rostra 166, 200

sacellum 118
Sacred Way (*Via Sacra*) 168,
199 (map)
sacrifices 49
St. Albans (*Verulāmium*) 100,
139
St. Paul 237
Salvius 140, 219
senatorial class 218, 255
Seneca 221
servī Caesaris 257
signifer 85
spīna 241

sportula 202
Stoicism 221
Styx 36
Subura 200–01
Sulis Minerva 16–17, 19

Tacitus 51, 101, 139–40
tesserārius 85
Tiber island 199–200
Tiber river 182, 199, 201
Tiberius 100
Tiro 255
Titus 181–82
arch of victory over Jews 168,
181–82
tombstones
of Avitus, Caecilius 145
of Cadarus, C. Lovesius 146
of Eumolpus, T. Flavius 257
of Flavia Quinta 257
of Flavia Philaenis 257
of Homerus, T. Flavius 257
of Rusonia Aventina 19
of Valens, L. Licinius 143
of Vitalis, Julius 19

Trajan 238
forum of 168
Christians 238
Trimalchio 256
Twentieth Legion (Valeria
Victrix) 101–02

Ummidia Quadratilla 239

valētūdinārium 116, 118
Venus 238
Vesta 151, 167
Vestal Virgins 151, 167
Vettii 256
via praetōria 116
via prīncipālis 116
via quīntāna 116
vīcī 120
vōta 51
Vulcan 238

Wroxeter (*Virocōnium*) 101

York (*Eborācum*) 121

Zosimus 256–57

Index of Grammatical Topics

Key: AL = About the Language; RvG = Review Grammar; RfG = Reference Grammar

Page references are given first, with paragraph references (i.e. references to numbered sections in the language notes and the Review Grammar) following in boldface; Roman numerals following page numbers denote sections in the Reference Grammar, which are sometimes followed by paragraph references.

In general, AL references are only to the *first* language note in this Unit on the grammatical topic in question: in a few cases, additional pages are cited.

nē *see* indirect
commands,
negative;
purpose clauses,
negative

neuter nouns
AL 43–44.**1–3**

nōlō (nōlle)
see verbs, irregular

nouns
RvG 262–64.**1–5**

oportet
see impersonal verbs

participles
present active
AL 10.**1**
RvG 280.**3**; 286–89.**1,
4–6, 8, 10–12**
RfG 307.VIII
perfect passive
AL 10–11.**2–8**
RvG 280.**4**; 286–89.**2,
4–5, 7, 10–11**
RfG 301–02.VI.**2, 3**;
307VIII.**1**
perfect active
(deponent)
AL 28.**2–3**
RvG 281.**1**;
286–89.**3–5,
7–12**
RfG 307.VIII.**2**
future (active)
AL 218.**1–3**
RvG 280.**5**
gerundive
see gerundive

passive verbs
AL 159–60.**2–4**;
176.**1–4**; 179.**1–3**
RvG 277–78.**1–7**
RfG 298.IV;
301–02.VI.**2–3**

personal pronouns
(**ego, tū**, etc.)
RvG 269.**1**

possum
see verbs, irregular

prepositions, cases used
with
AL 136–37.**1–5**

priusquam
RvG 293.**7**

pronouns
RvG 269–74.**1–11**
see also
demonstrative
pronouns;
determinative
pronouns;
īdem, eadem
intensive pronouns
personal pronouns
reflexive pronouns
relative pronouns

purpose clauses
AL 93.**1–3**; 163.**1–3**
RvG 291–93.**3, 6, 7**
RfG 303–04.VII.**3**
negative
AL 198.**3**

reflexive pronouns
RvG 269.**2**

relative pronouns
RvG 272–74.**9–11**

result clauses
AL 116.**1–2**
RvG 292–93.**5–7**
RfG 305–06.VII.**4**

sentence patterns
RfG 311.XI

subjunctive of the verb
AL 78–79.**1–4**;
RvG 279.**1–2**;
290–93.**1–7**
RfG 303–07.VII

subordinate clauses
RfG 303–07.VII

sum (esse)
see verbs, irregular

superlative
see comparison of
adjectives

taedet
see impersonal verbs

time, expressions of
AL 134.**1–3**

ut *see* indirect
commands;
purpose clauses;
result clauses

verbs
regular
RvG 275–80
RfG 298–300.IV
deponent
RvG 281–82.**1–6**
RfG 299.V
irregular
RvG 282–84.**1–8**
RfG 301–02.VI

volō
see verbs, irregular

word order
RvG 294.**1–5**

Time Chart

B.C.	BRITAIN	ROME	THE WORLD	B.C.
c. 3100–1166			Egypt ruled by Pharaohs	*c.* 3100–1166
c. 2100			Indo-European migrations	*c.* 2100
c. 1500			Minoan civilization at its height	*c.* 1500
c. 1450			Development of Hinduism	*c.* 1450
c. 1200			Exodus of Jews from Egypt	*c.* 1200
753		Foundation of Rome (traditional date) & rule of kings		753
c. 563			Buddha born in India	*c.* 563
c. 551			Confucius born in China	*c.* 551
509		Expulsion of kings & founding of Roman Republic		509
500–400			{ Persia invades Greece } { Golden Age of Athens }	500–400
390		Rome briefly captured by Gauls		390
336			Alexander becomes ruler of Greece	336
331			Alexander founds Alexandria	331
323			Alexander dies in Babylon	323
300–200		{ Rome gains control of Italy } { Wars with Carthage }	Building of Great Wall of China	300–200
218		Hannibal crosses the Alps		218
200–100		Rome extends rule outside Italy		200–100
58–49		Caesar conquers Gaul		58–49
55–54	Caesar's expeditions to Britain			55–54
49		Caesar is made "Dictator"		49
44		Caesar is murdered		44
44–31		Civil War between Octavian (Augustus) & Antony		44–31
30		{ Antony and Cleopatra commit suicide } { Rome annexes Egypt }		30
27		Augustus becomes Emperor		27
c. 4			Birth of Jesus	*c.* 4

A.D.	BRITAIN	ROME	THE WORLD	A.D.
14		Tiberius becomes Emperor		14
c. 29			Crucifixion of Jesus	*c.* 29
37		Caligula becomes Emperor		37
41		Claudius becomes Emperor		41
42		St. Peter brings Christianity to Rome		42
43	{ Invasion of Britain under Aulus Plautius } { Britain becomes province of Rome } { Vespasian leads second Legion against Durotriges }			43
45–57			Missionary journeys of St. Paul	45–57
54		Nero becomes Emperor		54
61	Revolt of Iceni under Boudica			61
64		{ Great Fire at Rome } { Persecution of Christians by Nero }		64
69		{ Year of Four Emperors } { Vespasian becomes Emperor }		69
70			Romans sack Jerusalem and Temple	70
75	Roman palace at Fishbourne begun			75
c. 76–87	Second Legion stationed at Chester			*c.* 76–87
78–84	Agricola is Governor of Britain			78–84
79		{ Titus becomes Emperor } { August 24 : Vesuvius erupts }		79
81	?Salvius arrives in Britain	Domitian becomes Emperor		81
83–84	Agricola's campaigns in Scotland			83–84
96		Nerva becomes Emperor		96
98		Trajan becomes Emperor		98
117		Hadrian becomes Emperor		117
208–11	Emperor Severus campaigns in Britain and dies in York			208–11
313			Constantine officially supports Christianity in Roman Empire	313
330			Capital of Roman Empire moved to Constantinople	330
400–500	Anglo-Saxons settle in Britain			400–500
410	Rome formally renounces Britain	Visigoths sack Rome		410
476		Last Emperor of Rome deposed		476
570			Birth of Mohammed	570
c. 643			Arabs conquer Egypt	*c.* 643
800			Charlemagne crowned Emperor of Holy Roman Empire	800
800–1100		Period of turmoil in Italy		800–1100

	BRITAIN	ROME	THE WORLD	
1066	Normans conquer England			1066
1143		Rome becomes an independent city-state		1143
1215	Magna Charta signed			1215
c. 1400		The Renaissance begins in Italy		c. 1400
1453			Turks capture Constantinople	1453
1492			Columbus arrives in America	1492
1497			Cabot explores Canada	1497
1521			Reformation begins	1521
1588	English defeat Spanish Armada			1588
1620			Pilgrims land at Plymouth, Mass.	1620
1776			United States declare their Independence	1776
1806			End of Holy Roman Empire	1806
1815			Napoleon finally defeated at Waterloo	1815
1837	Victoria becomes Queen of Great Britain			1837
1861		Victor Emmanuel II becomes King of a united Italy		1861
1863			Lincoln emancipates American slaves	1863
1867			Canada becomes a Dominion	1867
1914–1918			First World War	1914–1918
1931			Canada becomes a Commonwealth nation	1931
1939–1945			Second World War	1939–1945
1946		Italy becomes a Republic		1946
1952	Elizabeth II becomes Queen of Great Britain			1952

Quick Reference to Grammatical Information